Michael O'Leary

A Life in Full Flight

Alan Ruddock, a contemporary of Michael O'Leary's at Trinity College, Dublin, is a former business journalist with the *Sunday Times* and former editor of the *Scotsman*. He is currently a commentator with the *Sunday Independent*, Ireland's largest-selling newspaper.

Michael O'Leary

A Life in Full Flight

ALAN RUDDOCK

WITHDRAWN

PENGUIN
IRELAND

PENGUIN IRELAND

Published by the Penguin Group
Penguin Ireland, 25 St Stephen's Green, Dublin 2, Ireland
(a division of Penguin Books Ltd)
Penguin Books Ltd, 80 Strand, London WC2R ORL, England
Penguin Group (USA) Inc., 375 Hudson Street, New York, New York 10014, USA
Penguin Group (Australia), 250 Camberwell Road, Camberwell, Victoria 3124, Australia
(a division of Pearson Australia Group Pty Ltd)
Penguin Group (Canada), 90 Eglinton Avenue East, Suite 700, Toronto, Ontario, Canada M4P 2Y3
(a division of Pearson Penguin Canada Inc.)
Penguin Books India Pvt Ltd, 11 Community Centre, Panchsheel Park, New Delhi – 110 017, India
Penguin Group (NZ), 67 Apollo Drive, Rosedale, North Shore 0632, New Zealand
(a division of Pearson New Zealand Ltd)
Penguin Books (South Africa) (Pty) Ltd, 24 Sturdee Avenue, Rosebank, Johannesburg 2196, South Africa

Penguin Books Ltd, Registered Offices: 80 Strand, London WC2R ORL, England

www.penguin.com

First published 2007
3

Copyright © Alan Ruddock, 2007

The moral right of the author has been asserted

Set in 12/14.75 pt Postscript Monotype Bembo
Typeset by Rowland Phototypesetting Ltd, Bury St Edmunds, Suffolk
Printed in Great Britain by Clays Ltd, St Ives plc

A CIP catalogue record for this book is available from the British Library

ISBN: 978-1-844-88055-3

www.greenpenguin.co.uk

Mixed Sources
Product group from well-managed
forests and other controlled sources
www.fsc.org Cert no. SA-COC-1592
© 1996 Forest Stewardship Council

Penguin Books is committed to a sustainable future
for our business, our readers and our planet.
The book in your hands is made from paper
certified by the Forest Stewardship Council.

There is nothing more difficult to carry out, nor more doubtful of success, nor more dangerous to handle, than to initiate a new order of things. For the reformer has enemies in all those who profit by the old order.

– Niccolò Machiavelli

Business books are bullshit and are usually written by wankers.

– Michael O'Leary

Contents

Contents

1. The Black Hole

Michael Gerard Joseph Mary O'Leary was named after a grandfather, a grandmother, his own mother and the Virgin Mary. The names reflected the family's traditions – rural, Roman Catholic, conservative – and Michael O'Leary's early life was steeped in the values of home and family.

Born on 20 March 1961 in a maternity hospital in Dublin's Hatch Street, on the site of what became the office of the Euro Changeover Board, the second child and first son of Timothy ('Ted') and Gerarda O'Leary would be one of six children – three girls and three boys. For the first ten years of his life the family lived in a comfortable red-brick house in the centre of Mullingar, before moving to the greater freedom of Lynn, on the outskirts of the town, where his parents still live. No matter where they were, however, the rules were the same.

'Each of the girls got their own rooms and the three boys were always in a black hole of Calcutta,' Michael O'Leary has recalled. 'We didn't understand at the time. Apparently boys didn't need their privacy at all so we roomed together in the slum. The girls all had their rooms and they were all decorated in flowery wall-papers and posters of pop stars. We were always left in one room together to fight it out amongst ourselves.'

Both his parents hailed originally from Kanturk, a small town in County Cork, where his mother's parents were prosperous farmers. Timothy and Gerarda met and courted in their home-town, and were married in nearby Adare, County Limerick, in October 1958. Immediately afterwards they struck out on their own for a new life in the midlands, moving to Ballinderry, in County Westmeath, where Timothy's parents had helped launch Tailteann, a textile business, in the 1940s. Their new dream was not a farm, but business: Timothy was taking responsibility for his parents' textile business. Along with two local dentists and their wives, Timothy was now a major shareholder in the knitwear company located in Mullingar, Westmeath's county town, which lies about fifty miles west of Dublin.

Tailteann Textiles was a challenging venture. Ireland in the late 1950s was an economic backwater, a country that relied heavily on agriculture and that had failed, in its first thirty-five years of independence, to develop an industrial base. For Mullingar, a market town with a population around 5,000, the Tailteann factory had been an important development. It offered jobs – at its peak the factory employed more than 120 locals – and a sense of progress to a community that had lacked both.

Timothy O'Leary, bursting with ideas, was determined to run a thriving business and to provide a stable home for his new wife and their children. The first child, Ashley Concepta, had been born a year after the wedding, to be followed by Michael two years later. By the time their third child, Eddie, was born in 1962, Timothy had become more than just a shareholder, taking over as factory manager that year. A keen golfer, he had quickly become a well known and much liked figure in the local golf club, which at the time was considered one of the finest courses in the country.

'At the time there were very few wealthy men around,' said Albert Reynolds, an old family friend who went on to become the Irish prime minister. 'Like the rest of us, he was working. But he was always very well dressed and had a good car and all of the family were always well turned out.'

Gerarda O'Leary was typical of her generation – devoted to her family, deeply religious and fiercely protective of her children, particularly her sons. Donie Cassidy, who was a friend of Timothy and Gerarda and is now a member of the Dáil representing the people of Westmeath, remembers Gerarda as 'very religious' and heavily involved in the local prayer group. 'She wouldn't suffer fools lightly, and she certainly would be in no way accepting of anything except the highest standards.' Cassidy believes Gerarda was the 'dominant figure' behind her husband's successes: 'She was the driving force; she was one of the most determined people I ever met,' he said.

Michael O'Leary recalls, 'She was the stay-at-home mother, six kids, no help. Looking back I don't know how anybody did it, except they all did it in those days. But then she was very good. She'd do the garden, she was big into gardening and decorating houses, she was good at it. And with six kids they were frequently decorating houses. We'd trash the place,' he says.

Her influence remains a potent one. One former colleague remembers that Michael 'only put on a suit when she was coming to Dublin'.

In September 1965, aged four and a half, Michael O'Leary started school in St Mary's, a local national school for boys and girls. After three years he moved to the all-boy environment of the Christian Brothers school in Mullingar.

The Christian Brothers at that time often made heavy use of corporal punishment, but O'Leary does not recall a particularly violent schooling. 'I was only seven years old but I don't think of myself as an abused or a battered soul,' he says, 'but if I did get a belt I certainly got my spelling right the next day.'

Classmates recall O'Leary as someone who was able to defend himself. 'You always got the impression he was well able to stand up for himself; he would never let himself be put down,' said one. 'He wasn't the type to get into fights but he wouldn't let himself be put down.'

There were more than 400 boys in the school and class sizes were large. 'There were between forty and forty-five boys in any one class,' says Fergal Oakes, one of O'Leary's early teachers and now principal of the school. A classmate claims there were more than sixty boys crammed into one of their years.

O'Leary's contemporaries don't recall him as being particularly bright. 'He never stood out as being top of the class or anything,' said one. 'He would have been somewhere in the middle, an average pupil.' But O'Leary puts a slightly different slant on it: 'I was pretty good at school,' he says, 'but without having to try that hard.' What did mark him out was his dress. 'I remember he used to always stand out because he'd have a short-trouser suit and an Aran sweater that we didn't have,' recalls one former classmate. 'All the rest of us would be there in hand-me-downs from our brothers and sisters.'

Always a small child, O'Leary nevertheless enjoyed sports. The school's focus was on traditional Irish games – Gaelic football and hurling – and O'Leary participated in 'anything that was going'. But he steered clear of the Scouts – 'They wouldn't have let me in' – as well as arts and riding. 'I'm not into art, never have been. I've nothing on my left side [of the brain], or whatever side of the brain artistic stuff is on,' he says. 'And the only thing I didn't do, which the other brothers and sisters did, was the pony club. I could never twig riding horses. I couldn't ride one now. I could ride when I was younger but it just didn't do anything for me. So most of the other brothers and sisters were mad about riding horses. When they were doing things like the pony club I was playing soccer or golf or whatever.'

Summers were mainly spent at home in Mullingar. 'I certainly wasn't on a plane when I was a kid,' says O'Leary. 'We didn't go on holidays much because farmers tended not to go on that many holidays' – despite his father's business ventures, O'Leary still sees himself as a product of farming stock – 'and also with six kids I don't think the parents wanted to bring us on holidays. I remember some years we went away – we went down to the sea somewhere in Kerry at one stage and we went to Rosslare another year. But we certainly didn't go every year.'

O'Leary's memories of his childhood are, at best, sketchy. He has told interviewers that his early years were marked by the upheaval of moving home several times, usually after one of his father's business ventures had failed. '[My father] used to set up businesses that would be very successful for the first few years and then go bust,' O'Leary told Eamon Dunphy during an extensive TV interview. 'When he went bust, he would sell the house, and when he made money he would buy another house.'

Reynolds's recollections are similar. 'Ted would get an idea in his head, give it a good run, and if it didn't work turn to something else,' he says. 'He wouldn't be done down by failure at all.'

'He was always active,' O'Leary told radio interviewer Shane Kenny. 'The trouble, like with a lot of entrepreneurs, was that once he had set up a business he started to lose interest in it, or lose money, which was even worse.'

While growing up O'Leary moved house three times. Until 1972 the family lived in Mullingar's Harbour Street, the smallest of the homes he would occupy. The family then moved briefly to Clonard House, a large house on the outskirts of the town, the former residence of the Bishop of Meath and now home to the local tourist board. The following year they moved again, this time to Lynn, just outside Mullingar, where they stayed for the rest of his childhood. The moves were precipitated by the growing size of the O'Leary family, which by 1973 had reached its full complement of eight.

In other interviews O'Leary has praised his father as being a 'genius at setting up business' and has credited his parents with instilling his work ethic. 'I learned from my parents the value of hard work and I think that will always stay with me,' he told an interviewer in 1999.

Tailteann did eventually run into trouble, but not before enjoying a sustained period of success and expansion. In the early 1960s the business had received small government grants and had borrowed to expand, taking out a £20,000 loan in 1964 and a further £15,000 two years later. As the business grew, so the shareholders and directors changed, with more Dublin-based businessmen coming on board to replace the original investors. In 1970 the local paper ran a story commenting on the role Tailteann Textiles had played in putting Mullingar on the industrial map. Reflecting a more innocent age, every year a 'Miss Tailteann' was crowned at the staff Christmas party.

The company, originally based at Columb Barracks, in Mullingar, with 30 employees, relocated that year to a new factory on the Longford Road just outside the town, and the staff numbers grew to 120. The next year Timothy's mother, an original shareholder, handed her stake over to her son, making him the largest single share-holder and allowing him to become chairman of the company.

Over the next five years, however, Tailteann suffered as recession struck and oil prices soared. In November 1976, with its debts out of control, the Bank of Ireland appointed a receiver and the following year the company was sold for a nominal amount to a Dutch multinational.

2. Rites of Passage

The journey from Mullingar to Clongowes Wood College in Clane, County Kildare, takes just over an hour and a half, but when the thirteen-year-old Michael O'Leary set off for his new boarding school on a bright September day in 1974, he was entering a different world. In the 1970s, well before the economic boom that would create a new class of Irish wealthy, Clongowes was the school of choice for Ireland's well-to-do rural professionals and farmers, its dormitories filled with the sons of doctors, dentists, accountants and landowners, most of whom hailed from the nearby counties.

'The funny thing about Clongowes [is that] it is now a school for the rich and famous – multimillionaires' sons go to Clongowes,' says O'Leary. 'When we were there nobody was there. The year I left and my brother was still there [Sir Anthony] O'Reilly put two kids in for fifth and sixth forms and suddenly there was someone famous there. And Anto comes in the helicopter and lands on the under-thirteen pitch. It wasn't that kind of a [posh] place. There was no rich list in the 1970s. If you stood out for anything in Clongowes, except for rugby, you learned fairly quickly to stop standing out.'

Despite the perils of standing out at Clongowes, the school has many famous past pupils, including James Joyce; John Bruton, a farmer's son who would become prime minister of Ireland and the EU's ambassador to the United States; Paul McGuinness, an O'Leary contemporary and the son of a soldier who became manager of U2, Ireland's most successful rock band; and David Dilger, the chief executive of Greencore, one of Ireland's largest food companies.

Founded in 1814, Clongowes was the first Jesuit college for boys in Ireland, and its mission was to inculcate the Jesuit tradition in the thousands of boys who would enter its gates in the years to come. The pupils, privileged because of their families' relative wealth, would nonetheless be taught about their responsibilities to their communities and to God. Sport, particularly rugby and tennis, was an essential part of the formula.

O'Leary's first sight of Clongowes' impressive nineteenth-century buildings and grounds had come the previous year in 1973 when, as a gauche twelve-year-old who knew little of life outside Mullingar, he was brought to visit the school by his parents. 'I'll never forget the first time the parents took me around Clongowes. It had football pitches, soccer pitches, it had a swimming pool and tennis courts and I thought this was heaven. I had never seen a place that had so many sports facilities. I was delighted to go there. I didn't miss home in the least.'

In that, O'Leary was fortunate. Boarders rarely left the school during the term, with visits restricted to a few Sundays in the year and one weekend break at home for half-term. O'Leary settled in quickly, making friends who would stay with him for the rest of his life and participating enthusiastically, if rarely successfully, in as much sport as he could manage.

'Basketball and cricket were the only ones I didn't play,' he says. 'I hated cricket, couldn't understand bloody basketball but then I was about four foot nothing so for basketball I was kind of physically challenged. I was more likely to have been the ball. But I tried hard. So I finished up on most of the teams except for the rugby. I was tiny on the rugby pitch so I finished up on the super thirds for rugby, which was for the plodders.'

Academically O'Leary was an average student, never pushing himself too hard, but never struggling to make his grades. 'If you were in the top ten per cent you were a swot; if you were in the bottom ten per cent you were a moron, and much better off to be in the middle . . . In a fucked-up way, I was nobody in school,' O'Leary says. 'I was common Joe Soap. I'm still common Joe Soap, I just got lucky a couple of times.'

His one area of success, school friends claim, was in cross-country running. 'He was small, but he was gritty,' says one contemporary, 'and he could just keep running.'

While O'Leary settled into Clongowes, his father was trying to bounce back from the collapse of Tailteann. While the receivers would not be called in until 1976, the business had been dead in the water since 1973 and the elder O'Leary had already launched a new venture before Michael went to his new school. In February 1974, eight months before young Michael went to Clongowes, he had applied for planning permission to build a new factory on a one-acre site in Ballinagore, not far from Ballinagore House where he had lived briefly some thirteen years earlier. The locals, however, were not impressed.

O'Leary wanted to build a rendering plant – a factory that processes animal carcasses to produce bonemeal, tallow and other animal by-products. Rendering is a useful activity, but for those unfortunate enough to live close to a factory, it has one major drawback: it produces a foul smell. Three hundred residents organized a protest meeting against O'Leary's plans in April 1974. According to the *Westmeath Examiner*, O'Leary spoke to the protestors, congratulated them on the concern for their local area, but warned them they would regret blocking his initiative. Their determined resistance, however, forced O'Leary to withdraw his plans and apply instead for permission to build his factory near Castlepollard, a small town towards the Cavan border. The prospect of jobs in a community that had few was enough to quell any misgivings about the business.

'At the start they employed twenty-five or thirty people in Castlepollard, which was a godsend because in the 70s there was no one else giving employment, except for one other major employer outside of Castlepollard,' says Donie Cassidy.

One of Timothy O'Leary's earliest customers was Albert Reynolds, whose family owned C&D Foods, a pet food company. Philip Reynolds, who now runs the business, has three lasting impressions of O'Leary as a businessman. 'One: he was a difficult

man to deal with, always considered himself to be the expert and never wrong. He would not accept criticism of either his service or his product. Two: he knew the value of a pound and never accepted damaged or spoilt credit notes, and he made it his business to find a reason to visit around the time for payment and so collected his dues in person. And three: he was always looking for an angle, trying to be better, to do things different and do more and more business.'

Albert Reynolds too remembers O'Leary as 'a tough man in business, but he was very entertaining and I used to enjoy his company'.

The new factory, called Lickbla, was not the end of O'Leary's entrepreneurship. He was an avid property developer – 'He was always developing property, always buying and selling properties, and he was good at it,' says Michael – and he was prepared to try anything. He also dabbled in herbal remedies and in rabbits. 'He was commercially producing rabbits for the skins and rabbit meat,' says Michael. 'I didn't know where the rabbits were going; I was quite young. I remember all the white rabbits though. He'd kill them, I guess. That was what you would do with them . . . My father always had about three or four different businesses. He was brilliant at setting up businesses, crap at running them. So he'd set it up and run it for a couple of years, and then lose it. And he lost three or four. And looking back on it, the genius of the guy was that he was able to set up three or four different businesses in different industries. He was an entrepreneur in the true sense.'

In Clongowes O'Leary was shielded from the vagaries of his father's businesses and he has no memory of the Lickbla protests. He spent his days studying and playing sports, but as he grew older he found that there were two things missing from his idyllic world. 'For about six years I never saw a girl, and you couldn't drink alcohol,' he told an audience of students at an Irish university in 2005.

But when he entered fifth year, aged seventeen, all that changed. 'Up until then it had been all boys, with not a hint of a female within 5,000 miles of us,' he says with typical exaggeration. 'But when you got to fifth and sixth year there was a dance twice a year with the Dominican convent, Wicklow, and with Our Lady's convent in Rathnew, both of which have since been closed down. Everybody loved the dances.'

For the Clongowes boys and the convent girls, the dances represented a symbolic rite of passage. Sophistication, however, was not the order of the day. 'Talcum powder and Brut [the aftershave of choice for teenage boys in the 1970s] was as far as we got. I have no idea what we used to wear – jeans I would imagine,' O'Leary says.

The dances, like the rugby matches, were organized on a home-and-away basis, with the home dances taking place in the Clongowes concert hall.

'It was like a cattle mart,' says one of O'Leary's contemporaries. 'The music would start, the lights would go down, and off you'd go. You'd be praying for the lights to go down, but it was always the usual suspects who ended up with the girls. Invariably the rugby captain ended up with the best-looking girl.'

The pubescent O'Leary found it a daunting experience. 'It was fellas in one corner, girls in the other corner,' he says. 'It was like getting fifty fellas who'd been left in the desert for three months and showing them what the water table looked like . . . The sad thing was that in those days you couldn't miss, but the problem was that you didn't realize at the time that you couldn't miss. So we all went to the socials absolutely shitting ourselves, cos you had to snog one. If you didn't snog at a social you were gay. And there was no greater crime in Clongowes. But what we didn't realize was the girls were probably under as much pressure as we were, so you couldn't miss.' Plenty did, however.

Surprisingly, the priests and nuns took a back seat during the rituals. 'There was no one going around with a torch, though there would have been a patrol to make sure that you didn't disappear down to the gym hall,' says the contemporary.

If the dances were the social highlight for boys who spent the rest of their school lives in each other's company, rugby was the dominant passion. Under the leadership of Greg Dilger, now a stockbroker in Dublin, the Clongowes senior team was developing into a talented unit that would surprise the bigger Dublin schools in 1978 by winning the coveted Schools Cup for the first time in fifty years. Each match was an opportunity for the school to decamp to Dublin to cheer on its heroes, culminating in the triumph at Lansdowne Road on St Patrick's Day, when Dilger's team defeated Terenure College 19–6 in front of a crowd of more than 20,000.

Clongowes would repeat its cup victory four times in the years to come. Its success on the rugby field would change the perception of the school, and subtly change the nature of its pupils. While still the choice of the rural professional, Clongowes would also start to attract more and more of the children of Dublin's wealthy Catholic elite. Thirty years later Clongowes is Ireland's most exclusive private school; the largesse of its parents has delivered new buildings and a new state-of-the-art rugby pitch, now used by the Irish national rugby squad for training sessions.

In the summer of 1979 O'Leary was free: free from Clongowes, where he had spent most of the previous five years, free to experiment with girls, and free to drink as much as he could manage. He had applied himself to his Leaving Certificate examination and got a respectable set of results that allowed him to accept a place at Trinity College Dublin to study ESS – economics and social studies, the precursor of the modern business studies degree. But first he went to work. That summer was spent behind the bar at the Greville Arms Hotel in Mullingar.

Frank McKee, who was the manager of the hotel, remembers a confident young man he thought was destined to do well and to whom he recommended a career in tourism. O'Leary, though, had made up his mind to study business, and had opted for Trinity College over the more traditional choice, for Clongowes boys, of University College Dublin. Trinity, the older of Dublin's two universities of the time, was perceived to be the Protestant college, even though the vast majority of its students were Catholic. This sectarian perception of Trinity had been copper-fastened by John Charles McQuaid, Roman Catholic archbishop of Dublin from

1940 to 1972, who had instructed his co-religionists not to attend Trinity because of its Protestant ethos.

'It was always going to be Dublin,' recalls O'Leary. 'Everybody in Clongowes, all my pals, they were all going to Dublin. And it was only an hour from Mullingar. So it was only a question of would I go to Trinity or UCD. I chose Trinity. I just thought Trinity was cool and UCD was all industrial.' At the time Trinity students referred to UCD as a polytechnic, a derogatory term for a third-level college that did not share its sense of history or achievement.

In late September 1979 O'Leary arrived in Dublin to take up his place at the college. Michael likes to portray himself as an irresponsible student who spent his undergraduate years drinking and chasing girls. 'I did get a degree,' he told Eamon Dunphy in a television interview in 2003, in response to an inaccurate suggestion that he had dropped out of Trinity. 'In drinking, rugby and chasing girls, although I wasn't much good at that.'

'I learned absolutely squat about business,' he told students at the University of Limerick in 2005. 'I'll never forget, in Trinity they had this idea that we would read a lot around the subject and lectures, but the theory was that if they put industrial relations on at nine o'clock on a Monday and nine o'clock on a Tuesday we'd all show up nice and early. And if they put statistics on at five o'clock on a Thursday and Friday they'd keep us there till the end of the week. So of course we blew off Mondays and Tuesdays and we blew off Thursdays and Fridays and basically we fucked off around the centre of Dublin. So I learned very little in Trinity.'

For O'Leary's first year in the big city he moved into Hatch Hall, a Jesuit boarding house on the same street as the maternity hospital where he had been born. It was a ten-minute stroll from the Trinity campus; it was also less than a hundred yards from Hartigan's public house, situated just off St Stephen's Green, which would become O'Leary's local for the next four years. 'We went mad when we left school and went to college, everybody went mad. We were released out of a boarding school after six years, you couldn't help yourself,' he says.

O'Leary's madness was of the predictable kind. He and his friends, many of whom had chosen to study at UCD, would gather at Hartigan's, or the Pavilion bar in Trinity, which overlooked the college playing fields, or in the seedier surroundings of Trinity's canteen bar – a modern, bomb-shelter-like structure that sat incongruously to the side of the college's elegant Front Square. Early evenings in the pubs were followed by later sessions in Old Belvedere rugby club, 'and then there'd normally be a party in someone's house. It was fantastic, without a doubt the best fuck-up years of my life were in Trinity.'

Paying for the student lifestyle was not a problem. O'Leary received thirty pounds a week from his parents – a lavish stipend at the time – and also worked on Friday and Saturday nights in a hotel owned by his uncle, Noel O'Callaghan. O'Leary worked the late shift, from eight in the evening until four in the morning, serving drinks in the nightclub after the main bar had closed.

The cash he earned and the money he received from his parents allowed him to save. While most of his contemporaries were struggling with debts, O'Leary claims to have accumulated £5,000 during his college years. 'It wasn't that hard, actually,' he told a reporter for the *Sunday Business Post* in March 2001. 'My parents gave me the pocket money, and every time I saw the uncles and aunts they'd slip you a fiver too. I was rolling in it, to be honest.'

His network of friends slowly extended beyond his schoolmates. None had joined him in ESS, the course he had chosen to study, though a few had gone to Trinity. 'You had two groups of pals,' he says. 'The ones you went to school with – most of whom were in UCD – and another group in Trinity.' Invariably, the new friends came from similar backgrounds, and similar schools, like Glenstal, a boarding school near Limerick run by Benedictine monks, or Dublin's fee-paying Catholic schools.

A dutiful son, O'Leary found time to visit his parents in Mullingar, travelling home on the train until he solved his commuting problems by buying his first car, a purple Mini. 'Best car I ever drove,' he says. 'It was a babe magnet – not because it was a great car, but because you were one of the few people in college who actually had a car, even if it was a Mini. Our record was fifteen people one night, going to a twenty-first party in Howth. There were four of them sitting on the roof. And we drove from Trinity to Howth [in north Dublin, a twenty-minute journey]. You wouldn't fucking do it now, you'd be arrested long before you got there.'

O'Leary's summers were spent working in Mullingar. By now an accomplished barman, O'Leary plied his trade in the local hotel. He was one of the few students lucky enough to get work in his hometown. Ireland remained economically depressed. Most of his contemporaries went abroad each summer, working on building sites across Europe or travelling further afield to the United States to accumulate money for the following year, but O'Leary's skills as a barman ensured there was always a job waiting in Mullingar.

'I liked bar work; it was good fun, good money. I was good at it,' he says. 'I was fast, I'd get the drinks in and out. If you were good at it you'd go in in the evenings – I couldn't stand around all afternoon doing a shift from two till eleven at night. A lot of these places would want extra bar staff for nightwork, so I'd work the evening shift from six till maybe three in the morning. You'd get extra into your hand for working the nightclubs.'

O'Leary made his final break from the Jesuits when he moved from Hatch Hall into an apartment owned by his parents – another luxury denied most college students in 1980 – which he shared with his two oldest sisters. It was free, but it had its drawbacks. 'I couldn't bring back girls, but anyway I was useless with girls. I'd chase all day and catch nothing. Girls were the target in Trinity, they weren't friends. There were one or two but it was all very innocent in those days.'

3. Ryan's Dream

Four years of university life was enough for O'Leary. The time had come to make some serious money. In his final year at Trinity College he had worked hard for his examinations, the hedonistic lifestyle of the early college years replaced by a more sober work ethic. Life was getting more serious.

'I wanted to make money because we had financial problems when I was growing up and I remember my father being broke a couple of times,' O'Leary says. 'I would have murdered, I would have gone through concrete walls, to make money.'

Quite how he was going to make money, though, was a problem. His time at Clongowes and then Trinity had given O'Leary the quintessential attribute of middle-class boys with a private education behind them: innate self-confidence. Although Ireland in 1983 was in the midst of recession, with double-digit unemployment figures that encouraged tens of thousands of young men and women to emigrate each year, O'Leary believed that a well-paying job would fall into his hands. There were a few choice jobs for Irish graduates – a small number of management consultancy firms hired graduates each year, the accountancy firms took on trainees, and a few Irish companies, like Jefferson Smurfit, the paper company, ran graduate trainee programmes.

'When I finished college I thought, I'm a fucking genius here, I'll have my pick of these jobs,' says O'Leary. But he did not. Far from having his pick, he did not have a single approach until Stokes Kennedy Crowley, a Dublin accountancy firm, threw him a lifeline by offering him the opportunity to train as an accountant. He had no choice, no alternatives to consider. It was accountancy or nothing. In an Ireland where emigration was the norm for college graduates, an opportunity to train as an accountant was one of the most coveted positions for most business students, but

O'Leary was unimpressed. The training was tough, low paid and, worst of all in his mind, 'It was fucking dull.'

His Trinity degree granted him a number of exemptions from accountancy examinations, but he knew nothing about taxation. 'So they put me into tax and said, "Right, you can do the tax in twelve months." So I did tax, which was actually very fortuitous because in tax you were working on accounts all the time. I was never out counting washers or dipping oil tanks at midnight on New Year's Eve. It was, "Here's a set of accounts, how do we get the tax down?"'

O'Leary played the game. He turned up at work each day wearing a suit and tie and resolved to work hard and make a name for himself, racking up fourteen-hour days that could then be charged out to clients. His mentor in the tax department was Gerry McEvoy, a partner and widely respected tax expert who had a clutch of major individual and corporate clients. One of McEvoy's most important private clients was Tony Ryan, who had left Aer Lingus shortly after O'Leary first went to Clongowes to set up his own aircraft-leasing company, Guinness Peat Aviation.

Ryan had begun life as a train driver's son in Tipperary, left school at sixteen, then went to work at Aer Lingus. His twenty years at the company saw him work his way through the tiers of bureaucracy to reach the heady heights of middle management. And that was where he would likely have stayed – too much a maverick for the conservative company – if he had not struck out on his own.

In 1975 Ryan risked £5,000 of his own money to start his aircraft-leasing venture. Aer Lingus, Air Canada and Guinness Peat, a merchant bank, kicked in the other £15,000, and shared a 90 per cent shareholding. Operating out of the tax haven of Shannon, the airport on Ireland's Atlantic coast that was the early gateway to North America, Guinness Peat Aviation bought aircraft and then leased them to airlines. Instead of borrowing millions to buy new planes, airlines could get the planes they needed from GPA and pay monthly, leaving Ryan with the ultimate risk if the industry nosedived. In return, he earned handsome profits by charging the airlines more than it cost him to raise the money to buy the planes in the first place.

The bigger GPA grew, the better the rates it could extract from financial institutions to borrow money and the greater profits it could extract from the airlines that needed its planes. GPA became one of the most profitable finance machines in the world and turned Ryan into a multimillionaire.

O'Leary was fascinated by Ryan's success and instinctively drawn to him. Stories of how the two men came to work with each other are as numerous as they are apocryphal. One version has O'Leary sneaking into McEvoy's office on a Sunday and flicking through his contacts book until he found Ryan's home number. O'Leary, so the story goes, then called Ryan and told him how he could save him even more money. Another says that Ryan had spotted O'Leary when he was still at school with his son Declan, and had kept his eye on him ever since.

O'Leary, however, says that he 'wasn't friends with the Ryans in school. Cathal was two years ahead of me and Declan was two years behind.' In boarding-school terms, the two-year gaps were vast. 'I knew them in school, but I wasn't particularly friendly with them. I didn't go to their house or anything. The relationship with the Ryans started with Tony not through the boys.'

O'Leary says he made direct contact with Ryan while working for SKC. 'I called him up one weekend and said I think you can save some more tax by doing XYZ,' he says. They first met in 1984 when McEvoy brought O'Leary on a working visit to Ryan's home in Tipperary. Ryan was disappointed when O'Leary failed to reappear the following year, asked McEvoy what had happened to the restless young man, and was told that he had gone out on his own. Ryan liked hiring bright young men to work with him – Denis O'Brien, who would become a multimillionaire many years later by launching and selling a mobile phone company, cut his teeth at Ryan's side – and O'Leary's hunger and sharpness had impressed him. He made a mental note to pursue him.

Taxation was never going to hold O'Leary's attention for long. Partnership – the Holy Grail for accountancy trainees – held no interest for him, and he had scant respect for the men who ran SKC. 'They had some brilliant partners,' he says, 'but some of them were wankers, the greatest fucking gobshites.' O'Leary was in a hurry to make money. He was making a living at SKC, but no more than that. It was going to take at least another two years to pass all his exams and become a manager, and even then the rewards were not what he had in mind. 'I wanted it faster. I wanted to make a hundred grand, which seemed like, Jaysus, with a hundred grand the wolf wouldn't be at the door,' he says.

Eighteen months after joining SKC O'Leary walked out the door for the last time in the summer of 1985. Armed with a university degree and a grounding in tax law, he was determined to make his own mark and to make his own money.

While O'Leary pondered his next move, Tony Ryan was preparing for his greatest gamble. In June 1980 Ryan had drawn up his first proposal for a new airline, provisionally called Irelandia, but it had failed to get off the ground. Having made his fortune at GPA from airlines' inefficiencies, Ryan was confident that he could do better.

The prologue of Ryan's first proposal document noted that 'it is remarkable that Ireland is the least developed aviation nation in Europe'. Ryan also attacked Aer Lingus, the national carrier, for being Dublin-centred, claiming that 'token service is given in other cities'. Irelandia on the other hand planned to base its operations out of Shannon, home to Ryan's GPA.

In his proposal, which was pitched both at investors and at the government, which would have to grant his airline a licence to fly, Ryan argued that Ireland needed a second airline to force Aer Lingus to rationalize its own cost base, so that it would be ready to compete in what Ryan saw as the emerging low-fares market.

Ryan was ahead of the game. His experience in the airline industry and his knowledge of the US market had given him a glimpse of the future that others in Ireland and Europe could not see. He believed it was inevitable that Europe would follow the American lead and reduce the number of regulations that made flying such an exclusive and expensive business. It would take longer because Europe was a collection of independent states each with its own national airline, but he believed it would happen. Already, competition had spread beyond America's borders and into the transatlantic market, where Freddie Laker's Skytrain had slashed prices.

Ryan's original proposal claimed that Ireland and Portugal were the only two European countries which were home to just one airline flying international routes. In France, Air France competed with eight other airlines; in the UK British Airways had nine significant competitors and in Scandinavia SAS was fighting it out against five other airlines. In Ireland there was Aer Lingus.

Ryan argued that the Irish aviation market would soon have room for Aer Lingus and another airline half its size. And if that was not allowed to happen, then the new market would simply be served by foreign carriers, who would establish new routes between their home countries and Ireland once regulations were eased.

'The main objectives of a new airline are to profitably make low fares available to the public and prevent further foreign airlines dominating the market,' he said in his proposal. Ryan knew his plan would not be easy, and to underline his determination he quoted Machiavelli, the Italian master of politics. 'It must be considered that there is nothing more difficult to carry out, nor more doubtful of success, nor more dangerous to handle, than to initiate a new order of things. For the reformer has enemies in all those who profit by the old order.'

Ryan, though, believed he was up to the challenge. He had planned his airline's growth in four phases. Initially, Irelandia would offer flights from Shannon to New York, Boston and London. The second phase would see Irelandia using Shannon as a gateway to Europe, launching flights which would originate in New York or Boston, stop off in Shannon and continue on to European destinations. For phase three Ryan planned to increase the number of US destinations, and phase four would involve the creation of Middle and Far East services, 'perhaps with a weekly extension into Australia'.

The fares proposed – £160 return for a transatlantic flight, and

£40 for a return flight to London – were just a fraction of what other carriers were charging in 1980, but Ryan's plans were not immune to inflation; when a second draft of the Irelandia proposal was drawn up in August fares for the London route had risen to £50 return and New York had risen to £198 return.

'Irelandia would address itself to the demand of today's air traveller for cheap, no-frills, efficient travel,' Ryan wrote in a second proposal document in August 1980. 'It would compete aggressively with the foreign airlines which will otherwise dominate this aspect of Irish air travel and which cannot be successfully opposed at present.'

The keystone of Irelandia's operation will be low overheads, efficient operation and forceful marketing. The airline will be dedicated to the further development of Irish tourism and to the well-being of the south-west region . . .

Irelandia will respond to the deregulation philosophy currently implicit in American aviation policy and now gaining ground in Europe. Deregulation is a word that appears offensive to most national airlines; nevertheless, in the long term deregulation combined with competition is the only method by which the travelling public will enjoy low fares.

In his August proposal Ryan identified six 'hurdles': the procurement of government support and the necessary regulatory permissions, the assembly of talented staff and the formal establishment of the airline; the raising of the necessary finance; the building up of a network of supply services headquartered in Shannon; the inauguration of an aggressive marketing campaign; and the resistance that would inevitably be prompted by Irelandia's challenge to the status quo.

Ryan was right to be cautious. Even though the first phase of his plan was relatively modest, launching a new airline in the 1980s was a complicated, expensive and highly political operation. Ryan knew that getting a licence to operate routes between Ireland and the UK would be an uphill battle, and yet he also knew that winning the licence would be the least difficult part.

'The number of casualties in the airline business is enormous,' says Liam Lonergan, one of Ryan's early collaborators in the airline that became Ryanair.

There are very very few survivors and there are very few success stories. And the success stories tend to be people who had a considerable amount of money before they started. There are many airlines, innumerable airlines, big, small, medium, who have all just bitten the dust, some of them in rather quick time unfortunately. Never to be heard of again. And they have cost investors a great deal of money. It's a seriously quick way to lose money. It's like a black hole. It is something any sensible business person, if they knew the full commercial extent of running an airline, would run a mile from. Unless they've got more money than sense.

Ryan had the money and he thought he had the sense. His shareholding in GPA earned him millions each year in tax-free dividends and he was prepared to use that money to invest in other, riskier projects. 'Tony is not the sort of guy who salts away money for a rainy day. He is so confident, so arrogant some might say, that he never believes there will be a rainy day,' says one former colleague.

The road Ryan was preparing to take had been travelled over the previous seven years by Avair, an early competitor for Aer Lingus. Gerry Connolly, a young entrepreneur, launched Avair in 1978. Connolly's airline started life as a charter operator, but soon branched out into operating scheduled services within Ireland. Aer Lingus, which had failed to develop an internal network because it believed that it could not operate one profitably, was prepared to tolerate the existence of Avair, which did not threaten the national carrier as long as it stuck to routes within Ireland and could actually help it by ferrying passengers into Dublin for onward flights to the UK, Europe and North America.

In 1983 that tolerance came to an abrupt end when Connolly was granted licences by the Irish government to operate a number of routes from Ireland into British regional airports. For the first time Avair posed a threat to Aer Lingus, and its response was swift, brutal and very effective. Using the taxpayers' money that funded the national airline, it launched a predatory attack on Avair, opening new internal routes and slashing prices until the inevitable happened: in February 1984, less than six months after it went into direct competition with the state's airline, Avair was bankrupt. Aer Lingus had thrown down the gauntlet to all aspiring airline entrepreneurs in Ireland: if they tried to steal its market it would squash them.

Jim Mitchell, the government minister who had granted Avair its licence to expand, told the Dáil that he had refused to give the private airline a cash injection of £400,000 to save it from bankruptcy.

'Apart from the very difficult financial position of the exchequer,' Mitchell said, 'it would be totally contrary to established policy to subsidize a private airline.' He had no apparent difficulty, however, in subsidizing a state-owned airline so that it could use the state's money to undermine government policy.

Avair's collapse paved the way for Ryan to get his licence, but the risk could not have been more obvious: if his fledgling airline attempted to muscle in on Aer Lingus's market, it would concentrate its fire on him until he was broken. Worse, he knew that while the current government might be prepared to grant him a licence, Avair's demise had demonstrated that it was not prepared to stand up to Aer Lingus. It was a truly bizarre situation. Government policy was to encourage new competition in the airline market, albeit at a low level, yet the government's own airline was allowed to use public money to thwart that policy.

Avair was the most public victim of Aer Lingus's defiance, but Aer Arann, a small private airline that had been created in 1970 to fly passengers from Ireland's outlying islands off its Atlantic coast to the mainland, had also suffered at its hands. The airline had stumbled through the 1970s, losing money but surviving, operating charter flights, scheduled services and, during 1976 and 1977, allowing Captain Charles Blair, a former US Air Force pilot and husband of Maureen O'Hara, the Hollywood film star, to operate a forty-two-seat flying boat from Lough Derg, in County Tipperary. Blair's plane, the *Southern Cross*, flew under the Aer Arann licence and took tourists to the south and west coasts of the country for a flat £15 fare. By 1978 Aer Arann could offer a charter service to 32 airports across Ireland as well as destinations in the UK and Europe. It was hardly a threat to the national airline, but by 1982 Aer Arann, still in deep financial difficulty, had decided to expand and started a service from Galway to Dublin.

Once Aer Lingus attacked Avair by launching services and cutting prices across Ireland, it was inevitable that Aer Arann would be forced to retrench. In 1984 it withdrew back to its narrow routes, abandoned its expansion plans and focused instead on flying to the islands. Remarkably perhaps the airline never went under and has been able to resuscitate its ambitions in recent years. It now operates flights from a number of Irish airports to destinations across Ireland, the UK and one continental European destination.

Tony Ryan, his GPA millions burning a hole in his pocket, was prepared to take the fight to Aer Lingus at a time when Avair's experience would have discouraged most aspiring airline entrepreneurs. Along with Lonergan and another early collaborator Christy Ryan, a namesake but not a relation, Ryan would have the field to himself.

The airline would bear Tony Ryan's name and swallow his cash, but it would be owned by a trust of which he would not be a beneficiary. It was an arrangement that allowed him to honour his contract with GPA, which prevented him from owning an airline. Ryanair was, he said, for his children. Declan was working in the airline industry in the United States at the time, while Cathal had trained as a pilot. Both were appointed directors. Shane, the youngest son, was still at school when the airline launched, but he would too become a beneficiary of the trust that owned the company.

No matter the ownership structure, the new airline was very much Tony Ryan's baby, and he was determined it would be successful. His determination to launch a new carrier came, in large part, from his knowledge of what deregulation had already achieved in the US air transport market. Ryan's GPA leased planes to American operators, and Ryan excelled at predicting future growth patterns for the industry. He believed that deregulation in Europe would inevitably follow deregulation in the US, and he wanted to be one of the first to take advantage of the new regime. In the early 1980s Europe's aviation market was dominated by legacy carriers – state-owned airlines heavily subsidized by state coffers. State support had allowed these airlines to wallow in their own inefficiencies, and competition was nearly non-existent.

Aer Lingus and British Airways had no interest in increasing the size of the market on routes between Ireland and Britain; all they wanted was to extract the highest possible price from every passenger. Competition between the two was irrelevant, because at the end of each year the two airlines simply divided the revenues from the routes between themselves. There was no incentive for either airline to win business, because the spoils would be split.

Change had long been in the hands of the politicians, but there was an initial reluctance to embrace reform because they feared that competition would destroy the market rather than prove a catalyst for growth, a view encouraged by Europe's legacy carriers, which exerted exponential influence on their own departments of transport.

Aer Lingus, which knew it would feel the direct brunt of any new competition, had lobbied intensely against it, arguing that it would bring about its destruction and, by extension, that of Ireland's tourist industry. The airline insisted that the market would be cannibalized, not stimulated, by competition; that no more passengers would fly, but that the existing pool of passengers would just be divided up between more players at lower prices, causing every operator to lose money. While the airline was confident that it could squeeze out local competitors on the Dublin to Britain routes – Avair's speedy collapse into bankruptcy had convinced Aer Lingus's executives that they knew how to kill local upstarts – what it feared most of all was a transatlantic raid on its lucrative routes to the United States.

Aer Lingus's policy, and the policy of Ireland's department of transport, was unremittingly hostile to increased competition on the transatlantic market. The airline argued that competitors would simply cherry-pick the most profitable summer months, leaving the state airline to bear the burden and costs of an all-year service. It was determined to fight tooth and nail to protect its position: local competitors could be crushed by classic predatory pricing, and international carpetbaggers would be fought through the courts, through the Dáil and by a rule that forced transatlantic flights to stop at Shannon airport on their way to Dublin.

Irish consumers, who owned the airline, were never high on the Aer Lingus list of priorities. Its responsibilities were to its workers, who were heavily unionized, and not to its customers. The sheer size of the airline – it employed nearly 10,000 people in 1984 – gave it significant political power, but its near-monopoly status did not guarantee that it made profits.

Its patchy financial performance was used to demonstrate not that the airline was poorly run, but that the market could not sustain competition. Indeed the poverty of Aer Lingus's performance actually had government approval. Jim Mitchell, the minister responsible for Aer Lingus, told the Dáil in 1984 that 'for the first time since 1979/80 Aer Lingus have returned to profitability. The company are hopeful of making a net profit of £3 million in the year ending 31 March 1984 after taking into account an exchequer cost alleviation payment of £4 million to help the airline during a period of particular difficulty on the North Atlantic.'

In other words, Aer Lingus would make a profit of £3 million after receiving a cash injection of £4 million. It was, however, an improvement, as Mitchell explained. 'Compared with net losses of £13.6 million in 1980/81, £9.2 million in 1981/82 and £2.5 million in 1982/83 [the latter figure took account of an exchequer "cost alleviation payment" of £5 million], the company's expected results for 1983/84 represent a significant improvement, particularly against the background of the very difficult trading conditions which continue to prevail.' The government and Aer Lingus might have been fooling themselves, but the reality of the airline's poor

performance was difficult to hide. Because, apart from the cost alleviation payments the Irish government had also pumped in £15
million in 1983 and was about to pump in another £15 million
in 1984.

Aer Lingus had embarked on an expansion strategy that had seen
it invest in a host of non-airline businesses, like hotels, recruitment,
travel agencies, robotics and maintenance. Its senior management
team, headed by David Kennedy, then CEO, believed that the
cyclical airline industry was simply too risky and that the company needed to diversify to safeguard its earnings. It was a credible
strategy for the time, but it meant, says one former senior executive,
'that the core airline business was starved of investment and the
better managers were moving into the newer businesses, because
that's where the profit was. The fleet was getting older and that
was becoming a major problem.'

In reality, Aer Lingus's airline business was a sitting duck, waiting
to be shot by a competitor, but that competitor would need deep
pockets to survive the initial maelstrom that its arrival would
inevitably provoke, and would need strong political support within
the Irish government if it was going to get the breathing space to
survive. As the scale of the airline's difficulties began to penetrate
the minds of Ireland's public representatives, political support for
a more open market began to grow. To tip the balance, a crisis
was needed.

No sooner had Aer Lingus seen off Avair in 1984 than it was
embroiled in another turf war, this time across the Atlantic. Competition on the London–New York route had become intense
in the late 1970s and early 1980s, and the still tightly regulated
Ireland–US market was not immune to the pressure.

The Irish government controlled the price that airlines could
charge on the routes from the US to Ireland and it also controlled
the number of charter seats that could be sold in a given year at
lower prices. That ought to have been enough to ensure that Aer
Lingus was protected from competition and ought to have ensured
that Aer Lingus made money, but the Irish government could not

control what was happening in other countries, especially in Britain and the US.

Sir Freddie Laker, the British entrepreneur who had operated cheap charter flights to the US from London's Gatwick airport in the 1970s, had finally won permission to launch his cut-price Skytrain service from London to New York in 1977. Laker offered fares of less than GB£100 each way, making transatlantic travel possible for people who had never thought they would be able to fly. Laker was a people's hero, knighted in 1978 by the Queen, but his dream was undone by a combination of forces. Skytrain used McDonnell Douglas DC10s and public confidence in the plane was shattered by a series of fatal crashes which caused all DC10s to be grounded worldwide in 1979. Laker lost millions, but limped on until 1982 when his banks finally pulled the plug.

His legacy went far deeper than a five-year low-fares adventure. Laker had caught the public's imagination and made it possible for ordinary people to fly. He had changed the mindset: air travel did not have to be prohibitively expensive and competition could expand, not destroy, a market. The next year People Express launched a cut-price service from Newark to London. There were only a few flights each week, but the fare was a staggeringly low $79 each way, or about GB£100 for a return flight. Aer Lingus's cheapest fare that year was £399 return, or more than $600.

Neither Skytrain nor People Express were direct competitors with Aer Lingus, but they showed the travelling public that cheap flights were possible and created a hunger for discounts that the Irish airline refused to cater to. But if Aer Lingus would not discount, the travel agents would. They earned large commissions – up to 15 per cent on transatlantic ticket sales – and had plenty of room to cut prices if they were prepared to slash their own profits. And so the first price war started in the Irish airline business in 1983, under the noses of Aer Lingus and in direct defiance of government policy.

Neither government nor airline was amused. In April 1983 the Irish government took the unusual step of intervening in the market to prevent Liam Lonergan, the managing director of Club

Travel, selling a return ticket with TransAmerica to America for £299 against the government-approved rate of £399.

'We were [discounting] for about two years before [Aer Lingus and the government] got uptight about it. They made the usual noise – they threatened TransAmerica and said, "No, you can't do this." And that didn't work and they threatened us and said, "No, you can't do this." And we said, it's within the law – there's nothing in the legislation which says we have to sell at a certain price. They said, "We believe there is."'

Two months later the government took action against a travel agent who was prepared to discount Aer Lingus fares to London and Europe. In August the government moved again to stop Lonergan offering a £19 discount on an Aer Lingus flight to New York while in February 1984 it clamped down on an agent who was prepared to sell a full-price British Airways ticket but without forcing the customer to spend a Saturday night in the UK. In total, the government investigated nine infringements of its rules in seven months and, according to Ted Nealon, a junior minister with responsibility for transport, 'Satisfactory assurances were obtained from the airlines involved that steps were being taken to ensure that further infringements of the terms of the minister's approval would not take place.' Trouble was, the airlines might agree, but the travel agents did not.

Nealon and his colleagues were outraged by the defiance and sought an injunction in the High Court to stamp out the illegal discounting. The government won the action, but then lost on appeal in the Supreme Court, which decided that the government was within its rights to regulate the airlines but that it did not have the power to tell travel agents how to run their businesses.

So Nealon, encouraged by Aer Lingus, introduced legislation to fine and imprison travel agents who broke the rules. He argued that a free-for-all could 'lead to considerable instability in the market place, with discounting and other malpractices emerging on a scale that would undermine approved tariff structures and could have serious financial implications for airlines generally and for Aer Lingus in particular. In the long term, such a situation would only serve to put at risk the range of air services which Ireland enjoys, a development which would not be welcomed by either business or tourism.'

His argument was a perfect summary of Aer Lingus's views on competition: it would cannibalize, not stimulate, the market and must be stopped.

Nealon's proposal to fine travel agents up to £100,000 and imprison them for up to three years met a ferocious response from Des O'Malley, a senior Irish politician who was soon to break from Fianna Fáil to launch the Progressive Democrats, a party that would embrace economic liberalism. The government, he said, was

making a laughing stock of this country. [It is] the only government that I know of in the Western world at present who are bringing emergency legislation into their own parliament to push up air fares as much as possible. This is happening a week or two after the signature of an important bilateral agreement between the British government and the Dutch government which has been widely welcomed in both countries and has had the effect of reducing the return fare between London and Amsterdam to GB£49. But instead of increasing access to the country, making it cheaper for people to come here, we are introducing legislation which will ensure that our already extraordinarily high fares will be higher. We must be the only country in the world that puts people in jail for charging too little and for not making the maximum profit.

Although O'Malley was still unusual among politicians in taking a stand for liberalization, the debate had given voice to the campaign for lower fares and allowed economists, such as Trinity College's Sean Barrett, to highlight the enormous price discrepancies that existed between Ireland and the United States. In a newspaper article in 1984 Barrett pointed out the cost per mile of an airfare between London and Dublin was 39 cents, while the cost of a similar journey in the US, from New York to Buffalo, was just 12 cents a mile. On the west coast of America, where low-fare airlines were more prevalent, the costs fell lower still, with San Francisco to Los Angeles costing just 8 cents a mile.

'Barrett was probably the only public voice of any kind of stature making any comment on the nonsense that existed in the 80s,' says Liam Lonergan. 'There was a general acceptance at the time that Aer Lingus was always right, it wasn't Aer Lingus's fault . . . There was no recognition of [Ireland's needs] at all. If they had any recognition of Ireland being an island they would have deregulated airfares twenty years before that. There should never have been regulated airfares out of Ireland. The government had no concept whatsoever of how to encourage tourism, how to get people onto the island, or how to get them off the island.'

Lonergan's views were far from mainstream at the time. The government and Aer Lingus believed that Ireland being an island meant that it was essential to protect air services, because if carriers were allowed to compete they would collapse and Ireland would be left without an air link. The only sure way of keeping the market stable, they argued, was through state control. They did not trust the market and deemed air travel too important to be left to the fickle interests of investors.

Few apart from Barrett, O'Malley, Ryan and his collaborators embraced the idea that competition would create a more vibrant market and that tourism – one of the country's most important industries – would blossom rather than wither as a result. But slowly the evidence from America, where fares continued to fall and the numbers flying to climb, from a small number of competitive routes in Europe such as London–Amsterdam, and from the success of the transatlantic discounters in stimulating market demand, prompted the Irish government to dip a toe in the dangerous waters of deregulation.

Its first experiment – allowing Avair to fly to Britain – failed because Aer Lingus ensured that it failed. Without a change in government policy, a change that would see a government minister face down Aer Lingus's protestations and prevent predatory attacks on a newcomer, Avair's successors would also fail.

Pressure for change was also building fast outside Ireland and the catalyst for action had come from the courts. Just as the Irish government had introduced legislation in 1984 to outlaw discounting by travel agents, so too the French had moved to bring discounters to court. After the case, which the French government lost, the European Court of Justice was invited to determine whether aviation should be included within the European Community's strict rules on cartels and free competition.

To the dismay of the national airlines and the governments that owned them the court ruled that aviation should be subjected to the general ban on price fixing laid down under article 85 of the original Treaty of Rome. This increased pressure on Europe's senior politicians to finalize a new aviation policy. The days of bilateral agreements – where two governments carved up the airline routes between their countries and controlled both prices and capacity – were numbered.

Jim Mitchell, the senior minister responsible for Irish transport policy, had seen and heard enough. He had been converted to the benefits of aviation competition, but while he wanted competition he did not want another Avair fiasco on his hands. He had to ensure that the next licence he granted went to a company that had the funds and the leadership to mount a credible challenge to the Aer Lingus monopoly. Mitchell's strategy was not to undermine Aer Lingus, but to introduce a modicum of competition on regional routes between Ireland and the UK. Tony Ryan, a respected multimillionaire and recognized entrepreneur, fitted the bill, and so in May 1985 Ryan's Irelandia project, renamed Ryanair, became Ireland's second airline, with a licence to fly between a small airport in Waterford and London Gatwick.

Tony Ryan had his licence and was preparing for his first flights that summer but Michael O'Leary was oblivious to the dramas in the aviation industry. He had just one thing on his mind: money. He had for the moment rejected the corporate world, turning his back on accountancy and the slow path to wealth that it offered. His experiences at SKC had convinced him that the only way to make his way in the world was on his own.

'Those days there were only two ways of making money: retail or drink,' says O'Leary. 'I didn't have the money to buy a pub, so

I bought a newsagent. You could buy up old newsagents and do them up, extend the hours, bang up the turnover.' He found what he was looking for at Kestril Corner in Walkinstown, a tough working-class suburb of Dublin, and then went looking for the finance to secure the deal.

'The first person I looked up to in my business life was the bank manager of AIB in Walkinstown, who gave me a £25,000 overdraft to buy the shop. Boy did I look up to him,' says O'Leary.

The loan came with a penal rate of interest. 'My ass was grass if I didn't pay back this twenty-five grand overdraft in eighteen months,' he says. 'And at the time the annual rate of interest on personal overdrafts was 28 per cent . . . One of the advantages of that was that annual inflation was probably running not far behind 28 per cent,' he says with typical exaggeration.

With borrowed money and an acquired work ethic, O'Leary set about his business with the energy that would come to define him, motivated as much by fear of failure as determination to succeed.

He was confident enough and determined enough to turn down an opportunity to join Tony Ryan soon after he had acquired the newsagent. 'After I'd left SKC, Ryan approached me and wanted me to work for him, but at that stage I'd already bought the newsagent. Anyway I didn't want to work for GPA because GPA was huge, just like SKC. I didn't want to swap one big company for another big company.'

The Walkinstown shop was just the first step, soon to be followed by more corner shops. 'There was another one near the Submarine Bar in Crumlin. It has now been developed as a shopping centre and there was a third one which I had a stake in, out in Terenure,' he says. 'The main one was Kestril Corner.'

His business philosophy was straightforward. 'I bought mom and pop outfits,' he says. 'I'd open at seven in the morning, and close at eleven at night. Treble the turnover, treble your money.' With the shops, O'Leary learned the basic rules of running a business. 'A newsagent is a great business in that it's very small scale,' he says. 'So you learn day one that my costs are this, my sales are that and what's in the middle is my profit. So you are driving down costs, increasing sales and increasing your margins.'

Hard work was essential. O'Leary worked relentlessly long hours, opening and closing his shops, stacking shelves, serving customers and micromanaging every aspect of the businesses. And then he learned how to delegate. 'I ran the first one myself. At the end of the first year I put in a manager. Then I bought the second one, and put a manager into it as well,' he says.

'I was much more like Del Boy [the notoriously dodgy trader from the popular TV series *Only Fools and Horses*] than Dev in *Coronation Street*. I was going around in this van that had no back seat in it, going up and down to Musgraves [the wholesaler] getting all the cash and carry stuff. It wasn't very glorious.'

During his first Christmas as a shop owner in Walkinstown O'Leary proved that he had mastered the art of supply and demand and demonstrated a propensity to exploit which has stayed with him.

We had a turnover in the shop of about £1,000 a day, and being a greedy little bugger like I was at the time, we decided we'd open on Christmas Day. The staff weren't too happy – since it was just my younger brother and my younger sister I announced that the management had taken an executive decision.

I had this theory that people were stuck on Christmas Day for stuff to do, so we bought these big boxes of chocolates. And we stocked up on an unbelievable quantity of batteries. And we spent most of Christmas Eve trebling the price of batteries and the price of the big box of chocolates.

By lunch time on Christmas Day we had been cleaned out. Of everything. They bought cigarettes by the 200s, they bought the big boxes of chocolates. I had tripled the price of batteries and I still sold them out. And we took in about £14,000 in the day, fourteen times the normal turnover.

I have never had a sexual experience in my life like it. The feeling of having one wad of notes pushed down one side of my trousers and another wad of notes down the other, waddling out of the newsagent in

Walkinstown with about fourteen grand, hoping I wasn't going to be mugged going to the car.

O'Leary had tasted success and he liked it. His instincts had been proved right: he had the talent to succeed on his own, and he did not need to work for a large corporation to make his way in the world. He had learned the basic rules of business in the sharpest possible way – with his own money at risk. He had dealt with customers, grappled with stock and come to a conclusion that would stick with him for the rest of his business career: cost reduction was the key to profitability. If he could cut his costs – by working harder, buying smarter and opening longer – then his margins would rise.

Most of all O'Leary discovered what he had always suspected, but never tested to the full: he loved working, he adored making money and he was good at it. He would make whatever sacrifices were necessary to feed his obsession – long hours and inhospitable locations mattered nothing. Social and family life would be sacrificed to the greater god of Mammon. His appetite whetted, O'Leary was ready for his next challenge. He knew that he had learned a lot, but that there was much, much more to learn if he was to take the next step. Success did not sate him, it fuelled him.

4. Dash for Growth

While Michael O'Leary was striking out on his own, turning a profit by raising the price of batteries in a Dublin corner shop, Tony Ryan was launching his assault on the Irish aviation market. From the moment he had been awarded his operating licence in early 1985 Ryan and his partners had assembled a small team to launch the airline which they believed could in time become a serious competitor to Aer Lingus. Eugene O'Neill, a young former merchant banker who had worked as Ryan's personal assistant, headed the team, which first operated from a small prefabricated building at Waterford airport. Another key player was Christy Ryan, a former managing director of Aer Arann who had worked with Ryan at GPA and was godfather to his son Declan.

The airline's inaugural route would be from Christy Ryan's hometown of Waterford to Gatwick. That route was never going to make their fortune – Waterford in 1985 was a small coastal town known for its port and its hand-blown crystal glass, not a burgeoning metropolis – and Ryan decided to operate a fifteen-seat propellor aircraft which he brought in from GPA.

In July the new Ryanair took to the skies for its inaugural service, operating one return trip a day between the two airports. If Ryan managed to sell every seat on the plane every day of the week he would carry no more than 10,000 passengers a year – a tiny fraction of the overall market between Ireland and the UK – but it was a start. The initial response was encouraging: within weeks Ryanair had achieved load factors of 50 per cent – an impressive way of saying that an average of seven people flew on each leg of the route. Ryan was encouraged enough to double the daily frequency to two return flights and add a Sunday operation as well.

The Waterford–Gatwick route was always just an entry point.

Ryanair had to demonstrate to the Irish government, which granted the airline licences, that it could operate a simple route safely and efficiently. Ryan's target from the very beginning was the lucrative Dublin–London market. That, he knew, would be the real battleground with Aer Lingus, and Ryanair's entry as a competitor would inevitably provoke a ferocious response. Direct competition on flights to Heathrow was out of the question – apart from the expense of flying to a major airport, simply getting landing slots was beyond the means of a small start-up airline – so Ryan and O'Neill had to find an airport from which to launch a Dublin–London service.

Their choice was Luton, a small and underutilized airport which lay to the north of London. It could be reached by the M1 motorway, and by train from London's King's Cross station. Most important of all, Luton, though close to London, was technically not a London airport. If it had been a London airport, Ryanair would have been legally bound to charge fares in line with those of other airlines who were flying between London and Dublin. But as Luton was legally perceived as a different destination, and as Ryanair was the only airline flying to that destination, the only fares Ryanair had to match were its own.

Luton was not ideal – passengers would have to take a bus from the airport to the train station before travelling on to central London – but it was more than adequate for Ryan's purposes. It would allow Ryanair to charge whatever fares it chose and the journey time to London, at just over an hour, was not excessive. In December 1985, just five months after the first flights from Waterford, Ryan applied for and received a licence to fly between Dublin and Luton, with the new route scheduled for take-off from August 1986.

The route gave the airline its first opportunity to compete directly with Aer Lingus. Ryan was acutely aware of the significance of the development and described it as 'the most exciting route opportunity ever to be given to any independent airline operating into or out of Ireland'.

The breakthrough prompted Ryan to revisit his strategy for his airline. In January 1986 the revised business plan for Ryanair was completed. It envisaged an airline focused firmly on expansion with the resources to carve out a market. The company had set aside £1.5 million to develop its route network, which it hoped would soon expand to include a route from Shannon to Gatwick, and added a further £500,000 in buffer funding to cover any extra costs. Plans for services to America and Australia had been shelved in favour of developing short-haul services from Ryan's three favoured airports, Luton, Shannon and Waterford.

The company had high hopes for its Dublin–Luton route, commenting that even though Ryanair's flight time would 'admittedly be slower' than Aer Lingus (or 'marginally slower' as Ryan amended it by hand in his own copy of the proposal), their lower price would attract plenty of passengers. The proposed Shannon–Gatwick route was 'an essentially proven route', the document noted, but it was more vulnerable to price competition because Dan Air, a UK-based early pioneer of low-priced flights, held a licence on the route. On its one existing route, Waterford to Gatwick, the document noted that it was a 'fundamentally high yield route . . . with a proven traffic potential of at least 15,000 passengers annually'. But despite its 'fundamentally high yield', the business plan showed that the airline was heading for a loss of about £150,000 during its 'first formative year'.

The losses had eaten into Tony Ryan's original investment of £313,000, made by the trust which he had established for his sons, and within a year a third of his money – £109,000 – had already been lost. Ryanair owned fixtures and fittings valued at just £12,000, while the cost of establishing the Waterford route was £300,000. On the plus side, the airline also had stocks valued at £33,000 and debtors owed it £77,000. But it was also grappling with a £75,000 bank overdraft, and £211,000 was owed to trade creditors.

Despite its bumpy financial start Ryanair said that it was confident of making a profit of £600,000 in its second year, a profit which would be driven largely by the Dublin–Luton route. Route creation, though, was temporarily consigned to the backburner when

Ryanair's application for a Shannon–Gatwick licence was refused, leaving the airline to focus on the launch of the Luton route.

The expected demand for the new route meant Ryanair would need to serve it with more than a fifteen-seat turboprop, and as a short-term measure Ryan took in two ageing Viscounts which could handle forty-three passengers each. He planned to introduce a jet service as soon as he could, but his first priority was to get in the air and establish a presence.

The initial Waterford route may have been below Aer Lingus's radar, but Dublin to Luton was not. In the run-up to the route launch Aer Lingus and British Airways introduced a new cheap fare of £95 return, prompting Ryanair to introduce its first cheap fare of £94.99. Competition was already beginning to bite, and Ryanair's planes had yet to take off from Dublin.

Ryanair's first flight from Dublin to Luton was delayed for forty-two minutes, but finally, at 8.42 on 31 May 1986, FR201 taxied to the runway and took to the skies. It was a quiet start to a revolution that would change the fundamentals of European air travel.

The service quickly proved popular, and within weeks it was hitting its passenger targets. The response was so positive that the airline introduced extra flights. Its planes were small and slow, its destination airport was a long way out of London, but Ryanair tickets were cheap and, just as important, easy to get hold of – a new phenomenon for air travellers.

Now that Ryanair had a foothold, however slight, in the Dublin–London market, Ryan wanted more. The airline applied to the Irish government for permission to launch five more routes, with its expansion strategy based firmly on cherry-picking the busiest routes out of Ireland. Ryan wanted to fly from Dublin to Paris, Amsterdam and Manchester, as well as from Cork and Shannon to Luton. The choice of continental routes was based purely on existing traffic volumes. Figures from ICAO (International Civil Aviation Organisation) for 1984 showed that Paris and Amsterdam were the two biggest European routes from Ireland, accounting for 48.3 per cent of that traffic.

At the time the Dublin–Paris route was usually served twice daily – in the morning by Aer Lingus and in the evening by Air France. During peak season, July and August, there were four extra afternoon flights a week and an additional flight each on Saturday and Sunday. In its application to launch the new routes, Ryanair projected that on the Paris route it would stimulate the market by at least one third, and that Ryanair would carry 20 per cent of the newly enlarged market, giving it a projected 27,930 passengers and a load factor of 63.9 per cent.

The Dublin–Amsterdam route was served by just Aer Lingus, with Dutch carrier KLM operating no services. Aer Lingus operated two daily services – morning and evening. Despite facing no competition the national carrier had not fared well on the route – Ryanair said that the ICAO data for 1984 showed the outbound load factor was 'a disappointing 40 per cent'. Once again Ryanair projected a 33 per cent increase in the market, with Ryanair taking a 20 per cent share of the newly expanded market.

The Ryanair application stated,

Having seen the unprecedented demand for Ryanair's Dublin to Luton service, and bearing in mind the EEC's attitudes to competition in air travel within Europe and in particular the recent European Court ruling on air fares, it makes obvious sense to consider the extension of Ryanair's low-fare concept to other parts of Ireland and Europe besides Dublin and London; especially now that Ryanair has itself made the commitment to jets and high utilization of this equipment is key to success.

It said its early experiences on the Luton route 'vastly exceeded even our most optimistic predictions'. In its first week it carried 1,525 passengers (a load factor of 72 per cent), rising to 1,777 passengers and an 80 per cent load factor in week two. 'In week three the load factor was even higher,' it said, without specifying the numbers. It also claimed that Waterford–Luton had 'proved more popular than anticipated'.

Price would once again be Ryanair's weapon of choice, and on the continental routes it had plenty of room to manoeuvre. Aer

Lingus's return fare to Paris Charles de Gaulle airport was £434 – more than a return flight to New York – and Ryanair said it would charge just £159. It argued that price would stimulate demand and that if granted the new routes it would carry 340,000 extra passengers in the first year.

The applications were a clear signal of intent. Ryanair wanted to evolve quickly from a low-key regional operator into a serious potential competitor for Aer Lingus. Its business plan was consciously predatory – it wanted to identify Aer Lingus's most profitable routes and then challenge the national airline on each one, undercutting its fares and stealing its passengers. But Ryan knew too, from his study of the effects of US deregulation on the domestic market, that low fares stimulated air travel and encouraged people to fly. Ryanair would steal passengers from Aer Lingus, but it would also start to introduce a new generation of customers to the airline business.

Ryan was confident that the government would grant permission for the new routes, but Aer Lingus, already stung by Ryanair's success in attracting passengers to its Dublin–Luton route, was on full alert. The national airline now believed that Ryanair posed a serious threat, and after years of operating in the comfort zone of a stagnant but profitable market did not believe that the market would grow. Instead, it argued to government and to officials in the department of transport, Ryanair would simply cannibalize Aer Lingus's market and rob it of profits. The upstart, it decided, had to be stopped in its tracks.

At the time Ireland's department of transport was known as Aer Lingus's downtown office: the relationship between the department and the airline it owned was seamless. Aer Lingus executives were routinely asked to provide information for the department and allowed, in effect, to dictate government policy. Ryan's confidence that the new routes would be granted was entirely misplaced; he understood markets but he had no feel for the politics of the situation. The department of transport sought, and took, Aer Lingus's advice. The new routes would be refused.

The official reason for the refusal was that Ryanair had yet to prove itself as an airline. The Luton route, however, had quickly established itself. In Waterford early teething problems had also been countered. Poor weather conditions – Waterford airport is prone to fog – caused almost one in five flights to be diverted to other airports, but the introduction of the larger Viscount reduced the diversion rate.

Passenger numbers continued to grow as Ryanair introduced larger jet aircraft from the end of 1986. By early February 1987 the airline had carried its 100,000th passenger on the Dublin–Luton route. Ryan and his team were ready to expand further, but the rules of the day were that the government called the shots. New routes had to be approved, and getting that approval required convincing the department of transport that Aer Lingus, the fount of all its knowledge, was wrong.

A former Aer Lingus executive says that the airline was divided internally by the threat of competition, with conservatives arguing that it had to be killed at source and some liberal elements relishing the prospect of a livelier, expanding market. 'But management was dominated by the conservatives,' he says.

Ryanair had yet to prove itself to a hostile government but it had made its mark on an equally important constituency. The travelling public and initially the Irish media embraced the new company with an enthusiasm that unnerved its detractors. Eugene O'Neill, young, handsome and dynamic, captured the imagination; he was a David taking on the Aer Lingus Goliath, offering cheap flights and friendly service. His image was burnished by the skills of Anne O'Callaghan, his public relations adviser, who charmed the media and made it possible for O'Neill to shine. Significantly, too, the public wanted Ryanair to succeed because they had tasted low fares, and seen the immediate impact that Ryanair had had on Aer Lingus's fares, and they liked what they saw.

'Our customers were extremely forgiving because they genuinely wanted Ryanair to succeed,' says Charlie Clifton, who worked his way through the ranks at Ryanair from 1986 to 2002.

We had very very good public relations – Eugene was excellent at that – and the whole company really got a lot of public support. They could see that we were trying to break the monopoly. And they could also see that we were a bunch of kids as well, so it wasn't like you had crusty old folk who'd been there for years doing the stuff. We were just out of school, with no experience, trying to be as nice as we could. So you rarely got your head taken off. And people were pretty forgiving.

In just two years the company grew from being a one-plane operation out of Waterford into a serious player on the Dublin– London route. Its ability to survive, despite a deteriorating financial position, was a source of deep irritation to Aer Lingus. Hostilities were not restricted to the executive teams in both companies. Ryanair's young workforce was committed and passionate, and had no time for the patronizing disdain of the state-owned airline and its comfortable, well-paid staff. On the ground the battles were just as intense as in the boardrooms and Ryanair's people needled their Aer Lingus counterparts at every opportunity.

Clifton recalls the skirmishes, and Ryanair's minor victories still bring a smile to his face. When Ryanair moved into Cork airport in the spring of 1987, Clifton says, 'Aer Lingus acted as if it had owned that airport forever and then along came bright-eyed Ryanair. There was all sorts of messing. We'd say, "Can we have those stands there?" and they'd say snootily, "No, those are the Aer Lingus stands." We didn't have chocks for putting under the aircraft's wheels, so we merrily helped ourselves to the Aer Lingus chocks, then they'd come round and steal them back.'

To settle their differences, Ryanair eventually challenged Aer Lingus to a soccer match. 'We took them all out, eleven against eleven; we beat them 3–1 and we rang up the *Cork Examiner* and we got it put into the paper,' Clifton says, still pleased by the victory almost twenty years later. 'There were two brothers working for us, and there was something like eleven brothers in the family, and one of them played for Cork City and he came out for us. Of course the Aer Lingus guys didn't know who was working for Ryanair and who wasn't.'

Aer Lingus's naivety on the playing fields did not diminish its determination to put manners on Ryanair. It matched Ryanair's low fares with cheap, if difficult to obtain, headline fares of its own; it increased capacity on key routes; and it used aggressive marketing. The depth of Tony Ryan's pockets had kept Ryanair afloat, but Aer Lingus was determined to increase the pressure to breaking point.

O'Neill fought Aer Lingus with panache, positioning Ryanair as the cheeky, friendly alternative to the national monopoly and poking fun at it with effective advertising campaigns. Ryanair's youth and exuberance were in stark contrast to the stodgy, corporate middle-aged world of Aer Lingus; there was a swagger about the company, a confidence that comes naturally to the young and to those who have not had their ideals quashed by the dead hand of bureaucratic management.

If carrying passengers was the ultimate measure of success, then O'Neill was doing well. New route launches in 1987 had opened up the Cork–Luton market (although for the first few months the service had to land, taxi and take off again in Dublin en route because the British government still had the power to object to the new service), as well as routes from Dublin to Cardiff and Dublin to Knock, a new airport in the west of Ireland. The Knock service had been won in direct competition with Aer Lingus's new commuter service – a propeller-plane division which the airline established to compete with Ryanair – and the state airline responded by opening routes to the nearby airports of Sligo and Galway, a move that ratcheted up competition between the two airlines to a new, and more painful, level.

By the middle of 1987 O'Neill's Ryanair had carried its 250,000th passenger and with the addition of the new routes managed to carry 318,000 passengers in the whole of 1987. Its fleet of aircraft had been boosted during the year by the addition of three BAC One-Eleven jet aircraft from Tarom, the Romanian carrier, which were delivered in the early summer. That April Cathal Ryan had told newspapers Ryanair was heading for a 'substantial profit' and was expecting to have a hundred flights a week between Ireland and the UK by the summer of 1987, a fourfold increase on the summer of 1986. 'The public response has been incredible in Ireland,' he said.

O'Neill's marketing skills won him recognition from the media – Ryanair won the *Sunday Tribune*'s advertisement of the year award in 1987 for a campaign against Aer Lingus – and the admiration of his staff. The customers, too, were happy – the service was often as chaotic as the airline's finances, but in a country gripped by recession Ryanair's low prices won the airline many fans. Reservations, handled by phone and often scribbled on pieces of paper, were routinely lost, but the early Ryanair put a premium on customer relations.

'We were so customer-focused in the very early days that if you were a flight steward or stewardess and you clocked in for your flight maybe an hour beforehand and the flight was delayed, you'd be sent up to the boarding gate, and you'd float around the boarding gate talking to passengers, apologizing profusely and buying them a cup of tea or coffee. So people loved it,' says Clifton. 'It was very touchy feely. And, erm, pretty hopeless. People really liked that, but it was unsustainable.'

European expansion, however, remained elusive because of the government's refusal to grant new route licences. Ryanair's ambitions to get a foothold in the continental market were continually thwarted by the government's willingness to protect Aer Lingus from further competition.

Frustrated by his failure to win licences to Paris and Amsterdam Tony Ryan had dabbled with European expansion by paying £630,000 for an 85 per cent stake in struggling Luton-based London European Airways in late 1986. Ryan's original intention was to run LEA and Ryanair separately, with Cathal Ryan at the helm of the new UK operation. In January 1988, however, LEA was relaunched as Ryanair Europe, and began to cooperate with Ryanair, allowing the Irish airline to sell services from Dublin through to Brussels using Luton as a hub. Despite a steady trickle of Ryanair passengers, Ryanair Europe's attempts to start profitable services from London to Amsterdam and Brussels foundered quickly and the airline limped to eventual closure at the start of 1989.

The profit Ryan had envisaged for Ryanair remained similarly elusive, and by mid-1987 his airline had racked up losses of more than £2 million. The money itself wasn't a problem for Ryan – in 1987 alone his dividend from GPA had been in excess of five million – but he was becoming increasingly frustrated with Ryanair's swelling losses despite its rising passenger numbers, and with its failure to provide a serious challenge to Aer Lingus beyond the Irish Sea.

O'Leary too was getting restless. In the previous two years he had made about £200,000 from the newsagents – 'serious twine' as he puts it – but his interest in shopkeeping was waning. 'I was bored,' he says, 'but it was very good money. I wasn't overly concerned about the future. I just wanted to make a lot of money by the time I was thirty.'

He had, he says, no grand plan, just a hunger to make money. The shops were sold, and O'Leary invested his money and his energies in property dealing. 'I'd made very good money in the newsagents,' he says. 'I'd had enough of them and I sold them, bought some property, was making some nice money. That was the first time I didn't need to work for money.'

He felt invincible. Barely three years out of university, with a short career in tax affairs already in his past, he now had more money in his pockets than any of his contemporaries – and more, indeed, than many of the partners in the accountancy firm that he had left behind. He could choose his own future and decided that he still had plenty to learn. Smart, driven and ambitious, he decided to see whether Tony Ryan, who had courted him in the past, was still prepared to offer him a job – on O'Leary's terms.

O'Leary wanted to learn at the feet of a master, and money gave him the freedom to try his luck. He decided to offer his services to Ryan for free, asking only for a 5 per cent cut of any money that he made for Ryan in a year. Ryan didn't hesitate. O'Leary was hired as a personal assistant or apprentice with a bizarre array of duties ranging from the menial to responsibility for overseeing Ryan's private investments.

'I just wanted to see how somebody at that level operated,' he says.

Ryan was working at an international level; I had been working at a newsagent in Walkinstown. I'd already worked at SKC, so I'd seen a lot of big Irish business. But here was a guy who was going across the UK, across the US, across Asia. He had a global business and I don't think there was another business like it – maybe Jefferson Smurfit [the packaging giant] was close – but there certainly wasn't another business like it in Europe. He was the guy who started with nothing and was going all the way across the world. And I thought if I can't learn off this guy in a year or two . . .

O'Leary's learning curve was steep in his first year with Ryan.

Ryan's style was abrasive: he did not suffer fools, ruled his company aggressively and regularly savaged his senior executives at their weekly management meetings. He demanded excellence, worked obsessively long hours and was at the peak of his considerable powers. A consummate salesman and superb negotiator, Ryan also understood the dynamics of the airline industry better than the men who ran it. His ability to predict the industry's fortunes and to plan for future trends before they were apparent had made GPA astonishingly profitable, and its location in Shannon airport's business park allowed the shareholders to take tax-free dividends each year. The company had just reported profits of $25 million for 1986, and 1987's profits were expected to almost treble.

Under Ryan's dominance GPA was a battleground, with little room for the faint-hearted. Each week started with an 8 a.m. meeting at Kilboy, Ryan's farm in County Tipperary. The meetings were infamous for their bad temper. The cellar in Kilboy was the nerve centre of the operation. Filled with electronic equipment, it resembled NASA mission control, where Ryan could track the planes that he had leased and the movements of his GPA executives throughout the world and chart them onto large maps.

Anxious to be accepted as a serious player in world business circles, Ryan collected a heavyweight board of non-executive directors, inviting high-profile businessmen and statesmen to join GPA. The company was growing so fast and was making so much money that a stock market flotation was already a possibility; big names, he believed, would ease his company's acceptance and would enhance its burgeoning reputation. In April 1987 Ryan secured the services of a former Irish taoiseach, Dr Garret Fitz-Gerald, who had just retired from politics. FitzGerald was joined on the board by Sir John Harvey-Jones, who had just left ICI, the chemical company, and who had chosen the GPA appointment over a position on several other higher-profile boards.

While GPA prospered, however, Ryanair continued to struggle financially.

'I was trying to get involved in private investments,' recalls O'Leary, 'like the farm at Kilboy and Ryan's property investments. [Ryan] had a huge dividend income from GPA, and I had to advise on what to do with the money.' O'Leary had come in at a time when Ryan's personal finances were in some disarray. Money had been lost on a variety of failed investments ranging from an Irish Sunday newspaper to a jetfoil boat service, according to O'Leary.

Ryan had originally planned to base his new young assistant at his home in Kilboy, but that plan was abandoned because of Ryan's growing frustration with the financial problems at Ryanair. 'By the time I started there was a crisis at Ryanair,' says O'Leary, 'and I was sent in.'

The crisis stemmed from Eugene O'Neill's dash for growth. The young Ryanair managing director had decided to forge ahead with the airline's expansion into regional British airports, even though this would put him on a collision course with Aer Lingus. The Irish government was happy to approve Ryanair's expansion into the UK, but still refused to let it challenge Aer Lingus on the lucrative routes to continental Europe.

But for Ryanair the figures didn't stack up. Even though it was carrying more passengers than ever, it was also losing more money than ever. O'Neill's expansion strategy was being shot down in flames by Aer Lingus, which fought back viciously on price and by increasing flights, and Ryanair was increasingly exposed. It could not compete with Aer Lingus's apparently bottomless pockets and instead of standing on its own feet and trading profitably on the back of its passenger growth, it was fast becoming a costly embarrassment to Ryan. He needed to find out what was going wrong and how his pet project could be salvaged. And so he turned to his new assistant.

5. Pearly Gates

When Michael O'Leary first walked into Ryanair's central Dublin offices at the beginning of May 1988 it was, he says, 'like you'd arrived at the pearly gates'.

Although the airline had lost ever-increasing amounts of money since its launch three years earlier, its lavishly furnished offices screamed success. O'Leary recalls a 'gorgeous blonde chick at every desk', plush carpets, beautiful furnishings, and then the pièce de résistance: the chief executive's office, which was dominated by a 'huge big massive table' so large it could not be carried up the stairs; the windows had to be removed to get it in and the floor strengthened to support it. The effect was dramatic: instead of a sense of crisis, there was still a buzz of expectation. 'The place was a shambles and yet it was still amazingly sexy,' O'Leary says.

The young Ryanair was living up to airline tradition. It may have been the dynamic newcomer, the upstart that would challenge the Aer Lingus–British Airways duopoly over the Irish Sea, but it was going to mount that challenge with style. When it launched new routes, it would do so in the extravagant style so beloved of airlines at the time. Commemorative crystal glasses and gold-plated letter openers engraved with the name of the route and the date of the first flight were ordered by the hundreds to hand out to staff and passengers. Champagne flowed at the launch parties as the new airline wooed the media, projecting the image of a young successful company that was going to take the industry by storm.

It was an exciting, glamorous and chaotic place to work, a shaft of light in an Ireland that was still in the depths of economic gloom. It was also a company full of young people and run by young people. Eugene O'Neill, the chief executive, dressed sharply, courted the newspapers and projected the image of a new generation of Irish business leaders. Ebullient youth was replacing the stodgy corporate grey hairs, but it was not making any money. In its first year of operations Ryanair lost £4 million, followed by £5.5 million in 1986 and a further £7 million in 1987. The more passengers it carried, the more money it lost.

'The place was in a mess. There was no cost control. They were trying to be a me-too airline like everyone else and not really succeeding very well with it,' O'Leary says. O'Leary's role was to find out what was happening, and to ensure that further money did not flow into a black hole. It was a heavy responsibility for a twenty-seven-year-old with no experience of the airline industry, a man who had failed to stay the course in his chosen accountancy profession and whose only commercial success had been to turn a profit on a few corner shops. O'Leary had made no effort to study the airline industry before he walked through Ryanair's doors for the first time. His immediate objective was to stop the airline bleeding cash, not to understand the dynamics of a global industry.

At first, he could see no hope for Ryanair. 'No one had a handle on the finances and money was leaking out all over the place. All Ryanair was doing was cutting 20 per cent off the fares charged by Aer Lingus and British Airways and losing loads of money.' It took him less than a month to conclude that Ryanair could not be turned around and that it would continue to be a drain on Ryan's wealth. He had but one solution: close it down.

Declan Ryan agreed and both men travelled to Kilboy to tell Ryan their conclusions. He disagreed, refused to close the airline that carried his name and told them to sort it out. Ryan's stubbornness was not grounded in blind faith alone. GPA made its money by leasing aircraft to airlines across the world and Ryan knew how poorly those airlines were run. 'He made millions from their incompetence,' says O'Leary, 'and he thought he could do it better than them.' The trouble was, O'Leary adds, that Ryan may have thought he understood the industry but in truth he knew 'fuck-all' about running an airline. O'Leary knew even less, but he was to prove a better student than Ryan.

★

By May 1988, the month O'Leary arrived at the Ryanair offices, O'Neill was able to boast to the London *Times* that 'in one day we are taking more telephone calls than in a week last year. Competition has benefited everyone. All the airlines on the [Dublin–London] route are now carrying more passengers.' But while his confidence was high, his accounts were a mess.

Throughout the first half of 1988 O'Neill had pressed ahead with Ryanair's expansion, ignoring the financial returns and concentrating instead on driving his passenger numbers ever higher. On 1 March he launched a Dublin–Manchester service in direct competition to Aer Lingus, and by April Ryanair was operating fourteen flights a week on the route. Also in March O'Neill launched new services from Galway to Luton and followed that three weeks later with Shannon–Luton. In April, while increasing the number of flights on the Manchester route, O'Neill went head to head with Aer Lingus on the Dublin–Glasgow route as well, and in May, as O'Leary started his forensic analysis of the accounts, O'Neill pitted Ryanair against the national carrier once again, this time on Dublin–Liverpool.

It was a suicidal strategy. Following the first wave of European deregulation in 1987, which brought an end to the bilateral agreements that allowed airlines to carve up routes between themselves and loosened the restrictions on what fares could be charged, Aer Lingus had decided to build up its operations into and out of Manchester. This, the airline's management believed, was Aer Lingus's future in a world of unrestricted air travel. It would be a connecting hub for services to Amsterdam, Copenhagen, Hamburg, Milan, Paris and Zurich. In a foreign country, Manchester allowed Aer Lingus to compete directly with British Airways in a market more than ten times the size of Ireland.

Developing Manchester would be Aer Lingus's response as Europe cut back on the red tape and started to liberalize the industry. The 1987 measures were the third stage of a process that would carry on for another decade as European Union airlines were allowed to fly between other member states as long as they started in their home country. So Aer Lingus could fly from Manchester to Copenhagen if the flight started in Dublin. This allowed it to pick up passengers in Manchester for the Copenhagen leg of the flight, and it could also market the route in Britain. It was an elaborate response to the new freedoms on offer, but Aer Lingus believed it would be able to compete profitably in the bigger British market, catering to the millions in the north-west of Britain who did not want to travel to London to catch a European flight. It also had longer-term plans to link up with airlines in Asia and the Far East, but for the moment it was committed to becoming a European player. Ferrying passengers from Ireland to its new European hub was an essential part of the strategy and it was prepared to defend it with as much firepower as it could muster. O'Neill's decision to challenge it head on ensured a sharp response, just as his decision to chase Aer Lingus's other UK routes ensured that he would face a host of price wars, and not just one.

Aer Lingus responded to Ryanair's attack by cutting prices and increasing the number of flights on offer on the newly competitive routes. The response was so savage that some Ryanair executives began to suspect a conspiracy. 'You got the sense that Aer Lingus was happy to allow Ryanair to get these routes because it believed it could finish it off,' says one former Ryanair executive. 'It was like an ambush, and they gunned us down.' By July, just four months after Ryanair launched its Manchester route, the airline was forced to cut its flights there to eight a week. Three months later it pulled the route completely, its expansion strategy in tatters and its finances blown apart.

Ryanair's Glasgow challenge to Aer Lingus met a similar fate. The national carrier lowered its prices and timed its flights so that they took off earlier than Ryanair's. This was so effective that Ryanair abandoned the route in September.

The impact of the new routes – however short-lived – and the extra capacity and rising passenger numbers that they delivered had a further debilitating effect on Ryanair because they meant that the airline needed more planes. O'Neill, driven by the desire to expand no matter the cost, decided to order two new turboprop ATRs at a price tag of $18 million.

Watching from the sidelines, O'Leary could see that O'Neill's expansion strategy was putting the airline on course to self-destruct. 'They were opening routes fucking left, right and centre, the route network was nuts,' he says. 'They had no fucking schedule at all. O'Neill got blown off Liverpool because he went in twice a week and Aer Lingus was doing Liverpool three times a day. No wonder they blew him away.'

O'Leary is also critical of the state of the Ryanair fleet at that time. 'When I got here they had two BAE 748s, fifty seats; they had signed a lease with GPA for brand new ATR 42s which they didn't use; they were wet-leasing [taking both planes and crews] about six BAC One-Elevens from the Romanians. It was madness. It was all planes, planes, planes and no airline,' he says, because the strategy was chaotic.

The scale of the financial chaos started to become clearer once O'Leary started trawling through the paperwork. A Ryanair board meeting in July 1988 was told that the airline was on course to make profits of about £1 million, but O'Leary quickly shattered that illusion. 'It [the profit] was completely estimated,' says O'Leary. The airline did not have a proper system for collecting money that it was owed and was saddled with bad debts – unpaid bills from travel agents and customers that had to be written off ... It took little more than a cursory glance to realize that instead of making profits it was going to lose between five million and ten million.

The discrepancy between O'Neill's estimated profits and O'Leary's estimated losses was a rude awakening for Tony Ryan, and made a mockery of O'Neill's claims of success.

'There was a massive hole [in the Ryanair accounts],' O'Leary says.

The numbers were rubbish. There was nobody collecting cash. We didn't know how much money we had, except we had nothing in the bank. The bottom line was that if Ryan didn't give us a million by the next Friday we couldn't pay the wages. There was no cash in the company, and that was the problem ... The turnover in 1986 was

£4 million, and the cash at the end of the year was £18 million. The turnover in 1987 was £18 million and the cash at the end was £310,000. Where the fuck was our money?

We actually came to a point one night where we bounced a cheque to Aer Rianta for £24,000. They said if the cheque didn't go through on Friday they were going to put a yoke on the front of the plane [and seize it]. We had to call Tony and tell him we needed twenty-five grand or Aer Rianta were going to shut us down. Something had to give.

O'Neill, though, appeared oblivious to the source of the airline's crisis and the severity of the situation. 'Eugene said this is all the fault of Aer Lingus,' says O'Leary. 'He said if you allow me to sue Aer Lingus for anti-competitive [practices] in Brussels we will get 300 million in compensation and Aer Lingus will be ordered off the routes and all will be well.' The answer, thought O'Leary, was simpler: 'There is a hole in this fucking company.'

The Ryanair board's response to O'Neill's proposal to haul Aer Lingus before the Brussels competition authority was blunt. He was told that Ryanair depended on the Irish government for its route licences and could not sue the state-owned carrier. And the board had begun to recognize, too, that the problems went deeper than the crippling battle with Aer Lingus. O'Neill's time was up, and he was acrimoniously fired at the start of the summer.

'There was a meeting in a hotel, and Michael and Eugene were sitting beside each other on the podium,' says Charlie Clifton.

They announced that Eugene would be departing the company. They just said he was moving on to pastures new.

It wasn't evident to us at the time, but looking back it's clear that financial controls had been very lax under Eugene. The staff loved him because he was a bright shiny thing.

He'd give you anything. The purse strings were loose. For example, we were supposed to pay for our uniforms at the start – we signed up for it. Six months in he said look, don't worry about it, you've worked so hard. Of course that's nice, that's really nice. But nice costs money, and that's why we lost a shit load of money.

O'Neill's strategy of pursuing growth at breakneck speed had firmly positioned Ryanair as a serious player in the market – by the time he was fired the company had a 20 per cent share of the Dublin–London market – and had established the Ryanair brand in the marketplace. But success in positioning the airline had come at a very heavy price – one that he thought Tony Ryan was willing to pay. The early Ryanair never managed to shake off the sense that it was an indulgence for Tony Ryan, a plaything for his sons rather than a serious commercial operation. Money, so O'Neill thought, did not really matter in those early years because Ryan had plenty. The objective, he argued, was to build a business that would eventually make profits.

O'Neill was only partly wrong. Despite the millions he had poured into Ryanair, Tony Ryan was not struggling for cash. A few weeks after dismissing O'Neill, Ryan spent £35 million acquiring a 5 per cent stake in the Bank of Ireland, the country's most prestigious financial institution. O'Neill's problem was that the state of the airline's finances was hidden from view and investors, no matter how wealthy, hate surprises. Ryan had been led to believe that the airline's success in attracting passengers had started to translate into bottom-line profitability – O'Neill's wildly optimistic estimate that the airline would make profits of a million pounds that year had been unravelled late in the day by O'Leary – but the truth was different. Under O'Neill the company's accounts had become a black hole and his expansion strategy was fraught with risk. Instead of seeking out markets that were underserved, he had chosen to pitch Ryanair directly at Aer Lingus, inviting the national airline to strike back. It had, and had finished him off: Ryanair's ignominious retreats from Manchester and Glasgow were a sad epitaph for a man whose energy and charisma had put the airline on the map, but whose lack of basic financial acumen had cost him his job.

Bitterly angry at his ousting, O'Neill launched a series of court actions against Ryanair and, bizarrely, against Aer Lingus and its chief executive David Kennedy, claiming that they had all conspired together to reduce the value of his shareholdings in Ryanair.

O'Leary recalls the events with bewilderment. 'He then said he was removed because he wanted to sue Aer Lingus and the Irish government, and Tony Ryan wouldn't allow him . . . And then he said that we were cooking the books just to shaft his court case, and make it look like he was incompetent.'

Eventually O'Neill settled his case against Ryanair – the Ryan family bought back his shareholding in the company – and subsequently lost his action against Kennedy. A career that had promised so much had passed its zenith, and as O'Neill was dismissed, his legacy was already being dismantled. 'People would have been pretty loyal to Eugene and they would have been pretty shocked at his dismissal. The old guard left when Eugene left,' Clifton says.

But while O'Neill's exit from Ryanair was acrimonious, O'Leary sees the value in O'Neill's reign.

In a perverse way, if Ryanair had been run properly from the start, it would never have got off the ground. Eugene had a lot of faults, but he did such a good job with the marketing and he gave it great credibility from a standing start. If it had been started by a bunch of accountants it would never have gotten the credibility. And so in a fucked-up bizarre way, the best way to do it was to start with the panache and the style. Problem was, what they hadn't built into the model was a cheque for ten million to pay for all this pizzazz.

With O'Neill out, O'Leary was becoming a more powerful force in the company. His style was in sharp contrast to O'Neill's flamboyance. O'Leary worked from a modest office at Ryanair's Dublin city headquarters and was rarely seen at the airport. Most of the airline's staff had no reason to know he existed. Those who did were not to know that he was not even a company employee, but was instead personal assistant to the man whose money funded the company, even if that man's children held nominal control. O'Leary's role was to report to his master, not to the board or other executives. His brief was to watch over Ryan's personal investments, and Ryanair was the biggest and most expensive of them all.

'When he started he was very much shut away in head office,' says Clifton. 'The staff hadn't a clue who he was. He was another guy who worked in College Park, who was fairly high up. That was it. Nobody assumed that he was a hatchet.'

O'Leary's personal life was as understated as his approach to business. He drove a Honda Civic, a car more suited to students than business executives, and lived in an apartment on Morehampton Road in Dublin's Donnybrook, a low-key if affluent suburb near the city centre. He rarely socialized in Dublin, returning to his parents' farm in Mullingar most weekends. And while the young O'Leary grappled with the complexities of the airline industry – and any other problems thrown his way by Ryan – his father continued down his own entrepreneurial path, evolving from rendering plants and rabbits to his latest venture, making herbal remedies from nettles picked by students on the family's land.

O'Leary's working life did not, yet, revolve completely around Ryanair. His knowledge of the industry was thin and his responsibility was narrow. He was charged with finding out where the money was going, not with charting the airline's future. And as Ryan's assistant he still had other investments to divert his mind from Ryanair's difficulties, including Ryan's shareholding in the Bank of Ireland. O'Leary was not a candidate to replace O'Neill as chief executive and had no desire to take the job even if it had been offered. He did not want to become centrally involved in an airline that he believed had no future, and Ryan wanted to import a seasoned aviation industry professional to instil much-needed management discipline.

While he sought the right candidate he installed his son Declan as interim chief executive. Four months later Ryan appointed Peter (P.J.) McGoldrick to the position in October 1988. O'Leary would maintain his watching brief but remain in the background. 'P.J. McGoldrick was sent in as a fireman,' says one former executive. 'He was expected to stem the losses and turn it round. There was a lot of confidence that McGoldrick would be able to do it.'

McGoldrick had a track record in the aviation industry, but not one which was a natural fit with a commercial airline business. He had run an air transport company out of Stansted airport in Essex and had subsequently sold it to Trafalgar House, a British conglomerate with diverse interests in shipping, hotels and the Far East. Ryan, his reputation as businessman on the rise, had been invited to join Trafalgar's board, and when he came across McGoldrick he identified a 'fellow traveller', according to an executive who knew both men.

McGoldrick, at forty-nine, was substantially older than his predecessor and most of his workforce. He lived in Killaloe in County Clare, near Shannon airport, flying to work in his private plane. To the eyes of the people who worked under him, he lacked O'Neill's dynamism. 'He was not at all inspiring,' said one senior manager. 'An accountant would be a good description, not in relation to costs but in his manner. Kind of slow speaking, not dynamic at all. One time he called me into his office and delivered a speech which was supposed to be uplifting and I could hardly hear the guy.'

Tony Ryan, however, was not interested in charisma or people skills; he wanted a veteran who could stop his airline losing money. 'McGoldrick was a maverick and, as they say in Ireland, a bit of a chancer. He would take risks, and he would play right to the edge. He was not short of self-confidence, and he was in the Ryan mould,' says a Ryanair veteran.

McGoldrick's early priorities were to impose some order on the chaos within the airline. He needed to rationalize its route network, which had grown incoherently under the O'Neill expansion strategy; he needed to sort out the fleet and the schedules to make the airline more efficient; he had to kill off routes which were failing; and he had to impose some financial discipline. 'It would be easier to say what we didn't change than what we did change,' he said some months later.

The first step was to revamp the loss-making Luton-based Ryanair Europe. McGoldrick's solution was harsh. In January 1989 Ryanair Europe closed its Brussels office and abandoned its scheduled services.

Ryanair Europe's scheduled operations had been that most dangerous of hybrids – low fares with all the frills. 'It was patently obvious that that was the way not to go,' says O'Leary. Its acquisition, he says, had been a flawed response to Aer Lingus's decision to develop Manchester as a hub. 'The Ryans decided they would copy that strategy and they bought this bankrupt airline in Luton and relaunched it . . . It lost a fortune. It was all nuts, using Luton as a hubbing airport. It is hard to know looking back, with the wisdom of hindsight, how you could be so stupid in the first place,' he says.

From London, Ryanair Europe was facing competition from British Airways and Sabena, who pandered to business travellers who did not pay their own fares because air travel was an expense paid by companies. A remarkable 80 per cent of BA's passengers paid business-class fares, and Ryanair Europe had tried to compete by offering a similar quality of service but at a third of the price. Unsurprisingly, it had incurred heavy losses. McGoldrick had no option but to shut the service down before its losses dragged down Ryanair itself.

Back in Ireland McGoldrick embarked on a restructuring programme which included replacing the entire second management tier, revamping the accounts system and altering 'all basic systems from holidays to promotion'. He reordered the company into five coherent parts: Ryanair, the main airline, based in Dublin; Ryanair Europe, based at Luton airport and now reduced to small-scale charter operations; Ryanair Engineering, also based at Luton; Ryanair Fleet Management, established to manage the aircraft of the two airlines; and Ryanair Tours and Leisure, designed to move into the tourism and hotel sector of the travel industry.

'What we are doing is broadening the base of the group,' McGoldrick said in early 1989.

Instead of operating just the two airlines, we had to change direction and place the group on a strong and more viable financial footing.

The airline started to run into problems early last summer [1988]. It just didn't have the organization or structures to cope with the way business had grown. We had over-expanded our fleet. The company has now been restructured and we are on course for breaking even in the coming year.

On a pure business basis, what went wrong was that [Ryanair] expanded very quickly – it doubled its fleet within months. I don't think the organization and head office were able to keep up with that expansion and a lot of things fell apart because of that. On top of that you had fairly aggressive competition from other carriers, particularly in Manchester and Glasgow, where we made major losses.

It was a sanitized description of the company's problems under O'Neill, and it was economical with the truth by suggesting that Ryanair had only started to run into problems in the summer of 1988. That was when Tony Ryan had become aware of the scale of its difficulties, thanks to O'Leary's intervention, but they had been building from the start.

McGoldrick had taken over a company in crisis, that much was clear. What remained opaque was the depth of that crisis. Throughout 1989 the real devastation of the previous year became more and more apparent as O'Leary worked his way through the accounts. The previous July's optimistic forecast of profits had been replaced by the certainty of losses, but quite how deep those losses would be did not emerge until the following autumn.

In March 1989 the *Financial Times* reported that Ryanair's losses for 1988 were expected to be in the region of £2.5 million; in September that estimate had risen to £6 million, and when the results were finally announced in October 1989, a year after McGoldrick had taken charge, the figure was £7.34 million. It had been, a company statement said drily, 'a very difficult period'. Almost half of those losses had been incurred on the failed expansion into Manchester and Glasgow – a painful lesson in how not to compete with Aer Lingus and retrospective justification for the dismissal of O'Neill.

'I never wanted a battle with Aer Lingus. Ryanair has proved there is enough business out there for both of us. I'm not going to waste the Ryans' money fighting Aer Lingus,' McGoldrick told the *Financial Times*. He was confident that his overhaul of the company would produce substantial rewards, and he announced in October 1989 that the airline had responded well to treatment and was now on course to make a profit.

But his optimism would come to look as foolish as O'Neill's because he too was heading for abysmal losses in his first full year in control. Michael O'Leary, working quietly behind the scenes, would also feel the pressure. Despite his attention to the financial details of the business, he had failed to shed light on the airline's core difficulties. His master's investment remained a basket case, and O'Leary was expected to come up with solutions, and fast. His job, after all, was to mind Ryan's private investments and Ryanair's losses had become the most important part of his agenda. Until those losses were staunched, O'Leary would have little time to devote to what he really wanted to do: use Ryan's money to make more money, and take his 5 per cent of the action on the way.

6. Cohabitation

Michael O'Leary likes to claim that a 'cursory' look at Ryanair's accounts was all that he needed to understand the depth of the airline's problems, but it actually took the best part of two years for him to get to grips with the finances and help steer the airline towards stability and eventual profitability. 'The accounts were hopeless,' says one former director, 'and the management accounts were five or six months out of date. No one knew, or could possibly know, what was happening because the information was just not available.'

While O'Leary tried to unravel the financial mess, P. J. McGoldrick focused on sorting out the operational chaos that had enveloped the company, closing routes and shutting down Ryanair Europe. The route closures were morale-sapping for the young company but did not mean Ryanair was in full retreat. McGoldrick was pulling apart the flawed expansion plans put in place by O'Neill and also dismantling the equally misplaced ambitions of the Ryan family, who had wanted to expand into Europe before they had managed to secure the future of the core airline. But he still wanted to grow. His objective was to reposition Ryanair by retreating from the head-to-head competition on routes that was crippling the airline. He was also trying to maintain forward momentum by identifying routes that Aer Lingus would leave alone and where Ryanair had a chance of making some profit. So he went for new route launches in the early part of 1989 that brought services from Knock airport in the west of Ireland to Leeds/Bradford and to the new Stansted airport in Essex, as well as from Kerry airport to Luton. These were a far cry from the battles with Aer Lingus on the Dublin to Manchester and Glasgow routes, but they gave Ryanair the opportunity to expand while it regrouped.

At the end of May 1989 McGoldrick announced a further new

route, which would, as events unfolded, prove to be the most significant in the transformation of Ryanair from loss-making company into a profitable and viable European airline. Ryanair, he said, would fly from Dublin to Stansted – a move that would open a new front in the Dublin to London air war and which would pitch the man who claimed he wanted to avoid a fight with Aer Lingus into another struggle with the national carrier. This time, however, Ryanair would fight on the political as well as the commercial front.

In truth, McGoldrick had little choice but to challenge Aer Lingus again. It was one thing to withdraw from the ill-chosen fights over Manchester and Glasgow, quite another to allow Ryanair's growth to be dictated by fear. His dilemma was one of scale. McGoldrick knew that Luton airport, which had messy transport links to London and was in need of serious investment, could not provide the growth opportunities that Ryanair needed, if it were going to survive. The solution, he believed, was Stansted airport, a new facility in the middle of Essex which had been his base at his previous job as chief executive of Heavylift, an air cargo business.

Stansted was designed to be London's third airport. A gleaming modern building of glass and steel, complete with a futuristic monorail that took passengers from the main terminal building to the outlying airline gates, the airport had cost £300 million to build. The problem was that there weren't many passengers. Despite the hype that had surrounded its opening, Stansted had been shunned by the major airlines and had yet to finish its rail link to London's Liverpool Street station. Without the train, Stansted was simply too far from the British capital to attract scheduled airlines, and it had been forced to settle for the more sporadic trade of the charter airline market.

McGoldrick recognized that Stansted had the capacity to handle Ryanair's growth and saw an opportunity in the fact that it lacked the basic infrastructure to attract major airlines. This weakness provided a perfect platform for McGoldrick to strike an exceptionally good bargain with the British Airports Authority, Stansted's owners, who were keen to deal with anyone who promised passengers. Ryanair's finances may have been disastrous, but the airline had demonstrated its ability to sell seats, and anyway not even McGoldrick knew how bad the finances really were.

BAA and Ryanair negotiated quickly and without rancour. Sir John Egan, the former Jaguar boss who chaired BAA, was intrigued by the brash young Irish airline and was prepared to give it a chance, especially since he had few offers on the table. The deal was straightforward: Ryanair would pay a small fraction of the published landing charges and start its services in the spring of 1989.

Unfortunately for McGoldrick, Aer Lingus had also spotted the opportunity that Stansted offered. It had moved first, acquiring landing rights and launching services in early 1989 from Dublin. When Ryanair launched services from Knock and then from Dublin, Aer Lingus immediately made plans to increase its once-a-day service to twice daily to heap pressure on its competitor. It was then, at the end of May 1989, a year after O'Leary had arrived, that Ryanair's fortunes started to change, marginally but very importantly, for the better. Ireland's department of transport denied Aer Lingus permission to increase its number of flights. For the first time since Ryanair's launch in 1985 there was official recognition that competition might actually be good for Irish tourism, as well as a willingness to prevent a competing airline from being driven off a route by a bigger rival.

Seamus Brennan, the new minister for transport, was intuitively more open to the idea of competition than his predecessors, and officials in the department could no longer ignore the fact that Ryanair's emergence as a force in the market had stimulated traffic between Ireland and England. The number of passengers travelling by air between Ireland and the UK had risen sharply each year since the new airline started operations – doubling from 1.5 million in 1985 to more than 3 million in 1989 – and thereby destroying Aer Lingus's argument in the early 1980s that a new competitor would simply cannibalize the existing market.

Brennan and his department officials had no intention of supporting Ryanair directly, but they were prepared to draw Aer

Lingus's predatory teeth. 'The department was very supportive of Aer Lingus at that time and it dominated the airports and the routes,' says Brennan.

Ryanair had just started up, and was losing money and doing badly, servicing regional airports like Knock, Waterford, Galway. It was seen as an outsider, a small player.

I could see that there was a clear contradiction in my position as the official owner of the national airline and also as the industry regulator. You can't be a referee and play on one of the teams at the same time. And that was what was going on in Irish aviation – the referee played on one of the teams.

He recognized that Ryanair under McGoldrick had moved away from confrontation by abandoning the routes to Glasgow and Manchester, and had also observed that Aer Lingus had forced it off the Knock–Dublin route. It was time, Brennan reasoned, for cohabitation. There was room, as McGoldrick had argued, for both airlines in a growing market, and competition had demonstrably increased the size of that market.

Aer Lingus, however, did not read the signs. Conditioned to believe it had an inalienable right to run air services out of Ireland, it remained committed to killing Ryanair. If it could not add more flights, it would compete on fares and schedules. Since it was state-owned, Aer Lingus had never been subjected to the commercial pressures that dictate the fortunes of private companies. It knew that it would not be allowed to fail, and successive Irish governments had pumped in millions of pounds to keep the airline flying.

Armed with a conviction of its own invulnerability, Aer Lingus was now prepared to use Irish taxpayers' money and its own profitability in the late 1980s to defeat government policy, and it was supported in its rebellion by the trade unions which dominated its workforce and intimidated its management. Unions and management were united in their hatred and fear of Ryanair, the unions because a successful, non-unionized private airline could disrupt their own cosy arrangements with the national carrier, and the management because they believed, wrongly, that Ryanair's success could only come at their expense.

The pressure reached breaking point in the summer of 1989. Despite the public confidence of the Ryanair management, privately they now knew that the airline was in deep crisis. The rate of its losses had slowed in 1989, thanks to McGoldrick's route closures and O'Leary's tightening grip on the airline's finances, but it was still losing money at an alarming rate. Tony Ryan knew that if the airline were to survive he would have to invest a further £20 million, and he would not do so unless there was a realistic chance that the airline would be given the breathing space to grow profitably. The situation was stark: unless the uneven David and Goliath struggle with Aer Lingus could be halted, Ryanair would have to fold. O'Leary recommended, once again, that Ryan cut his losses, but the GPA chief executive decided on one last roll of the dice. He would try to persuade the government that Ryanair deserved another break.

The late summer months are traditionally a good time to meet members of the government – at least those who have not disappeared on their summer holidays. August is a month when formal politics in Ireland ceases, the Dáil is in recess and the country at play. If a minister is in the capital, he has little pressing business to fill his day. Seamus Brennan, the transport minister, had no trouble making time for Tony Ryan.

Ryan brought McGoldrick and O'Leary with him and outlined a simple case: their airline could survive only if the minister was prepared to build on his decision to block Aer Lingus from increasing its frequency on the Dublin–Stansted route. Ryan needed much more: he wanted Brennan to make a very conscious decision in favour of a two-airline policy by carving up the routes across the Irish Sea between Ryanair and Aer Lingus. This would not be the two-airline policy of the past, when British Airways and Aer Lingus shared the routes across the Irish Sea and divvied up the cash each year. It would be a policy based on competition, not on collusion, which would give both airlines the opportunity to compete for business but which would prevent them from destroying one another by dividing Britain's airports – and particularly London's airports – between them.

Ryan was not asking Brennan to hand over Aer Lingus's traditional route to London's Heathrow airport; he just wanted the national carrier to stop using its apparently limitless resources to kill his own company by using predatory tactics on shared routes. He wanted space to survive and space to grow, and that meant getting Aer Lingus out of Stansted. If Brennan was not prepared to stop Aer Lingus's predation, he warned that Ryanair would close and the tourist industry, which had begun to flourish after twenty years of stagnation, would wither once more. The choice was stark.

'It was made quite clear to me that Ryanair was about to shut,' says Brennan.

We were bombarded by Ryanair at that time, being told that it was going to close, that it was losing millions. The figure six million was in my mind – that's nothing nowadays but it was big money then. I'm not sure how they told me but they got the message across in phone call after phone call, letter after letter, meeting after meeting. There were calls from Tony Ryan and from their accountancy people. They were all chasing the department, not just me, and they were backing their claims with financial statements.

Luckily for Ryan, Brennan was one of the few Irish politicians at the time who was instinctively in favour of competition – an instinct that he would trust again in the future. In the early 1990s state-owned companies were a dominant force in Ireland's then lacklustre economy. More than 60 per cent of those in work were employed, either directly or indirectly, by the state, while unemployment levels were persistently high.

Brennan listened to Ryanair's tale of woe and decided to act. 'They were in big trouble and they convinced me and my officials that the company was about to close. Could they have been bluffing? They would have had to get past all the top people in the department, most of whom would have loved to have seen them going bust, they would have had to get past me, past the department of finance, even the media.'

Financial help was not on the table, though Ryan did ask if a handout would be considered. 'They never got any money from us,' says Brennan. 'It was out of the question, because Aer Lingus got our money.' Instead, Brennan and his officials settled on a radical new policy for the Irish aviation sector, a policy which for the first time recognized that the country's interests would be better served by having two native airlines carrying passengers into the country rather than just the single state-owned company.

'If you think about that today, imagine having a two-newspaper policy or a two-anything policy. It should have been an any amount of airlines you like policy,' says Brennan. 'The climate was such that I couldn't even say let's open the market for any airline that wants to fly to Ireland. I couldn't say that because Aer Lingus was so dominant and powerful.'

The two-airline proposal then went to the Irish cabinet, where it had to clear another significant political hurdle. Charles Haughey, Ireland's then taoiseach, represented a north Dublin constituency, as did Bertie Ahern, then minister for labour. Since Dublin airport is situated in north Dublin, the two men's constituencies were home to thousands of airport and airline employees. The national interest, when it came to aviation policy, often had to take a back seat to the more pressing political realities of winning elections.

Haughey and Ahern, says Brennan, took a lot of convincing before they would sign up to the new airline policy, but luck was still on Ryanair's side. Unusually for a major political decision, Brennan was moving at speed, and the August holidays, followed by the slow return to mainstream politics in September, meant that Ryanair's opponents were asleep. Aer Lingus knew that Ryanair was in crisis but did not believe that the government would actually lift a finger to help its rival.

Caught unawares by Brennan's speed, the state airline failed to lobby aggressively before the cabinet meeting that would decide

Ryanair's future. Then, to its shock and genuine horror, the two-airline policy was announced as a fait accompli and there was nothing that could be done to reverse it.

'There was,' says Brennan, 'absolute murder. Aer Lingus employees were picketing my office, calling for my resignation and making all sorts of accusations.' Some insinuated that Brennan had introduced the new policy because Tony Ryan had made a large donation to Fianna Fáil, Brennan's political party. Others claimed that Brennan had benefited personally – a charge that he rejects angrily.

'There were conspiracy theorists around that decision,' he says.

People asked, 'How much did he get from Tony and the lads?' And the answer is nothing. Not a red cent, ever. Not a free trip to a football match, not a fucking ha'penny, not even a postcard. I did not make that decision because of them, I didn't care who they were.

They could have been Mexicans as far as I was concerned. Or Chinese. I just saw a small company who wanted to fly people to London at a cheaper price. It was £208 to fly to London in 1989. Here was an airline that came along and said we'll do it for half that. And I was supposed to shut them down? I said why the blazes should we have one airline, I don't understand it, I don't care if we have forty airlines.

Prompted by Brennan, the Irish government decided that Ryanair should be the sole Irish carrier licensed to operate from Ireland to Stansted and Luton airports and that Ryanair would also be the sole carrier on the Dublin–Liverpool and Dublin–Munich routes. Aer Lingus, meanwhile, was awarded exclusive rights to service Heathrow and Gatwick, London's two major airports, as well as Paris and Manchester.

The effect of the new policy was seismic. 'I went to the cabinet, I simply said "Aer Lingus have three London airports and Ryanair have one, well let's give them two each." The nub was to take Aer Lingus out of Stansted. I think history has shown that that was the right decision,' Brennan says.

It was, on balance, an equitable carve-up: the national carrier was guaranteed no competition on its traditional and highly profitable routes to Heathrow and Gatwick, London's largest airports, while Ryanair was protected from predation on its routes to the new Stansted airport. Irish tourism, so Brennan believed, would be the winner.

But for Aer Lingus it was a dramatic setback. It had lost its status as the only airline that mattered in government policy-making, and its competitor had been thrown a lifeline by Aer Lingus's owner. It was, the senior management and unions believed, a betrayal. Cathal Mullan, Aer Lingus's chief executive, said the change of policy was 'very serious. Without a Dublin–Stansted operation, our capacity to generate increased tourist numbers from the south-east of England will be totally inhibited.'

If that had been the airline's sole intention, then it is possible that Brennan would not have acted. But it was evident that Aer Lingus had become dangerously obsessed by Ryanair's success in building a market that it had always argued did not exist. Simply put, Aer Lingus had been wrong, and its errors had deprived the state, its owner, of a booming tourism industry. Aer Lingus had to be saved from itself, and the safest way of ensuring that it focused on its real business rather than on killing a competitor was to separate the two airlines and cushion them from each other for a period of time.

Aer Lingus's attempts to drive Ryanair out of business were by then proving ruinously expensive. Aer Lingus's profits had peaked at £52 million in 1988/89, but the battle with Ryanair cut those profits almost in half in 1989/90 and by 1990/91 they had tumbled to just £8.3 million. The airline's dwindling profits (and eventual fall into substantial losses) were not caused by Ryanair's existence, but by Aer Lingus's chosen response.

As Des O'Malley, then leader of Ireland's Progressive Democrats, said,

Aer Lingus's management failed to recognize the changing environment in European air travel that deregulation had brought about and had failed to change its corporate culture. While paying lip service to the new competitive era, Aer Lingus still hankered after what they consider the good old days of collusion between state-owned airlines to maintain high prices, to keep out competitors, and to discourage increased business. They have compounded the original strategic error of trying to block competition by an obsessive follow-on policy of trying to kill off their new domestic competitor, Ryanair. So obsessive did this policy become in recent times that it has virtually bankrupted their core aviation business. There was an irrational targeting of the new Irish airline, which they sought to put out of business at all costs. They pursued Ryanair everywhere, even to the small provincial airports, which they would not touch until the new airline went into them. Instead of going out to develop their own business, Aer Lingus chose the soft option of matching fares with all competitors and trying to prevent other airlines from developing business for the benefit of the country.

If Brennan saved Aer Lingus from destructive competition, he also gave Ryanair a real opportunity to emerge from years of loss-making. McGoldrick said the change in government policy represented 'a coming of age for Ryanair, a recognition that we have a role to play'.

Fifteen years later O'Leary takes a more conservative view of the impact of the deal. 'The concession itself didn't actually amount to a lot,' he says. 'Aer Lingus owned Heathrow and Gatwick, we were in Luton and Stansted. The deal was Aer Lingus got Heathrow and Gatwick and we got Luton and Stansted. We got Liverpool and they got Manchester. And that was it . . . The deal was only crucial in persuading Tony [Ryan] to put in more money. He said he was not putting in another ten or twenty million if the government was going to keep on dumping on him.'

The exclusive right to fly to Stansted was not a guarantee of success. While Stansted had clear potential, it was an airport entirely without a track record, had no experience of low-fares airlines and, even more worryingly, was unknown to the vast majority of British travellers.

'Ryanair was in a very difficult position,' recalls Peter Bellew, who ran a tour-operation company in the UK. 'When they opened up in Stansted, it too was literally just opening. I put a proposition to Ryanair that we'd do inclusive packages, your flight, your accommodation, your car hire, whatever, based around the concept of low, fixed airfares.' Ryanair jumped at the idea, and soon Ryanair Holidays was born. The tour operator, which had previously offered ferry holidays, brought out a brochure featuring all the destinations Ryanair flew to in Ireland. In 1989/90 Ryanair Holidays carried 10,000 people – a small but profitable slice of Ryanair's total traffic for that year.

'It was a great success,' says Bellew.

They were really good holidays, because it was the first time there had been low-cost, high-volume holidays by air, from England to Ireland, because Aer Lingus was very expensive. For the Punchestown races in 1991 we brought about 700 people – which at the time was a lot.

It was good cash flow for the airline. This was great because they were getting paid for these seats about eight weeks before they got paid for normal seats.

By the end of 1989 McGoldrick was confident that the airline had turned a corner. In November, in an interview with trade magazines, McGoldrick said that the two-airports deal had been a resounding success for both airlines and predicted that Ryanair was 'on course to do better than break even this year. We are determined not to lose money.'

We have almost all been winners as a result of liberalization and the relaxed bilateral [that] was signed between the governments in Dublin and London. Aer Lingus is making more money and so is the Irish Airports Authority. It just goes to prove that competition does work . . . This year, the airlines will carry a total of 750,000 passengers, with present load factors running at around 78 per cent. We have our heads down and are working our way out of our troubles.

But his confident assertions would prove a nonsense: Ryanair eventually reported losses for 1989 of just under £5 million, despite

McGoldrick's corrective actions and the late benefit of the two-airline policy. His confidence was not based on simple bravado; the harsh reality was that just two months before the end of Ryanair's financial year, and eighteen months after O'Leary had been sent in to find out what was happening to Tony Ryan's money, the airline's senior management had no idea about the company's underlying financial performance.

McGoldrick's confidence in the future was to prove more valid than his belief in the present. With the two-airline policy secured and with wider deregulation of European aviation on the way, he was entitled to dream of expansion, growth and profits.

We see an expanding regional operation to more European points from the existing airports in Ireland, a build-up of our charter operations based on the BAC One-Eleven and the A320, and a possible move into long-haul charters with the Airbus A340. And we would like to get into scheduled services from Britain into Europe at some stage in the future.

Provided we keep ourselves slim and the utilization of our aircraft up, we will be capable of taking on anybody when the European Economic Community frontiers go down at the end of 1992.

Winning a respite from the struggle with Aer Lingus was only part of the battle. If Ryanair was to survive and Tony Ryan's latest £20 million investment was not to be wasted, the company simply had to get to grips with its elusive finances.

O'Leary was trying to learn about the business, to get a feel for where money was being spent and how it could be saved, but instead of studying the industry by reading books and poring over financial statements, he started to work on the ground. 'Michael had the beginnings of an enthusiasm which went on and on,' says Clifton. 'You'd see him in on Saturdays and Sundays and he'd be helping board flights and stuff like that. But Michael was pretty poor in those days at being one of the boys, something he's tried to become later. He would appear on the ramp, and he'd be something of a stranger. He wasn't well known at that stage. And he'd appear on the ramp and people would be doing their job and saying who the fuck is this guy.'

Scrabbling through the undergrowth of the company, O'Leary started to work out where the money was flowing to, and how it could be saved. He had yet to formulate the rigorous business model that would transform Ryanair into the leanest and most profitable airline in the world, but he could identify waste and he could identify ways of doing business more cheaply.

It was not, he says, about saving paper clips but about instilling discipline. 'It's the decision that one guy down in operations can make on one Friday evening on leasing in an aircraft that can cost you £10,000 or £20,000 at a stroke,' he says. 'It's those decisions that we had to clarify and clear up in people's minds.'

O'Leary replaced the marketing department with an outside public relations agency and renegotiated contracts which had never been questioned; insurance costs and fuel costs were hammered lower as the airline grew and started to exploit its new market power. 'It was all about getting rid of the lunatics who were running the asylum and putting some order on it,' he recalls. 'I was doing a lot of the ripping and burning and slashing at the lower end, which you couldn't have done if you were the CEO.'

Nothing was too small to escape O'Leary's attention, whether it was the cost of aviation charts (he discovered that Ryanair was paying for maps of the world rather than for the small number of charts it needed for its routes) or the cost of its planes. O'Leary had the nerve to question Ryanair's arrangements with GPA, and discovered that instead of getting favourable terms from its owner's company, it was being screwed.

'The guys down in GPA couldn't be seen to do a soft deal for Ryanair so they raped Ryanair. And the muppets in Ryanair thought, ah well, it's GPA and they'll look after us because of Tony Ryan. And so Ryanair spent its entire life being ridden by everybody when everybody assumed it was getting looked after because of the connection with Tony Ryan.'

Caution and cost-cutting were the watchwords through 1990. Route launches were kept to a minimum as McGoldrick and

O'Leary concentrated on developing their existing routes and maximizing passenger numbers and aircraft efficiency while assiduously cutting waste.

Towards the end of 1990 Declan Ryan, Tony Ryan's eldest son and Ryanair's then managing director, decided it was time for O'Leary to immerse himself in the operations of the airline. He asked Hamish McKean, the operations manager, to 'take O'Leary under his wing' and teach him how the airline worked. O'Leary was not amused. He had already spent much of the year finding out for himself what worked and what did not, and he 'absolutely didn't want to be taken under anyone's wing', says McKean, who suggested that O'Leary be sent away for training. 'Michael responded with several expletives in a very short sentence,' McKean recalls. 'He took that as a very huge insult. Michael would rarely take advice from anybody.'

Tensions had been building between O'Leary and Declan Ryan, and the company rumour mill rumbled with speculation that Tony Ryan would sideline his own son and wanted O'Leary to take over from him as managing director. For the moment, though, Declan was still in the post and in a position to assign an unwilling O'Leary to McKean for a couple of days a week for four or five weeks.

With McKean O'Leary learned about how 'ops' worked – rostering, dealing with pilots and crew, making the best use of planes and controlling fuel. 'On the logistics side he was an eager pupil,' says McKean. 'On the technical side, he couldn't be bothered with it. He just regarded aircraft as a vehicle for generating revenue, carrying passengers – didn't care how it was done. He did not take well to being told anything.'

During this time Ryanair was renegotiating its fuel contracts, and O'Leary sat in on the meetings. 'He was very confrontational in fuel meetings, effing and cursing and swearing, quite bizarre behaviour,' recalls McKean.

Aviation is a very conservative business, a bit like banking or accounting. You would expect people to be in black or navy suits, polished shoes, all of that. So him turning up to these meetings in jeans and open-neck shirts was unusual . . . People didn't take him seriously at all. They just questioned his sincerity. The feedback was, 'Who the hell is this guy? Who does he think he is telling us that we can't charge this?' He was demanding parity of price with BA and larger carriers who had huge quantity. But it worked, we got almost parity with BA. He was effective in shocking people into realizing that we were a small carrier but an emerging force in aviation.

Soon O'Leary's influence would be felt on a wider scale. In early 1991 he moved from Ryanair's administrative headquarters in College Green to the airline's offices at the airport. He quickly turned his attention to catering, a key cost for the airline. Charlie Clifton was installed as catering manager, and O'Leary spared few words when giving him his brief: 'Cut the fuck out of it.'

There was certainly a lot to be cut out of it. 'When I arrived into the catering department there would be meal presentations, there would be a meeting about the tray, the quality of the tray . . . Then there'd be, would you get cloth, would you get plastic, would you have rotatable or disposable equipment, knives and forks, stainless steel, would you have them branded, would the glasses be branded?' Clifton recalls.

Within months Clifton and O'Leary had made sweeping changes: the catering department was reduced to a fraction of its former size with most of its functions outsourced to Gate Gourmet to save money. 'It was pretty obvious what had to be done at that stage,' Clifton says. 'Which was even if you're serving smoked salmon and it's ridiculous, you might as well get the smoked salmon at the best possible cost. At this stage there was no talk about just not serving smoked salmon.'

Ryanair had another stroke of good fortune in January 1991, when British Airways announced that it was pulling out of its Irish routes after forty-four years. The move was out of character for the British giant. 'This is the first time BA has ever moved off a route as a result of competition,' said Michael Bishop, head of rival airline

British Midland. BA had operated flights from London to Dublin, Cork and Shannon and from Birmingham to Dublin, but after many months of vicious price competition BA concluded the routes were 'uneconomic'.

Less than two weeks after BA announced its withdrawal Ryanair seized the opportunity to announce extra services to and from Stansted. From 28 April the airline would operate six flights a day from Stansted to Dublin, three a day to Galway and Waterford, and one a day to Kerry and Knock. The Stansted expansion came at a cost to Luton, where six destinations were cut, leaving daily services to Dublin, Knock and Cork. Never a man to understate his decisions or achievements, on 5 February P. J. McGoldrick told journalists, 'The decision to operate into Stansted represents the culmination of a twelve-month turnaround by the airline.'

Hammering costs remained top of the agenda; just days before the Stansted announcement Ryanair pilots were forced to take severe pay cuts or lose their jobs. Ryanair's top pilots, who were earning £35,000, lost £6,000. Lower-salaried pilots were harder hit, losing about £5,000 each on salaries of £20,000. The pilots' union IALPA was not impressed at the airline's rationalization: 'The pay cuts mean that some pilots will now be on salaries lower than the average industrial wage,' said its president Ted Murphy.

Pay cuts were soon followed by staff cuts. Hamish McKean recalls,

One day I received a bundle of letters addressed to staff members who were to be made redundant. There was no prior warning given – the letters appeared at about 12.15, and I had to tell the ten or twenty staff by one o'clock.

I couldn't get hold of McGoldrick so I managed to get Declan, who had signed these letters, and I was told that they had to be sacked, and if you don't you will be sacked. We knew there was something afoot but certainly not the large-scale redundancies that were foisted upon me with a total lack of consultation.

By April 1991 Ryanair and Aer Lingus were once again locked in a battle that seemed to be strangling both airlines and the pilots' union called on them to form a quasi-partnership to avoid the mounting job cuts and financial losses. 'In a global context, the skirmish now being fought on the Irish Sea routes is more expensive than any airline can afford,' said IALPA spokesman Ross Kelly.

The wheel had turned full circle, and once again Ryanair and Aer Lingus were scrapping for supremacy, but this time there was one crucial difference: Ryanair had finally stopped haemorrhaging cash. O'Leary had forced through swingeing salary reductions – Ryanair's pilots swallowed cuts of up to 37 per cent – and the air of excited expectation he'd experienced on his first day had been replaced by an atmosphere of doom. Ironically, just as the company's survival prospects looked brighter, its employees started to fear the worst. The results for 1991 showed a small profit. It may have been just £293,000, artificially boosted by the sale of Ryanair's stake in a tourism business – the underlying business was still losing money – but it was a remarkable turnaround after years of steepling losses which had accumulated to more than £20 million.

At the end of the year McGoldrick resigned – a decision that came as much from him as from Ryan, who recognized that he had served his purpose. He had inherited an airline in financial chaos and on the brink of collapse, and had led it, painfully and slowly, to the point of profitability. His low-key leadership, combined with his industry savvy, had dovetailed effectively with O'Leary's war on costs throughout the company. It was without doubt a harsher place. The touchy-feely customer service of the early years, the sense of youthful adventure, had been replaced by a steelier resolve. Ryanair would survive, but its transformation from upstart to major player had changed the nature of the company as well as its financial performance.

O'Leary's role in the company was formalized with his appointment as chief financial officer, but still he did not want to step up to the top job. In a bizarre move Ryan instead appointed Paddy Murphy, a veteran of the Dublin business scene who had been chief executive of Irish Ferries.

His reign was doomed even before it started. At the end of October it was reported that his brief was 'to improve the airline's marketing, strengthen its corporate identity, improve the quality of service and develop stronger links with tourism officials in Ireland and Britain'. It was a momentary lapse, and so clearly at odds with the airline's still urgent need to reduce its costs even further while boosting passenger numbers that it could not last long. Sure enough, within six weeks Murphy had gone. O'Leary had been deeply unimpressed.

Murphy's replacement did meet with O'Leary's approval. Conor Hayes, a former accountant who had been chief executive of the Almarai Group in Saudi Arabia, started his new job in January 1992. Together, he and O'Leary would take Ryanair to the next logical stage of the airline's development – its metamorphosis into a truly low-cost, low-fare airline that would revolutionize air travel in Europe.

7. The Last Handout

Conor Hayes, a thirty-five-year-old who had spent the previous five years reviving the fortunes of a food company in Saudi Arabia, knew little about Ryanair when he accepted the post as chief executive in the autumn of 1991. His expertise was and remains instilling financial discipline in troubled companies and nursing them back to health – a company doctor in all but name.

His background fitted Ryanair's needs. While Ryanair and commercial airlines were an unknown quantity for Hayes, he had experience of the aviation business. His years as an accountant with the Dublin firm Stokes Kennedy Crowley had exposed him to the intricacies of aircraft leasing, first through work for GPA and later for IAS, the aircraft leasing company run by Gerry Connolly, the man who had founded Avair. Ryanair was, from what he could see, a major challenge but an opportunity he could not turn down. It was a welcome route home – he had a young family and was keen to return to Ireland – and the job offered a reintroduction to the Irish business market. Opportunities to return were few in 1991, and he was eager to seize the chance,

When Hayes officially took the reins as chief executive in December 1991 the company remained in a critical condition. It could claim a market share in excess of 20 per cent on the Dublin–London routes following British Airways' withdrawal from the market the previous year, but it was still losing money.

The Irish government's embrace of the two-airlines policy two years earlier had given Ryanair crucial breathing space and had helped reduce its losses, but the airline remained vulnerable. The modest profit in 1991 had been generated not by the core business of flying people but from the sale of a shareholding in a small hotel business; at the operating level the airline was still losing money and Tony Ryan was increasingly worried that despite the remedial work of the McGoldrick regime his airline remained doomed. He had kept it afloat two years earlier because he had hoped and believed that the removal of Aer Lingus from the Stansted route would give his airline an opportunity to carve out a profitable route network, yet the hoped-for profits had yet to materialize. If Ryanair could not be made to stand on its own feet, he would be forced to make further cash injections. He had, friends say, reached the end of the line. There would be no more money for Ryanair; if it could not survive on its own, he would admit defeat and retreat, selling the airline if he could find a buyer, closing it if he could not.

'Hayes was brought in, and O'Leary given a more prominent role, so that there was clear distance between the Ryan family and any potential disaster. Hayes's appointment has to be seen as a damage limitation exercise for the family rather than a vote of confidence in the company,' says one former manager.

Ryan had already been badly bruised by the losses the family had incurred during its ill-fated venture into London European Airways. Cathal Ryan, his eldest son, had been appointed executive chairman of LEA and was closely associated with its failure. Declan had stepped up to the mark to run Ryanair after McGoldrick's departure and Ryan was not prepared to see the main company fail under direct family stewardship. If it had to close, it would not be with a Ryan at the helm.

Hayes's immediate priority was to find out what was happening, and to do that he had to put in place accurate and timely financial reporting systems. Despite Michael O'Leary's presence at the company for more than three years, the detailed financial information compiled for senior management and the board was months out of date. This had to change and quickly if the company had a hope of survival.

O'Leary's early firefighting had highlighted the financial chaos at the company, but he had not radically altered its course. He had brought greater discipline to contract negotiations, had lowered costs and eliminated waste, but he was still being diverted into family business in his role as Ryan's personal assistant and had not come to grips with the minutiae of the company's accounts. Hayes brought different and essential skills. Where O'Leary could highlight waste, he could implement a basic accounting system that would deliver the numbers on which they could start to plot a survival plan.

With Hayes on board as chief executive, O'Leary started to devote more of his time to the airline and the two men became a firm double act. For the majority of the staff Hayes was the man in charge, but higher up the management chain it was clear that the company was being run by two men, not one. 'Part of the time Hayes reported directly to Ryan, and part of the time to O'Leary. It was a strange relationship. O'Leary was both the conduit to Tony Ryan, and reported to Hayes as well. But for all its peculiarities, it worked,' says a former member of the senior management team.

'To be fair, it was a partnership,' says Brian Bell, who advised the company on its marketing and public relations at the time. 'Conor doesn't get the credit he deserves for the work he put in. They were good cop–bad cop. Michael was the bad cop and Conor was the good cop . . . They were very much on the same wavelength about what needed to be done. Both of them were cost cutters, they were accountants looking at how to make the bottom line work for them. They set out with the same aim.'

Hayes had been faced by serious financial difficulties when he had arrived in Saudi Arabia to run Almarai. Its accounts had been chaotic and it was losing money. In five years Hayes had transformed it into profitable order, and he tackled Ryanair with the same attention to detail. He drove through a rigorous internal accounting regime that forced transparency onto Ryanair's accounts. 'In a matter of weeks we went from having information that was five months out of date to [information] that was just five days old,' says a former financial adviser. 'It was a phenomenal turnaround, and it was not cosmetic. Hayes's system delivered monthly accounts for every line of the operation, and they were updated weekly. Basic stuff, perhaps, but it had never happened at Ryanair before.'

Meanwhile, O'Leary's profile in the company grew, as did his reputation for ruthlessness. 'I saw him fire a financial controller, a young guy, in the office next to where I was waiting for him to come into our meeting,' says a former colleague. 'He was screaming and shouting at this guy, how incompetent he was, and he could clear his desk and take himself back to wherever he came from.'

Hayes and O'Leary were men on a mission, and nothing would be allowed to get in their way. For Hayes, Ryanair was his chance to prove to the Irish business world that he was a force to be reckoned with. He did not see it as a long-term post – he signed a two-year contract and had no intention of extending it – but it gave him the opportunity to showcase his talents. If Ryanair had to close, Hayes could demonstrate his ability in an orderly retreat and perhaps find a buyer; and if he could save it, then his ability to turn around financially troubled companies in Ireland would be made. For O'Leary it was just as personal: if he could turn around the airline, then he would make his fortune.

The previous summer O'Leary and Ryan had struck an improbable deal.

'I kept trying to get out,' recalls O'Leary. 'I thought it [Ryanair] was a stupid business, and it was also very high profile. I didn't want a high profile; I wanted to make lots of money but not be known. That was the way my family would operate, there was no credit for being in the papers.' Ryan, though, wanted O'Leary to stay with Ryanair. O'Leary had agreed but only on condition that he was paid 25 per cent of any profits the airline made above £2 million.

Ryan has subsequently described it as the best deal he ever negotiated, but O'Leary was just copying his master. 'I did the deal because it was a copy of what Tony had originally done in GPA. I didn't need to be a genius; I wasn't blinded by inspiration,' he says.

The scale of Ryan's generosity indicates that he had no concept of how successful Ryanair could become. He believed that it had a future as a niche airline, competing aggressively with Aer Lingus on the Ireland–UK routes and on some continental European routes, but his ambitions did not run to European domination. After years of losses funded from his own pockets, Ryan hoped for stability followed by modest profitability. O'Leary had already shown that he could identify problems, and Ryan had enough faith in his young protégé to believe that he could, if motivated properly, guide the company to health. O'Leary's original deal – that he would work for free as long as he got a cut of the profits – revealed his hunger for success and money, and Ryan dangled both as an incentive to satisfy both their needs. He wanted a successful airline that no longer drained his personal reserves, and O'Leary wanted money.

O'Leary believed that profits were possible if unlikely, but he had no idea that he could turn Ryanair into a money-making machine. 'I thought that if I got it right I could make some decent money, but not a fortune,' he says. 'I thought in a good year we'd make a couple of million and I'd get 250 grand, and there you go, more money than I could imagine, I'd be rich. But at that stage it was as likely to go bust as it was to make a million quid.'

The deal remained a secret. Hayes was unaware of O'Leary's cut of future profits when he joined the company, though he knew that there was an understanding between the two men. He assumed that O'Leary was on a profit-share deal, and knew that his relationship with Ryan went far beyond Ryanair, but he did not probe. His responsibility was to turn around an airline, not worry about who would benefit.

For O'Leary, the agreement changed everything. He now had a tangible stake in the airline's future. He was not, yet, an owner of the business, but the profit share was as good as ownership – better, in fact, while Ryanair remained troubled, because it involved no responsibility for current losses. Ryan's incentive strategy had an immediate effect and was a powerful motivator. O'Leary had always wanted to be his own boss. When Ryan had first sounded out O'Leary about working for him he had offered him roles at GPA, his aircraft leasing company. O'Leary had consciously turned down those offers and had offered instead to work as his personal assistant, determined to learn the art of business so that he could make a fortune for himself, not for others. It was an unusual role, and a vague title. 'Personal assistant' conjures up the image of a valet or batman – a servant who helps his master dress, irons his shirts and perhaps manages his social diary. Ryan, though, used the term for young hungry men who worked for him on his private investments, his eyes and ears on current and future investments while he toured the world for GPA. Now O'Leary had an enormous incentive to make Ryanair work, because he knew that every penny saved, every extra seat sold, was potentially money in his own pocket. He was determined to work harder than ever, and threw himself into the business.

'I thought his life was very strange,' said Brian Bell. 'His whole life seemed to revolve around work. He was always there early in the morning, he was always there late in the evening. I heard stories of him being in on Saturdays reading a book at his desk and helping out the baggage handlers on Sunday. He played football with the staff and he didn't seem to have any personal life outside it.'

O'Leary did not have all the answers to Ryanair's problems, and Tony Ryan was well aware of that fact. So in early 1992, just after McGoldrick's departure, Ryan dispatched O'Leary to America to learn what he could from the master of low-fare airlines, Southwest.

Set up in 1971 as the original low-fare operator, Southwest had just reported after-tax profits of $26.9 million for 1991, a considerable feat when rocketing oil prices were inflicting heavy losses on most airlines. Southwest was a roaring success story, a story which Ryan was keen to repeat on his side of the Atlantic, and so he sent O'Leary to meet Southwest's hard-drinking founder, Herb Kelleher.

While O'Leary's recollections of his meeting with Kelleher vary, the central importance of Southwest's experiences to Ryanair's evolution remains clear. In December 1998 in an interview with the *Financial Times* O'Leary placed Southwest at the heart of

Ryanair's success. 'We went to look at Southwest. It was like the road to Damascus. This was the way to make Ryanair work.'

O'Leary spoke and drank to excess with Kelleher that night, and the two hit it off. 'I passed out about midnight, and when I woke up again at about 3 a.m. Kelleher was still there, the bastard, pouring himself another bourbon and smoking,' O'Leary told an audience of Boeing workers in 2004. 'I thought I'd pick his brains and come away with the Holy Grail. The next day I couldn't remember a thing.'

Kelleher admired O'Leary's focus and determination, but Southwest's secrets did not come tumbling from the great man's lips. They did not have to. O'Leary had spent two days studying Southwest's operations from the ground and had begun to understand what it took to make an airline work. He watched the speed of the Southwest turnaround – the amount of time that a plane spent on the ground before being dispatched skyward again with another load of passengers. Where other airlines took an hour and a half, sometimes longer, to turn their planes around, Southwest did it in less than thirty minutes. He studied the check-in, where Southwest passengers were boarded speedily without seat numbers, and he studied the prices the airline charged.

The results, he says, were not 'rocket science'. Southwest was obsessive about its costs. It reduced its staff training and maintenance costs by flying just one class of plane, the Boeing 737. It made those planes work harder than anyone else's by keeping them in the air longer and on the ground idle for as short a time as possible, flying more routes and carrying more passengers.

Scores of American airlines had come and gone in the previous decade, victims of overexpansion and poor financial control, but Southwest was a model of controlled expansion. It grew each year, adding more routes and more planes, but it did not rush and it kept a tight grip on costs. Its turnaround times meant that it could fly more routes in a day than other, less efficient airlines, giving it a simple productivity edge that translated into greater profitability. It could achieve much faster turnaround because it chose to fly to smaller airports than its rivals: airports like Love Field in Dallas,

Texas, which were uncongested and required only a few minutes taxiing by a plane from its stand to the runway. Unreserved seating meant that passengers could be loaded swiftly from either end of the plane, and the effect was to make airline travel more like bus travel. It was cheap, fast and uncncumbered by mystery. O'Leary could see the model was sound. More importantly, he could see that the model was transferable to Europe. There was no magic ingredient, no special American factor that made a Southwest possible in Texas but impossible in Ireland and Europe. The arithmetic could not have been simpler: keep your costs lower than anyone else's, your planes working harder and your prices low and you could beat any competitor on any route.

Southwest had demonstrated that low fares actually worked. Just as Ryanair's arrival on the Ireland–UK routes had stimulated rather than cannibalized the air travel market, so Southwest's experience across its route network had shown that low-cost air travel boosted the overall market. Its success had come from serving new markets, but also from competing on traditional inter-city routes already served by traditional airlines.

O'Leary could see it worked. His challenge was to distil the best of Southwest's model and then adapt it to the realities of Ryanair. It was the genesis of a revival plan.

Hayes had a plan too but it was a more basic one. He had recognized quickly that Ryanair needed more paying passengers. The previous Easter Ryanair had run a successful seat sale – promotional prices on the Dublin–Luton route had been cut from £49.99 to £34.99 and tickets sold fast – but the promotion was seen as a once-off initiative to boost seat sales ahead of the traditionally busier summer season. Hayes thought it was worth trying again, but met resistance within the company. 'Everyone said he was mad and pleaded with him not to cut fares,' said one former executive. 'The only person who backed him unequivocally was O'Leary.'

O'Leary's exposure to Kelleher had convinced him that low fares were an essential part of the formula that Ryanair would have to adopt if it were to claw its way to profitability, and Hayes, desperate to drive passenger volumes higher, was determined to gamble. Consciously Hayes borrowed his lowest fare – £29 each way – from Southwest Airlines' by now famous $29 fare from Dallas to Houston and then set higher fares at ten-pound gaps, with fewer restrictions applying as the price rose, and launched it as a 'Happy Days' promotion in early February 1992.

It was an instant success. Later that month he doubled Ryanair's Dublin–Stansted services from twelve to twenty-four flights daily to cope with the increased demand and a week later he announced plans to launch a new service between Stansted and Shannon in April. The low fares were held for a second month, and then a third.

Ryanair, almost by accident, had become a genuine low-fare airline, and low prices, matched by even lower costs, were now being recognized as its most potent weapons. It was a discovery born of desperation rather than planning. O'Leary had yet to formulate his Southwest-lookalike model and Hayes was chasing volume not a strategy, but it worked. Ryanair could not compete with other airlines on service, but it could compete aggressively on two levels: price and the frequency of its flights. The key to success would come through implementing the flipside of a low-fare structure – Ryanair would make money on low fares and high frequency only if its costs were low and its productivity high. And so Hayes and O'Leary started to dovetail effectively. While O'Leary concentrated on driving down costs, Hayes worked on price and frequency. By May 1992 Hayes felt confident enough to tell Reuters that while the profit for the previous financial year might be small, 'this year our profit will be measured in millions . . . I can't prove that [we have the lowest costs in Europe],' he said, 'but I know I can sell a twenty-nine-punt flight to London at a profit even if it's a small one.' Hayes said that his competitors would need to charge seventy punts to make a profit.

Hayes's low fares had already had a dramatic impact on Ryanair's Dublin–London market share, which had leapt from an average 15 per cent on the route in 1991 to a remarkable 26 per cent by

April 1992, the third month of the low-fare initiative. 'My target is that in eighteen months we will have stabilized at 25 per cent of the London–Dublin corridor,' he said. Unlike rival airlines, which advertised cheap fares but had few available, Ryanair was actually delivering its lowest fare to the majority of its passengers. By the end of the year more than 50 per cent of all seat sales were at the lowest available fare, decisive evidence that price was hugely significant in stimulating demand even on mature routes.

The success of low fares was also forcing Hayes and O'Leary to look closely at Ryanair's fleet of aircraft, which in 1992 was a modest collection of eight leased BAC One-Eleven jets and three propellor-powered ATR 42s. A larger fleet was vital if the airline was to grow by launching more routes and increasing the number of flights on its existing routes, and McGoldrick had placed orders for new Airbus A320s and ATRs.

Hayes, however, cancelled the orders and decided to wait. Acquiring new planes is always a gamble – on the one hand, they give airlines the firepower to expand, but they also bring a heavy financial burden and put the company under intense pressure to sell the newly acquired seats. The gamble only pays off when an airline's acquisition plans are perfectly in tune with its route expansion plans. Hayes was still uncertain about the airline's direction and did not want to end up with the wrong mix of large and small aircraft. 'What we've got to do is put this business on a viable footing, then we'll see what fleet we need,' he said.

The accountant in Hayes was never far from the surface. While he was keen to lower fares and increase the number of flights on offer, he was equally determined that no individual flight should lose money. His solution horrified airline traditionalists. Hayes insisted that no flight should be allowed to take off until it had been given clearance to go by Bernard Berger, the man in charge of flight operations. He was instructed by Hayes to run the financial slide rule over every flight. If the total revenue from the seats sold on the flight added up to more than the costs of running the flight, Berger let the plane fly. If it fell short, then the flight was cancelled and combined with the next flight.

Twice in the early weeks of the new regime flight managers ignored the order and let planes take off without clearing the numbers with Berger. On each occasion the person responsible was fired. After that, the rule was implemented with religious fervour. 'Flight consolidation was commonplace, but it was only possible because we had such frequency, particularly on the Stansted service. You could cancel the 18.30 and push everyone on to the 19.30 – so no one lost out hugely,' says one former employee.

It was ruthless but very effective. Passenger numbers climbed on the back of low fares, leaping from 650,000 in 1991 to 850,000 in 1992, and while more people flew, O'Leary worked tirelessly to ensure that the costs of flying them were kept low. By working the planes harder, making more trips, achieving faster turnaround times at the airports and by restricting service costs – planes were cleaned by the cabin crew not by contract cleaners, while toilets were emptied after a number of flights rather than after each one – O'Leary chipped away at the cost base and kept productivity high.

The formula worked, and the cash started to accumulate. It was too early to relax, but for the first time since the airline had been founded it was trading profitably and management knew exactly what was happening within the company they ran.

'It was still a small company, but it was run very personally by Michael and Conor: they ran it like a sweetshop, not an airline. Everything was at their fingertips; they knew everyone and they knew the cost of everything. It was micromanagement in action,' says a former colleague.

It was also management by instinct rather than by design; there was still no grand plan of how Ryanair could be transformed into a consistently profitable airline. O'Leary had been down the road to Damascus, as he described it, but it was one thing understanding how Southwest managed to operate successfully and quite another to impose that structure on Ryanair overnight. Hayes and O'Leary were making progress through trial and error, both convinced that low fares and low costs were the only way forward. Their instincts were sound, but they were still a long way short of delivering a business plan that could pave the way for the airline's expansion. Hayes was conscious of airline deregulation, but still not sure what impact it would have on the European market and was trying to balance the needs of strategic planning with the day-to-day pressures to reduce costs and seek out profit. It was a daily grind.

The two men were hunting for profit centres, prepared to chase American tourists flying to Stansted with American Airlines, dabbling in the charter holidays market, offering connecting flights to European cities through a marketing tie-up with Air UK and even contemplating franchised route operations for the bigger European carriers. 'With deregulation of the industry there's going to be amalgamation and the big operators cannot fly the thinner routes profitably,' Hayes said in an interview. 'It will be in our best interest to find those routes and do the appropriate deals with people.'

The strategy, what there was of it, was to scrabble together a profitable business from the chaos that had gone before. Nothing was ruled out as Hayes and O'Leary fought to make money in a market which was highly competitive on the domestic front and increasingly imperilled internationally by rising oil prices and war in the Middle East.

'You've got to remember that from Michael's and Conor's point of view, and from the company's point of view, this was backs against the wall stuff,' says one former manager. 'It was their way or no way and they were dead, dead right. Some people from the previous era just didn't get it. But forget the stuff about developing a low-cost model, because it wasn't even close to that back then. This wasn't about low cost, this was about survival.'

For O'Leary, the battle for survival was wearing him down. Despite the profit-share deal he had struck with Ryan, he was growing restless and frustrated. 'I was trying to get out,' he says. 'I wanted out all the time.'

O'Leary had been persuaded to stay at Ryanair by the prospect, however slim, of making his personal fortune if the airline could be turned around, but 'a year or two in Ryanair, there was no action'. Instead of making money, O'Leary was cutting costs. It was, he says, 'a pain in the arse. My role in Ryanair from 1988 to 1991 was stopping it from losing money – it wasn't looking to make Tony [and, by extension, himself] money.'

On paper his deal with Ryan had seemed good but 25 per cent of nothing was not what O'Leary wanted. His time, he felt, would be more profitably rewarded by chasing his 5 per cent share of the profits that could come from using Ryan's millions to invest in more exciting businesses. 'I had had four years of this place on the brink of bankruptcy; we had gotten it back to making a small profit, and I had had enough,' O'Leary says. A small profit was not what O'Leary had in mind. He was chasing bigger dreams, and Ryan was on the verge of floating GPA on the stock market, selling shares to institutions that would generate hundreds of millions of dollars for him to play with. The choice was a simple one: stay at Ryanair and work like crazy to turn a modest profit or help Ryan spend his fortune. In O'Leary's eyes his job at Ryanair had been completed. The airline had stopped haemorrhaging cash and was no longer a drain on Ryan

And so he stepped away from Ryanair in the first half of 1992, devoting most of his energies to his role as Ryan's personal adviser. Hayes was left to fly solo, and he relished the challenge. By the summer of 1992 Ryanair was finally heading towards genuine trading profits for the full year. Hayes's 'Happy Days' fares had worked, stimulating a sharp increase in demand, and costs had been brought down to levels that made it possible for the airline to make money on fares which would have bled its rivals.

Tony Ryan should have been able to breathe a sigh of relief. The money pit had been filled in. It might be many years before he saw a decent return on his eight years of investment, but at least there would be a return. By then, though, Ryan had a far bigger worry on his hands than the fate of Ryanair. The airline's losses had always been an irritant, but profit had not been his prime motivation when he established Ryanair. Ryan had wanted a business for his sons and he had the essential wealth to make it happen. But that summer the wealth generator of the previous fifteen years fell apart spectacularly and Ryan did not even see it coming.

It should have been the best summer of his life. At the start of the year GPA was the largest buyer of new aircraft in the world, and had advance orders for more than 400 planes, worth more than $20 billion. It leased aircraft to more than forty airlines and its profits, which had hit $280 million in 1991, were forecast to rise to $380 million by 1995. GPA's board was packed with business and political luminaries of the time, and the company's shares changed hands at fancy prices in private deals. GPA executives were renowned for their swagger and hard work, travelling an average 140,000 miles a year to secure leasing deals for their aircraft, spending more than 170 days away from home on average and earning exceptional money for their troubles. It was a gruelling lifestyle, and one that O'Leary had rejected, despite the rewards, because he did not want to be trapped into life as a company executive. Just as he had shunned the opportunity to work his way through the ranks at SKC, so he shied away from becoming just another executive in a large corporation. He wanted to make money, but he wanted to make it on his own terms.

Now GPA was preparing for a stock market flotation that would value the company at more than $2 billion and would make Ryan's shareholding worth more than $200 million. On the day the company was due to float, Ryan was going to pocket an extra $38 million as a fixed success fee, and would still enjoy a heady dividend stream from his shareholding. The flotation was also going to be a significant boon to GPA's founding shareholders Aer Lingus and Air Canada, who both stood to make huge profits, and to many senior managers who had acquired shares in the company over the years.

GPA's shares were to be sold in an ambitious global exercise, with investment banks finding homes for shares in Tokyo, London and New York as well as the other main European and Far Eastern financial centres. During the final six weeks leading up to flotation day on 7 June ripples of discontent were felt across the markets. There were mutterings that the share sale was being priced too high – GPA hoped to achieve $22 a share, but the market was indicating that it would only pay $16 to $18. And although GPA had survived the traumas of the Gulf War – indeed Ryan was keen to float that year precisely because GPA's resilience during a period of crisis demonstrated how robust his company had become – investors fretted about the financial security of some of GPA's major clients. The problem could have been dealt with in the market's time-honoured fashion – by reducing the price at which the shares were to be sold – but Ryan refused to budge.

O'Leary watched the drama unfold but was powerless to intervene. Ryan did not employ O'Leary to tell him how to run GPA or how to negotiate with investment banks. Those close to the negotiations in the run-up to the flotation give different accounts about O'Leary's input. Some maintain that he, like Ryan, was exceptionally bullish about GPA's share price and shared the arrogance that persuaded Ryan to stick to his guns. Others claim that O'Leary was horrified by GPA's hubris and could not understand why Ryan would not just float the company at any old price and let it find its own level in the market.

GPA's astonishing profit performance had been based in large part on Ryan's ability to outsmart the markets. He and his managers had accurately predicted the patterns of aircraft demand and had converted those predictions into massive orders for new aircraft when others were too timid to take the plunge. When demand for air travel met Ryan's predictions, he had the planes that the airlines needed. GPA's executives believed that they were invincible, masters of their universe, and would brook no outside interference. Their self-belief was their undoing.

O'Leary says he will 'never forget the rows over the share price. Goldman Sachs advised a price cut and Tony and the rest of them went berserk.'

Although GPA was only trying to raise $850 million in fresh capital, it had planned to borrow a further $3 billion on the back of its new liquidity – money urgently required to meet its forward aircraft purchase commitments. The complexity of the share offer, which involved securing commitments to buy shares from institutions on three continents, made a difficult situation worse, but in the end it came down to price.

'I'd have sold the shares at any price just to get the thing away,' says O'Leary. 'Tony was going to collect a bonus on flotation of more than $30 million and I told him to forget about the price and just take the money, but he wouldn't.'

On the day that GPA's shares were meant to start trading on the world's stock markets, the sale was cancelled. Ryan's refusal to lower the sale price had had a ripple effect across the markets, and potential buyers – particularly in the US and London – simply refused to pay the asking price. If the shares had been listed on the stock market, the overhang of unsold shares would have caused the price to collapse, leaving those who had actually agreed to buy shares with substantial losses. Ryan had no option: he had to cancel and watch his world implode.

The unravelling of the flotation proved disastrous for a company that relied heavily on its ability to borrow vast sums of money from the money markets. Deprived of the ability to raise fresh borrowing on the back of the flotation proceeds, GPA was left in a deep hole. Worse, the pummelling of its reputation had made its creditor banks circle nervously. In a business that depended on the ability to borrow money cheaply and in vast amounts, confidence was everything. That June, as the share flotation crashed, confidence evaporated and banks started to look more closely at the company's creditworthiness.

Maurice Foley, Ryan's right-hand man, left the company weeks later and predators started to sniff blood. Before long the inevitable happened: robbed of its power to borrow the money it needed, with its commitments to buy planes unmeetable and with the aviation market still in Gulf War turmoil, GPA was taken over by GE Capital, the financing arm of the giant American conglomerate General Electric, in a deal that left Ryan lamenting that he had been 'raped' by Jack 'Neutron' Welsh, GE's aggressive chief executive.

'GPA collapsed because Tony and the boys couldn't help themselves fighting over the share price,' says O'Leary. 'And, looking back, they had called everybody's bluff for about ten years. This was the one time they were outside of their own business, and they were dealing with the bankers in London.'

Ryan was not a man to hide his sense of betrayal. He believed, and still does, that GPA's flotation was destroyed by the vicious rivalry that existed between American and Japanese investment banks, which shared responsibility for selling the company to international investors. 'People say I'm arrogant and sure I am. But you should see those arrogant sons of bitches on Wall Street,' he said in an interview two years later.

Ryan was retained by GE to see through the takeover, but it was scant consolation. His empire had gone and the vultures were on his back. Like many other GPA executives and directors, Ryan had borrowed money to acquire extra shares in GPA, believing that the flotation price would exceed the price they paid and leave them with easy profits. Now the shares were close to worthless. Without the sale proceeds and the bank loans that would have followed, GPA was a company saddled by liabilities and future obligations to buy planes with money that it did not have. Instead of sitting on a pile of shares worth hundreds of millions of dollars, Ryan owed Merrill Lynch, the US investment bank, $35 million. If Merrill Lynch collected all its money, Ryan would be a broken man.

'You'd think that a man who enjoyed such wealth for so long would have put something away for a rainy day,' says one former acquaintance, 'but Tony is not the sort of man who salts away money in case he fails. He never expects to fail or contemplates disaster.' Ryan had gone from vast riches to relative rags and Ryanair, the airline he funded but which he always maintained was his sons' company and not his, became his most valuable asset. It was time for it to perform.

With GPA in tatters, Ryanair regained its place at the forefront of O'Leary's attention. He would help Ryan steer his way through the GPA aftermath, but there was no longer any immediate prospect of making his fortune by investing the Ryan millions. They had vanished and Ryan now owed rather than owned millions. If

O'Leary was to make his mark, it was Ryanair or nothing. So he returned full time to the airline, determined to make it work.

With the ruthlessness that would become his trademark, he could see that GPA's weakness represented an important opportunity for Ryanair. The airline wanted to cut out three of Ryanair's loss-making routes – from Galway, Kerry and Waterford – and get rid of the three turboprop planes that served them. All three were leased from GPA, and O'Leary knew that there would never be a better moment to get out of the contracts – whose terms were never favourable to Ryanair – as cheaply as possible.

O'Leary and Hayes took enormous pleasure from what they did. While GPA's executives were still reeling from the flotation disaster and fighting fires on all fronts, Ryanair announced that it was handing back the planes. GPA refused to accept them, arguing that the airline had to honour its contract, but Hayes and O'Leary refused to budge. 'They said they'd fly the planes to Shannon, park them on the runway and then call a press conference and announce to the media that GPA was trying to destroy Ryanair,' says a former employee.

GPA backed down, the planes were returned and Ryanair agreed a break payment of just £5 million, £10 million less than the penalties that should have been incurred under the terms of the contract. Hayes then organized a meeting with Maire Geoghegan Quinn, the minister for transport, whose constituency included Galway airport, to tell her of Ryanair's decision to cease flying to Galway, Kerry and Waterford. On 1 August the airline announced that the services would cease on 1 September. In a statement the company's board described the withdrawal as 'regrettable', but 'an inevitable consequence of both the continuing recession in the United Kingdom, which has had such an adverse impact on traffic numbers, and the worldwide recession in the aviation industry'. It described the routes as 'economically unviable' and said it would redouble its efforts to increase services to Cork, Knock and Shannon, where passenger numbers had already climbed by 55 per cent in the first six months of the year. All three were in the same geographical areas as the airports being dropped, with Knock and

Shannon relatively close to Galway, and Cork not far from either Waterford or Kerry – which in turn was close to Shannon. It was a route rationalization that made commercial sense: passenger numbers were strong at the three airports being retained, and the existing traffic on the other routes could be diverted to them.

The media missed the significance of the route cull, interpreting the withdrawals as a signal that Ryanair was in terminal decline. In fact, they arose from a hard-nosed strategy focused on profitable routes that was actually proving to be the airline's salvation.

Seamus Brennan's controversial two-airline policy had given Ryanair the breathing space to build a profitable business by removing head-to-head competition with Aer Lingus on its key routes to London's Stansted and Luton airports – a compromise that had also protected Aer Lingus's routes to Gatwick and Heathrow. It was, however, a deal with a deadline: Brennan had agreed a two-year moratorium, not an indefinite one. The power of government to intervene in the airline business was also in steady decline, because the staged liberalization of Europe's aviation market was already under way and would reach a new milestone the following year.

Flight International, an aviation trade magazine, reported, 'Speculation that Irish operator Ryanair is in trouble has re-emerged following the announcement that it is to shut down its London service to three regional Irish airports . . . Until now, Ryanair has had the stated aim of becoming Ireland's leading carrier to regional airports . . . This leaves the airline largely dependent on the Dublin–Stansted route at a time when Aer Lingus is preparing to fly into Stansted from next year.'

It was a threat that Hayes and O'Leary were already moving to close off.

The crisis in the airline industry did not halt Europe's slow progress towards deregulation and by the time the next tranche of liberalization came into effect in 1993 the industry was showing early signs of recovery. Fifteen years after US deregulation, the concept of low-fare airlines had also finally made its way across the Atlantic.

Dan Air, a British-registered company, became the first genuinely low-fare European airline to live, and die. Originally a charter airline, Dan Air had transformed itself into a low-fare and relatively low-cost scheduled carrier, but it could not achieve profitability. It fell to earth in September 1992 and was subsumed by British Airways the following month.

As the *Financial Times*'s Lex column wrote in September 1992,

There is a clear lesson in the plight of Dan Air for would-be liberalisers of Europe's aviation industry. Here, after all, was a relatively low cost airline which ought to have been a model beneficiary of the open skies policy pursued by Brussels in recent years. Instead its parent company, Davies & Newman, now finds itself in apparently life and death talks . . . The reason is largely the dire economic climate and delayed hopes for economic recovery. But Dan Air's failure to gather momentum as a scheduled carrier highlights the difficulty of breaking into markets dominated by the big national flag carriers.

The reality was that the national carriers still held a massive advantage over aspirant airlines: they controlled the landing slots at the major airports. As the *FT* explained, 'BA's hold over slots at Heathrow has provided it with an inestimable advantage in developing its European network.'

The 1993 deregulation package brought with it the concept of a European rather than national airline – this was 'open skies' within the European Union, allowing any airline registered in a member country to operate without restriction in all other member countries of the union. For Ryanair this was the package that at long last made it possible for the airline to build on its ambitions. Price controls – which required airlines to have their fares approved by their governments – had disappeared, and airlines were now free to charge what they wanted rather than seek government approval for their fares. Airlines could also fly to and from anywhere in Europe. Ryanair had avoided price control of its fares by operating services where none had previously existed – like its early Dublin–Luton route. This had given it access to the London market, but because Luton was technically not a London airport, there had been no price constraint.

But despite the freedom that the previous waves of deregulation had brought, the basic make-up of the aviation market in 1993 was not significantly different to what it had been in 1990 or even 1985. By 1993 there were twenty-two independent airline operators in Europe, but Greece, Finland, the Netherlands, Luxembourg and Spain all had no competition for their flag carriers. Competition was advancing more rapidly in some areas – there were five jet airlines in both the UK and France, and two in Ireland. The real catalyst for change in the market was the 1993 reform, which at last spurred developments in the European aviation market.

In 1993 four large airlines (using jets with seventy seats or more) entered the market, but seven large airlines exited. Between 1994 and 1997 thirty-three large airlines entered the market and a further eleven smaller-scale operations upgraded to larger aircraft. But twenty-four airlines ceased operations. It was a sign of the new order: competition would bring change and opportunity.

The roller-coaster ride had begun.

Tony Ryan's life had been turned upside down by GPA's collapse in the summer of 1992, but for Michael O'Leary and Conor Hayes life was getting better and better. Hayes's price cutting and O'Leary's cost cutting had taken Ryanair to the promised land of real profitability by the end of 1992. For the first time in its short history the airline would be able to announce genuine trading profits, rather than a surplus cobbled together by selling assets.

Ryanair announced a trading profit for 1992 of £850,000. The real profits were substantially higher – almost £3.5 million – but Hayes and O'Leary, prompted by Ryan, decided to conceal the extent of the airline's remarkable recovery. 'They just plucked a number from thin air that year,' says one former colleague, 'and I remember one of them saying that 850,000 sounded good because it was exactly the number of passengers we'd carried.'

Their coyness was unusual, but GPA's collapse had altered

Ryan's priorities. Merrill Lynch, to which he owed $35 million, was pressing hard for a settlement of his debts and he was determined to hand over as little as possible.

According to those close to the negotiations, Merrill decided to deal directly with Ryan rather than allow the two main Irish banks – Bank of Ireland and AIB (Allied Irish Bank), its syndicate partners on the loan – to lead the talks. Ryan played a cunning game. Even though Ryanair was legally outside his direct control, he offered a large stake in the airline to Merrill Lynch in exchange for a write-off of his debts. But the bank was not prepared to take shares in a company which appeared to have no prospects of success.

'Merrill wanted some cash, not a share of a loss-making airline,' says one of Ryan's associates. The airline industry, though limping out of the recession of the early 1990s, was still in trouble and Ryanair had a history of losses. Had Merrill's bankers looked closely at the company's accounts for 1992, which were published in early 1993, they might have noticed that the underlying cash position for the year was far better than the headline profits indicated – Hayes had thrown money at depreciation charges to keep the profits down – but they were not interested.

The negotiations between Ryan and Merrill Lynch would drag on for another year, but while Ryanair's real level of profitability may have been concealed from the bank, it was uppermost in O'Leary's mind. He knew that his profit-sharing deal with Ryan would start delivering dividends very soon. He was just thirty-two years old, and was about to make his first serious money. He knew that his life was changing and he could afford to indulge himself.

In May that year Patsy Farrell decided to sell Gigginstown House, just outside Mullingar. The asking price for the house and 200 acres was £580,000. Gigginstown, an unpretentious Georgian mansion built in the 1850s for the Busby family and designed by John Skipton-Mulvany, needed renovation, but its setting was what O'Leary coveted. Robert Ganly, the auctioneer who handled the sale, described the house as being 'grand and honest' and remembers it as a typical Irish country house – 'It needed work,' he says, 'like most country houses of the time.'

O'Leary had always wanted his own home in Mullingar, where his parents had lived since he was a small boy, and Gigginstown was too good an opportunity to miss. Within a month of the house being put on the market, O'Leary had made his move. He negotiated briefly, knocked a few thousand off the asking price and struck a deal. 'I don't remember him being particularly aggressive or particularly difficult. It all went relatively smoothly,' Ganly says.

O'Leary says that when he bought Gigginstown

I was probably to the pin of my collar to pay for it. I grew up on a farm and I'd always known that if I ever had the money I wanted to have my own house, my own farm. Then I got lucky and got more money and I wanted a grander house.

The house itself isn't massive. People go on about this magnificent mansion. It is a very nice family home – it is not one of these big palatial mansions, nor was it built to be. It was built as a sort of a weekend house for someone in Dublin, but on a grand scale. I wouldn't want my kids rattling around in a ginormous fucking mansion. My house isn't small but it feels fairly compact. If you have kids and the kids are growing up and bringing friends back, you don't want them to think they are arriving in Buckingham Palace.

It was to prove a bargain buy – over the next twelve years house prices in Ireland rose tenfold as the economy went into a period of double-digit growth – but in 1993 large country houses were slow to sell and relatively inexpensive to buy.

Gigginstown was to become his oasis, a private retreat from the self-imposed frenzy that Ryanair had become, but not yet. For his first few years as Gigginstown's owner O'Leary continued to spend most of his working week in Dublin, visiting his estate at weekends. He had plans for the house and for the land, but first he wanted to bank some 'serious cash'.

While O'Leary was completing his purchase, Hayes was preparing his exit. On 23 June 1993 Hayes formally tendered his resignation as chief executive, though he would continue in office until the end of the year.

His departure was not a surprise: he had been contracted to do a specific job with a specific time limit. By the time he left Hayes would have completed two years at Ryanair and could take much of the credit for transforming the airline's fortunes. His determination to impose rigorous and timely financial reporting had made it possible for him and O'Leary to fully understand the company's problems for the first time, and his desperation to drive up passenger numbers had seen him experiment with, and then embrace, low price and high frequency as his twin weapons. By the end of his second year Ryanair was carrying close to one million passengers a year.

Hayes had pruned out underperforming routes, had been prepared to take tough political decisions like withdrawing from small regional airports, and had insisted that every Ryanair flight that left the ground covered its costs. Most importantly of all, he had imposed financial transparency on a company that had never had it before.

There was little debate about his successor. Michael O'Leary had returned to Ryanair after his sabbatical working for Tony Ryan and was now committed to making his mark at the company. He had been appointed chief financial officer on his return, could see that the company had turned a significant corner and had a 25 per cent stake in its future profits. He also knew that there were no other options. For the moment Ryan was a broken man, consumed by bitterness at the demise of GPA and robbed, as he saw it, of the millions that were his right. Ryan would recover spectacularly from his fall from grace, but it would be on the wings of Ryanair. Ryan's eldest children Cathal and Declan had tasted high office already and were happy to leave the airline's leadership to O'Leary. He knew the company better than anyone, had played a key role in its recovery and was ready and willing to take charge. Hayes's low-fare strategy, though born of desperation rather than strategic cunning, had set the airline on its way and, just as importantly, it meshed with the business philosophy which O'Leary had learned from Herb Kelleher's Southwest. The basket case had become a viable proposition, and O'Leary was perfectly positioned to take advantage and build the business. The liberalization of the markets gave him the opportunity to expand, and the work done by Hayes and himself had given him a stable company.

Hayes's final months at Ryanair were not idle; he became embroiled in a major political battle with the European Commission, the Irish government and Aer Lingus.

Ryanair's success in winning market share by cutting prices was only just beginning to translate into profits, but through its loss-making years it had managed to wreak havoc at Aer Lingus. Already buffeted by the international aviation recession, Aer Lingus received a further hammer blow in the summer of 1992 as a major shareholder in GPA. Instead of banking heady profits from the flotation, it now had to write off its investment and swallow the losses. It would have been painful in a good year, but by now Aer Lingus was bleeding cash on its operations.

The state-owned airline's instant solution to its crisis was typical of a company used to monopoly and unsuited to the challenges posed by competition. Bernie Cahill, Aer Lingus's chairman, decided he should get rid of the competition by buying out Ryanair, and was also preparing a survival plan for Aer Lingus that would require the Irish government to pour in £175 million to repair its balance sheet. Without the cash injection Aer Lingus would be bankrupt, and if it could not kill off Ryanair, it would be unable to return to profit on the Ireland–UK routes.

In May, a month before Hayes tendered his resignation, Cahill approached Tony Ryan about a possible deal. He was, he said, prepared to offer £20 million for Ryanair – a price which he thought would tempt Ryan to cut his losses. O'Leary and Hayes were delegated to deal with Cahill, a decision that riled the Aer Lingus chairman as he believed he should be dealing with the main player.

Accounts of the meeting between the three have taken on the mystique of an urban legend, with Hayes and O'Leary cast as young mischief-makers determined to wind Cahill up with no intention of ever selling. In the legend, Hayes and O'Leary pushed Cahill all the way, forcing him to edge up his offer and yet, each time he raised it, they came back looking for more. Finally, they demanded £29 million, saying that Ryan would not settle for a penny less. And then Cahill realized what was happening: the figure had been chosen not because it was Ryanair's real price, but because it echoed the £29 fares that Ryanair was using to lure passengers onto its planes. Cahill had been played for a fool and was furious, the story goes.

O'Leary, however, remembers it differently. He says the negotiations were serious and based on Ryanair's profits the previous year. Cahill, he says, was told the company was his for £20 million. 'There was no 29.99, this was a serious discussion.'

It was not, however, a discussion between equals. Cahill, a veteran of the Irish business scene, had to deal with Hayes and O'Leary, and according to some who knew him he took an instant dislike to the 'young upstarts'. 'After meeting Cahill a couple of times, it came back to us that he thought we were just a pair of young pups. Who did we think we were telling him what he had to pay?'

A former Aer Lingus executive agrees with O'Leary. 'We heard that Bernie was high-handed. A deal was on the table, but it just did not happen.'

The proposed deal fell apart. 'When you try to do these sorts of deals, they either gather momentum or they fade away,' says O'Leary. 'It could have happened very quickly,' he says, acknowledging that Ryanair was genuine about the sale. Neither he nor Hayes, however, was convinced that Cahill was serious, and they refused to allow Aer Lingus access to Ryanair's accounts, because they feared that Cahill might simply be after information about the company. Those close to Ryan say that he might have sold, but for the first time since he had founded the company it was beginning to make serious profits and he knew that Cahill wanted to shut it down and destroy his legacy rather than invest and build it.

Months later, on 5 October, news of the takeover talks finally broke in the media. The *Irish Times* carried a front-page report headlined 'Ryanair rejects £20 million bid by Aer Lingus'. According to the report, 'A valuation of £20 million is understood not to have been acceptable to Ryanair and it then refused Aer Lingus access to its books because it believed the national carrier was only on an information-gathering exercise,' a version of events that mirrored the fears of O'Leary and Hayes.

Cahill was apoplectic about the leak. He was about to go public with Aer Lingus's survival plan and did not want his efforts to save the airline sidetracked by speculation about buying Ryanair, especially since the mooted deal had been dead in the water for almost four months. Two days later, after intense pressure from Cahill, the *Irish Times* retracted its story and published a correction: 'The Irish Times accepts that no bid was made or rejected.'

The story was true, but it was inconvenient. The *Irish Times*, which prides itself on being Ireland's paper of record, buckled under pressure and published a retraction that it knew was false. 'Aer Lingus was furious about the story,' recalls Jackie Gallagher, its author. 'It maintained that while there had been discussions, there had never been an actual bid. That is why the correction was specific to the headline – if there had been a formal bid the paper could have stood its ground, but at the time there were a lot of connections between the paper and the airline and so the correction was published.'

Two weeks later the reason for Cahill's anger became abundantly clear when Aer Lingus announced that 1992/93 had been the airline's worst year ever. 'The period since my last report was the most traumatic in the 57-year history of Aer Lingus,' he said in the group's annual report. Annual losses were an eye-watering £109.7 million while the airline's debts were £540 million. Cahill attributed the company's dire performance to 'the impact of worldwide recession which rocked the airline industry, the impact of the failed GPA flotation, the high cost base and the declining average yield per passenger'.

The GPA debacle had forced a write-off of £43.9 million. Restructuring charges were just short of £100 million and the airline had just ten days left to finalize negotiations with its trade unions to save £50 million a year. If it failed to meet the deadline, it would not qualify for state aid, which had been tied to Aer Lingus's ability to reform itself.

Carefully, Cahill avoided mentioning the impact that Ryanair's aggressive pricing had had on the national airline's performance. Far better to blame international crises than look closer to home. Cahill could avoid talking about Ryanair, but the industry knew where Aer Lingus was being hurt. In November Tony Brazil, the outgoing president of the Irish Travel Agents' Association, said that Aer Lingus was losing ten pounds on every passenger on the Dublin–London route because of Ryanair competition. It was being forced to charge fares that it could not afford. 'This blood-letting must end as surely to God the two parties can see where it is all leading.'

Hayes and O'Leary decided, after much discussion, not to oppose Aer Lingus's request for state aid, but Hayes was given the task of ensuring that the money came with strict conditions about how and where it could be used. Rescuing a state-owned airline was one thing, but using state money to prey on Ryanair was quite another.

Hayes spent the last months of his tenure as chief executive compiling Ryanair's dossier on the matter for the European Commission. He was determined that Aer Lingus should not be allowed to use taxpayers' money to subsidize its existing routes. The state aid was, Ryanair argued, permissible if it gave Aer Lingus a last, one-off chance to reform itself, but not if it was used to further distort competition and imperil Ryanair.

This was a genuine fear not mere posturing. Under Cahill's survival plan Aer Lingus was planning to launch its own low-fare subsidiary, to be called Aer Lingus Express. This, Cahill hoped, could compete with Ryanair on price, leaving the main Aer Lingus company to compete on service.

'We believe that this specific proposal [to launch Aer Lingus Express], which envisages the misuse of a State subsidy to add capacity on our route network, is incompatible with the EC's transport competition and state aid rules,' Hayes said in the submission. He wanted a requirement that Aer Lingus should be forced to operate all routes profitably from the following year and not from 1996, as was proposed in the Cahill plan. Hayes also asked the commission not to approve any EC aid for Aer Lingus flights from Ireland's regional airports – a subsidy which could be applied to commercially unsound routes that would otherwise not be flown by an airline but which the government deemed essential public services. He pointed out that Ryanair had initiated such services but had been forced to withdraw from them because of Aer Lingus's predatory pricing – a direct reference to its decision to withdraw from Galway, Kerry and Waterford airports.

It was a war that Hayes could not expect to win outright, but he chalked up battle victories nevertheless. The Aer Lingus rescue plan was hemmed with conditions that Ryanair had proposed and which O'Leary could police in future years to ensure that the private airline, which had only just managed to make decent profits, would not be squashed by state subsidies. 'Aer Lingus's strategy will, if unchecked, lead ultimately to the demise of Ryanair, albeit at enormous cost to Aer Lingus, since Ryanair simply does not have the resources to continuously fight subsidized competition,' Hayes said.

While Cahill's excuses for the national airline's difficulties were centred on international crises not under his control, his solution was single-minded. Aer Lingus's new strategy was to have low fares when competing with Ryanair on routes to London and higher fares and yields on other routes to the UK where the airlines did not compete. Aer Lingus hoped to charge premium fares to London's Heathrow and cut its prices on flights to airports that Ryanair did serve.

Hayes and O'Leary were also prepared to show the Irish government and the EC that Aer Lingus's rescue would not be victimless. In a pre-emptive strike they announced forty redundancies on 29 October, saying Ryanair 'must now take all necessary measures to prepare for the inevitable increase in subsidized competition from Aer Lingus when they receive (as we expect they will) the £175 million of state aid from the Irish taxpayer'.

Aer Lingus tried to strike back, with Executive President John Griffin writing to the *Irish Times* to claim, 'Contrary to the notion that the national airline is another subsidized semi-state company, the public record shows that the Aer Lingus Group produced net profits of £120 million between 1986–92, after payment of interest, taxes and dividends to government.' He neatly ignored the massive subsidies which had flowed into Aer Lingus over the previous years, and the fact that all those profits had been lost subsequently, but then the truth was rather more painful.

Griffin then attacked the validity of the low-cost, low-fare phenomenon:

The public record shows once again that the very low pricing policy established by this new private company [Ryanair], now publicly acclaimed, was not a basis on which to build a viable new airline. In 1989, only four years after starting up, it had to appeal to the government for assistance. Aer Lingus was effectively made to bail it out by having to surrender three routes to Ryanair, on a monopoly basis – all in the name of competition!

Incidentally, apart from its monopoly on the Stansted route, Ryanair also enjoys subsidies there, which are not available to Aer Lingus at Heathrow, underlining the precarious economics of the airline business in this country at the moment.

Griffin's defence of Aer Lingus and its need for state aid was understandable, if tendentious. Ryanair had been saved from likely collapse by the government's adoption of a two-airline strategy in 1989, but it had not received taxpayers' money. Its 'subsidies' at Stansted were actually negotiated reductions in charges, granted because the airport's owners were anxious for business. Griffin also ignored the fact that Ryanair had survived despite the best preda-tory efforts of the state airline, which had used state money in a determined attempt to send Ryanair the way of Avair, its bankrupt predecessor. He was reflecting the exasperation felt by the tra-ditional airlines, which had grown accustomed to a world devoid of competition.

Griffin and his colleagues still believed that state-owned airlines were members of a gentlemen's club. They did not compete aggressively, they could charge what they liked and they could turn to their governments for cash whenever cyclical crises blew a hole in their bottom lines. Airlines, in their view, were not just commercial operators; they were an extension of government policy, providing an essential public service (in Ireland's case air travel between an island nation and the rest of the world) as well as being a substantial employer.

Aer Lingus would get its government aid this time, but it would prove to be the last handout. From now on the company would have to stand or fall on its ability to compete, and O'Leary was just about to up the ante.

8. Bread and Water

On 1 January 1994 Michael O'Leary finally stepped out of the shadows. For the previous five years he had been at the heart of the airline's transformation, but he had operated below the radar. He was known within Ryanair but barely registered outside it. Now he was to assume official leadership of a company that he had helped drag from near bankruptcy to profitability, a role that he had combined with the sometimes all-consuming pressures of dealing with the sporadic crises in Tony Ryan's business affairs.

His rise was greeted with some internal trepidation. 'Some were delighted to hear it, some weren't,' recalls Charlie Clifton. 'They were scared he'd be cutting costs and cutting us. That it would be bread and water.' Ryanair's employees were right to be wary; the new chief executive was messianic about cost control. He was also convinced he could transform Ryanair from a successful niche airline into a serious European contender.

O'Leary first needed to develop a new relationship with Ryan. The collapse of GPA had destroyed Ryan's aura of invincibility and threatened to eliminate his wealth. The great man of Irish business was on his way down while O'Leary, his protégé bagman, was on an upward curve. He had chosen to stay in the background at Ryanair for years, first as Ryan's eyes and ears, later as finance director and deputy chief executive. He had, as he reminds anyone who interviews him, wanted to shut the airline down but Ryan's stubbornness had kept it flying. He had walked away from it for a time, only for his hopes of striking gold with Ryan's millions to be dashed when GPA collapsed. He had returned to the airline, knowing that it was his only remaining opportunity of making serious money. He had in his pocket his previous deal with Ryan which promised him a 25 per cent share of any future profits above £2 million – a deal struck when the prospect of the airline being closed seemed more likely than recovery. Under Conor Hayes, however, Ryanair had stabilized and edged its way to profit, and O'Leary was prepared to sweat blood to take it to the next level. His routine was relentless: he arrived early in the office, left late, smoked heavily and drank coffee incessantly. He lived in his apartment in the Dublin suburb of Sandymount during the week, escaping some weekends to Gigginstown, but his real life was at Dublin airport, guiding the fortunes of the company he now directed.

From 1988 to the end of 1993 the battle at Ryanair had been for control of the company, but not in the sense of boardroom struggles and jockeying for power; it had been a more basic battle. Hayes, who had just left, O'Leary and their management team had been fighting for control of the airline's finances, slowly instilling order where there had been chaos. Loss-making routes had been closed, financial controls had been imposed, costs had been reduced, but the strategy that was to mark out Ryanair from the rest of the competition over the next decade had yet to emerge. Under first McGoldrick and then Hayes elements of that strategy had fallen into place, but it had not been pulled together into a coherent business model that could be the template for the future

Slowly, the policy of low costs and fares had become the dominant if still bare approach. Hayes had experimented successfully with low fares and high frequency, and it had stuck. What had evolved at the airline, through trial and error, was a way of doing business profitably – a gigantic breakthrough, but it had not yet been fleshed out into a business model that O'Leary could call his own.

His Ryanair was now lean, understood how to reduce its costs, had a clear idea of what it wanted to become – an airline that could expand profitably – and what it needed to do to get there, but its corporate clear-headedness was not the result of a eureka moment. O'Leary had visited Herb Kelleher, Southwest's charismatic founder, two years earlier and had left with an understanding of the dynamics of the low-fare industry, but he had not yet converted his knowledge into a strategy.

O'Leary's impact on the company was incremental: he was determined to make each day better than the day that went before it. 'Looking back it looks like we were some kind of genius turnaround artists whereas in fact the company was in such a sorry state that all we did was try to keep improving it day by day, week by week. And it has kept improving,' he says.

By the time O'Leary decided to take the chief executive's chair he had started to put flesh on the survivalist strategy that had secured the airline's future by pointing it down the road of sustainable profitability. 'He started to develop a plan based loosely on Southwest,' says Clifton. 'The dynamic guy on top, single fleet-type, good culture and cheaper than everybody else.'

Within days of his appointment at the start of 1994 the new Ryanair began to emerge into public view, though few in Europe would have recognized the significance of what O'Leary was attempting. Throughout that year he rolled out a series of initiatives that, taken together, created the modern Ryanair. The business model that was to become the envy of low-cost airlines across the world has been refined since, but the fundamentals were laid down in 1994, and the first signs of O'Leary's emerging vision for the airline and what it could achieve in Europe had become apparent by the end of the year.

Ryanair was metamorphosing from a small, if profitable, Irish airline into O'Leary's creature: an airline that could challenge, create a market and defeat Europe's dominant national airlines.

For O'Leary there would be no honeymoon period in his new role. Ryanair had just survived a bruising battle with Aer Lingus, a battle that had plunged Aer Lingus into heavy losses, but Ryanair's success tempted yet more competition to join the market. On 4 January British Midland launched a price war on the Dublin–London route by introducing a return fare of £69, a 50 per cent cut on its existing price and a serious challenge to Ryanair. Six days later Richard Branson's Virgin group joined the fray when it teamed up with Cityjet, a struggling Irish start-up which serviced London's City airport from Dublin. The Virgin deal was effectively a franchise: Cityjet would continue to operate the routes but would use Virgin livery, uniforms, catering, maintenance and other support services.

Branson's arrival and British Midland's low fare meant that Ryanair would have to fight even harder for customers, and would have to find new ways of reducing its costs so that it could offer still lower fares than its competitors. The years of attrition with Aer Lingus had hardened the airline and its management team; they knew they could fight, and they knew they could survive. The early reliance on Ryan's then bottomless pockets had been replaced by the bare bones of a business model which could see off challengers with a straightforward proposition: Ryanair's lower costs allowed it to make money from fares that caused the larger airlines to bleed. Ryanair's sticking power now came from its competence, not from its benefactor.

By 1994 Aer Lingus was on the verge of ruin. Under pressure on its core Ireland to Britain routes, where its market share had declined sharply to less than 50 per cent in 1993, Aer Lingus was also being pummelled on its profitable transatlantic routes, as more and more passengers availed themselves of lower fares from London to the United States and shunned its service. Time too was against Aer Lingus. Europe's steady deregulation of its skies meant not only greater freedom for new independent airlines like Ryanair, but also a looming curb on the amount of money governments could pour into their ailing national airlines. Aer Lingus had had one last chance of getting its hands on a sizeable state subsidy and no time to waste.

The European Commission, after intensive lobbying from the Irish government, had approved the £175 million rescue package. Bernie Cahill promised that costs would be slashed by shedding workers and boosting productivity, and Aer Lingus committed itself to maintain capacity at 1993 levels. Its objective, so it said, was to reinvent itself as a lean, modern airline rather than to use the state's money to blow its competitors out of the skies, and it would raise money by getting rid of much of its non-airline business, like its hotel chain and human resources company.

But O'Leary suspected that the state aid would be used to subsidize a fresh round of predatory strikes against its competitors, and he was determined to stop that happening. With that determination, another key element of the modern Ryanair model was about to fall into place: the aggressive and noisy pursuit of competitors and anyone who stood in the airline's way. At the beginning of 1994 O'Leary complained to the European Commission that Aer Lingus was already using state aid to distort competition by 'fare dumping' – charging ludicrously low fares – on certain routes. His argument was that Aer Lingus could only charge those fares because it was using taxpayers' money to subsidize them.

The commission listened and acted. On 4 February officials from its competition office raided Aer Lingus headquarters in Dublin airport. In a statement Ryanair said it had 'supported Aer Lingus in its application for state aid, primarily in the hope that it would lead to fair play in Irish aviation, and on the grounds that Aer Lingus would, as a condition of receiving state aid, be obliged to cease its practice of "below-cost selling" on those routes where it faces competition from Ryanair'. The statement continued:

It is a matter of great regret to Ryanair that this has not happened. Indeed, in the four weeks since it received this state aid, Aer Lingus has, as it has done in the past, engaged in widespread 'below-cost selling' and seat dumping practices on those routes where it faces competition from Ryanair.

Is it reasonable that Aer Lingus, which has received vast amounts of state aid, should be allowed to use taxpayers' money to subsidize temporarily reduced fares until Ryanair is driven out of business, and then, as it has done in the past, raise the fares to levels which are profitable for them, but will put air travel to the UK once more out of the reach of the vast majority of Irish people? This type of 'dirty tricks' must stop.

Brian Cowen, the Irish minister for transport in charge of winning Europe's support for his government's rescue of Aer Lingus, said that it was 'regrettable that it was deemed necessary [to raid the headquarters]. I don't dispute the competency of the com-

mission to act in that way, but it could have been done otherwise.'
O'Leary, though, had made his point. Aer Lingus, if it wanted to
survive, would have to learn to compete on a level if vicious
playing field, and he would stop at nothing to prevent it regaining
its old dominance of the skies between Ireland and Britain.

On 13 January 1994, less than two weeks after O'Leary started
work as Ryanair's chief executive, it was reported in the aviation
trade publication *Airclaims* that the airline was planning to replace
its existing fleet of aircraft and switch to the Boeing 737. This was
the plane that Southwest had used to develop its low-fare empire
in America. Ryanair chose the 737 because, apart from its reputation
for needing little maintenance and an enviable safety record, it could
be configured to carry the ideal number of passengers for the company's market. Just as importantly, operating a single type of aircraft
delivered savings across the airline, from maintenance to training
and simple flexibility: all crew members, pilot or stewardess, could
be moved seamlessly to any aircraft in the fleet.

Two weeks later the airline made its decision public. It was
acquiring six second-hand Boeing 737–200s, each with a capacity of
130 passengers (26 more than the existing 104-seat One Elevens).
Ray MacSharry, the former European Union commissioner who
was now Ryanair's chairman, said that Ryanair was 'now a major
Irish airline, with significant expansion plans for the next three
years. This 737 fleet will provide us with a unique platform upon
which to develop and expand our existing markets.'

For Ryanair it was a major step: not only would the Boeings
deliver savings, they would also bring credibility to a still young
airline. Boeing was the most respected brand name in the aircraft
business and O'Leary believed it would resonate with customers
if, when they booked a Ryanair flight, they knew that they would
always be flying in a relatively new, high-quality aircraft, rather
than the mixed bag used by most young airlines. The decision to
embrace the 737 set O'Leary on a course from which he would
not deviate. The move would reduce a range of costs within the
company by streamlining the training of pilots and staff, by reducing

maintenance costs, by simplifying reservations with a standard layout, and by increasing capacity on every route they flew by almost 30 per cent.

By the time the 737s were delivered 'it was penny pinching to the extreme' says Charlie Clifton, as O'Leary worked the airline to the bone to pay for his new machines.

I remember when the first 737–200 came in I was head of inflight operations and we discovered that we didn't have any safety cards for the new aircraft. They're specific to the type of aircraft – some 737–200s have 130 seats, some have 121, and they sent over lots of cards with 121 seats on it instead of 130 seats.

Unbeknownst to anyone, the night before myself and the cabin services manager found a stick-on that you could put on these cards that would cover out the old bit and put on the new bit. So we were in the office writing away and sticking the new bit on to each of these cards to put on the aircraft. Michael popped his head around the door and was really pleased: 'Good, good, good lads.' You were so conscious of doing this sort of stuff – instead of saying we'd go out and order 150 brand spanking new cards, you just tape over the old bit.

By October 1994 Ryanair had taken delivery of five more 737s, bringing its fleet to eleven, and it had phased out all its other planes by not renewing lease agreements. The single fleet-type had arrived and O'Leary's Ryanair was taking shape.

Declan Ryan says that the decision to acquire the first six Boeings was 'the real turning point for the company. If you had to identify one decision, that was it.'

O'Leary agrees. 'That was the big one,' he says.

Ryanair was now positioned to mount an inexorable challenge on the Ireland–Britain routes, which still accounted for the bulk of its business, but it was also, far more significantly, ready to test the continental European market.

On Valentine's Day 1994, ten days after the raid on Aer Lingus headquarters, O'Leary turned up the heat once again, announcing

Ryanair's simplified fare structure. Advance purchase requirements would be reduced to a single day – on most airlines the cheapest tickets had to be purchased at least fourteen days in advance – and Ryanair was abolishing the rule that travellers had to spend a Saturday night at their destination to get the cheapest fare.

The changes were seismic. Fare restrictions were used by the national airlines to create the impression that ticket prices were generally cheap, while in reality the cheapest fares were hard to come by. O'Leary's decision to strip away the rules gave Ryanair a critical edge in a market where it could now claim a 30 per cent market share and where it now carried more than 1.2 million passengers each year. Its route network was still small – in March 1994 it offered services from Dublin to Liverpool, Luton, London Stansted and Munich; from Luton to Cork, Galway, Kerry, Knock and Waterford; from Stansted to Galway, Kerry, Knock and Waterford; from Liverpool to Knock and from London Stansted to Munich and to Shannon – but it was no longer a bit player struggling for survival. It was a profitable airline gearing up for expansion, and the greater capacity of its Boeing 737s would increase the pressure on O'Leary and his team to sell seats.

If the new planes were to be worked productively Ryanair had to develop new routes, and O'Leary was pushing ahead with his expansion plans because he needed to keep the planes flying for as long as possible, with as many passengers on board as he could sell tickets to. He had set his sights on new routes to Manchester and Glasgow's Prestwick airport. First, however, O'Leary wanted to reduce the costs of that expansion by negotiating exceptional deals at the airports he wanted to serve.

Three years earlier he had played a role in the negotiations with Stansted airport that had paved the way for Ryanair's survival. It was a deal that had benefited both sides, because Stansted was a new airport with a need for customers. Now O'Leary had to persuade established airports that discounts were the way forward, arguing that passenger growth would compensate them for lower charges.

His negotiations with Prestwick airport, situated outside Ayr, about thirty-five miles from the centre of Glasgow, were to prove a template for the deals that followed. When the details of the deal became public in April 1994, industry experts accused PIK, the owners of Prestwick, of 'economic suicide'. The airport, which had not had a scheduled service for the previous five years, had agreed to waive all landing, passenger and air-traffic control charges in order to win O'Leary's business. The *Sunday Times* estimated that the deal would cost PIK about £600,000 in its first year and £850,000 in subsequent years, but PIK Managing Director Paddy Healy was unrepentant.

We are incurring the costs to get us into the scheduled passenger game again. Prestwick will again start to appear in international airline time-tables on travel agents' computer screens. The new service will bring a flow of scheduled passengers we do not have at present. We will make money from our duty-free, catering and car parking facilities which we operate ourselves. At the end of the first year we will have more money in the till than if we had not done it.

We have done our sums carefully. What we are doing is cutting costs to the bone to promote low-cost air services. We are taking a long-term view.

The industry was not convinced. 'The extra income to be generated from duty-free, catering and car parking will at best be marginal compared to the costs incurred by PIK in providing the services to the airline,' said one commentator quoted in the *Sunday Times*.

O'Leary, though, had got what he wanted: a deal that took his cost base lower still, which allowed him to offer cheaper fares and which gave him the routes that his new fleet needed if it were to be productive. He also believed that the deal would work for Prestwick – there was little point, he argued, in carving out a deal for Ryanair which would force airports into bankruptcy. He was simply shifting the airports' thinking from a low-volume, high-cost model to one predicated on high volume and low cost. His part of the bargain was to deliver the volume by persuading passengers to take to the skies. Better still, the welter of publicity that had surrounded Prestwick's decision to grant Ryanair cheap access to its facilities meant that the Scottish public knew that a low-fare airline had moved into their country without O'Leary having to spend a pound on marketing the new service. The Ryanair name was known and its message was clear: cheap flights.

Much to Aer Lingus's horror, O'Leary trumped his Prestwick coup by extracting dramatic discounts from Manchester airport as well. According to Tim Jeans, then head of marketing at Manchester airport and later Ryanair head of marketing, Manchester had been trying to attract Ryanair ever since it realized how much traffic the airline was putting through its neighbour, and rival, Liverpool airport. Jeans began talking to Ryanair towards the end of 1993, and in January 1994 he flew out to Dublin to meet the airline's new chief executive.

'The meeting itself was quite bizarre,' Jeans says. 'Apart from anything else, my attempts to go across to Dublin incognito, by going through Liverpool and booking on Ryanair, were thwarted because I chose the one day in Liverpool when it was snowing.' His flight cancelled, Jeans had to switch to an Aer Lingus flight out of Manchester.'Who should I run into but a group of fairly senior managers from Aer Lingus, all of whom I knew well. They said, "Why are you going to Dublin if you're not meeting us?" So I was rumbled before I even took off.' When Jeans arrived at Dublin airport he met Ryanair's head of route development, Bernard Berger, finance chief Howard Millar and finally Michael O'Leary.

'They just spent three hours telling me how much they didn't want to fly to Manchester,' Jeans says. 'And I almost said, well if you don't want to fly that much then, okay, I'll go back . . . I was never going to accept the first proposal they put to me. And I said, look, I'm not in a position to commit to that sort of level of pricing, but I said I'm not going to close the door on you either, so I'll go back, talk to my colleagues, and we'll talk again.'

A deal was eventually agreed, and three weeks later Ryanair announced it was flying to Manchester. The price Ryanair negotiated was 'substantially below the deal with Aer Lingus', Jeans says, but the airport quickly offered the flag carrier the same terms. But Jeans was soon to learn that getting Ryanair to sign on the dotted line was only half the battle. The airline had, he says, a lengthy list of demands involving ticket desks, slots and services, and argued about every aspect of the deal. 'There was a point where I almost said, just don't bother,' Jeans says, such was his level of exasperation. But he held his temper and Ryanair added Manchester to its route network.

Slowly but inexorably O'Leary was changing the nature of the airline business: low fares demonstrably stimulated air traffic, and airports benefited from the increased numbers of passengers. If airports wanted volume, then they had to lower their costs and change their way of doing business, because the only way to generate volume was by offering low fares. Prestwick, Manchester, Luton and Stansted had seen the logic, and before long others were queuing up to revitalize their terminals.

O'Leary's arguments were simple and compelling for those airport operators just outside the mainstream. He offered them what they needed: passengers. The operators, he argued, would make their money on the ground, from shops, restaurants, car parks and transport to and from the airport. It is an argument that he has refined over the years, but the fundamental insight hasn't changed: low-cost airlines should not have to pay to bring passengers to airports, which are captive retail markets.

For O'Leary cut-price airport deals meant he could fulfil another mission. 'Some airlines enter a new route and aim to make a profit in three years. We will not enter a route if we cannot break even in three hours and grow the market by at least 100 per cent,' he said.

Tony Ryan had still not repaid Merrill Lynch the $35 million he had borrowed from them to acquire shares in GPA, and he could not afford to pay. He refused to contemplate personal bankruptcy, but he also could not afford the embarrassment and ruinous expense of a foreclosure by the American bank. Needing desperately to negotiate a settlement, he turned to his personal assistant of five years, Michael O'Leary.

'Those Merrill boys were bastards,' says O'Leary, 'but eventually we ground them down.' For weeks O'Leary battled for a settlement, flying to New York to hammer out terms. Eventually, in the early autumn of 1994, he reached it. Ryan would repay $4 million to Merrill Lynch, and the bank would write off the remaining $31 million. Critically, it was a clean-break agreement: there would be no clawback against any wealth Ryan might accumulate in the future. It was a remarkable deal, particularly since Ryanair's transformation from loss maker to profit centre – albeit on a small scale – was clearly complete.

Ryan now needed to raise the $4 million, and O'Leary came up with a neat solution – one that did not become public for another three years. The airline needed five more Boeings to complete its fleet transformation and maintain its growth. O'Leary negotiated a deal whereby Ryan would acquire the jets for $20 million and then immediately trade them on to the airline for $24 million, booking himself a $4 million profit that would pay off his bankers. It was in effect a direct payment by the airline to its founder, but it was never disclosed as anything as straightforward. Ryan had bankrolled Ryanair for its first seven years, spending more than £20 million to keep it afloat, and the time had come for payback. 'The company paid the debt to Merrill Lynch,' a financial adviser confirms, 'but it was more than he was due at the time. Tony had kept the place going when anyone else would have shut it down. He had poured in money, and now he needed some back.'

Ryan, finally, was free from the GPA debacle and also free, thanks to the deal with Merrill Lynch, to take a stake in what was rightfully his. The bank had missed an opportunity to acquire a stake in a company which was soon to be worth billions, and Ryan would waste little time before joining the board and assuming the chairmanship, as well as major shareholding, in the restructuring which would precede its eventual flotation three years later.

By the autumn of 1994 O'Leary had thus secured his bases and his boss's finances. Ryanair was not yet the dominant player in the

Dublin to London market, but it had more than 30 per cent of the traffic, had opened new routes to Glasgow and Manchester and was above all profitable. His mixed-bag fleet of 104-seat jets and turboprops had been replaced by a homogenous fleet of Boeing 737s, which carried 130 passengers each, and he was beginning to fill the planes. Ryanair, which now employed just 500 people – compared to the more than 7,000 employed by Aer Lingus – had a turnover of £75 million, carried almost two million passengers and had the lowest cost base of any airline flying between Ireland and Britain.

'We make 92p net profit per passenger and claim to be the lowest-cost airline in Europe,' said O'Leary. 'Our strategy is about running the airline the way people want. Low fares, high capacity at busy times, flexible tickets. There are only three layers of management. No secrets. No dogma. No unions. I drive buses at the airport, check in passengers, load bags and get a good kicking when I play for the baggage-handlers' football team. The only thing I will not do is fly aircraft.'

Despite the changes throughout 1994, Ryanair was still pursuing a predictable and relatively traditional route network. It flew from a number of minor airports, but its primary source of passengers and profit was from major cities like Cork and Dublin to other major cities like London, Glasgow, Manchester and Liverpool. Some of his destination airports may have been on the fringe – Prestwick, Stansted and Luton were all some distance from the cities they served – but they were not significantly more distant than traditional airports like Gatwick and Heathrow.

O'Leary could sense greater opportunity, and he was hungry to try.

'Continental Europe is a market with over 300 million people most of whom are now paying outrageously high airfares. I assure you that this is a market which Ryanair will not ignore but I cannot reveal our strategy today,' he said that autumn. He predicted that after 1997, when many of the remaining restrictions on airlines in Europe were due to be lifted, 'short-haul, cost-efficient, point-to-point airlines will sprout up throughout Europe. They will, in

a short space of time, change the face of European air travel . . .
From 1996 onwards continental Europe will be at the forefront of
our plans, but whether the Ryanair assault will come from Dublin
or London, we have yet to decide.'

His optimism was not universally shared, however. Air UK's
director of planning and industry affairs, Phil Chapman, told an
IATA conference on aviation economics that the chances of a
European airline replicating the success of Southwest in America
was virtually non-existent. 'Governments still support many of our
national carriers and in some countries the social implications of
allowing a major carrier to fail or to dramatically reduce costs is
nearly impossible,' he said.

'But,' Chapman added, 'set against this is the political desire to
see low airfares to satisfy voter aspirations. Many of these carriers
dominate their home markets, and with the structural advantage it
is difficult to see how a real threat can be mounted by a low-cost,
no-frills company. The numbers travelling by air in Europe are
not sufficient to allow a real high-frequency, low-cost service to
take place.'

Chapman underestimated the single-minded determination of
O'Leary. He was right to foresee the difficulties which lay ahead
and the determination of the flag carriers to retain their stranglehold
on the market, but deregulation had already changed the game.
The flag carriers would survive, and would continue to subsidize
their European operations with the profits they made on intercontinental routes. Chapman also underestimated the European
public's as yet untested appetite for low airfares.

Ryanair, even in its earliest and most chaotic period, had shown
that competition would stimulate a market. In its first ten years of
existence the number of people flying between Ireland and Britain
had more than doubled. Ryanair had grown the market for everyone, but its ability under O'Leary to contain its costs and lower
fares had made it impossible for rivals to compete profitably. Existing airlines could not match Ryanair's costs because they were
laden down with the historical costs of serving a different type of

aviation market. Overstaffed and heavily unionized, national airlines were imbued with the ethos of public service, not profit. It
was far easier for a new airline, without the baggage of the past, to
adapt to a changing market and keep its costs at a level that could
not be matched by its rivals.

The airline's success at new or previously underutilized airports
like Stansted, Luton and Prestwick demonstrated that travellers
would fly to relatively inconvenient locations if the price was right,
and marked the beginning of an airport strategy that would turn
the air travel market on its head.

Aer Lingus's experience should have been a salutary warning to
the flag carriers that O'Leary would have to face down in the years
ahead. It had tried to use its power as a state-owned company to
blow the upstart out of the skies, but it had failed to understand
the most basic of business lessons. In order to compete, it had to
charge less, and unless it was prepared to bring its costs into line
with those of Ryanair, it was doomed to lose millions on every
head-to-head challenge. In 1994 Aer Lingus did not have the
stomach for bloodletting on a serious scale. The airline's survival
plan envisaged job cuts, but not a scale that could guarantee
survival.

O'Leary was on his way; nothing, it seemed, could derail the
ambition of this man who had helped salvage a company from
near-bankruptcy and was now driving it relentlessly to dominance
of a new and fast-growing market. The results for O'Leary's first
year as chief executive would show that he had almost trebled the
airline's reported profits to £5.68 million. Its arch domestic rival
had been seen off and would not be able to mount a credible
challenge for another nine years, while in Europe the slow but
sure pace of deregulation meant that further opportunities were
just around the corner.

9. Takeover Talk

During Michael O'Leary's first year running Ryanair Tony Ryan licked his wounds in the tax haven of Monaco, to where he had retreated after the GPA debacle. Then, in February 1995, Ryan bounced back. His brooding done and his debts settled, he was co-opted onto the airline's board and it was announced that he would take over as chairman the following year, on 1 January 1996, when Ray MacSharry's term was due to end.

Ryan had bankrolled Ryanair from its launch, had installed his sons as shareholders and directors while his brother Kell ran a division out of Stansted, but he had never been legally allowed to acknowledge the airline as his own. His contractual arrangements with GPA forbade Ryan from owning an airline, a problem surmounted by his decision to place ownership in a trust whose beneficiaries were his sons. When GPA collapsed, he still needed to keep his distance so that Ryanair could be kept out of Merrill Lynch's grasp. Only now could he claim what was his, and he wasted little time. 'He had fantastic experience and was very amenable to the airline business,' one long-serving director recalls. 'Not a single person had a problem with it. Michael and Tony were buddies and they are to this day. He was his pa.'

O'Leary would once again be working directly for Ryan, but in his first year as CEO his confidence and stubbornness had grown. O'Leary believed that Ryanair had barely touched its potential. His battles in Europe would, he foresaw, be reruns of Ryanair's successful battles with Aer Lingus. In each market O'Leary would be faced by overstaffed, poorly managed, state-owned airlines lacking the commercial wit or the political ability to compete with a lean, hungry aggressor.

Ryan, meanwhile, could see dollar signs. By 1995 Ryan had invested almost £20 million to keep the airline afloat in its early years and to fund its expansion once it had stabilized. In return officially he had received not a cent, though the airline had structured the airplane purchase deal in 1994 that had allowed him to pay off his debts to Merrill Lynch. But in his own mind he was still owed, and the time had come to collect. Ryan wanted cash and Ryanair was all he had left to sell. While O'Leary plotted expansion, Ryan plotted a sale that would generate millions for his family and put him back where he belonged – among Ireland's wealthy business elite.

His timing, though dictated by events outside his control, was impeccable. On 14 February the *Irish Times* pointed out that 'Dr Ryan has joined the board at a time of rapidly rising profits at Ryanair', adding that the airline's 'profit is understood to have been substantially higher in 1994' than it had been in 1993. Conflict between Ryan and O'Leary was becoming inevitable. O'Leary was making more money than he had thought possible from his profit-share agreement – in 1993 and 1994 he had made his first million pounds from Ryanair, and would earn a further £6 million through 1995 and 1996 – but he had no shareholding in the company. A sale would benefit the Ryans but could put an end to O'Leary's new-found income stream.

For both men one thing was clear: Ryanair had to maintain its upward momentum. Success was a virtuous circle, creating higher profitability and greater visibility for the airline, which in turn whetted the appetites of potential investors and buyers as the money rolled in. For a time at least Ryan and O'Leary were thus on a parallel mission. The tactics remained simple: hammer down costs, drive up profits and maintain relentless pressure on Aer Lingus. Whenever the state-owned airline tried to break free of the constraints imposed upon it by the European Commission in 1993 Ryanair cried foul.

In March 1995, a month after Ryan had joined the board, O'Leary lodged a formal complaint with the commission, alleging that Aer Lingus's plans to buy a new fleet of jet aircraft to operate on some of its Ireland–UK provincial routes breached the capacity restrictions placed on the airline. O'Leary's complaint was eventually dismissed, but his intervention caused delay and maintained pressure, allowing Ryanair to push ahead while its rival stumbled.

In April O'Leary announced that he was creating more than a hundred new jobs across the company – hiring pilots, cabin crew, reservations staff and ground crew as Ryanair geared up for expansion on the routes between Ireland and the UK. Passenger numbers continued to climb throughout 1995, with the routes to Prestwick proving remarkably popular while the airline's share of the Dublin–London market continued to rise.

O'Leary was also now beginning to get the public recognition he deserved. In an interview with the *Irish Times* in May Tony Ryan waxed lyrical about his young chief executive's talents. O'Leary, he said, was 'probably the best chief executive I've ever worked with', and according to the newspaper report Ryan attributed 'much of the success of Ryanair' to O'Leary. The example he gave of what O'Leary had actually done at the airline, however, revealed the shallowness of Ryan's appreciation of the company's transformation under O'Leary. Instead of highlighting the cost controls, the deals with airports, the renegotiation of contracts, the fast turnaround times achieved by Ryanair aircraft or the switch to a fleet of Boeings, Ryan credited O'Leary with first proposing that the airline stop serving food on its flights.

'The family were appalled,' Ryan told the newspaper. 'We told him the passengers would go spare. He went ahead anyway and nobody complained. The time saved in serving food is now spent selling duty-free. I think Ryanair is now the biggest retailer of Jameson [whiskey] in the world.'

Shallow, yet also insightful. O'Leary was clearly the airline's dominant force and Ryan family opposition to his plans wilted when he stood firm. The company was run O'Leary's way and Ryan's sons did not stand in his path.

Tony Ryan, however, was a more robust figure and had plans of his own.

In 1995 the routes from London to Scotland were dominated by British Airways and British Midland, and fares were as expensive

as Dublin–London had been in the late 1980s. The train service
between London and the two major Scottish cities of Glasgow and
Edinburgh was also slow and expensive, and O'Leary reckoned
that there was potential to stir up the market, and do it noisily.

It was widely known that the EU was planning to bring in new
rules that would grant foreign airlines the right – known as cabotage
– to operate domestic flights in another country.

'We wanted to get first-mover advantage on it, in case anyone
else wanted to have a go,' recalls Tim Jeans. 'It was very difficult
to determine, when cabotage came along, whether there would
be a rush to get onto the best domestic routes that everybody else
had. Everybody thought that cabotage was the nirvana, particularly
for someone like Ryanair with no domestic market in Ireland and
the potential to have such a large one in the UK.'

Jeans says that Ryanair briefly considered reincarnating the airline's previous UK-based company, Ryanair Europe (formerly
LEA), in order to establish itself on internal UK routes before
liberalization opened the door to everyone else, 'but LEA had
gone horribly wrong, and in many ways nobody wanted to revisit
the failure. We didn't do failure by then.' Instead, Ryanair took
a 45 per cent stake in Ryanair UK, which had been set up by
Cathal Ryan in 1985 and been dormant for several years. The
company was registered in the UK and authorized by the UK's
Civil Aviation Authority.

As the airline's only British senior manager, Jeans was put in
charge of the new company, through which Ryanair planned to
launch a service between Stansted and Prestwick on 26 October
1995. More than ten years later he still recalls fondly the route's unconventional birth. 'Stansted–Prestwick was a convoluted thing.
It was confusing even for us. That was the great thing about
Ryanair. It genuinely didn't care an awful lot for convention. The
idea that we could construct this elaborate design to get around
the regulations appealed to everybody's taste.'

But it didn't take long for Ryanair's cheekiness to arouse the
anger of its rival carriers. The first skirmish came two weeks before
the new service was due to commence when British Midland

threatened to bring a case before the UK Office of Fair Trading. BMI objected to what it claimed was Ryanair's misleading advertising. 'Whilst your flights are scheduled from Stansted to Prestwick, your advertising campaign description is "Glasgow to London". This gives the clear impression that the flight is to be from Glasgow Airport, whilst Prestwick is some 35 miles away,' it said in a letter to the company, claiming that Ryanair's advertisement was in breach of the Control of Misleading Advertising Regulations 1988, Article 2 (2).

Jeans's response at the time was succinct: 'I was astonished to read the letter from British Midland as I had always considered them to be the great champions of competition in the airline business. I have made it clear that Prestwick is one of the two designated Glasgow airports under IATA regulations and we have no hesitation in using that designation in our literature, just as our sister company has done for over a year on the Dublin routes.'

Ryanair cleared that first hurdle, but a more serious one was about to be thrown in its way. If Ryanair UK was to operate the route, it needed to have an airline operator's certificate from the Civil Aviation Authority, but it could not get one in time for the first flights. Instead, O'Leary had arranged for GB Airways, a UK-registered and -certified company, to operate the flight, using an Irish-registered 737 leased from Ryanair. It was an obvious ruse, a deliberate attempt to drive a coach and four through the regulatory rulebook, and O'Leary's rivals went on the attack. British Midland was joined by Air UK and British Airways in a joint complaint that GB Airways could not use an Irish-registered plane if there were British-registered planes available.

Unfortunately for Ryanair, there were – but they were the smaller BAC One Elevens rather than the 130-seat Boeing. Bookings for the new service were already running at more than 1,000 a day and if Ryanair was forced to use the smaller plane, just under a third of the passengers on every flight would have to be turned away.

'It would have been chaos,' says O'Leary, and for once he contemplated defeat. The weekend before the first flight was due to take off he engaged in desperate negotiations to salvage it, but as the problems mounted he seriously considered suspending bookings and running up the white flag. Frantic telephone negotiations between O'Leary, Jeans, Prestwick's managing director Hugh Lang and the UK department of transport came to nothing and the impasse continued through the next three days.

In the end, after tense negotiations and Ryanair threats to cancel the inaugural flight, the UK department of transport offered the airline a way out. Ryanair was given a ten-day dispensation to run an internal UK service. After ten days Ryanair would be allowed the more usual permission for extended cabotage. This meant that the flights from Prestwick to London, or from London to Prestwick, would have to start in Ryanair's home country of Ireland. 'We had to construct this elaborate operating device where the route was loaded as a Cork–Stansted–Prestwick and in theory we were only allowed to load half of the passengers on the Stansted–Prestwick link,' recalls Jeans. 'But it was all a load of absolute nonsense, because the plane didn't operate that way and there was no cap on the passengers carried – and nobody checked either.'

For O'Leary it had been an irritating and only partly successful fight: Ryanair had made the headlines and copper-fastened its reputation as an aggressive young airline which championed lower fares, but the partial victory was unsatisfactory. He had not won the right to run internal UK services, but had instead won a messy compromise that allowed him to schedule flights within the UK but only if they originated and terminated in Ireland. No one might have been checking, but this was not a firm basis for expansion.

A more significant fight was shaping up at Luton airport. In March 1995 a new low-cost airline was registered by Stelios Haji Ioannou. Other low-cost airlines would come and go, but easyJet was the one which would prove the biggest thorn in O'Leary's side.

It started as a small affair, flying from Luton to Edinburgh and Glasgow with two leased Boeing 737–200 aircraft, and it contracted in everything from pilots to check-in staff – hardly a threat to Ryanair's growing might. But Stelios, as easyJet's owner and founder came to be known, was the son of a billionaire Cypriot shipping magnate, and his fortune gave the airline a level of financial backing that few airlines, or companies for that matter, could match. The easyJet challenge was to prove a slow burner – the first routes were not launched until November 1995, and the airline did not mount a serious effort until it ordered twelve new Boeing 737s in September of 1997.

While O'Leary tried to channel his energies into his expansion plans for the UK and European markets, he was being distracted on the home front by Tony Ryan's obsession with building a new commercial airport at Baldonnel, the military airbase on the south-west fringes of Dublin.

Ryan claimed the new airport would be a 'low cost' alternative to the proposed second terminal at Dublin airport, which was expected to cost £200 million. It was not a new idea – Gay Mitchell, a senior politician within the Fine Gael party, had published a development plan for Baldonnel almost a decade earlier – but Ryan backed his idea with the promise of hard cash. Ryanair, he said, would invest £50 million in the new airport – an enormous amount for a company that had only just started to make profits and which still carried accumulated losses of more than £10 million from its earlier troubles. 'We would design the Dublin City South terminal to facilitate the flow of passengers at a rate four times as great as most other airports can manage,' Ryan said in May 1995. 'This would be achieved by doing away with complex ticketing and other clumsy, time-consuming, unnecessary and costly processes.'

Armed with plans drawn up by two firms of architects, Ryan began to bombard Transport Minister Michael Lowry with details of how cheap and effective Dublin City South airport would be. And, seeking to neutralize any local opposition to the project, Ryan organized public presentations in Newcastle, Rathcoole, Blessington and Naas. He projected that the airport would generate 10,000 jobs, handle 6.5 million passengers a year within a decade and would be a 'low-cost gateway to Europe'.

O'Leary viewed Baldonnel as a Ryan plan rather than a Ryanair plan. 'O'Leary was against it for business reasons – business reasons underpin all of his decisions,' says Tim Jeans. 'The airline didn't need the fixed cost of an airport.' In any case, Ryan's dream was to be short-lived. On 25 January 1996, after a brief cabinet discussion, Lowry vetoed Ryan's proposal, which he said would not be in the interests of the aviation sector or the economy. Lowry claimed in a statement that Aer Rianta, the state-owned airports authority, had 'developed plans for extending the terminal building [at Dublin airport] to enable it to cater for the forecast demand of about 14 million passengers by the year 2005. Dublin Airport has the capacity, therefore, to cater for traffic demand for several decades well beyond 2000.'

Within five years, however, Aer Rianta's projections would look hopelessly conservative. Tony Ryan was incensed by the government's decision and launched an immediate counter-strike. 'Ryanair,' he said, 'must now reassess totally its future plans and its Dublin base. In the short term all expansion out of Ireland is being shelved and other fundamental strategies are being reviewed. The company's new service between London and Glasgow is perhaps a template for the airline's future development.'

But whatever his chairman might say, O'Leary was pressing ahead with his own plans. Three months later, in May – still, presumably, the short term Tony Ryan had spoken of – Ryanair announced three new routes out of Dublin, to Cardiff, Bourne-mouth and Leeds Bradford. Apart from a new Stansted–Knock service, announced in December, they were the only route launches of 1996. The following year O'Leary announced seven new routes; four of these were out of Dublin.

Ryan might bluster, but his chief executive was not taking any notice.

Although Michael Lowry had rejected Ryan's plans for Baldonnel, he was not an instinctive opponent of Ryanair. 'Within the department you still had a core of the public service who were brought up in the old way, which was the protection of the state monopolies. They worked with them and they worked for them.'

I didn't see Ryanair as somebody to be loathed, I saw them as having a genuine cause, I could see their operation as having enormous benefits. It was clear to me that the only hope we had of increasing the accessibility of air travel to the public and encouraging more people to come into Ireland was through the low-cost model. I was very conscious that there was a need for competitive forces within the airline market, and Ryanair were the only ones that were successfully attempting to bring that competition to the sector. I was unashamedly a fan of Ryanair.

And if he wouldn't deliver a new airport, he could deliver a better deal at the existing Dublin facility. Shortly after rejecting the Baldonnel plan Lowry instructed Aer Rianta to lower its charges at Pier A – used by Ryanair – by more than 25 per cent, and in November he asked the airport authority to look at the possibility of reducing charges even further.

'I did that because when Ryanair made a submission it was quite evident that, compared with other airports which they were using, Dublin's charges were excessive,' says Lowry. 'And I also felt that Ryanair had a point, and it was quite clear to me that Ryanair meant what they said when they told the department that they were going to invest and create business in airports that responded to their needs, and that gave them the no-frills service that they required.'

Lowry's plan was met with public criticism by the opposition transport spokesman, Seamus Brennan, but ten years on Brennan admits that his objections were more about politics than policy.

Aer Rianta, meanwhile, was not happy. Its chairman, Noel Hanlon, despised Ryanair and reserved special loathing for O'Leary, who treated Hanlon with naked contempt. 'I think O'Leary respected him [Hanlon] at the start,' recalls one senior Ryanair manager, 'but he didn't respect him for long.' The manager recalls one particular meeting he attended with O'Leary and Hanlon. 'The meeting was just a shout-fest. Hanlon was a rude man. O'Leary is rude in a different way. Hanlon was much ruder but his language was slightly less colourful.'

The two men were natural opposites. Hanlon had been appointed to Aer Rianta because of his political connections and not his competence. For Irish politicians the boards of state-owned companies were places to deposit friends and supporters who needed reward. It was not about financial gain – remuneration was token – but status, and Hanlon revelled in the role of chairman of one of the state's most successful companies. O'Leary thought little of him and did not bother to hide his feelings.

Lowry's instructions to Aer Rianta outraged Hanlon, who did not understand why a state-owned company should favour a private company that was stealing market share from another state-owned company. 'Hanlon has since called me the worst minister for transport he ever had, but as far as I was concerned Aer Rianta had a golden nugget, a monopoly, and had become too comfortable. Initially Aer Rianta had been a company of great vision but it gradually lost its way. The management became aloof, and grew old with the system,' Lowry says.

Five years later, in May 2001, a Dublin newspaper, the *Sunday Business Post*, claimed that the lower airport charges had been worth €40 million to Ryanair. The story, which bore the fingerprints of Aer Rianta's public relations department, played on the fact that Lowry had subsequently been forced to resign his ministerial post after revelations that he had avoided paying tax. Discredited and under investigation by a tribunal of inquiry, it was not difficult to impugn his damaged reputation further by suggesting he had been overly generous to Ryanair.

Like all good smears, it had a grain of truth. Had Ryanair managed to grow passenger numbers for five years and continued to launch new routes at the previous higher charges, then it would have had to pay that €40 million. But the lower charges were available to any airline that wanted them and there was no way Ryanair would have continued its expansion from Dublin if the charges had remained high.

'There was no ulterior motive,' says Lowry. 'It was, as I saw it, in the interests of Aer Rianta. I was for creating greater activity. I was for creating volume and quantity. Aer Rianta had become something like Aer Lingus in the sense that they could effectively decide and govern what prices they wanted for everything. My only consideration in making those decisions was to get a better deal for the consumer.'

O'Leary, however, was already thinking of different consumers, and in particular those prepared to travel from the UK to Europe.

Since 1993 Ryanair had been raking in money. The profit figure for 1992 was closer to £4 million than the reported £850,000, while in 1993 the profits had been substantially higher than the reported £2.03 million and the upward momentum had continued throughout 1994 and 1995. O'Leary's basic strategy – a strategy started by Conor Hayes – was piling up the cash, but O'Leary knew that he could not rest. He and the company had survived a bruising war with Aer Lingus; Ryanair was an established player in the Dublin to UK market, a new player on the Scotland to London market and also had a toehold in Europe.

The real competition, however, was only just beginning. Europe's economies were recovering from the deep recession of the early 1990s and entrepreneurs were beginning to realize the potential of the market. EasyJet was already up and flying in the UK and in January 1996 Debonair, the brainchild of Franco Mancassola, announced that it would be flying from Luton to five European destinations from 1 May. But Mancassola, like many of those who would follow, was about to make a critical error. He believed there was a middle ground, a place between the expensive national flag carriers and the rock-bottom, no-frills service operated by Ryanair.

Debonair, he said, would not be a 'no-frills' airline, though it would be cheap.

We want to be an innovator, not an imitator. We are not targeting any specific sector, but our airline will appeal to cost-conscious, discerning business travellers who value punctuality and reliability and want no compromise on comfort. Debonair will equally appeal to people who have time on their hands to explore Europe – to students, retired people who want to explore the beauty of Europe's cities and holidaying families who want a change from the traditional hot summer resorts.

It was a mission statement that sounded good but delivered little. In the emerging battle for Europe's newly liberated consumers, free at last to choose between competing airlines, and free to fly rather than travel overland or by boat, the battleground was price not service. Millions of Europeans who had never flown before and never expected or wanted airline meals or 'free' drinks on forty-five-minute flights, were prepared to fly if it were cheap. Traditional airlines, and those who had worked in them, never quite understood that price mattered so much; they thought that flying was an experience rather than a travel choice. Sure enough, Debonair went out of business in October 1999. Mancassola blamed its demise on Go, BA's low-cost airline, saying it was not a genuine low-cost operator as it was backed by BA's resources. As the *International Herald Tribune* commented at the time, 'The consensus is that Debonair was doomed . . . by a defective strategy. By raising fares and adding frills to attract business travelers – separate check-in, free drinks and snacks in the front of the cabin – Debonair may have fatally compromised the promise of no-frills: Keep it cheap, keep it simple.'

British Airways, the first of Europe's flag carriers to be privatized, had kept a wary eye on deregulation and the emergence of the low-cost operators. By 1996 it had taken on Cityflyer Express, Loganair, Manx Airlines and Brymon as franchise partners – small airlines that operated in BA colours, wore BA uniforms and operated routes that the main airline did not service. For the Ryan family, still desperate to recover its fortune following the crash of GPA four years earlier, BA offered an obvious route to extracting some cash from its airline.

On 22 April 1996 the Dow Jones news service reported that the Ryan Family Trust had confirmed it was in talks with a 'major international company' to sell 25 per cent of Ryanair. A company statement said the investment would 'enable Ryanair to continue its expansion of low-fare air services in Europe'. Contracts were to be finalized by May, a press release said, and industry sources said the stake would cost £10 million, valuing the airline at £40 million.

'A price was agreed with BA,' says a senior Ryanair figure, 'but the deal fell down on technical issues.'

The price was significantly higher than the newspapers believed – BA was prepared to pay £25 million for a 25 per cent stake, which would have valued Ryanair at £100 million – but even that would have seriously undervalued the company. The true level of its profitability justified a price tag of closer to £300 million and if BA had struck the deal it would have been a bargain. It could also have sounded the death knell for Ryanair's growth.

'I was a staff member at the time, and the news kind of trickled out that this might have happened but it didn't happen. It had fallen apart by the time the staff heard of it,' recalls Charlie Clifton.

It would have been a huge change for all the people who'd been there: you'd have been marching in an entirely different direction, you'd have become 'BA-ified', uniform and corporate. In simple terms it would have squashed any of the competition, which was I presume part of the purpose. It would have been bad for morale and a number of people would have left. But equally I'd say quite a number of people would have been delighted. BA would have brought security – that's brilliant, we're working for 'the world's favourite airline'. At the time [we thought] the company had only just got into profitability, and people would have been happy to run for safety.

But it was not to be, and BA abandoned the negotiations, turning its attentions to its own internal problems. Tony Ryan's dream of at last seeing a return on his investment would have to wait for another day.

10. Stepping up, and down

British Airways' interest in buying Ryanair had whetted Tony Ryan's appetite for a sale. He knew that the airline he had founded was now a remarkably valuable property, and he also knew that if it were to expand even further it would have to broaden its shareholder base. Ryanair would need more planes and more people if it were to take its successful business model out of Ireland's skies and into Europe, and that would require deep pockets. The search for a partner or, failing that, the pursuit of a stock market flotation that could release cash for the family, was on in earnest.

In April 1996, shortly after the talks with BA had broken down, Ryan received a call from Paddy Blaney, a former vice president at GPA. Blaney had met David Bonderman, an American corporate lawyer and investor with a track record of successful investments in the US airline industry. Ryan had met Bonderman years earlier during the negotiations to salvage the US airline America West, which had leased planes from GPA. He knew Bonderman was a serious player.

Bonderman was not a typical American businessman. A former civil rights lawyer, lover of rock music, eclectic dresser and canny investor, he was far more suited to O'Leary's informal but obsessive style than to the grey corporate world. Bonderman's personal interests were as varied as those of Texas Pacific Group, his investment vehicle, which looked for value investments in companies as diverse as Del Monte foods, Beringer wine estates, Ducati the Italian motorcycle manufacturer, America West and Continental Airlines, and retailer J. Crew.

Blaney told Ryan that Bonderman was in Europe looking for investment opportunities, and that he was toying with the idea of investing in Virgin Express, Richard Branson's new European low-cost carrier. Blaney had mentioned Ryanair to Bonderman, and he had shown interest. Perhaps, he suggested, Ryan could do worse than set up a meeting.

Declan Ryan was dispatched to make contact in early March and Bonderman, intrigued by what he heard, travelled to Dublin with a team of advisers. For a week they pored over Ryanair's operations, probing its business model and examining its management team. Very quickly Bonderman recognized that the Irish airline had developed a model that had the robustness to take on Europe and exploit the opportunities that deregulation would bring.

'Bonderman understood what had happened in the US market after it had deregulated in 1978, and he knew what was necessary for an airline to survive and prosper,' says a Ryanair executive who was involved in the negotiations. 'Fundamentally that came down to cost control. Bonderman knew that the lowest-cost operator would always have the competitive edge, and he could see from O'Leary's operation, and from the books, that Ryanair was ideally positioned. Its attention to cost was phenomenal and, just as importantly, he warmed instantly to O'Leary.'

Securing Bonderman's investment was top of Ryanair's agenda, but the company was still focused on extracting extra revenue from its business wherever it could, with no opportunity deemed too small or too bizarre to merit its attention. In June 1996 it became the first European airline to sell advertising on the exterior of its planes.

The idea had been hatched by Tony Ryan over a dinner with Nick Sheele, the chairman and chief executive of Jaguar. Sheele agreed to pay £120,000 to get the Jaguar livery on a Ryanair 737. Once Ryanair had agreed the price with Jaguar, the aircraft was sent to Birmingham to be painted.

'The Jaguar guys were so precise about it, they had to make sure the leaping Jaguar was exactly 33⅓ per cent off the horizon to make sure of the perfect jaw,' Charlie Clifton recalls. 'Then the big day came and we said we'd have the launch in Birmingham. The idea was the aircraft would be towed out of the hangar, there would be two sports cars, photos, Tony, Nick Sheele, lots of pretty girls draped over the cars, and the aircraft in the background. Fantastic.'

But there was one major hitch – the final part of the painting had to be carried out in the south of England, and the plane became stranded down there.

'I arrived in to work, got a call to say the aircraft is broken down in the south of England. Tony arrived and I said the aircraft is tech [broken down],' says Clifton. 'Tony said, "Relax, don't be a pessimist. It'll work out fine; the aircraft will be there." I said, "It won't be, I bet you it won't be." And he said, "It will, I'll bet you. What do you want to bet?" And I said, "A pound?" and he said, "Okay, I'll bet you a pound."'

When Clifton and Ryan arrived in Birmingham, there was no aircraft so they carried on with the photo shoot and digitally added the plane afterwards. But two months later, while Tony Ryan was in the middle of negotiations to secure Bonderman's investment in the company, Charlie Clifton got a note through his letter box: 'Dear Charlie, please find one pound for my indebtedness in relation to our bet. Regards, Tony Ryan.'

After a slow start, exterior advertising went on to provide a solid revenue stream for Ryanair, with companies such as Kilkenny beer, Hertz and Vodafone following Jaguar.

By August 1996 Bonderman and the Ryans had finally consummated a deal, and at a price which reflected Ryanair's real profitability and not the carefully constructed numbers published for the previous three years which had helped conceal Ryanair's real profitability from Merrill Lynch during its negotiations with Ryan over his debts. Bonderman, through a specially created subsidiary, would acquire 20 per cent of Ryanair for £26 million, a price that valued the airline at £130 million.

Bonderman used just £1 million of his own money to buy the stake, and funded the rest of the deal with debt – an astute move that would see the value of his equity stake rise from £1 million to £250 million in the years to come. It was, Bonderman said later, his 'best ever investment', but for Ryanair his involvement was just part of a package that would transform the airline over the next two years.

Tony Ryan was ecstatic with the Bonderman deal, which valued his family's stake at almost £80 million. At long last he could smell the money. Eleven long years of struggle and near-bankruptcy were about to pay off in spectacular style, as long as he did not manage to repeat the mistakes that had destroyed GPA. O'Leary, for one, was determined not to let him, but Ryan did not yet know quite how determined. His days as chairman were numbered, but he was oblivious to the threat.

As a stock market flotation grew ever closer, O'Leary was a man on a mission and Ryanair was his obsession. He still arrived early, often starting work at six in the morning, and left late. He lived for the company, working weekends and bank holidays, surviving on coffee and cigarettes and snatched meals from the Ryanair canteen. Those who knew O'Leary at the time recall him as being singularly focused on Ryanair, to the exclusion of almost everything else. He did have a long-term girlfriend, but the relationship was not thought to be serious.

O'Leary's obsession meant that by the end of 1996, just three years after he had taken the reins as chief executive, the airline was indisputably his. He was not yet an owner in the real sense – he shared in the profits, but had no shareholding but the company reflected his character and ran to his beat. 'He was in control of pretty much everything that went on,' says Conor McCarthy, who joined Ryanair as operations manager in October 1996 after a successful career in Aer Lingus. 'There was a team of us who backed up Michael, [but] we carried out mainly Michael's bidding. If you wanted to do something and Michael didn't want to do it, you could be pretty sure it was never going to happen.'

McCarthy, accustomed to the slow, bureaucratic world of Ireland's state-owned airline, was immediately struck by the informality of Ryanair, and also by its sense of purpose.

On my first morning I went into Michael's office [and he was] dressed in his characteristic jeans and shirt. He took me round the office, introducing me to the different people. All pretty informal, but as he was showing me round he was also asking them about particular issues he wanted to chase up. So he'd say, 'This is Conor, he's just joined us as director of group operations. Oh, by the way, how did you get on with that crowd yesterday? I saw you meeting them. Did you get a good deal out of them?' He used it, not just to introduce me, but to catch up on what was going on. I got an immediate feeling that it was a no-nonsense organization with no fat.

O'Leary's growing dominance created a conundrum for the Ryans. The arrival of David Bonderman as a 20 per cent share-holder meant that a stock market flotation for Ryanair was now inevitable. The airline needed cash to buy more planes, and Bond-erman would be looking for a swift return on his investment; a flotation would be the simplest solution to both needs. O'Leary was crucial to the airline's future, but as an employee he stood to gain nothing from the flotation. It was an issue which would have to be resolved, and not in the normal way by offering stock options to the management team.

There was also a second problem to be overcome: O'Leary's lucrative profit-share deal had become unworkable. 'The profit share had become an embarrassment and it had to be unravelled,' says O'Leary. He knew that the scale of his reward would become public knowledge during a flotation process, when all relevant financial information on Ryanair would be revealed to potential investors and, more significantly, to his fellow executives and the rest of the Ryanair workforce. His price for walking away from an annual bonus that had netted him £20 million by the end of 1996 was a 25 per cent share of the company, with Bonderman on 20 per cent and the Ryan family taking 55 per cent. Eventually O'Leary settled for 22 per cent.

As Bonderman signed off on his investment that August, O'Leary had begun preparations for the riches that were about to come his way. He created Garnham, an off-the-shelf company, with himself as a director alongside Howard Millar, who had joined Ryanair in 1992 as a financial controller. Two months later, in October 1996, O'Leary's mother Gerarda replaced Millar as a director and the following July Garnham acquired just over twenty-two million shares in Ryanair – representing his stake in the airline – for a token consideration of less than £1 million. In a reversal of the normal entrepreneurial model, O'Leary had won his share of the company after leading it to triumph, rather than by gambling everything on a dream. His wealth and shareholding had required no risk other than his time; not once had O'Leary had to put his own money into the company or mortgage his house to keep the company afloat.

With O'Leary firmly installed for the long haul as a significant shareholder, Ryanair became fixated on growth where only recently it had been concerned with nothing more than survival. Its short-term priority was to prove that the low-cost model, which was now demonstrably successful on routes between Ireland and the UK, could shift to a far bigger stage: continental Europe.

For the international investors who would be wooed ahead of a stock market flotation, European expansion was critical. All the work done in the previous decade to secure Ryanair's position as a profitable player on the Ireland to UK routes would count for little if O'Leary could not prove that his model could be transferred profitably to mainland Europe – a continent with a population larger than that of the United States; with a host of traditional, and expensive, national airlines; with virtually no experience of low fares; and, perhaps most significantly of all, with an increasing number of countries falling into the embrace of the European Union. A single European market would need a mobile labour force if it were to prosper. Cheap and frequent flights would be an important part of that.

European consumers knew nothing about cheap air travel. Unlike the American consumer, who had benefited from low fares for almost twenty years – and even longer in some states – Europeans had been fed a diet of expensive, restricted air fares on a small number of airlines which tended to be owned by their governments. Travellers in Ireland and Britain understood what low fares and competition meant because they had enjoyed the benefits of competition for a decade. But if continental Europeans wanted to fly, they could choose between an often prohibitively expensive scheduled flight or, during the holiday seasons, an inflexible charter flight – a package holiday that required them to buy accommodation as well as an air ticket.

O'Leary, alongside a small number of new, similarly inclined operators like easyJet, had to re-educate a continent if they wanted to create a market. Time was not on their side; re-education had to be swift, the message simple and easily understood. O'Leary needed shock tactics, not subtle brand building, and his weapons of choice were publicity stunts and advertising campaigns designed in the heat of the moment but which followed a basic pattern.

The early battles with Aer Lingus had instilled in Ryanair a sense of being the underdog. O'Leary might be a fan of Manchester City football club, the perennial underachiever in a city dominated by the success of its more famous rival Manchester United, but his motto was drawn more from the terraces of Millwall FC, a relatively small London club known in the 1980s for the violence of its supporters and their chant: 'Nobody likes us but we don't care.'

O'Leary did not care who liked him as long as his messages got through: Ryanair is cheaper than the competition; traditional airlines rip you off. He did not want to be loved, he did not want to win awards for best airline advertising and he was certainly not trying to win any popularity contests. All he wanted was instant brand recognition. He had to create a mass market for a product that few in Europe understood and that his competitors – with their political clout, massive advertising budgets and, critically, their grip on the major airports – would be determined to undermine as soon as they recognized the threat.

Unfortunately for them – for Lufthansa in Germany, Sabena in Belgium, British Airways, Air France and Alitalia in Italy – they underestimated O'Leary and, despite the evidence from the United States, they underestimated the business model he was creating. One after another they fell for his stunts, allowing themselves to be sucked into skirmishes that only O'Leary could win, dismissing him and his airline with an arrogance that was as breathtaking as it was self-destructive.

O'Leary's tactics mirrored the man: irreverent, effective, often outrageous but never expensive. In September 1996, shortly after a Sudan Airways plane was hijacked and flown to Stansted, O'Leary rushed out an advertisement showing a picture of the hijacked jet with the catchline, 'It's amazing what lengths people will go to, to fly cheaper than Ryanair.' The ad sparked a flurry of complaints and was dropped, but not before it had the required impact. Outrage, as O'Leary was discovering, always translated into media coverage, and that coverage translated into sales. One cheap advertisement could generate far more interest and consumer response than any expensively conceived and executed marketing campaign.

The tactics, honed in Ireland and Britain over the previous years, would now be turned on Europe – as soon as O'Leary could establish some routes. The pressure was on; the clock was ticking down on a stock market flotation and Ryanair needed to be a European, not an Irish, airline by the time the roadshow to sell the shares got under way in the New Year.

At the end of November Ryanair bought six second-hand Boeing 737s from Lufthansa, increasing its fleet to seventeen. The $60 million price tag, financed by loans from a consortium of Irish banks, was a big commitment for the airline, but it laid down its marker for expansion. By then, too, O'Leary had a strong base on which to build – the airline had just reported pre-tax profits of almost £5 million for the fifteen month period to March 1995, on a turnover of £99 million. This was a one-off adjustment to the traditional annual accounting period so that Ryanair could change its year end to the end of March from the end of December – a convention for many stock market companies.

The new planes were to be used to launch O'Leary's assault on the mainland European market. He told journalists that Europe would be 'a big part' of the airline's future, but refused to be more specific than confirming plans to fly to two unnamed 'non primary' airports in mainland Europe: 'We don't want to forewarn our opposition.' In fact, O'Leary would have found it difficult to be more specific even if he had wanted to reveal his hand, as he had yet to finalize any deals with airports on the continent.

The task of finding the new routes fell to the new operations manager Conor McCarthy, Tim Jeans and O'Leary himself, who went on a three-day whirlwind tour of Paris, Brussels, Stockholm and Copenhagen. McCarthy and O'Leary had no real interest in talking to the major airports in these cities – they knew that they would find it impossible to strike a deal – and focused instead on small airports that few people had ever heard of. 'There was no question that we would go into major gateways,' says Tim Jeans. 'One major issue was price, and the other was timing. You cannot get an aeroplane in and out of Charles de Gaulle airport in Paris in under an hour, and we needed turnaround times of twenty-five minutes or less.'

For Ryanair's early European routes O'Leary had decided that capital cities, with their large populations, were important, yet access had to be cheap and turnaround times fast. Paris – continental Europe's most visited city and near Disneyland's European theme park – was an obvious first choice; Brussels, the home of the European bureaucrat, was equally attractive; Scandinavia, however, would be a shot in the dark.

'We spoke to Orly [Paris's second main airport] and they treated us with considerable disdain,' says Jeans. 'I remember the little Peugeot 106 they sent out to meet us, with the office junior aboard, and that was about as far as we got. We didn't darken Orly's door again.' Instead O'Leary chose Beauvais, a tiny airport forty miles west of Paris, close to the horse-racing centre of Chantilly. There were no rail links – air travellers would have to continue their journey by bus, taxi or hired car – and virtually no facilities. Beauvais was a runway with a shed, but for O'Leary it would be Paris.

In Belgium Ryanair had similar problems. The options were Ostend and Antwerp. Ostend was operationally unsuitable because the runway was too short, and Antwerp was too far from Brussels. The solution was Charleroi, thirty miles south of the Belgian capital and very like Beauvais: a runway where sheep grazed alongside with a terminal building served by sporadic charter flights. It, too, could only be reached by road. Skavsta, in Sweden but sixty miles away from Stockholm, completed the trio of international destinations that O'Leary would use as his guinea pigs for low-cost travel in Europe.

McCarthy remembers the pace of the deal-making. 'We covered the airports in three days and managed to do a deal with three of them. We didn't even really try to do a deal with the big airports because we knew they just didn't have the psychology or mentality to do that sort of business.' In May 1997 Ryanair would launch routes from Dublin to Paris-Beauvais and Dublin to Brussels-Charleroi; the following month it would launch Stansted to Stockholm-Skavsta. The routes would be sold as capital-to-capital services even though the airports were up to two hours drive from the capital cities they were serving and the prices would be rock bottom.

In the autumn of 1996 O'Leary had begun talks with Kerry airport about the possibility of starting a service from there. Ryanair had previously withdrawn from Kerry in September 1992, along with Galway and Waterford, because of 'lack of demand', but four years later the climate and the airline had changed. Ireland was emerging from years of recession into a period of remarkable economic growth, low fares had proved to be as much of a market stimulant in Ireland as they had in the United States, and airports were beginning to realize that the only way to encourage traffic was to strike deals that made low fares possible.

Kerry is in a far-flung corner of Ireland's south-west, but it also lies at the heart of the Irish tourist market. That seasonal business provided a useful basis for an air route, but it was the growing prosperity of the region that provided the second, more important ingredient: locals keen to travel throughout the year. Kerry airport wanted part of the Ryanair action, and a tour operators' conference in Killarney provided the chance.

'As part of trying to get Ryanair to start a service we chartered a plane off of them to fly the people free of charge from Dublin down to Kerry,' says a former executive at the small airport. 'A lot of their senior people flew down on it. A lot of them hadn't been in Kerry before and on the day they just said, "Jesus, we should be flying down here."'

After that Kerry talked to Ryanair 'on and off', and in November 1996 Ryanair decided that it was ready to push ahead with the route.

'It all happened very fast, as it does with Ryanair,' says the executive. He says that Peter Bellew, the airport's marketing manager, received the call from Ryanair and was tasked with tracking down Denis Brosnan, the airport's chairman, who was in Chile that day. Bellew told Brosnan that Ryanair was 'hot to move' and Brosnan agreed to meet them just two days later in Dublin. 'Brosnan cut his journey and came straight off the transcontinental flight. He got off the plane and walked down in the rain with Bellew into Ryanair. It was very interesting because Denis wasn't going to leave the building until they had agreed to do it. Not in a hectoring way, he just kept talking and talking and talking.'

Brosnan was no hick from Ireland's Wild West. Like O'Leary, he represented a new generation of successful international businessmen. He had created Kerry Foods, a multi-million-pound food ingredients empire which was spreading its reach into North America, and he was a match for O'Leary. 'Jesus, would you not clean the place up and get yourself a suit, Michael,' he said at one point during the negotiations.

The new route was signed off later that day, and the first planes took off the following June.

By the beginning of November 1996, just three months after Bonderman had joined the company as a director and major shareholder, the chairman was being eased out. 'Tony was being sidelined, and we fought quite hard to maintain his chairmanship,' says Brian Bell, one of Ryan's media advisers, who had previously worked for Ryanair. 'At one stage Michael wanted Tony completely off the board, and our advice for Tony at the time was to stay put.'

Ryan, O'Leary had decided, would be a liability for the company when the time came to sell it to the stock market. GPA's collapse four years earlier was still fresh in his mind and, he thought, in the minds of the investment community. Ryan, no matter how much he had invested and how visionary he had been, was a symbol of hubris, arrogance and stock market failure.

'Tony was quite dispassionate about it,' says Bell. 'He took soundings from various people. Michael was saying to him that the feedback from the UK was that if he stayed he would be a liability because of GPA. We did our own research on Tony and we found that was rubbish.' O'Leary, though, was not for turning. He believed that Bonderman was the obvious choice to take over from Ryan as chairman. Bonderman had the respect of the market in the United States and his reputation for sound investments combined with his knowledge of the airline market would command respect in the UK.

The name Ryanair, O'Leary felt, was bad enough; having Ryans on the board was worse, but having Tony Ryan as chairman was just impossible. 'You wouldn't have been able to float it,' he says. 'Tony didn't realize that. But Bonderman brought us huge credibility in the States, a lot more than we knew at the time. A lot of this is just luck, but the judgement call had to be made.'

Ryan was determined to stay on the board but prepared to concede the chairmanship. He had too much at stake to risk another market failure: this was his chance of financial redemption and an opportunity for his children to be secure for life. He had thought GPA would deliver that security, and now he had a second chance he was not going to let it slip. It was a blow to his ego, but his wallet was more important. In the end, says a fellow director, 'It was all quite amicable. We were a small regional airline, so we needed someone bigger for when we floated. The board was fully supportive of putting Bonderman in as chairman, and it's been proved right since.'

One of Ryanair's investment bank advisers says that the banks did not apply pressure for Ryan's removal, but were more than comfortable with the choice of successor. 'It wasn't an atypical decision by a company that was planning a flotation. Bonderman had written a fairly sizeable cheque to get involved, so it's not unusual for the new financial investor to say, "I'm now going to control the business and control the board and be the chairman." So part of it was related to the fact that Bonderman had arranged this capital,' he says.

Ryan's resignation and Bonderman's appointment in his place

were announced on 19 November 1996. Three days later O'Leary tried to play down rumours of a rift in the company by telling the *Irish Times*, 'Dr Ryan indicated some time ago that he wanted to step down as chairman in the medium term.'

While he had been replaced as chairman, Ryan remained umbilically linked to the company, which still bore his name and which, through his nearly 60 per cent shareholding, he still controlled. 'I don't think it would have made much difference if Ryan had stayed,' says the investment banker. 'There's not much difference in perception between chairman and majority shareholder. The flotation would still have been successful – GPA was in the past and the market has a short attention span.'

By the end of 1996 O'Leary had completed the transformation of the airline and of his own fortunes. Bonderman had been installed as chairman and his presence gave Ryanair instant credibility in the financial markets. Ryanair was progressing smoothly to a flotation: its profit performance was strong, its route network was growing, six more planes were joining the fleet and European destinations had been lined up for the following year.

O'Leary's profit-share deal would earn him more than £8 million in 1996 – indicating the scale of the airline's improvement – but this would now be transformed into a major shareholding in an airline that would soon be worth hundreds of millions. For the moment O'Leary appeared to have everything that he had ever wanted, but it was not, and never would be, enough. 'Michael just has to go on and on, succeeding and accumulating,' says one former colleague. 'It's just the way he is. It's too simplistic to say that it's all a game; it's far more serious than that. He makes money, and he succeeds, because that is what he does. There is no endgame, no point at which he steps aside and smells the roses. He is perpetual motion, restless, insatiable, driven – but by what? Who knows? It's just what he does, and it's all he knows.'

11. Out-of-Town Airports

Nine years after he had first been asked to sort out Ryanair, Michael O'Leary remained a largely anonymous figure in Irish life. Ryanair was still a private company and flew under the radar of the financial media. Coverage of the airline's progress from loss maker to serious profit generator had been muted, and scrutiny of the man who had led that transformation was underwhelming. The scale of O'Leary's wealth was unknown even to his closest colleagues. All that was about to change.

David Bonderman's arrival at Ryanair had altered the dynamics of the company. Until Bonderman had invested, Ryanair had been a small and moderately successful regional airline. It could have stayed that way: a small, profitable, niche operator. Bonderman's investment, however, heralded a far more ambitious strategy.

Publicly, the company tried to dampen speculation that flotation was imminent. In early January Tim Jeans tackled the gossip by saying that he had 'read with interest the speculation about a stock market flotation, but would stress that it is just that – speculation. We have recently announced the acquisition of six Boeing 737 aircraft from Lufthansa which were financed by the traditional methods of cash and bank finance. These will be sufficient for the medium-term expansion into Europe, so there is no pressing need for finance on any grand scale. When you have a guy like David Bonderman coming on board the industry tends to start putting two and two together. I feel that this time they may have come up with five.'

Behind the scenes, though, Ryanair's executives were moving with pace. Within weeks of Jeans's attempt to downplay speculation, O'Leary was in New York to talk to major investment banks about a flotation, an exercise known as a beauty parade. 'We went for a day, and all the major banks were pitching,' says

O'Leary. Each bank was trying to convince O'Leary and Bonderman that it would be best suited to take the Irish airline to the stock market, and in time-honoured fashion bragged about how much it could sell the company for. 'The lowest valuation was $600 million and the highest was $3.5 billion,' says O'Leary. 'Crazy stuff. We went with Morgan Stanley, who were somewhere in the middle.'

The valuations bandied about by the Wall Street bankers were far in excess of Ryanair's assumed value. Bonderman's investment just six months earlier had valued the company at about £130 million, yet now, at the start of 1997, bankers reckoned that the lowest achievable price was $600 million. That valued O'Leary's stake alone at more than $100 million, enough to catapult him, age thirty-six and still single, into the top rank of Ireland's wealthiest individuals.

On 9 February 1997 the speculation ended and the countdown to the stock market began when the *Irish Times* announced that Morgan Stanley had been chosen to 'pilot Ryanair through' its flotation.

For O'Leary, life was about to change irrevocably. The anonymous obsessive who spent his life at his desk was about to be thrust into the limelight. While potential investors would sift through his financial accounts, hunting for signs of weakness before they committed their millions, Ireland's media was about to discover a new target.

Just as O'Leary was about to embark on his new life, hawking his company to global investors while dealing with his new-found celebrity status at home, his former life as Tony Ryan's personal assistant came back to haunt him. In 1992, when O'Leary was still doubling as Tony Ryan's assistant, Cathal Ryan had allegedly assaulted Michelle Rocca, a former Miss Ireland and the mother of his child. Ireland's justice system grinds slowly, and it was not until February 1997 that the case finally opened in Dublin's High Court.

It was, inevitably, a media circus. Rocca was a photogenic celebrity, and by the time the court started hearing evidence she had become the partner of Van Morrison. Cathal Ryan's celebrity status was also assured; since the high-profile collapse of GPA the Ryan family had been regular fodder for the Irish media. Tony Ryan's rise and fall had been chronicled in detail, and his financial resurrection with Ryanair had added extra spice. Cathal Ryan, too, was flamboyant in his own right. A pilot with all the stereotypical attributes of the breed – he was seen as an arrogant playboy – he was grist to the media mill.

The trial had everything the media could have wanted – sex, violence, bizarre humour, celebrities at war and a rare glimpse of the lifestyle of the rich and pampered. In the trial's opening statements the court heard that Ryan and Rocca had begun dating in 1988 and in April of 1991 had had a daughter, Claudia. Rocca's lawyer told the court that Ryan had assaulted her in the early hours of 22 March 1992 at a party at Blackhall Stud near Clane in County Kildare. Rocca said that at the time of the incident she and Ryan were still a couple though they were living apart. Rocca was left badly bruised, the court heard, and Cathal Ryan had never apologized to her. 'He did send his daddy, Dr Tony Ryan, with flowers to say sorry,' her lawyer told the court.

When Tony Ryan had apologized for his son, Rocca told him that she would not allow Cathal to see his daughter Claudia again. Ryan wanted some arrangement made for access and Michael O'Leary was dispatched to talk to Rocca. His role was uncomplicated: he was to offer cash and get Rocca to agree a settlement that would allow the Ryans to see Cathal's daughter.

The court was told that in April 1992 O'Leary brought Rocca a document to sign. In return for agreeing access, the Ryans would provide £1,000 a month maintenance for Claudia and a further £5,000 one-off payment for Rocca. She signed on the dotted line but later said she had not realized that the document included a clause which stipulated that she could make no further claims against Cathal Ryan.

O'Leary was called to testify. 'Tell me more about being the Ryans' bagman,' the lawyer began. 'If the Ryans wanted someone to, say, go to the shop for a bag of sugar, would that be you?' O'Leary was not amused.

The case was finally settled in mid-February with the court awarding £7,500 to Rocca and finding Ryan guilty of assault. The case was a tawdry embarrassment for the Ryans but it gave O'Leary a public profile as the Ryanair flotation drew nearer. In March the *Irish Times* did its numbers and estimated that the airline would be worth £250 million when the shares were sold. That, the paper realized, would value O'Leary's stake at about £50 million, making him one of the wealthiest men in the country.

For O'Leary, the self-styled one of the boys, a chief executive who wore jeans and open-necked shirts and mucked in with the baggage handlers for a weekly game of football as well as helping out with the bags from time to time, the focus on his wealth was uncomfortable. 'His big personal concern was, I'm a man of the people and can mix it up with the best of them, and I work harder than anyone else,' said one source close to the flotation. 'Once you are a rich guy in Ireland all of a sudden you've gone from labour to management. People, as opposed to saying, "This guy's the man," say, "Rich bastard."'

Publicity, however, was unavoidable. In April the *Irish Times* decided that the time had come to publish its first major profile of the rising star of the aviation world. Of his life before Ryanair the paper said, 'He began his career in KPMG, then trading as Stokes Kennedy Crowley, having graduated from Trinity College Dublin with a business degree. He worked in taxation for two years, but hated it. He left and dabbled in property, bought a couple of newsagents in Dublin, turned them around, made some money and sold them at a profit.'

On his personality the report said, 'Publicity shy or not, Mr O'Leary is not afraid to fight his corner,' referring to his campaigns against Aer Rianta and his frequent denunciations of Aer Lingus. The newspaper also speculated about O'Leary's relationship with Tony Ryan: 'O'Leary was undoubtedly once very close to Dr Ryan. Sources say this is no longer the case, that in some ways O'Leary has sought to distance Tony Ryan and his family from the business they founded.'

O'Leary was clearly being billed as the star of the flotation, the

unconventional, publicity-shy chief executive who had transformed the company and would now lead it to greatness. But his
own attentions were on simpler pursuits. That spring, while New
York beckoned, O'Leary started a hobby – a rare departure for a
man who seemed to devote every waking hour to his business.
O'Leary decided that Gigginstown needed some purpose, so he
decided to create his own herd of prime Aberdeen Angus cattle,
prized for the quality of their meat.

'At the time, I didn't want to be in Charolais [a popular breed for
indulgent farmers] because Tony Ryan and Tony O'Reilly and all
those guys were into Charolais. I didn't want to be pricking around as
the latest idiot with his Charolais cows,' he says. 'I wanted something
which was a native breed to Ireland, which means Whitehorns or
Angus. The Angus were easy calving, they are very easy to handle.
For someone who farms two days a week they were perfect.'

While he didn't tell journalists about his new passion, he was
quick to suggest that he was planning for a life more ordinary.
O'Leary, uncomfortable with media attention and conscious that
his privacy was a thing of the past, lusted for a return to the quiet
life where he could accumulate money without attention. He was,
after all, publicity shy, as the *Irish Times* had said. Ryanair, too, did
not need media attention in Ireland. It had already achieved a
market presence; its planes were full and its name was known. At
a press conference in February O'Leary showed how little of what
was to come had been planned when he said, 'You're probably
wondering why we're suddenly talking to everybody for the first
time in ten years. When this is finished we'll probably disappear
for another ten years.'

Some chance. The flotation would change his world, forcing
O'Leary onto a global stage to sell the company. The game was
just beginning, and he was to be the central player. Instead of
disappearing to his private world of cattle and country, O'Leary
was about to become the Duracell bunny of European aviation.

The prospect of flotation had concentrated O'Leary's mind even
further on cost reduction. Investors would want to see profits, and

they would want to see evidence that the Ryanair model was continuing to evolve. O'Leary decided it was time to tackle one of his biggest and most irritating costs: the commission paid to travel agents on every Ryanair ticket they sold.

For the moment O'Leary was interested only in shaving the commission from 9 to 7.5 per cent, but it was a radical move at the time and the Irish Travel Agents' Association, which represented 340 agents across the country, was not going to give up its money without a struggle. Within days of O'Leary's decision to cut their commissions, there were mutterings in the trade about a boycott of Ryanair, but this was not O'Leary's only move against the travel agents. In January 1997 he had also set up Ryanair Direct, a telemarketing operation which he hoped would cut the travel agent out of the loop completely. Helped by a £2.5 million government grant, Ryanair Direct hoped to handle five million customers by the end of its first year in operation, and each ticket it sold would be free of agent commission.

Telemarketing was not a new idea, nor was O'Leary the airline innovator. The British low-fare airline easyJet had blazed the trail by painting its reservations number on the side of its aircraft and had been determined from the outset to control its own bookings. O'Leary, naturally cautious, watched and waited. Only when he was convinced that it would work did he follow easyJet's lead.

Ireland's travel agents were not happy. In March Ryanair opened negotiations with the ITAA but the talks broke down without agreement. 'There was no headway made in those talks, none whatsoever,' recalls P. J. Brennan, who was head of the ITAA at the time. 'I still think it was an exercise that we had to go through. It would have been very remiss of us to sit back and do absolutely zilch.'

In public the row quickly turned nasty. At the end of March Ryanair angered agents by faxing advertisements for Ryanair Direct to their offices and rumours flew around the industry that Ryanair was harassing and intimidating individual travel agents. Brennan, though, remembers little acrimony at subsequent meetings. 'We didn't go in with pitchforks or anything like that, and they didn't arrive with them either,' he says. 'We weren't being told what we wanted to hear, but there was no hitting the desk or anything.' O'Leary was central to all discussions. 'There would have been five or six Ryanair people there, but I can't remember who else was there because Michael was such a focal point,' recalls Brennan. 'He would have done 99.99 per cent of the talking.'

With no compromise on the table, ITAA's members voted on 4 April to refuse to handle sales of Ryanair tickets when the new commission rates were imposed by the airline. A week later their planned confrontation was sabotaged by Ireland's Competition Authority. Prompted by O'Leary, it wrote to ITAA and said that a boycott of Ryanair would be anti-competitive, and the organizers would face immediate court action.

The Competition Authority was not bluffing. It followed up its letter with a raid on the association's headquarters, and demanded personal assurances from ITAA's leaders that they would not seek to damage Ryanair's business. Pat Massey, a member of the Competition Authority at the time, says that authority staff found enough evidence during the raid to justify court action against the travel agents. 'The raid started at nine or ten in the morning, and lasted until four or five,' he says. 'ITAA seemed surprised to see us.'

The Competition Authority decided to proceed against ITAA, but it was settled on the steps of the court. 'All a court could have done was force the ITAA to give an undertaking not to continue any anti-competitive behaviour/boycott, and the ITAA gave that undertaking to CA the morning of the court case,' Massey recalls.

O'Leary had been handed a simple victory by the Competition Authority, which had carried out its raid on the ITAA offices following an anonymous complaint. 'I have no proof or information as to who [the complaint] came from, but it wouldn't surprise me if it came from Ryanair,' says Brennan.

Two weeks later, at an extraordinary general meeting of its members, ITAA said it would pursue legal action against the airline, but this never materialized. The agents had been defeated with barely a shot fired. Ryanair cut its commission on 1 May and travel agents were forced to comply. Some retaliated by introducing legal surcharges on Ryanair sales, but they could not refuse to sell the tickets.

'It's a matter of conjecture really as to whether there was a boycott or not,' says Brennan. 'I suppose travel agents acted individually in the sense that they felt that their business was threatened and when people feel that their back is against the wall and their business is threatened, you know, people do things off their own bat, and maybe sometimes they're not the right things.'

Soon they had all come back into line. Ryanair was a popular airline with passengers and a source of revenue, even at a reduced rate of commission. The agents could not afford to boycott it.

For O'Leary it was a gratifying coup. He had made a relatively painless assault on his cost base, had seen off an industry boycott, and at the same time had established his own direct sales operation. It was also a popular victory with consumers and with potential investors. By defeating the ITAA O'Leary had made it possible for airfares to fall further, and he had also demonstrated to investors that Ryanair was serious about cost cutting and not afraid to fight its corner.

Ryanair's use of small, out-of-town airports was a crucial element in keeping costs down, but there was no guarantee that passengers would want to fly to them. So while Ryanair might be landing in Beauvais, its passengers needed to believe they were flying to Paris.

O'Leary and Jeans had travelled this road before. Prestwick, a long way south of Glasgow, was still Glasgow as far as IATA regulations were concerned, just as Stansted, in Essex, was a London airport. For the new destinations, all Jeans had to manage was a simple sleight of hand.

'We had to make sure that they were designated by IATA as Paris and Brussels and that they were included in the three-letter city codes,' recalls Jeans. 'At the time the airlines operating to those airports had to vote on them being included in the city designation.

So the airlines operating to Beauvais had a vote – and so we had the only vote. We were the lone rangers in Charleroi too.'

Beauvais was Paris and Charleroi was Brussels because Ryanair said so, and IATA's own regulations – which allowed the airlines serving the airport to decide on what it should be designated – made the claim easy to ratify and impossible to refute. 'Our competitors were then ready and able to take us to advertising standards and things like that and say you're not flying to Paris you're flying to Beauvais. But we were manifestly flying to a designated Paris airport,' says Jeans. And that was the key: despite the protestations of its rivals, Ryanair could legitimately market its flights as London to Paris.

On 1 May 1997 Ryanair launched into Europe, offering cheap fares to Paris and Brussels from Dublin. Only when passengers landed did they discover they were in fact more than an hour's drive by coach from the city centres, but few grumbled. The price was right, the airports were uncluttered, and the journey time into town was little worse than they had come to expect from the main airports.

The first phase of European expansion was under way.

Weeks after the successful launch of the routes to Paris and Brussels, Eugene O'Neill re-emerged. Ryanair's second managing director, he had been fired by Ryan in 1988, shortly after O'Leary had arrived to sort out the troubled airline's finances. He had launched a number of court actions against Ryanair and the Ryan family, claiming he had been unfairly dismissed and had been conspired against. The last of the cases was settled in 1995, with O'Neill receiving a payment of £83,000 from Ryanair, on top of an earlier settlement of £735,000 for his shareholding in the company.

Now Ryanair looked set to float, O'Neill was back for more money. In mid-May he claimed that when he accepted the 1995 payment he 'was not of sound mind and was incapable of understanding the provisions, the nature and effect of the said settlement or of properly giving his assent thereto'. O'Neill also wrote to the Securities and Exchange Commission in New York, repeating his allegations, which included wrongful termination, breach of contract and the oppression of a minor shareholder. Ryanair responded by issuing a statement claiming that O'Neill had a history of proceedings against the company and other parties 'and these have been long since resolved and settled'. O'Neill would be seen off, but Ryanair was facing another obstacle, which was not going to be quite so easy to get around.

Every company preparing for stock market flotation or an initial public offering (IPO) must produce a prospectus, outlining its key statistics, past performance, any risks to its business and its future objectives. The problem for Ryanair was that its prospectus painted a picture of a company which was very different from the one the media and its own staff had expected.

Ever since its launch Ryanair had played the underdog, the undernourished upstart sticking it to the giants Aer Lingus and British Airways, but the prospectus told a different tale. Ryanair was in rude financial health, and had been for the previous three years.

Annual passenger numbers were up to three million for the year ended 31 March 1997. The average load factor stood at 72 per cent, well above the industry average, and the yield per average seat mile (ASM) was £0.113, compared with ASM operating costs of £0.110, which meant that Ryanair was making money on every passenger. It also had impressive ancillary revenue – £7.3 million from inflight sales of drinks and duty-free for the twelve months to March 1997. That year also saw a significant contribution from a new moneyspinner – the airline's deal with the Europcar rental agency brought in more than £2 million. The airline was also dedicated to pursuing other revenue streams. 'Ryanair offers a variety of ancillary, revenue-generating services in conjunction with its core transportation service,' the prospectus noted, 'including on-board duty-free and beverage sales, charter flights, cargo services, travel reservation services, advertising, travel insurance and car rentals.'

Ryanair now had thirteen aircraft, all of them Boeing 737–200s with an average age of fifteen years, and was scheduled to acquire six second-hand aircraft of the same type at the end of 1997. The airline's flight network had grown to more than a hundred scheduled short-haul flights, serving eight airports in England, three in Ireland, one in Scotland and one in Wales. But dry descriptions of revenue streams and routes paled beside two eye-popping figures. The first was Ryanair's profitability before tax, which had reached £23.6 million in the fifteen months to March 1996 and £26.09 million in 1997. And the prospectus also revealed the bonus payments to O'Leary: £8.9 million in 1995/96 and £9.75 million in 1996/97.

Ryanair's financial advisers were prepared for a backlash once the information in the IPO prospectus became public knowledge; indeed the document itself admitted, 'A variety of factors, including but not limited to, the Company's recent profitability and disclosure of the level of executive director bonuses, may make it more difficult to maintain its current base salary levels and current employee compensation arrangements.' But the reaction was much more hostile than expected.

As soon as details of O'Leary's remuneration package became public, the Irish and UK media whipped itself into a state of frenzy. On 11 May a headline in the *Sunday Tribune* asked, 'What does this man do? Walk on water?' The trade unions, which had been shunned by O'Leary and were not represented at the company, were equally unimpressed and keen to make a point. 'If Mr O'Leary's latest annual bonus of £10 million was shared between the 700 staff instead, they would have got about £14,000 each,' said Paul O'Sullivan, an official with SIPTU, Ireland's largest trade union, which represented workers at Aer Lingus and Aer Rianta, and which wanted to gain access to Ryanair. 'Ryanair has pleaded the poor mouth, but the fat cats at the top creamed off the money that could have been used to pay the workforce a decent wage. Bad conditions don't apply to pay alone. Regarding staff, Ryanair operates like a revolving door. There is little or no job security and a climate of fear operates,' he maintained.

The union's opportunism was hardly surprising. 'SIPTU jumped on it straight away,' says one senior manager.

Their typical line at the time was that these poor underpaid guys have been worked to the bone and are badly paid, and this guy gets an absolutely immoral amount of money out of the company at the same time. It almost made out that they were working the salt mines in Silesia. But at the end of the day Michael was essentially the guy who took a company that was bankrupt and turned it into a profitable entity, and he had a share in that, so it wasn't a salary for him really.

Inside Ryanair the news about O'Leary's pay also sparked outrage, but he seemed oblivious to the resentment when he joined some management colleagues for lunch in the staff canteen a week after the information about his bonuses had been published. 'A group of us were having lunch and just having a chat about different things,' says one former executive, 'and Michael says, "Hey, did you see the newspapers there, did you see your man Schumacher, he earns ten fucking million a year." And he was saying, "It's fucking crazy, ten million dollars. For driving a car around a racetrack. Mad." And all of us looked at each other. Here was a guy who had just earned seventeen million pounds, which was about thirty million dollars at the time, in three years, and he was saying he couldn't believe what Schumacher earned.'

Privately, O'Leary was bothered by the revelations. 'It was a big concern for Michael. He was very private about his wealth and he never would have come across as a wealthy guy in 1996,' says one former colleague.

O'Leary did not flash his cash. He had plans for Gigginstown and was prepared to dabble in cattle and horses, but ostentatious displays of wealth were not his style. In business he was no different. O'Leary was happy to earn bonuses, but he despised corporate excess. The company was run as leanly as he could manage, and he was not going to allow his standards to slip when he and his executives, accompanied by their Wall Street bankers, went on the road to sell the company. When he set off on the two-and-a-half-week investors' roadshow in early May O'Leary insisted that he and his team stay in modest hotels and travel on commercial flights and not a private jet.

'Michael did not just suggest that everyone flew on a commercial flight, it was a requirement,' says one of those involved in the flotation. 'Companies preparing for a flotation would typically use a private jet. So if there is not a flight from Boston to Milwaukee at 8 p.m. on a Monday you don't have to worry about it, because the jet is waiting. It costs an extra $55,000 to $70,000 but it's worth it because you get to see an extra twenty-five investors.'

O'Leary was having none of it. 'Everyone stayed in dirt-cheap hotels. Michael said, "We're not staying in the fancy Morgan Stanley Four Seasons," so they stayed in some pretty grim places. It wasn't as bad as sharing rooms, but it was close. And part of Michael's big focus was that when Ryanair pilots travel and when Ryanair people travel they stay in dirt-cheap hotels and they fly economy class. So, he said, we are flying economy and we are not staying in fancy hotels.'

O'Leary was focused on the company's image. He wanted to portray a lean, hungry company that knew how to cut costs and deliver low fares. There was no room for hubris or self-indulgence. 'There was very little fun on the roadshow No mad dancing, no strippers, no heavy drinking. Michael's reputation as a workaholic travelled with him. He was working unbelievably hard,' says a colleague. O'Leary had to live that image so that his executives and his bankers understood the message. And he wanted the Ryanair staff to know that the management lived as frugally as they were forced to.

O'Leary was also determined to ensure that ordinary Ryanair staff would share in the proceeds of the flotation, and in May the company revealed details of the share options scheme for its 1,000 employees. A total of four million shares would be handed out. 'The staff grant was not atypical, but in Ireland it would be more typical not to have done it than to have done it,' says a source close to the company. 'O'Leary was pushing for it, and the board was too; they wanted to make sure the employees were happy.'

But the share allocations did not win favour with all of Ryanair's employees. 'The senior management, the guys just behind the executive team, were very unhappy,' says one management source.

They had seen what O'Leary had earned from the company in the previous three years, and they wanted a larger slice of the business for themselves.

While the Irish obsessed over O'Leary's money, American investors were unconcerned. 'It wasn't hard to defend in the US at all,' says one source close to the float. 'It's like the anecdote where an Irish guy and an American guy walk down the street and they see this guy's huge house up on the hill. The American guy goes, "Some day I'm going to get that house," and the Irish guy goes, "Some day I'm going to get that fucker."'

The Americans were also more receptive to O'Leary's disregard for business norms, and did not seem to mind that he did not wear a suit and peppered his conversation with swear words, though it did give Morgan Stanley some cause for concern. Senior executives discussed at length whether it was acceptable for the Ryanair CEO to use the F-word so frequently, but in the end the bankers decided not to coach O'Leary on his language. 'The decision in the end was that O'Leary runs a very successful business, so we're going to coach him in terms of what works and what doesn't work on the selling of a business,' said a Morgan Stanley executive. 'But he is very charismatic and extremely dedicated to driving the growth. So we didn't really try to convince him not to be Michael O'Leary.'

'O'Leary's behaviour was very full on,' remarked one source in the US.

O'Leary didn't wear a suit, which was very unusual at the time. He met with over a hundred institutions and several hundred people. I'm sure there were a couple of people who were put off by it, who were certainly surprised, including investment bankers, salespeople, investors. But people didn't really complain about him. If he had only done five-minute presentations maybe. But after thirty, forty-five minutes, you realized that he was extremely focused, extremely bright, and that the business was very fast-growing. And he happens to swear a lot, but it's part of the culture.

Investors try to focus on business results, not table manners.

They had a lot to focus on. Ryanair's prospectus was crammed with detail, yet for the American investors who were critical to the success or failure of the flotation there was a simple message.

'In the early 1990s the new management team, including the current Chief Executive and the then executive directors, commenced the restructuring of Ryanair's operations to become a low-fares no-frills airline based on the operating model pioneered by Southwest Airlines in the US.' Ryanair, Morgan Stanley and O'Leary were saying, is the European Southwest: a low-cost airline which will deliver unrivalled and unbroken profit growth for many years to come.

Southwest had developed a strong following in the US investment community. 'Southwest was doing well as a company, so it was very good as a comparable stock,' said one of Ryanair's financial advisers. 'A big part of the pitch was what Southwest has done in the US we are going to do in Europe.'

For a company which had barely dipped its toes in the European market and had faced collapse five years earlier, this was, to say the least, an ambitious claim. For some, the Southwest analogy was nothing more than a stunt; cynics said it was a wild claim which sounded good – was easy to justify on the surface but of little substance because Ryanair was such an unproven carrier.

O'Leary disagrees strongly. 'Ah shit no,' he says, offended at the suggestion. 'Southwest was a big guiding thing for me. Before I heard about Southwest I had seen two airlines in Ireland, Ryanair and Aer Lingus, both of which were blindingly incompetent. They had complicated check-in, business class this, travel agent that, all the rest of that crap, and were turning planes round in an hour. Then you went to Southwest, banging aircraft out after fifteen minutes. They were phenomenal, passengers loved it.'

The prospectus did not hold back on the risks facing the business. 'Ryanair is very vulnerable to a change in demand in the Ireland to UK market,' it noted, '39.9 per cent of passengers carried in 1997 were Dublin–London (46.2 per cent in 1996).' The size of the airline, which had 'smaller/fewer aircraft than some potential or actual competitors', was a risk, as was the fact that future growth depended on the ability to acquire additional aircraft. The prospectus also said that Ryanair's ageing fleet (average age fifteen years) could leave the airline vulnerable if new regulations or standards on aircraft maintenance were introduced. Investors were advised to be cautious about Ryanair's ability to expand – 'there is no assurance that Ryanair's low-fares, no-frills service will be accepted on new routes' – and even if the model worked, then Ryanair's ability to manage growth became a risk, as did airport access and charges, and competition.

The airline's dependence on Michael O'Leary and other senior managers was also highlighted as a concern. 'Ryanair's success depends to a significant extent upon the efforts and abilities of its senior management team . . . and key financial, commercial, operating and maintenance personnel,' the prospectus noted. 'Ryanair's success also depends on the ability of its executive officers and other members of senior management, none of whom has any prior experience of managing public companies, to operate and manage effectively, both independently and as a group.'

The risks did not deter investors. They understood the Southwest story – a tale of unbroken profit from a Texas airline which had helped prompt deregulation and profited hugely in its aftermath by keeping its fares low, its costs lower and its customers happy – and they wanted to be a part of the European revolution that Ryanair promised to deliver.

Despite five years of progressive deregulation, the European market had not caught fire like the US had after 1978. Aviation expert Dr Markus Franke says that by 1997, 'In theory every carrier in Europe, or in EC Europe at least, could . . . fly within every other country. But nobody was really doing that.' Between 1992 and 1997 the number of international routes within Europe rose by 13 per cent – notable but hardly seismic – and the amount of competition on those routes had increased only moderately as well. Progress had also been unspectacular on domestic routes. Investors understood the potential if the sleeping giant could be woken, and the scene was set for Ryanair to expand. All it needed was the money the flotation would provide to buy more planes, and the belief that the business model that had proved so successful on the Ireland to Britain routes could be exported to Europe.

The roadshow was a success. 'The management did a great job selling the story,' says one of the bankers involved in the flotation. 'O'Leary and his deputies [Michael Cawley and Howard Millar] are very good salesmen.'

While the senior executives sold the company, back in Dublin the flotation remained an abstract concept to most of the staff until very close to the event.

'There wasn't a huge build-up to it. Michael was very much business as usual. Keep the show on the road, and let us, the financial people, look after making sure the flotation goes successfully, and everybody else make sure that the company runs smoothly. For the staff it was, like, we're gonna float, there's an American guy who's bought 20 per cent. That's great. What does floating mean?' says Ryanair veteran Charlie Clifton.

Most of the staff got either 2,500 share options or £2,500 in cash. 'It floated at £1 97 so the shares were a better bet, but the cash looked better to those who knew nothing about the markets,' says Clifton. 'It took a lot of explaining to some staff members, and a lot of people said no, I don't trust that stuff. Give me two and a half grand in cash, thank you.'

Two weeks before the flotation O'Leary promoted Clifton to Ryanair's senior management team. 'I didn't even know what it meant,' says Clifton. 'Michael said, "Good news, we're going to make you a director. By the way we'll be floating; by the way you're getting this many shares." I was clueless about it. It was only later that the penny dropped. He had his reasons for promoting me though. It was, like, here's Conor [McCarthy], one I've poached from Aer Lingus. And here's Charlie, one I've grown myself.'

The share options also gave Ryanair something which had previously been sorely lacking in the airline – stability at the top. With the options, senior managers were tied in for three years. 'The good news is you get X number of shares, the bad news is you've gotta stay three years before you get them,' says Clifton.

'Nobody knew the upside potential,' says Tim Jeans. 'I bought quite a lot of shares as well as the share options because I knew we had a good company. Because of what had happened with GPA the shares were priced to go,' he says. And up they went. Ryanair floated at 2 p.m. Irish time on 26 June. 'It was a landmark day,' says Jeans. 'There was a massive TV on the first floor, with a link-up to Wall Street. There was a graph on the TV. The shares started at 1.95 and the graph started off at the bottom left hand of the screen. By the end of the day it was at the top right. There were lots of very happy people, people who could buy their first car or put a deposit down on their house.'

'We all watched the flotation on TV at work,' says Clifton, 'and there was a big party. It was hugely successful on the first day. It was a great day, it was fantastic. And I remember asking Michael what does it mean, and he said it's like paying off your mortgage. He was floating around, delighted.'

The following day newspapers reported that the offering was more than eighteen times oversubscribed at the initial level of 195 pence. The price immediately soared to 250 pence, and was trading at 315 pence in after-hours trading, valuing the company at £380 million, and O'Leary's share at almost £70 million.

O'Leary's pragmatism was on show the following week. 'It had been the most successful flotation in Ireland,' says Jeans. 'And then at the management meeting the following Monday it was not mentioned once. Life moved on; we'd done the float and that was that. Nothing changed, except that we had all these millions on the balance sheet.'

12. A New Beginning

Once seen as plucky Davids fighting mighty Goliaths, O'Leary and Ryanair were now clearly successful and highly profitable. The scale of O'Leary's bonus package over the previous two years had shocked even his closest colleagues and thrown him into the media spotlight as Ireland's wealthiest young chief executive. Anonymity had been stripped away and replaced by instant recognition. Ireland's economy was growing dramatically and O'Leary personified the new breed of entrepreneurial managers putting the country on the world stage. Just as significantly, the flotation re-energized Ireland's trade union movement, which had been excluded from the airline since its launch and which now realized that it had to gain a foothold in the fast-growing company.

Ryanair's decision to be a non-unionized company had been an important element in the early business plans developed by Tony Ryan for his new airline. Instead, Ryan had hoped that all those who worked for the airline would become stakeholders in the company, owning shares and participating in its profits. As the company, if not its profits, grew, the unions failed to make inroads. Ryanair, from its launch, was a young and exciting company with a remarkably youthful workforce – the average age of staff was under twenty-six – who had no experience of the trade union movement and felt no need to be represented by them. A culture of direct contact and negotiation between management and employees was easy to maintain in the company's early years when numbers were small, and the flexibility this gave Ryanair was essential to its development because employees were not hemmed in by restrictive union conditions on job definitions. There were no boundaries; in a crisis – and there were many – employees were expected to help out wherever they could.

As the company grew, the non-union culture became embedded.

While the youth of the workforce played its part, it was also significant that Ryanair was fighting for survival in those early years against the predatory attacks of Aer Lingus. The national airline was heavily unionized and Ryanair's employees saw it as the enemy. They did not have common cause with the workers of an airline that was trying to put them out of business, and there was little appeal in being represented by the same unions which represented the very different interests of Aer Lingus workers.

The unions, too, underestimated Ryanair's ability to survive. Imbued with the same arrogance which characterized the early responses of the Aer Lingus management to the threat posed by Ryanair, they expected the new airline to fail. Why battle to sign up union members in a company that was never going to last, and which, if it did survive, would threaten the livelihoods of existing union members in the state airline?

Their complacency was shattered by the facts that emerged during the lead-up to the stock market flotation. Ryanair's success was relatively new-found – its first genuine trading profits had only been recorded four years earlier – but it was demonstrably a survivor and was also, by 1997, a significant employer with just under 1,000 workers. The unions now wanted a slice of the action and decided to agitate. It was an important fight for the union movement, which was belatedly beginning to realize the threat that Ryanair posed to its former monopoly at Dublin airport, where the vast majority of workers were union members. Aer Lingus and Aer Rianta could not make a significant management decision without union agreement. But if the unions wanted to maintain their grip on the airport, they had to gain a foothold in Ryanair.

They wasted no more time. The weekend after Ryanair shares started to trade, O'Leary was faced with the threat of strike action from a small number of baggage handlers at Dublin airport. They demanded significant pay increases, claiming that they were earning substantially less than other baggage handlers at the airport. A small number of Ryanair's handlers joined the ATGWU, a transport workers' union which represented many workers at the airport and at Aer Lingus.

For the first time in Ryanair's history a strike was on the agenda. The initial ultimatum was averted by O'Leary's decision to meet his workers – but not the trade union – to discuss their demands. Keen to defuse the discontent as quickly as possible – a strike so soon after the flotation would have been a deep embarrassment, as well as being costly – O'Leary offered the baggage handlers an increase in basic pay and further productivity-linked increases which he argued were worth up to 20 per cent.

Conor McCarthy, head of operations, assured the handlers that their wages would not be allowed to fall behind the rates paid by other companies. 'You will be earnings competitive,' he told them. For the moment the increases bought peace and McCarthy could also assure the company's shareholders that they represented just 'a tiny percentage' of Ryanair's costs. But if the baggage handlers had been mollified for the moment, the union had not. Although excluded from the negotiations – Ryanair maintained that it was happy to recognize unions but preferred dealing directly with its own employees – the union was not about to give up on the bigger battle to gain negotiation rights at the airline. O'Leary had won the first skirmish, but the fight was only beginning.

The decision to float the company in the United States as well as in Dublin imposed tight financial constraints on O'Leary, forcing him to prepare quarterly financial statements for investors as opposed to the six-monthly reports which the Irish authorities required. With any newly floated company, the first results are a significant event and O'Leary had to prepare to meet his shareholders – or at least their representatives in the investment community – on 11 August. His performance would be critical to the continued upward momentum of the share price and would set the tone for his future dealings with the markets. The flotation was not an end but a beginning; O'Leary would need access to more money from the markets to fund his ambitions.

Building up the airline's fleet was a key priority. Ryanair needed planes to fly the expanded route network promised in the IPO document. The previous month it had purchased an extra Boeing

737–200. The aircraft was fifteen years old, acquired from Portuguese flag carrier TAP for about £5.9 million, and was due to be delivered in November. Four other aircraft were due by the end of the year, which would bring the fleet to twenty, but they were stopgaps – planes to meet the airline's immediate needs not provide it with the platform for aggressive expansion.

O'Leary's profits announcement did not disappoint. Profits before tax for the three months to the end of June were £5.7 million, some 30 per cent up from £4.4 million for the same quarter the previous year; turnover was up by 34 per cent (to £41.3 million), and load factors on the new European routes were above 75 per cent. Surprisingly, perhaps, O'Leary chose to be downbeat and cautious in his commentary – a theme that he has followed ever since. The official statement said the company did not expect 'this level of increase to continue consistently through each quarter' because of seasonal factors and because five more aircraft were to be added by the end of the year. He said that trading conditions 'continue to be tough' and that in coming months Ryanair would 'shoulder further challenges by increasing the size of our fleet by one third, and opening up new routes, despite facing continued intense price competition throughout our network'.

'We have a job to do and it is never easy making a living flying people for fifty-nine pounds,' he told journalists. He insisted that his comments and the official statement that accompanied the results should not be seen as a profits warning, and that the airline was still on course for growth. And at that first results meeting he also laid down the mantra that would be repeated every three months: 'We want to increase our business by 25 per cent to 30 per cent a year and to keep cutting out costs.'

After studying the results, stock market analysts set their estimates for Ryanair's full-year pre-tax profit at £35–40 million, a range with which O'Leary said he was 'comfortable', but the caution in O'Leary's words had an effect: Ryanair's shares fell by 20 pence to £3.70 because of what analysts termed 'a negative tone'.

O'Leary's reasoning was sound. Far better to cool expectations and then deliver news that was marginally better than expected than to overexcite the markets and then disappoint them. Aggressive with his competitors and increasingly bullish with the media, O'Leary knew from the start that the markets required more sophisticated handling. The low-cost airline industry, not just Ryanair, remained an unproven phenomenon in Europe and could still only point to the success of Southwest in the United States. The market was in its infancy and the national flag carriers still dominated the skies, the airports and the regulators. For the moment Ryanair was a flea on the elephant's back, a serious competitor for none but Aer Lingus and not even considered a threat, let alone a rival, by Europe's major airlines.

Expansion was now the key target. At the end of August O'Leary announced that Ryanair was to abandon cargo services from 14 September. Cargo had tumbled as a percentage of the airline's turnover in the previous five years and now accounted for less than 1 per cent. Loading cargo on a plane compromised aircraft turnaround time and by the autumn of 1997 there was plenty of competition with easyJet putting up a particularly strong challenge.

The airline had just six aircraft but big plans. In September it announced it had secured a deal that would triple its fleet over the next three years with the acquisition of twelve Boeing 737s. EasyJet also said it was exploring the possibility of establishing hubs in continental Europe. This would make it one of the first airlines to take full advantage of cabotage, which had come in with the final wave of deregulation earlier that year. Originally easyJet said it was considering setting up in Amsterdam and Athens to compete directly with KLM and Olympic Airways, but in the end Geneva was chosen as its first base, and it arrived there in July 1999, with Amsterdam's Schiphol airport following in 2001.

Ryanair, for the moment, saw its bases at Dublin and Stansted as its engines for European growth. Between May and November 1997 it added seven routes to its network to bring the total number to twenty. Three of the new routes – Dublin–Bristol, Dublin–Paris and Dublin–Brussels – had been launched before the flotation, with the first flights on 1 May, in an effort to prove to the market that

Ryanair was serious about rolling out its model in Europe. The next two new routes, Stansted–Kerry and Stansted–Stockholm Skavsta, began flights on 12 June. The Stockholm route was Ryanair's first foray into Scandinavia, and its first from Stansted to a continental European airport. It was an unusual choice. O'Leary had consciously avoided the summer hot spots of Spain and southern France – markets well served by seasonal charter airlines – opting instead for a route that had less obvious appeal but which had other attractions. Flights to and from Scandinavia were notorious for their high prices predicated on the relative prosperity of the Scandinavians.

Barry Barrable, a former baggage handler who had risen through the ranks to become a sales manager, was given the responsibility of opening the route in Sweden and generating demand. His budget was close to zero. 'Michael just told me to go there and make a noise and get us noticed,' he says. So Barrable went on a promotional blitz, using students to hand out flyers and then organizing a demonstration outside the Stockholm offices of SAS, the flag carrier for the Scandinavian nations, against its high prices and praising Ryanair's low ones. The media bit, and Ryanair got the launch publicity it required.

Within weeks the route was a success. 'Skavsta might have been in the middle of nowhere,' says Barrable, 'but Stansted wasn't. And that was the key. London is a huge magnet for foreign tourists, and for the first time people in Sweden had an opportunity to get there without being scalped in the process by SAS.' Skavsta's success prompted the announcement of a second Scandinavian route: Stansted to Torp, a small airport that would serve Oslo, which would start flying from 3 November. That day Ryanair also started a new route from Dublin to Teesside, bringing the total to twenty.

In mid-October Ryanair announced that it was in talks with Boeing and Airbus with a view to acquiring between twenty and forty new short-haul aircraft – either Boeing 737–700s and 737–800s or Airbus A319s and A320s – which would either double or triple the airline's existing twenty-strong fleet. It was O'Leary's most audacious move in his four years as chief executive, and it underlined the scale of the company's vision. Less than six months after floating on the stock market, O'Leary had put in train a series of plans which would at least double the size of the company and change its profile from a cheap and cheerful operator running a fleet of second-hand planes.

Staff recruitment was also a priority, and the company managed to use its selection process as a means of generating publicity. The *Irish Times* reported that applicants for cabin crew positions, who were interviewed at Jury's Hotel in Dublin, were urged to sing their CVs. The paper quoted the airline as saying, 'The interview technique is designed to weed out any "wilting flowers" . . . singing is a fairer procedure than relying on good looks and examination results and prepares them for their high-pressure job.' Applicants could also be asked to do role plays, mime or speak on a given topic, but the quality of the singers' voices, 'some of which would defy music criticism', was not a criterion for selection.

Publicity stunt or not, Ryanair's recruitment carried a serious message. Expansion was a reality not a management pipe dream. In November O'Leary faced the stock market analysts for the second time as a public company CEO and was able to reveal steady progress. The figures showed that pre-tax profits (for the half-year) had risen to £18.6 million, up from £12.4 million for the same period in 1996. Turnover for the half year came in at £96.9 million, up 36 per cent on the first half of the 1996 financial year.

Ryanair's results were far ahead of the rest of the low-cost contingent. Debonair reported a half-year loss of GB£5.5 million on sales of just under GB£18 million in November, while Virgin Express reported profits of GB£6 million for its first nine months. Michael Cawley, O'Leary's chief financial officer, told analysts and journalists that while the results were good, they could be, and would be, much much better. He pointed out that the airline was continuing talks with Boeing and Airbus on the purchase of new aircraft, which would be delivered in 1999. Cawley also said at least four new routes would be launched the following year, one out of Dublin and the remainder out of London. In fact, five new routes were launched in 1998, four from Stansted and one from Prestwick.

Ryanair's profits and the growing realization that low-cost airlines had a future in Europe had increased speculation that competition was about to reach new levels of intensity. In October British Airways had confirmed that it was studying the possibility of setting up its own low-cost operator and by the end of the year it was clear BA was intent on launching the new airline, originally dubbed Blue Skies. O'Leary, though, professed to be unfazed. When asked about BA's plans, his response was brief: 'They must be smoking too much dope.'

O'Leary was pleasing the markets, but there was no pleasing the trade unions at Dublin airport. The temporary ceasefire negotiated during the summer broke down acrimoniously at the end of the year with the baggage handlers claiming that O'Leary had reneged on his promises. Paul O'Sullivan, a union organizer, says their main grievance was pay. 'Initially the basic issue was that they had been made a promise by Ryanair that they'd get at least the same money as the baggage handlers at Servisair.' But there were other concerns too. 'The company refused to use equipment for the safe handling of bags,' he says. 'They wouldn't use conveyor belts to lift the bags from the trucks to the hold on the plane. Ryanair refused. This was a company that paid Michael O'Leary millions of pounds but they refused to buy what every other company saw as essential for health and safety.'

It was a clash of culture rather than safety, however. To achieve fast turnaround times Ryanair had dispensed with the traditional method of loading and unloading bags. Conveyor belts slowed the operation, and so its handlers used their hands, and their muscles, to transfer the bags at speed. As a result of their working conditions baggage handlers suffered frequent back injuries, for which there was no sick pay. O'Sullivan says, 'We talked to them [the handlers] and explained that unless we had a situation where we would have basically 100 per cent support there was little point in doing anything, given Ryanair's track record with unions.'

O'Sullivan claims that between September and December fifty-nine of the sixty Ryanair baggage handlers at Dublin airport became SIPTU members. 'The only one who didn't was a relation of Tony Ryan's,' he says. 'During that time Ryanair didn't contact SIPTU to tell us to stop recruiting but they tried to pull people aside and put them off joining.' SIPTU's efforts to meet Ryanair were dismissed by the company. 'We wrote to them before Christmas and asked to meet O'Leary,' says O'Sullivan. 'They wrote back and said the company would only deal with their own staff.'

By the beginning of 1998 both sides were squaring up for a confrontation. The trade union was incensed at being treated with conscious disdain, and the baggage handlers were frustrated that nothing was happening about their pay. O'Leary was determined that a trade union would not dictate to his company, and he was prepared to face it down.

On 9 January the baggage handlers staged a three-hour strike, and O'Leary and his managers stepped into the breach to load the planes. A series of three-hour work stoppages continued throughout January. The Irish media came out in force behind the baggage handlers, with one columnist accusing O'Leary of 'hypocrisy of the highest level' for the way he was treating his staff. But the impact of the strike remained largely confined to newsprint. Ryanair insisted it had not been forced to make any schedule changes, denied charges that it had imported workers from the UK to cover for the strikers, and remained implacably opposed to negotiations with the trade union.

Ethel Power, then head of communications for Ryanair, says the baggage handlers had not succeeded in influencing the opinions of Ryanair's other 950 staff. 'Was there this feeling of support for the baggage handlers?' she says. 'No. They were basically on their own in that people didn't consider that their so-called issue was of great relevance to anybody else. Everybody in Ryanair felt the same: you worked hard, you were well paid for it.'

Getting nowhere with O'Leary and making little impact on

Ryanair's operations, the union went for escalation. Three-hour work stoppages became six-hour stoppages by the end of January and the union also announced that it was preparing a detailed submission for the Labour Court on its claim for recognition and higher pay. What had started as a fight on behalf of Ryanair's lowest-paid workers for better pay was becoming a political battle for the right of the trade union movement to be represented and recognized in any company they chose. Ryanair was the battleground, but it was a much broader fight for the union movement.

Ireland's economy was booming and thousands of new jobs were being created each month. Giant American corporations, particularly high-tech companies like Dell, Intel and Microsoft, were choosing Ireland as the centre for their European operations, but there was a catch. Not many of the new jobs were unionized because few of the new investors in the Irish economy wanted unions on their factory floors. Since the jobs were both welcome and high paid, few workers objected and the trade union movement was on the slide. Still dominant in Ireland's public sector and in the media, the unions were becoming less and less relevant to the booming private sector.

The Ryanair dispute was fast becoming a cause célèbre. The unions called on political support from Ireland's left and then tried to promote a boycott of Ryanair by the travelling public. The National Union of Journalists, whose members were expected to be reporting dispassionately on the dispute, was among the first of the trade unions to weigh in behind the baggage handlers, passing a motion calling on the government to introduce legislation to 'ensure the right of each worker to trade union representation' and for 'punitive sanctions against employers who refuse to recognize this fundamental human right'. The journalists' union also called on its members not to use the airline 'as long as it refuses to recognize the right of workers to be represented by a trade union' – a call that remains in place to this day.

Despite their waning power on the shop floor, Ireland's unions exerted extensive political power through their control of the public sector, and had participated in a series of national wage agreements that had become known as social partnerships – deals between government, unions and employers to moderate wage demands in return for reductions in personal and corporate taxes.

Social partnerships, which had come into being a decade earlier when Ireland had been mired in recession and high unemployment, had assumed cult status by the late 1990s and were seen as key contributors to Ireland's changing economic fortunes. They had, according to the wisdom of the time, delivered industrial peace and moderate wage inflation and as a result had encouraged foreign firms to invest with confidence.

Subsequent studies by academics would show that the impact of social partnerships on industrial peace had been overstated, and that trends in Ireland were no different to those in other European countries which had not engaged in similar deals. Wage moderation, too, was a figment: in the booming private sector the national wage deals simply provided a floor for pay negotiations, and actual salaries reflected market demands not centrally agreed deals. In reality, social partnerships were elaborate structures for the government of the day to negotiate with its own employees. But because they had such elevated stature, the price of every agreement was the appointment of trade union officials to every government committee. Social partnerships had played a role in selling Ireland as a stable economy and a member of the European Union to American firms that wanted to take advantage of the growing European market. Ireland's attractiveness went far beyond deals with unions, however. It had a young workforce – almost half the population was under thirty – which was well educated and English speaking. Economically, it had benefited from a devaluation of its currency in 1993 and from low interest rates as it headed for membership of the euro. Money was cheap, and exports competitive because the exchange rate was artificially low.

The deals had obtained political prominence and power for the unions, but had had little impact on the private sector, which responded to market forces rather than grandiose national plans. It did, however, mean that Ryanair's local difficulty with a small number of baggage handlers would become a national story and would, for only the second time since its launch thirteen years earlier, cast Ryanair in a poor light. Instead of being the people's champions, Ryanair and O'Leary were now evil capitalists, making fortunes for the management while threatening the social partnerships, which were believed to be such a fundamental factor in the nation's success.

John Tierney, a union leader, caught the mood when he attacked Ryanair's behaviour as a 'flagrant breach of the letter and the spirit' of the latest social partnership deal. 'This is all the more unacceptable at a time when Ryanair claims to be one of the most profitable airlines in Europe and has awarded its executives multi-million-pound bonuses and share option benefits.'

It was a potent combination: a lavishly rewarded chief executive, a highly profitable company and a dispute over the rates of pay of the lowest-paid workers. The NUJ's Ryanair boycott set the tone for the media coverage of the dispute, which was weighted heavily in favour of the baggage handlers. The *Mirror*'s story of 9 February, ' "Why won't he talk to us?" – Ryanair's striking workers in plea to airline boss Michael O'Leary', was typical of the flavour of newspaper articles of the day, consisting almost solely of Ryanair handlers and union representatives bemoaning their plight. 'We have given years of loyal service. We dug in when it mattered most. This dispute is very stressful on all the lads. We just want to be treated with a bit of respect.'

The *Irish Times* ploughed a similar furrow. On 13 February it gave prominence to union claims that baggage handlers who had been working normally had been subjected to threats of violence, by phone, by Ryanair management. The phone calls were part of a 'growing campaign of intimidation and bullying, both of our people who are working normally and, worse still, of their families', according to Paul O'Sullivan. O'Leary denied the allegations but grew increasingly irritated at the media's willingness to publish union allegations as facts, and to ignore or downplay his denials.

Ethel Power says the dispute was in part the result of a media obsession with doing down Ryanair.

There was a hunger out there nationally for a story about Ryanair. Michael O'Leary was doing too well. If Michael O'Leary was in America or in another country he would be invited home to Ireland, Dublin Castle would be opened to him, because he had created such a big company, such employment, contributing so much to the economy and transforming the tourism business. But because he was here living in Ireland and niggling the government every now and again, he didn't fit.

Almost a decade later, O'Leary is still incensed by the media's treatment of his company.

The coverage was all about [how Ryanair] was denying the workers rights. We were saying the majority of the workers are working, the majority of the workers don't want union recognition. Nobody was writing that. It was all 'Support the workers.' The reason we kept flying and the bags kept getting loaded for about twelve weeks was because the majority of [our employees] were working. [The tone was] always, 'The union confirms, Ryanair claims.' We learned, midway through it, to answer every bullshit allegation they made. But you don't always get a chance to answer the allegations; you're not even allowed to put your point of view.

Ryanair's quarterly financial results, announced in mid February, further fuelled anti-Ryanair sentiment in media and political arenas. All the financial indicators were good – profits were up by almost £3 million to £8.1 million for the three months ending 31 December 1997, compared with the same quarter in 1996, while passenger numbers grew by 30 per cent to just under a million for the quarter, due to the success of the new Paris and Brussels routes. The market responded well to Ryanair's figures, with its share price rising by ten pence to 405 on the Dublin stock exchange. Two weeks later O'Leary announced six new route launches, all from Stansted. The routes – to Venice, Pisa, Rimini, Carcassonne/Toulouse, St Etienne/Lyon and Kristianstad/Malmö – were a significant breakthrough for Ryanair, increasing its route network by 30 per cent to twenty-six routes and giving the airline a serious presence in the continental European market.

But Ryanair's fight with the unions had created a growing army of critics who were quick to use the airline's success against it.

At a debate on transport and tourism at the European parliament in Strasbourg, Irish MEPs joined forces to condemn Ryanair's treatment of its workers. Mary Banotti, a Fine Gael MEP, said that Ryanair was now 'the most profitable airline in Europe' and slammed the fact that it was still paying lower wage rates than less profitable firms. 'Let us not hand out kudos to a company whose industrial relations practices are unjust and whose profits were built on the generosity of its employees.'

Labour's Dublin MEP, Bernie Malone, chimed in at the same debate, maintaining that Ryanair's treatment of its workers was tantamount to an abuse of their human rights. 'It is deeply ironic that Ryanair, which has benefited enormously from the economic principles set out in EU treaties, for example the commitment to air liberalization, is doing its damnedest to infringe corresponding social principles.'

The dispute signalled open season on the airline. Now that it was in the limelight, previously unexplored aspects of the company were coming under scrutiny from the media and from politicians. Landing-charge discounts were first in the firing line, and at the end of February Transport Minister Mary O'Rourke was forced to admit, in answer to a parliamentary question raised by Democratic Left TD Eamon Gilmore, that Ryanair had saved £8.5 million between 1989 and 1994 because of landing-charge discounts. O'Rourke had taken up the post in January, replacing Brian Cowen, who had spent a very brief and unremarkable time at transport. Now she was quick to point out that Aer Lingus and other airlines had also benefited from similar discounts, but she said that she would be talking to Aer Rianta about the levels of the discounts.

Just days later the media stumbled upon another gem – the fact that Ryanair had been getting large rent discounts for its Dublin airport office space from the state. Ryanair's offices had been built on state land by Darley Ltd, a subsidiary of Tony Ryan's children's trust fund, in 1992. Darley had brokered a deal with then Transport Minister Maire Geoghegan Quinn that saw the government agree to waive the site's £192,000 a year rent until 2004, and only charge 50 per cent of the usual rent from 2004 to 2010. When news of the agreement become public, O'Rourke announced she was launching a full inquiry into the circumstances of the deal.

The unions were quick to claim the inquiry as a victory. 'This is the end of the honeymoon for Ryanair,' a spokesman said. 'We are delighted to see they are finally under scrutiny after appearing for so long to be so innocent. We have received hundreds of complaints by Ryanair staff across the board since it was set up. They are people we represented yet we have been totally disregarded. The company has even ignored the Labour Court. We see this as the opening of the floodgates and the end of the cosy relationship the company has enjoyed with the state.'

The lines of battle were clearly drawn. The unions wanted to breach Ryanair's union-free policy and establish for themselves the right to represent its workers – and then, by extension, every private sector employee in the country. Politicians from all parties were slow to recognize the threat that the unions' agenda could pose to Ireland's burgeoning economy and were all too easily prepared to support the unions' demands.

O'Leary was not a soft target. Although he was still relatively inexperienced as a chief executive, and even less prepared for a full-scale public battle after spending most of his time below the public's radar, he was not prepared to concede an inch. If Ryanair was to achieve its minimum objective of 25 per cent annual growth it was essential that it continue to attack its costs and lower its fares. Competition was growing more intense, the airline was committed to acquiring new planes and developing new routes, and O'Leary needed the flexibility that only a non-unionized labour force could provide. He did not want to be trapped by detailed agreements on wages and conditions that would require negotiations every time he wanted to try something new. Stubbornly, too, he refused to allow Ryanair to become a trophy for the unions.

The unions increased the pressure on the company by calling a two-hour protest outside its Dublin airport headquarters at the end of January. The protest drew a crowd of up to 1,000, though

Ryanair claimed it was about 500. 'It was just a demonstration to show Ryanair workers that they were not on their own,' says O'Sullivan. 'Ryanair management were at the windows on the fifth floor. The Garda asked them to move from the windows, and they refused. I remember the inspector from that day, he was absolutely furious. Then people started shouting abuse and the strikers shouted back.'

O'Leary's sense of mischief was also beginning to emerge. Non-striking Ryanair workers, encouraged by their chief executive, used megaphones to chant 'Heigh ho, heigh ho, it's off to work we go' from the upper windows of the head office building. The crowd responded with shouts of 'Scabs' and the Irish police, unused to aggressive disputes, expressed concern at Ryanair's 'provocation' of its striking workers.

'Bollocks,' says one former executive. 'What were we meant to do? Allow a tiny minority, egged on by a union with a big political agenda, to derail the company? We were not going to lie down.'

The following week the dispute escalated further. 'Ryanair delivered letters to everyone saying if they didn't report back for normal duty they were going to be fired,' says O'Sullivan. 'It was a threatening letter and it was perceived as such.'

The baggage handlers held a meeting that Thursday, and agreed to report for duty on the Friday at 6 a.m. But as that Thursday progressed, O'Sullivan says he learned that Ryanair had taken steps to revoke the airside passes – passes legally required to go through airport security – of the handlers involved in the dispute. 'I established during Thursday that the airport passes were the property of the airport authority, not Ryanair,' says O'Sullivan. 'I asked the airport authority if they had revoked the passes. They confirmed they hadn't.'

The next day, O'Sullivan turned up at the airport with the baggage handlers. 'Ryanair had someone at the post instructing airport police not to let people through,' he says. 'I contacted the person in charge of the airport and established that they had no authority to refuse access and they were finally allowed through on the stipulation that I accompany them. So I did that and went with the workers to the normal place where they would check in for work, the breakroom.'

Soon after the workers, accompanied by O'Sullivan, got to the baggage handlers' hut they got a message from airport police, at 6.30 a.m., that Ryanair management wanted them to leave. 'So the shop stewards rang looking for management,' says O'Sullivan. 'They wanted management to explain; the baggage handlers said they would talk to Ryanair on their own. Management wouldn't come down. Finally management stopped answering the phones. I had Conor McCarthy's mobile phone number, from his time in Aer Lingus. He answered and said, "How did you get my number? You shouldn't be ringing this number." Then he hung up.'

As the confrontation intensified airport police evicted the baggage handlers from the hut, and the group made its way back to the union offices. 'They were a very resolute group of people,' says O'Sullivan. 'We had long discussions and we decided to set up a picket.'

O'Sullivan says the picket was to be placed at the gate Ryanair workers passed through next to head office, 'to confine the impact and not to affect the airport'. But by mid-afternoon the picketers had to find a new location. 'Ryanair told Aer Rianta to have the picket moved off their land,' says O'Sullivan. 'Aer Rianta was saying, "You have to go out to the public road, which is the roundabout." I kept saying, "No, that doesn't make sense, there's no point in doing that."'

Aer Rianta threatened to go to the courts to have the picketers removed, according to O'Sullivan, so they moved on, and pickets were placed at the main airport entrance at three or four o'clock. It was there that the picket began to grow. 'At about five or six o'clock the people on the picket line were joined by a group of women cleaners,' says O'Sullivan. 'One said the guys picketing could be her sons. The airport was a small place and when word spread that others had stopped work others came out and stopped work too.' The Ryanair handlers were joined by Servisair handlers, British Midland handlers, Aer Lingus handlers and other airport staff.

Ethel Power says the media reporting coaxed other groups out on strike. 'It was given an unfair amount of airtime, because there was a feeling in the media that they wanted this to blow up,' she says. 'They wanted 1,000 people from Ryanair out protesting; they didn't get them, so what they did was they got the next best thing, they got the Aer Rianta people out protesting and the AL people out protesting. So that did give the media a story . . .'

The next day, a Saturday, the weather was cold and the ground was muddy, but the picket began again at 6 a.m. with even more groups weighing in, and it swelled to 2,000 workers refusing to cross the line, as well as taxi and bus drivers who refused to pass the roundabout, leaving passengers to walk half a mile with their luggage. At lunchtime Aer Rianta decided to shut the airport when emergency fire workers declared themselves off duty.

Bewildered by the airport management's docility, frustrated by its refusal to confront its workers and its failure to have a contingency plan, O'Leary watched the situation unfold from his first-floor office. 'What they [the unions] got up to in the end was a joke,' he says. 'They closed the airport, CIE [the bus company] was dumping all the ould ones down the roundabout. A couple of our cabin crew got physically assaulted by the headbangers down there. We are the only airline flying. Eventually Aer Lingus walked off, security staff walked off, the whole thing came to a ball of wax.'

Bertie Ahern, the taoiseach, was furious, and said the airport closure would make Ireland an international laughing stock. But he was also not prepared to confront the unions, and refused to send in the army to replace the striking firemen, even though their action had been illegal.

Power says the protest did provide some wry amusement for the Ryanair workers who were not involved. 'When Dublin airport was closed down all Ryanair employees were working, except for the baggage handlers,' she says. 'It actually was quite laughable on the day because the strike closed down the competition and the airport, not Ryanair.'

The picket at the airport's roundabout continued throughout Saturday, but the picketers were back on duty on Sunday morning.

O'Leary still refused to negotiate and declined to be drawn into the political storm, turning down requests to meet Ahern at the taoiseach's office.

We got a call from the taoiseach's office asking us to enter talks with the union. We said, 'Fuck off and open the airport.' It was his job to keep the fucking airport open. There was nothing he could do, it was very tense, very difficult circumstances. So we said, 'Tell him to send in the army and open the fucking airport.' The only thing that Bertie wanted on the Sunday when it was closed was for me to come down to Government Buildings at six o'clock. He wanted me there in time for the TV news, so that the message would be, 'O'Leary summoned to Government Buildings for crisis talks.' So I said, 'No, fuck off. Go fucking open the airport.'

O'Sullivan says that neither he nor any of his union colleagues had any interaction with Ryanair or O'Leary, and confirms that pressure to resolve the dispute was being driven from the highest political levels. 'The taoiseach's office was trying to talk some sense into him at that stage,' he says.

In Government Buildings the situation was becoming tense. 'Everyone was saying that the only one who could talk any sense into O'Leary was Mary Harney [the tánaiste],' recalls one insider. Ahern was desperate for a compromise. He hammered out a deal which would see the baggage handlers abandon industrial action and resume normal duties if Ryanair signed up to an inquiry into the dispute, which was to be headed up by former trade union leader Phil Flynn and former employers' leader Dan McAuley. O'Leary agreed but refused to move an inch on union recognition. 'These recommendations will result in an orderly return to normal working by these employees without compromising Ryanair's principle of only dealing with its own people directly,' he said.

On 12 March Conor McCarthy felt compelled to write a piece for the *Irish Times* detailing the company's position. He began by slamming the media coverage of the dispute. 'Since the industrial action began nine weeks ago, the media have virtually ignored the fact that 961 of Ryanair's 1,000 people have defied intimidation, abuse and hostile publicity by continuing to work normally,' he wrote. 'However, following the unlawful events of last weekend, Ryanair feels that we owe it to the 97 per cent of our employees who worked normally, to state our position to your readers.'

He also attacked Aer Rianta and Aer Lingus for their actions which had led to the closure of the airport. 'It was not Ryanair which indulged in the unlawful activity which shut Dublin Airport last weekend,' he wrote. 'It was Aer Lingus and Aer Rianta employees who engaged in unlawful secondary action, by blockading Ryanair's aircraft and our passengers for two hours on Saturday morning (and again on Sunday morning), and by withdrawing the fire cover at Dublin Airport from 1 p.m. on Saturday, therefore preventing Ryanair and all other flights from operating.'

But McCarthy's wrath was by no means confined to old foes Aer Rianta and Aer Lingus.

Even worse were the shameful scenes of intimidation at the entrance of Dublin Airport on Sunday, as efforts were made to block and intimidate many of our 961 staff, who wished to work, from doing so. The behaviour of some taxi-drivers – who dropped young Ryanair employees in full uniform at the airport's entrance, forcing them to walk through a baying mob who subjected them to gross abuse and intimidation – was unforgivable. If these are low-paid employees, with poor conditions, why would 961 of them brave the bullyboys last weekend?

For the unions the baggage handlers' dispute proved to be a dismal failure. They had shut Dublin airport and organized an impressive array of political and media support, but O'Leary had stood firm. There would be no union presence in Ryanair, and O'Leary was free to continue to cut costs and expand the airline at his own pace. As the pickets had gathered outside his offices, he had been finalizing the details of his most aggressive expansion, which would be announced within 48 hours of Dublin airport reopening for business. On 10 March news broke that Ryanair had agreed to buy twenty-five new planes from Boeing, with options for a further twenty.

It was a massive order for a still small airline, more than doubling its fleet size, while the options would allow it to treble in size over the next eighteen months. The new planes would all be Boeing 737–800s, capable of carrying 189 passengers, fifty-nine more than the 737–200s. The total value of the deal was estimated at £1.4 billion – making it easily Ryanair's biggest ever transaction.

'I can't say what the discount is, for confidentiality reasons, but no airline pays the full price for new aircraft,' Cawley told journalists.

For Ryanair, the deal was the culmination of months of negotiations with Boeing and rival aircraft manufacturers Airbus. Chris Buckley, a vice president of Airbus who was involved in the Ryanair negotiations, says Ryanair effectively played Airbus and Boeing off against each other, with Conor McCarthy and O'Leary spearheading Ryanair's negotiating team. McCarthy was already known to Buckley and his Airbus colleagues in Toulouse from his days at Aer Lingus. But O'Leary was an anomaly.

He might have said '*Bonjour*' once on a visit to Toulouse [Airbus headquarters] but everything else was very much in English. The negotiations were earthy and very direct. He was certainly not somebody to waste any time at all on detail or unnecessary issues. It was all very much focused on doing the right deal for Ryanair as efficiently as possible.

In 1997 we really had the opportunity to do a deal there and we lost that opportunity. Ryanair came to the conclusion that the A320 would work very well for them and in November 1997 Michael O'Leary sent me a letter saying that Ryanair would like to go with Airbus. He set down lots of terms for Airbus to make so that Ryanair would do a deal with us. And he said, 'Chris, if Airbus can deliver these terms then we would be prepared to recommend them to the board.'

The 'terms' Ryanair wanted involved a 'further but fairly small reduction in price', Buckley says. He recommended to his colleagues that they did whatever it took to secure the Ryanair deal, 'but unfortunately not everybody agreed with me, so we did not deliver on the terms'. Airbus's loss was Boeing's gain.

★

The new planes represented a coming of age for Ryanair.

'This new fleet of aircraft will allow Ryanair to compete head on and beat any low-fare competition from Europe's major airlines, and enables us to maintain our planned capacity growth of 25 per cent per annum,' O'Leary said at the time.

'It was an absolute landmark,' says Tim Jeans. 'We had been flying with ten- to fifteen-year-old hand-me-down 737s, and in many ways they defined the company – they were cheap, they were reliable, they sat 130 people and they allowed us to compete with Aer Lingus and British Airways. But ordering the new 737–800s, that put us in a different ball game. There was huge pride and massive excitement. It was a turning point – we could now compete with the flag carriers of Europe.'

In less than a year O'Leary had engineered a staggering transformation, from a small family-owned airline that competed in a small, if busy, piece of airspace over the Irish Sea, into a publicly quoted European airline with new planes, new routes and unbridled ambition. At home the trade unions had been seen off and the overwhelming majority of his workforce had stayed loyal. Stansted was proving a successful gateway into Europe and the Ryanair brand was beginning to become as well known in Stockholm as it was in London.

13. Pre-emptive Strike

Ireland's economic blossoming in the 1990s turned a nation accustomed to hiding its meagre wealth into a nation of ostentatious spenders. Economic growth was, by European standards, staggering: in each year from 1994 to 2000 the Irish economy grew by almost 10 per cent net, a spurt that spawned a new generation of multimillionaires.

In 1997 Ireland's fast-emerging wealth prompted the London *Sunday Times* to devote part of its annual Rich List survey to the Irish phenomenon. That year the paper could only find seventy-five Irish people worth individually more than £6 million; the collective worth of the seventy-five was just over £4 billion. O'Leary, whose salary and bonuses were unknown while Ryanair was a private company, made his first appearance in the list in 1998, joining the top ten Irish with an estimated worth of £140 million. That year the newspaper commented, 'A noticeable feature of this year's list is the high proportion of young self-made millionaires. A new breed of entrepreneurs has leapfrogged over older money. These were led by newcomers [like] Michael O'Leary.'

For some, recognition in the *Sunday Times* Rich List was an important symbol of arrival, but for O'Leary it was meaningless. His life was dominated by work at Ryanair, which was all-consuming during the working week, and his farm in Mullingar, which took up most of his remaining hours. O'Leary did not parade his wealth or indulge public passions. But his life had changed course over the previous year. He had become one of the most recognizable Irish voices and faces, and his fame, or infamy, was spreading to the UK and onto the continent. The Irish public was being introduced to something it had never experienced before: a chief executive with attitude.

O'Leary did not play by the normal rules of polite engagement.

He was prepared to state his case robustly, to argue, harangue and provoke. Along with his stubbornness or intransigence, O'Leary had an extra quality that gave him a marked edge: he did not want to be a bosom friend of prime ministers, or an accepted member of the business elite or the most loved man of his generation. All he wanted was for his business to prosper.

His calculation was simple: if Ryanair was to keep growing, it had to become a household name. He was not prepared to spend (or as he would see it, waste) tens of millions of pounds on advertising campaigns if he could reach people more directly. He recognized that at least part of the success of Southwest came from the high profile of founder Herb Kelleher, the hard-drinking, chain-smoking Texan who gave the airline personality and whose flamboyant behaviour generated publicity. O'Leary could never be a Kelleher – he lacks his charisma – but he could nonetheless give Ryanair a definition of its own.

'I think he felt that it was important to give the airline some personality,' says Charlie Clifton, a long-standing executive at the company.

Not at the start, because it was important to do the knitting at the start. But later, when people were comparing Ryanair to Southwest, they would look at us and say, 'Right, who's gonna run it? Are you trying to say we're really like Southwest but we've got a dull accountant running the company?' It wouldn't have washed. Michael knew he had to lead from the front, but I suspect he took that on reluctantly rather than egotistically. He'd been trying to keep out of the limelight for a long long time.

On one level his new-found fame made O'Leary uncomfortable and presented a threat to his low-key and unremarkable life. He wanted to be seen as an ordinary person, wanted to maintain the myth that he was just one of the boys. But he had also realized that recognition could be used to the advantage of his airline – people's interest in him translated directly into newspaper coverage, which in turn translated into free publicity for Ryanair and lower marketing budgets. He would happily prostitute himself for the cause, because whatever benefited Ryanair, benefited him. 'I don't mind dressing up in something stupid or pulling gormless faces if it helps,' says O'Leary. 'Frankly I don't give a rat's arse about my personal dignity.'

O'Leary was conducting a series of noisy re-education seminars for Europe's travelling public. The concept of cheap air travel was still relatively alien outside the British and Irish markets where Ryanair had already made its mark. O'Leary had to change the way travellers thought about airlines, had to strip away preconceived notions about both cost and service, and he had to do it fast if he was to fill his soon-to-arrive fleet of Boeings with fare-paying passengers.

The primary message was price. In every fight he picked O'Leary would portray himself as the people's champion fighting against fat, cosy, cosseted and expensive national airlines. The secondary message was simplicity: you pay for what you get, so do not expect traditional levels of service. In O'Leary's new world order planes were buses; there would be no more romance about flying, no exclusivity and no luxury. Airlines were no more, and no less, than a means of getting from A to B simply and cheaply, and they were now available and affordable to everybody.

Over the years O'Leary had become increasingly unhappy about Aer Rianta's charges at Dublin, which he claimed were the highest Ryanair paid in Europe – a claim repeatedly denied by the airport's managers. As a destination, Dublin worked for Ryanair – 40 per cent of the airline's turnover was from flights in and out of the city – but as an airport, it did not. His solution was simple: build a new terminal at Dublin, attached to the same runway but with different management and lower charges. Competition, which had breathed life and lower prices into the airline industry, should logically be extended to airports. If airports had more than one terminal operated by rival companies then the terminals would compete on price and service for the airlines' business, rather than charging take-it-or-leave-it monopoly rates.

He was not alone. Ulick and Desmond McEvaddy, two Irish entrepreneurs, through their company Huntstown Air Park, had already approached the government with a view to building a new terminal on land they owned near the existing airport but had met entrenched opposition from Aer Rianta, who had tied the McEvaddys' proposals up in lengthy legal wranglings. Growing impatient with the delays, O'Leary decided that while what the McEvaddys were proposing was compatible with Ryanair's needs, the plans were moving too slowly. The best solution, he thought, was for Ryanair to build its own terminal. And so in mid-May he submitted the first plans for Terminal Ryanair to Ireland's department of transport.

Before submitting the plans, O'Leary had tried to rally support at a Dublin Chamber of Commerce meeting in mid-April, telling the assembled crowd of businesspeople that Ryanair was prepared to spend £20 million on the new terminal as a way to break 'the totally unfair and appalling monopoly of Aer Rianta'. The move would also make good financial sense for Ryanair, O'Leary said, because the airline was paying Aer Rianta £10 million a year to use Dublin airport, so the airline would recoup its investment in just two years. Ryanair's terminal would be built on Aer Rianta land which adjoined the airport and would have enough gates to allow Ryanair to operate more flights, O'Leary said. And, eager to capitalize on his public image as the champion of the consumer, he added that the new terminal would mean cheaper fares for those flying from Dublin airport.

Convincing the business community of the merits of his proposals was a relatively easy challenge, but O'Leary was to have a much tougher time winning over Mary O'Rourke, the minister for transport, who would ultimately decide the fate of the plan. O'Rourke hailed from Athlone, in the same electoral area as O'Leary's Mullingar home. The pair had met occasionally at local events in Westmeath before O'Rourke came to transport, but didn't know each other 'in any meaningful way', O'Rourke says. Once she took over the transport ministry their contact became much more frequent, and O'Leary soon became a thorn in the minister's side. 'I wasn't long in the office when he made contact with me,' she says.

There was often twenty letters a day. All that is quite silly, I mean if you want to write one punchy letter that's grand, but twenty letters a day, that's silly.

I have never met anyone like him in my life. It is not persistence – I've met persistent people – he is obsessive, about himself and his business. He's not interested in a good business relationship, or a social relationship, he is interested in none of those things, it's just me me me me. I just think he is a horrid, horrid little man.

The hostility was mutual. 'She's an idiot,' he says. 'I'm very supportive of people who come from the [Irish] midlands but I'm not supportive of an idiot no matter where they come from. Most politicians are idiots, but if you look on the scale of idiocy she'd be right up there at the top.'

O'Rourke was prepared to meet O'Leary to discuss his proposals, but the omens were hardly inspiring. A privately owned terminal would be a direct competitor to the state's own operator, and required O'Rourke and her cabinet colleagues to take a decision that would inevitably spark serious confrontation with the trade unions that controlled the existing airport, and would provoke political opposition both within and outside the government parties. Either way, there would be no fast decision. The wheels of Ireland's public service churn slowly, and a decision on something as momentous as a second terminal for the country's largest airport would not be swift.

O'Leary had commercial logic on his side – a second terminal would give Dublin airport room to grow – but his battle with the unions at the start of the year, and in particular his refusal to engage with Bertie Ahern when he wanted to appear to be solving the crisis, had set O'Leary on a course to conflict with the Irish government. Ahern's hostility was made evident in a barely concealed swipe at O'Leary in May, when he hit out at managers 'who don't seem to believe in social partnership but who have done very well out of a strong economy' and attacked 'people who weren't around ten years ago' who had been 'jumped up a bit' by economic growth and 'who are now telling us how we achieved what we collectively achieved'.

The lines had been drawn: O'Leary could expect no political support for a plan that would deliver extra jobs and extra tourism to Ireland, largely because that plan was opposed by the trade union movement, whose grip on Dublin airport would be loosened by a privately owned second terminal. For the moment it was a confined battle, one that pitched O'Leary as the people's champion against a government that refused to deliver better and cheaper services for consumers, and while it undoubtedly alienated O'Leary from the political establishment, it gave him and his company precisely the profile and media coverage that he had hoped for.

In the summer of 1998 Ryanair bolstered its route network further by launching three new routes into Italy – Stansted to Venice, Pisa and Rimini – and two new French routes – Stansted to Lyons-St Etienne and Carcassonne/Toulouse. The routes followed Ryanair's now established approach of selecting remote airports and hammering out favourable deals on landing charges, pro-motional and marketing incentives and grants. Each time the offer was the same: We can deliver passengers, what can you do for us to make it worth our while?

The small airports were chosen for a number of straightforward business reasons: they were underused or barely used at all, meaning Ryanair had no competition on the route and also guaranteeing swift turnaround times for their aircraft; they were typically distant from the main cities they were expected to serve, creating opportu-nities for Ryanair to earn more money from its passengers through deals with car-hire companies, hotels and bus operators, as well as drawing passengers from a greater hinterland. Starved of passengers and planes, they were desperate to please them and were prepared to charge little or nothing for their services and to subsidize Ryanair's arrival.

For Venice the airline flew to Treviso airport, some nineteen miles from the city centre – a short walk in Ryanair terms – and little more than a shed attached to a runway. The airport at the destination Ryanair dubbed Carcassonne/Toulouse is on the out-skirts of Carcassonne but more than fifty miles from the region's major city, Toulouse. Similarly, a flight to Lyon–St Etienne leaves passengers quite close to St Etienne but some forty miles away from Lyon. Pisa's airport is close to the city centre – but the main city in Tuscany is Florence, some fifty miles away. Meanwhile, Rimini airport is quite close to Rimini, but quite far from anything else of interest.

For Ryanair each route was but another notch on an ever-expanding belt, but for the five chosen cities the launches were far more significant. 'It's equivalent to somewhere like Longford [a small town in the Irish midlands], that doesn't have an airport, and suddenly has three million people coming in every year,' says Ethel Power, who helped organize the route launches that summer.

On the launch day for the three Italian routes Ryanair arranged a trip for the press, who would be accompanied by O'Leary and Power on a visit to the airports. Power remembers the reception Ryanair received that day in Italy as the best day of her three years at the airline. Coming in to land at Rimini, 'We saw the runway and we saw a big guard of honour of all the fire engines down along it,' Power says, 'And then as we came in close to land we saw thousands and thousands of people on the apron – breaking security really, they shouldn't be on the apron – waiting for Ryanair to arrive. They were waiting for God; Michael O'Leary was God coming to these places. I still remember the cheers that went up. Seventeen different television stations had come to see who this man was.'

O'Leary was not overcome by the occasion. The crowds may have wanted to see him, but he had a blunter message that he wanted transmitted on the news programmes. 'The first thing we did when the door of the plane opened was to carry out a massive sign that said simply, "Londra, 999,000 lira" [about £40]. We held that up before Michael came out of the plane because that's the shot we wanted on every television camera. We didn't want pictures of Michael, we wanted pictures of 999,000 lira. That's what hit them. They were used to paying millions of lira to fly to London,' Power says.

On the ground, the Italians had gone out of their way to welcome the new airline. 'Every single tourism organization had rolled out and they were giving a big party. We do the press conference, then an hour later we're back on the plane, on to Pisa, touch down, repeat the sign, greet thousands of people, and then on to Treviso.'

For O'Leary it was another day's work, but a hard one. He preferred the office to the road, found the meeting, greeting and posing exhausting. He played to the crowds and to the press to get the news coverage and to transmit the message, but it was tough. The Italian job, though, had pleased him. 'At the end of the day he said, "Well done,"' Power says. 'But "Well done" from Michael O'Leary means you did a fantastic, amazing, amazing job.'

Ryanair's presence in the Italian market was a clear shot across the bows of Alitalia, which was already teetering on the edge of collapse and insatiable in its demands for capital from the Italian government. Of the major flag carriers, it was one of the most vulnerable to attack from the low-fare airlines, and one of the least capable of making a competitive response. By choosing small regional airports O'Leary avoided direct competition on comparable routes, but the challenge was serious.

In mid-June, after almost a year of hints and speculation, Ryanair announced plans to list its shares on the London Stock Exchange, to complement the listings in Dublin and New York. About £50 million in new shares was to be offered to the market, and the airline's main investors were to sell another £50 million worth of their shares, so £100 million in total would be available to London investors. All three major shareholders were sellers – David Bonderman and the Ryan family were both to sell the equivalent of 2.4 per cent of the company, while O'Leary was to sell 1.2 per cent of the company, about 8 per cent of his £130 million stake.

There was some confusion about the motivation for the share sale, which came just a year after Ryanair's original £300 million flotation. In his first interview with the Irish press, Bonderman told *Irish Times* journalist Cliff Taylor that this was an 'ideal time' for Ryanair to issue new stock. 'This will enable us to expand the shareholder base here in Europe as we expand our route network in Scandinavia, France and Italy,' he said. Michael Cawley told journalists that the funds from the sale would be used to finance new aircraft purchases. But earlier that month O'Leary had told UK trade magazine *Commuter/Regional Airline News* that money wasn't the primary motivation for the London flotation. 'We want to raise awareness, broaden our shareholder base and give our existing UK shareholders a means of holding shares in the company,' he said. 'We are still perceived as Irish, but 75 per cent of our traffic does not originate in Ireland, and 40 per cent does not even touch Ireland.'

In truth it was a combination of all those factors, and the timing was also advantageous. Rival easyJet was starting its third year, and while the airline had yet to publicly report profits, confidence was high and it had just acquired 40 per cent of Swiss charter airline TEA Basel AG, which went on to be renamed easyJet Switzerland. Several new players were also entering the fray, most notably Go, the much-anticipated low-cost operation of British Airways, which began flying on 22 May 1998. BA's commitment was a sign that low-cost carriers were here to stay and not some passing craze.

Go's initial three routes – Stansted to Rome, Milan and Copen-hagen – were picked because they were not served by either easyJet or Ryanair. Go's chief executive, Barbara Cassani, was keen to position her airline away from low-cost carriers such as Ryanair. 'Low price will not mean low service,' she told journalists in April. 'We have excellent staff and we are hoping to encourage people who have not previously travelled far in Europe to fly with us.'

Ryanair professed to be unconcerned by Go's appearance. 'Go was never going to be a threat to Ryanair,' says Power. 'At that point in time BA was the biggest fat cat around – BA were never going to show Ryanair how to run a low-cost airline. Did we have sleepless nights about Go? No.'

Ryanair's London offering came to market on 10 July, when twenty-one million ordinary shares were placed at £5 per share. The placement was a resounding success, with demand for the shares more than five times oversubscribed. The Ryan family grossed GB£34 million, as did Bonderman, after each decided to offer an additional 1.15 million shares to the market to satisfy the heightened investor demand. O'Leary stuck with his 1.8 million share sale, and grossed GB£10 million, which he claims he duly deposited in his local post office.

He had plans for the money. Between 1995 and 1998 O'Leary had carefully restored his home. Now he wanted luxury. He asked Westmeath County Council for permission to renovate the existing courtyard buildings and to add a swimming pool, terrace and leisure centre. The development would more than double the size of the house, turning what had been a comfortable family home into a luxurious retreat. He also sought permission to build a dressing room and bathroom adjoining the master bedroom – an expensive storage solution for his undemanding collection of jeans and check shirts.

Controversy was never far away, no matter how successful the international expansion. The baggage handlers' dispute, which had been on ceasefire since the end of February, had not been resolved. In July the Labour Court findings on the dispute that had shut Dublin airport loomed over Ryanair, and O'Leary knew that he would come in for heavy criticism. He decided on a pre-emptive strike against the bad publicity by issuing share options to all 1,000 employees to a total value of £20 million. It was the first time that an Irish public company had granted shares to all its employees directly, rather than through an ESOP scheme, in which the shares are held in trust.

The details of the share grant were to be finalized on 12 June, when Ryanair was to publish its full-year results. Michael Cawley said the scheme would be salary-related, with employees on higher salaries gaining more shares. O'Leary was keen to add that the share option scheme was in addition to basic pay increases of between 3.25 per cent and 5 per cent, which were significantly ahead of the increases agreed in Partnership 2000, the national wage agreement struck between the government, employers' representatives and trade unions. 'We are determined to continue to try to create substantial wealth for our outstanding people, by encouraging them to become long-term shareholders in Ryanair,' O'Leary said.

It was a smart tactic. O'Leary wanted to demonstrate that his people could do better without a trade union, and he wanted to show that everyone in the company could benefit from its success. It also fitted neatly with Tony Ryan's early philosophy that every employee should be a stakeholder in the business. Events, though, conspired to dilute its impact. While O'Leary sought positive coverage ahead of the Labour Court report, news that Ryanair had received £23 million in rebates from Aer Rianta since 1994 delivered the opposite.

The scale of the rebates was revealed in an answer to a parliamentary question from Tony Killeen, a Fianna Fáil representative from County Clare. Ryanair's rebate was not too far ahead of the £21 million received by Aer Lingus, but given Ryanair's persistent complaints about Aer Rianta's charges the revelation was damaging for the airline's credibility.

Aer Rianta, which was now on a war footing with Ryanair because of its proposals for a competing terminal at Dublin airport and its incessant criticism of the organization's charges and management competence, was willing to stoke the controversy. A spokesman said Aer Rianta had originally been reluctant to disclose details of the scheme for commercial reasons, but that it 'suits us in some ways to have the figures out in the open . . . It annoyed the hell out of us to have Michael O'Leary going on about our high charges when Ryanair was getting rebates on that scale.'

A week after the revelation about the rebate, the Labour Court report was released. It showered criticism on both Ryanair and SIPTU, saying both parties must bear responsibility for the 'chaos and eventual closure of Dublin Airport'. It said their 'intransigence' led to a situation which had brought hardship and inconvenience to 20,000 passengers. Ryanair was criticized for its failure to make a meaningful effort to resolve the dispute, and the report cited the company's refusal to participate in a Labour Court inquiry and its rejection of government invitations to cooperate with an independent inquiry into the dispute before the airport's closure. Ryanair had gambled that the protest would be short-lived and would collapse if there was no outside intervention, the report concluded. It also urged Ryanair to review its personnel policy to allow at least limited union recognition, and said the company should 're-examine and clarify its policy and attitudes' towards the Labour Court and Labour Relations Commission.

The unions, though, came in for even harsher criticism, with the report noting that SIPTU, the main union at the airport, had 'inexplicably' failed to use its vast knowledge and experience of industrial relations and collective bargaining in the crisis. It said the union had allowed a major disruption to occur over an industrial dispute that involved a relatively small number of Ryanair workers and it criticized the union for 'creating confusion and uncertainty, deliberately or otherwise, among its members on the reasons and purpose of the strike'. It had also failed 'to consult or communicate effectively with its members in Ryanair'. Damningly, the report found that 'by its statements, [SIPTU] left itself open to allegations that it had a wider agenda' and that far from being spontaneous, the walk-out at the airport had been 'instigated and encouraged by SIPTU activists in airport-based companies. Such action cannot be condoned.'

Aer Rianta also felt the lash. The report found a 'negative attitude' to Aer Rianta's performance on the part of other airport users. 'In the opinion of airport users Aer Rianta did not have effective arrangements in place to maintain a safe and secure environment for passengers, airport operators and their staff during the weekend of the dispute,' the report noted. 'Most airport-based companies were especially critical of airport police, who are employees of Aer Rianta and members of SIPTU', for joining the strikers.

O'Leary was uncharacteristically quiet the week the report came out and delegated responsibility for public relations to Cawley. He chose Dublin newspaper the *Sunday Business Post* for his one interview and stuck rigidly to the company's mantra. Ryanair, he said, had no problem with recognizing a union if the majority of staff wanted it, which they did not — a stance that sat uneasily with the fact that the majority of Ryanair's baggage handlers had, indeed, wanted union representation. O'Leary, however, did not see his workforce as autonomous units; union recognition would require majority approval from all the staff, not majorities from separate groups of workers. He also defended Ryanair's decision not to engage with the Labour Court earlier on in the dispute. Cawley, meanwhile, admitted that the airline had failed to manage the media as effectively as it could have. 'The biggest flaw in our campaign was on the PR side,' he said. 'We didn't manage it well – in fact we made a complete mess of it. We never anticipated thirty-nine people could get so much exposure and oxygen.'

In September 1998 Ryanair suffered a setback in another of its long-running battles. This one dated back to December 1994, when the airline had taken a case to the European Court of First Instance, challenging parts of the Irish state's £175 million aid package for Aer Lingus, which had been sanctioned by the European Commission the previous year.

Under the terms of the agreement, payments of £50 million in both 1994 and 1995 were contingent on Aer Lingus achieving cost reductions of £50 million. Aer Lingus fell short of this target by £7.6 million, but the commission accepted that Aer Lingus could have the £100 million because 'substantial progress' had been made. Ryanair disagreed, claiming that since the conditions had not been met the aid should not have been paid. Ryanair also argued that the commission's decision to overlook the fact that Aer Lingus flights from Dublin to UK provincial cities were run at a loss meant that the aid was in breach of EEC rules.

For O'Leary it was just another front in his battle with Aer Lingus. In 1993 he and Conor Hayes, then Ryanair's chief executive, had opposed Aer Lingus's plans to set up their own low-cost airline, Aer Lingus Express, claiming that the proposed carrier would represent illegally subsidized competition and could 'ultimately lead to the demise of Ryanair, albeit at enormous cost to Aer Lingus'. The plan was eventually shelved by Aer Lingus. In 1995 Ryanair complained about Aer Lingus's plan to introduce new planes on their Dublin–London routes, asserting that the number of seats on the planes would break the terms of the 1993 state aid agreement. His legal challenges were guerrilla tactics, designed to distract Aer Lingus from the serious business of competition, and launched because he knew that the bureaucratic mindset at the state-owned airline would devote money and management time to refuting the allegations – far more time than he would spend on making them. His actions were not frivolous – he always had a point to make, however narrow – but they were vexatious.

In September 1998 the European Court of Justice eventually ruled that while Aer Lingus had been in breach of the conditions set out, the commission was entitled to exercise a degree of 'discretion' on the matter. Regarding the loss-making routes to the UK, the court said that while the government was obliged to ensure that such routes were not subsidized, that did not mean that a group like Aer Lingus could never operate a route at a loss. Aer Lingus could keep its money and its routes, but O'Leary still claimed vindication because the commission had upheld his argument that taxpayers' money should not be used to subsidize loss-making routes. The court, though, ruled that Ryanair should pay all the costs of the action.

For Ryanair the setback was minimal. It had made record profits of £39.8 million for the year ending 31 March 1998, on a turnover of £182.6 million. The airline had also just announced pre-tax profits of £9.2 million for March–June 1998, up almost 20 per cent on pre-tax profits for the same quarter of 1997. Aer Lingus, in contrast, was still struggling, with its operating profits wiped out by the losses it had incurred selling a subsidiary and its heavily unionized workforce denying it the flexibility to adapt to the escalating challenges posed by Ryanair and other low-fare operators. Once again the state airline was lurching towards crisis, while O'Leary drove Ryanair to a new level.

Yet another series of battles arose from the EU's plan to end the sale of duty-free goods between member states, which was set to come into force in 1998. Stansted airport feared an immediate fall in its retail revenues and decided to repair its finances by hiking landing charges by 15 per cent. O'Leary was having none of it. On 23 September he announced that Ryanair would halt its expansion from Stansted if BAA, Stansted's owner, forged ahead with the proposed increase in charges. 'If BAA goes ahead with this, we will not start any more new services through Stansted,' he said. 'We will go to an airport that is more growth orientated.'

At the time eleven of Ryanair's twenty-four routes were from Stansted, and the airport had been the focus of much of its European growth, with recent route launches to new Italian and French destinations. But O'Leary said future growth could easily be from another British airport such as Luton or Birmingham, or from an airport on the continent. The threat to Stansted was deadly serious, says Tim Jeans. 'At the time, and to this day, there was capacity at Luton,' he says. 'We wouldn't have pulled out of Stansted but we could certainly have driven future expansion from Luton.'

A week later O'Leary showed no such restraint when he threatened a total withdrawal from Dublin airport – Ryanair's biggest base, with five planes and fourteen routes – if charges there were not reduced. He made the threat after Ryanair's AGM, describing Dublin as the most expensive of the twenty-five airports used by the airline. As with Stansted, the row was created by Dublin's reaction to the impending cessation of duty-free sales. Where the UK airport wanted to raise landing charges, Dublin wanted to end its rebate scheme, which rewarded airlines for reaching pre-agreed growth targets by reducing landing charges.

'Our total payments [to Dublin airport] amounted to about £8 million this year,' O'Leary said. 'If those rebates go, those will rise to about £15 million every year.' He said that Ryanair was looking at a number of solutions to the problem at Dublin airport, including building its own terminal, and that the airline was 'indifferent' to whether a deal was done at Dublin or not, pointing out that the future was in European growth, which could just as easily be managed from the UK.

'If it [a deal at Dublin airport] is not done by Christmas, we will be gone,' O'Leary said. 'The government has to make up its mind what it wants to do.' It was a wild threat – Ryanair would expand elsewhere, but it would not pull out of a large and profitable market because its growth potential was being curtailed.

Aer Rianta was publicly unconcerned about O'Leary's threat – which was made less potent by Richard Branson, head of Virgin Express, who said he would be happy to fill any gap left by Ryanair at Dublin. 'If Ryanair pulls out over landing charges we'll take over,' Branson told journalists. 'I've no wish to undermine Ryanair or put them in a negative position, but if they really did pull out we'll step in. It's a very competitive market today.' In the event, Ryanair did not withdraw a single route from the airport, but Dublin did not get a new route from Ryanair for another three years.

O'Leary meanwhile stepped up the pressure on Stansted by announcing a ten-year deal with Prestwick in early October. O'Leary could now argue that he had a second viable base from which to drive growth in flights from the UK to continental Europe. But when Go announced that it was planning a major expansion from Stansted in early September, Ryanair's attitude towards the airport changed. Go claimed to be hiring up to 200 staff and said it was in talks with several new European destinations. Far from suspending growth from Stansted, all of the seven new routes launched by Ryanair the following year were either to or from the airport, and the dispute about landing charges was fudged.

For O'Leary, part of the beauty of low-cost travel was that it generated huge volumes of travelling passengers. While they were on his planes they represented a captive audience, sitting in their seats for an hour or more with nothing to do and with plenty of money to spend. The psychology of the early travellers – one that has receded as low fares become the norm across Europe – was that the money they had saved by flying Ryanair could be spent on other things: hotels, hired cars, restaurants, gifts. O'Leary wanted to get his hands on as much of that spare cash as he could, maximizing his revenues from every passenger.

In the 1996 fiscal year ancillary revenue had contributed 17.2 per cent of total revenue, but by 1997 it had fallen back to 11.8 per cent, partly as a result of Ryanair's abandonment of cargo and charter flights. However, in October 1998 Ryanair embarked on a new stream of ancillary revenue – a tie-in with car rental company Hertz.

Hertz approached Ryanair about the possibility of a deal, and Michael Cawley and Tim Jeans were dispatched to see what could be done. 'Other airlines were already doing it, so our deal was not particularly special, other than the fact that our commission rates were probably higher. And we felt that because we were still the young mavericks, it was nice to have the imprimatur of somebody like Hertz,' says Jeans.

The initial deal between Ryanair and Hertz involved Hertz offering preferential fly-drive rates to Ryanair passengers and paying the airline a percentage of the sale price. 'The great thing was that the secondary airports created a vast market for car hire,' says Jeans. 'Because how were people going to get from Carcassonne to wherever? It became part of the Ryanair folklore that if you were hiring a car you had to sit at the front of the flight and leave your wife and children struggling with the baggage so you could be first in the queue at the car hire desk, otherwise if you were at the back of the queue you'd be waiting well in excess of an hour.'

Ryanair's other ancillary ventures – Ryanair Telecom, Ryanair credit cards and even Ryanair mortgages – would come and go, but the deal with Hertz has gone on to become a staple of Ryanair's revenue. By the 2005 financial year car hire accounted for 15 per cent of all ancillary revenue and 5 per cent of total revenue. At the time the deal was not seen as monumental. 'There wasn't any particular bunting put up in the office,' says Jeans. 'It was just another deal.'

14. Opening New Fronts

On 6 November 1998 the *Irish Times* published a letter from Michael O'Leary.

There is something incongruous in the Tourism Minister's speech of Monday evening last in which he warned the tourist industry here 'not to get too greedy and price itself out of the market'. Yet while he is warning the industry, the Government-owned airport monopoly Aer Rianta is planning to significantly increase charges to airlines at Dublin next year by doing away with existing rebates and discounts.

Both Ryanair and Aer Lingus have confirmed that if Aer Rianta's charges rise, then traffic growth will cease, and new route development plans will have to be reviewed. We need lower charges at Dublin Airport because this will mean lower air fares, more visitors and more jobs. If tourists are not to be fleeced next year, then the Government should start at its own Cabinet table and require Aer Rianta to lower existing charges. Ryanair for its part will respond with lower fares, and new routes from European destinations.

O'Leary's next step was to launch a £200,000 campaign to get the public involved in Ryanair's quest for lower charges at Dublin airport. In mid-November the airline asked its passengers to fill out a form designed as a ballot paper, where a vote for Ryanair was a vote for more routes, more passengers, more tourists and more jobs and a vote for Aer Rianta was a vote for the opposite. A vote also guaranteed passengers entry to a draw for a weekend for two in New York.

'I think we have to get the public voice, to bring to the consumer's attention this campaign, because that is what we need to influence the politicians,' O'Leary told journalists. 'When the public makes its views known, the politicians tend to listen.'

Aer Rianta remained unmoved by Ryanair's latest stunt. 'Traffic is going to grow by 1.2 million passengers this year – just 0.2 million of that is from Ryanair,' said the airport authority's public relations manager, Flan Clune. 'Ryanair is part of the growth but no longer the total.'

Two days after the votes campaign began Aer Rianta chief executive John Burke sent a letter of his own to the *Irish Times* in response to O'Leary's letter of 6 November. 'Airport charges are one of the smallest elements of all the costs involved, accounting for just 3 to 4 per cent of airline operating costs,' Burke wrote. 'It is not credible to suggest that a charge which is lower than the local bus-fare to an airport would influence a decision on whether to take a holiday or not. This debate has much more to do with Ryanair's profitability than it has to do with tourism.'

Burke argued that Aer Rianta would not be retaining its discount scheme at Dublin airport 'simply because, with double digit growth, there is no need . . . Ryanair, on the back of a spurious tourism argument, is lobbying for its current average payment of £1.93 per passenger to Aer Rianta to be reduced to a flat 50p. A 50p airport charge would do little more than cover the electricity and gas bills at Dublin Airport. No other airline is looking for nor would expect such a deal. I am sure Mr McDaid [the tourism minister] was not referring to Aer Rianta when he mentioned greed.'

Two weeks later Ryanair took another swipe at Aer Rianta, this time claiming that the airline had cancelled plans to operate five new routes from Dublin to mainland European cities because Dublin airport was 'too expensive'. Ryanair claimed the new destinations would have been in Germany, Italy, Sweden, Norway and the south of France, with fares starting at around £70 return. The *Irish Times* reported that Ryanair had confessed that there was no way to independently verify that it had ever planned the routes, because the routes had only been discussed internally at Ryanair.

'Those routes weren't planned to the extent that we had them all scheduled and the aircraft allocated,' admits Tim Jeans. 'It was reasonably clear that it was going to be some time before Aer Rianta would be brought to heel. But it would be fair to say that had there been a breakthrough we would have done the routes. Airports all over Europe would have bitten our hands off to fly to Dublin.'

Ryanair gained some ground in mid-December when the EU heads of government acceded to a request from the Council of Europe and postponed the abolition of duty-free sales, which had been scheduled to happen on 30 June 1998. With the immediate threat of abolition removed, Aer Rianta's plans to do away with discounts were harder to defend, and opposition politicians began to pressure Transport Minister Mary O'Rourke into urging the airport authority to reconsider.

Its chief executive John Burke went on a PR offensive, giving an interview of his own to the *Irish Times*. The reporter noted that Burke's style 'differs radically from his high-profile opponent on airport charges, Michael O'Leary', and referred to Burke's 'soft voice' and 'the initial impression of shyness'. Burke was keen to set the record straight on Ryanair.

Firstly, it is too simple to say that Ryanair was the sole driver of growth at Dublin Airport over the past decade. They have brought a very welcome increase in passenger numbers and we have always acknowledged that. But they were helped to a large degree by a more favourable economic climate, by a drop in fuel prices equivalent to £20 per passenger and by government protection on some key routes to the UK. We in Aer Rianta were also as supportive as we could be, as we had been looking to introduce competition to Aer Lingus for some time ourselves.

And he was unwavering on the issue of charges. 'I would say we are reaching a point where our charges for a broad range of services are too low,' he said. 'As for airport landing charges, they only represent about 16 per cent of our total revenues. We are not aware of any commercial airport anywhere in the world where that proportion is as low.' Burke was also dismissive of Ryanair's complaint that Dublin airport was the most expensive of the twenty-six airports the airline dealt with.

Most of the airports they talk about are on the European continent and have a throughput of fewer than one million passengers per year, so they are not comparable. Why wouldn't a small secondary airport offer discounts to attract greater custom? But in our case where we are a mature commercial airport that is investing over £200m to expand facilities and cope with passenger numbers, it doesn't make sense to offer discounts any more.

Aer Rianta commissioned a report by accountants Price Waterhouse Coopers which found that higher charges were necessary to secure the airport's long-term future. O'Leary promptly dismissed the report as 'irrelevant' because it referred only to published airport charges, 'which none of the airlines actually pay, as Aer Rianta is well aware'.

O'Leary stewed, knowing the battle over Aer Rianta's charges would take months if not years to resolve. Withdrawing from the airport was not a viable option – despite its allegedly high charges, Dublin airport was one of Ryanair's biggest profit centres. But O'Leary wrote off Dublin for route launches. For the moment Stansted was where the future would lie, with Jeans expected to deliver sustained growth. The dynamics at Dublin also counted against O'Leary. In the UK and Europe Ryanair was used to being the dominant player in its negotiations with airports. Its growth had been hugely important to Stansted's emerging reputation as a viable London airport, while at smaller European airports like Charleroi and Beauvais Ryanair was the only reason the airports had prospered. In Dublin, however, Ryanair was still just a small player. It was important to Aer Rianta as a customer but not as valuable as Aer Lingus. The balance of power lay with the airport operator, not with O'Leary, and this was not a situation he was used to or comfortable with. So he railed and he blustered, but without leverage there was little he could do other than chase expansion away from Dublin.

In February 1999 O'Leary announced phase two of Ryanair's European expansion. Six new routes were announced from Stansted to destinations in Germany, France and Italy. Dublin was sidelined, and O'Leary goaded Aer Rianta, saying he would happily introduce ten new routes to the Irish capital over the next two years if only landing charges were reduced. 'The 1999 Stansted launches were the most significant of all the launches,' says Tim Jeans. 'Unless Ryanair could crack the UK to Europe market we were never going to grow beyond being a niche carrier to and from Ireland.'

The launches were to be staggered between April and July as Ryanair's new Boeing 737–800s came into service. The destinations – Genoa, Turin and Ancona in Italy; Hahn, which was to be Ryanair's Frankfurt; and Biarritz and Dinard in France – were chosen through a methodical selection procedure. 'They did very extensive research,' says Andreas Helfer, manager of the airport at Hahn. 'They employed a UK specialist company to cover all the potential airports in Europe, and they made a short list and then very comprehensively went through all of those airports.'

Flughafen Hahn had begun life as a military airbase. When Ryanair first began talking to the airport authorities, in late 1998, Hahn had just been designated a civilian airport but had no commercial traffic. The possibility of attracting airlines seemed remote; Hahn is seventy miles from Frankfurt, so when Ryanair appeared the airport management welcomed them disbelievingly. But doing business with Ryanair was to prove a challenge for the airport's new owners, Fraport AG. Fraport also owns Frankfurt's main airport, and the managers were used to dealing with full-service carriers. 'We had to learn the business concept behind Ryanair,' Helfer says. 'It was completely new in Germany at the time.'

Helfer says Ryanair were 'very very tough' negotiators. 'They were always very straightforward. They tell you what they want and ask whether you are prepared to give it to them or not. And if it's not okay then they leave you and you are not partners any more.' To the delight of Helfer and his Fraport colleagues Hahn eventually struck a ten-year deal with Ryanair. A near-dormant regional airport would, at a stroke, become a destination for hundreds of thousands of passengers.

If Hahn was delighted, Lufthansa, Germany's dominant airline, was unamused. 'We were ambushed by Lufthansa,' recalls Tim Jeans. The German airline decided to take Ryanair through the German courts, arguing that Ryanair should not be allowed to refer to Hahn as Frankfurt and seeking injunctions to prevent it from advertising the service. 'We had no German lawyers. We employed Caroline Baldwin, who was made the German sales manager, and Caroline was a fluent German speaker and gave us invaluable advice into the way Germans did business. But clearly what she didn't have, because she wasn't a lawyer, was an insight into the German legal system.'

So 'We winged it,' he says. Winging it, O'Leary style, meant fighting outside court. Ahead of a court case in Cologne O'Leary ran a free-ticket promotion on the Ryanair website, but with a twist. As Jeans recalls, O'Leary's message was, 'If you come to the courthouse in Cologne with a banner insulting Lufthansa we'll give you a free ticket on one of our flights from Hahn. A motley crew of a dozen Germans turned up – it was hardly the world's biggest demonstration – but by the time a dozen or so Ryanair staff turned up, armed with helpful placards disparaging Lufthansa, the riot police were called out because they thought that there was going to be a massive demonstration.'

The tactic worked. As word spread of the peculiar scenes outside the court, the media got interested. 'By the time the case was finished we were pursued out of the courtroom by six television cameras,' says Jeans. 'And by the time Ryanair took its first flight from Hahn, there wasn't a German with a pulse that didn't know that there was a low-cost airline flying from this place that purported to be Frankfurt but manifestly was not.'

Ryanair got an easier ride in France and Italy. 'Alitalia wouldn't know how to be predatory,' says Jeans. 'They were always in trouble and they were always in retreat. We didn't challenge Alitalia on any routes. Initially we flew to places like Pisa where they didn't fly. Before we came, if you wanted to go London–Pisa you went on a charter flight and people were being ripped off royally.'

In the early days France was a similarly soft market for Ryanair.

'Air France were in denial; they thought that if they woke up it would all have been a bad dream,' says Jeans. 'They had ceased serving the French market from London. By the time we came in they only served Lyon, Nice and Bordeaux and Paris. They were feeding their Paris hub from provincial UK airports. French airports were neglected.'

But in Scandinavia, where Ryanair had launched flights a year earlier, Ryanair had a hostile reception. SAS, indignant at having to share a market it had monopolized for decades, threatened to sue Ryanair over what it termed 'misleading advertisements'. The Ryanair ads, which appeared in Scandinavian newspapers, compared SAS and Ryanair's prices on the Oslo–London (or Torp–Stansted in Ryanair's case) route.

Encouraged by the hostile fire he was drawing from incumbent carriers and by third-quarter results, announced in early February, which once again showed record profits, O'Leary plotted more route launches. The more the flag carriers complained and took him to court, the more publicity O'Leary generated for Ryanair and the more passengers he attracted to his low fares.

He needed them; the new planes from Boeing were about to arrive. On 20 March, O'Leary's thirty-eighth birthday, Boeing delivered Ryanair's first new 737–800, with four more due later that year. It was a momentous occasion for the airline. For the previous fourteen years they had survived on a range of second-hand aircraft, from the first propeller craft, through the BAC One-Elevens, to the ageing Boeing 737–200s. Now the airline would have the latest planes to mount its assault on Europe.

O'Leary tried to put the delivery to good PR use, promptly announcing the new plane would fly neither to nor from Dublin, because of the ongoing Aer Rianta stand-off. It was a gambit to garner a few column inches, but it was an empty threat. Within a month the *Irish Times* had spotted the shiny new plane on the Stansted–Dublin route.

For several weeks now skywatchers have been reporting that Ryanair's new plane is indeed flying in and out of Dublin. This week, Ryanair confirmed this was the case, but described the journeys as 'proving flights' – the test-runs used by new pilots. The flights are, however, carrying fare-paying passengers on board. Ryanair now says this plane will not be used in Dublin for long, and that when the summer schedule starts, it will be moved to Stansted for routes to the Continent only.

Foreign airlines might have been easy prey for O'Leary, but at home the media had grown wise to his stunts.

Less than two years after Ryanair launched its route between Stansted and Kerry, with the route a success and tourism numbers on the rise, Kerry airport was looking to expand. The expansion would need funding, and the airport's management decided the best way to secure that funding was a £5 'development levy' to be paid by all departing passengers from 1 May.

In April O'Leary took to the newspapers and airwaves, denouncing the charge – which would add 6.25 per cent to its lowest fares of about £80 on the route – as 'unworkable' and urging passengers to refuse to pay it. A former Kerry executive says the airport was surprised by Ryanair's reaction. 'On the [first] anniversary of our first flight [June 1997] we said to Ryanair, "Listen, we're going to bring in this thing,"' he says. 'They said, "Grand." They didn't seem too perturbed. And then they just decided against it, I think on the basis that if this was successfully introduced in Kerry this would happen everywhere and it would be a bad precedent for Ryanair to accept it.'

He was right. What was the point, O'Leary thought, of winning lower airport charges if a small-time operator like Kerry could then turn around and introduce new levies on his passengers? If he allowed Kerry to charge his passengers five pounds, how could he prevent them charging ten? Or object if Treviso or Charleroi introduced similar charges? Kerry had negotiated low landing charges with Ryanair in good faith, and Ryanair had delivered the passengers. The airport's opportunity was to make money from those passengers by selling them goods and services, not by slapping on levies.

The Irish media, however, was instinctively sympathetic to Kerry and growing tired of O'Leary's relentless hostility, with the *Irish Independent* reporting, 'Ryanair, the discount airline, has declared war on yet another Irish airport.' O'Leary did not care about the media's attitude and rolled out another pamphlet campaign, distributing 20,000 'No to Kerry levy' leaflets on Kerry–Stansted flights. 'They handed them out for about a week,' says Bellew. 'We just thought, fair enough, if that's what they want to do. We weren't happy about it, I suppose, but it was just a bit of a nuisance.'

The leaflet's impact was limited to the felling of a few trees, and the levy stayed, for the moment.

A year on from the IPO, Ryanair was still perceived as a family firm. The Ryans were no longer the airline's sole shareholders, but about 27.7 per cent of the airline's stock was still controlled by Tony, Declan, Cathal and Shane Ryan. At the end of May 1999 the company moved to correct that, announcing that the airline's major stakeholders would sell a total of 15 per cent of Ryanair's equity valued at about GB£168 million. The Ryans would reduce their holding by a third, leaving them with just over 17 per cent of the stock, and Ryanair would become a more attractive proposition to investors, who often shy away from companies where families exert a dominant influence. Bonderman was to almost halve his interest, reducing his 6.3 per cent stake to 3.2. O'Leary disposed of 1.5 per cent of the company, retaining a 9.3 per cent stake.

The timing of the share sale was critical to its success and Ryanair opted to synchronize it with the announcement of its fourth-quarter results for 1998. The results once again showed record highs, with a 20 per cent rise in adjusted net earnings (to £37.7 million) and a 28 per cent rise in turnover to £182.6 million, and earnings per share up 11 per cent to 27.47 pence.

Ryanair also had good news on its protracted row over Dublin airport charges. Aer Rianta had insisted it would cease all rebates for airlines, but at the end of May had submitted a plan to Transport

Minister Mary O'Rourke that would allow operators of new routes a 75 per cent discount on charges for the first year and a 50 per cent discount for year two. The compromise offer represented some progress: Aer Rianta was clearly prepared to encourage new routes with lower charges. But the plan fell short of Ryanair's demands, and the market responded negatively to the news: the airline's share price dropped 14 per cent, to GB£6.69. It was a short-lived plunge. The sale of the Ryan family, O'Leary and Bonderman shares proved a resounding success, with the share price closing at an all-time high of GB£7.30 on the day of the sale.

The Ryans, who had almost lost everything five years earlier after the collapse of Tony Ryan's Guinness Peat Aviation, grossed £137.3 million, Irish Air grossed £34.3 million and Michael O'Leary got £16.6 million.

Dublin, Stansted, Kerry and then Manchester. Early in 1999 Ryanair's five-year deal with Manchester airport came up for renewal. The airport seized upon Ryanair's improved financial position to demand higher landing charges. O'Leary was not impressed. 'Michael decided that he would withhold some of the increase whilst in theory we would continue to try to negotiate a more acceptable cost base,' says Tim Jeans. 'Ryanair had delivered on all its promises in Manchester, and Manchester then flexed its monopoly muscles, hid behind the fact that it had to charge all airlines the same, which of course is nonsense because there are all sorts of one-off arrangements.'

O'Leary's tactic of non-payment worked well for a few months, but by June Manchester airport had had enough. On 19 June flight 553 from Dublin arrived in Manchester fifteen minutes ahead of schedule. The airport staff directed the plane, with 126 passengers on board, to a taxiing area for impounded planes. The airport then sent a blunt message to Ryanair: pay us what you owe us – rumoured to be about £500,000 – or you won't get your plane back. The passengers and crew were allowed to disembark but the plane had been seized.

O'Leary caved in. The debt paled in comparison to the value of his Boeing 737 and to the chaos that would hit Ryanair's schedules if it was deprived of a jet. Within five hours of the seizure Ryanair's bank had given a verbal guarantee that the debt would be paid, and the plane was released.

The airline was quick to criticize the airport for its actions, claiming the non-payment had been a 'clerical error'. But, Jeans says, the seizure had longer-term implications for the airport. 'It did have an impact on our relationship with Manchester ever after.' Ethel Power agrees:

We were not expecting it as we had done a lot of business with Manchester airport. Basically it was Manchester airport being bolshie, as Ryanair would always be negotiating lower landing fees, and in my opinion it was an airport manager saying, 'I'll fix them.' But really it could have backfired in their face as Manchester airport had an awful lot more to lose than Ryanair. In our world it was a one-minute wonder – bill was paid and away we went.

Manchester manager Jim Stockton was unrepentant. 'I agree the powers we exercised were severe but they were justified in the circumstances,' Stockton told journalists. Seven years later, his views haven't changed. 'If we hadn't acted as we did, we would never have been paid what we were owed, and the scale of the debt would have grown each day. We had no choice.'

In August of 1999 the military airfield at Baldonnel in west Dublin returned to the spotlight when Defence Minister Michael Smith brought forward plans to sell off parts of it. Tony Ryan, who had first proposed setting up a commercial airport there in 1995, latched on to the news, terming it a 'very positive development'. But O'Leary was quick to distance Ryanair from the future of Baldonnel, pointing out that it was 'important that the Ryan family's plans for Baldonnel do not cloud the debate' on the second terminal at Dublin airport. It was a rare public spat between the two men, but O'Leary's motivation was clinical.

'Michael would have been annoyed that we were perceived to be fighting on two fronts,' says Charlie Clifton. 'His view was, "Get Aer Rianta to give us a deal; don't let them off the hook." Aer Rianta did start to say, "What are we talking to these guys about when they're pissing off down the road to Baldonnel?" And that's what he didn't want to happen. Michael's view was succinct: "Draw a line on Baldonnel, we're never going to get it."'

O'Leary tried to drag the question of a second Dublin airport terminal back to centre stage in early August in a 445-word letter to the *Irish Times*. He began by congratulating the paper's editor, Conor Brady, on an editorial which recognized the value of tourism to the Irish economy. 'Unfortunately the Aer Rianta monopoly represents a far greater threat to the health of our industry than Bord Failte [Ireland's tourist agency],' he wrote.

The facilities at Dublin Airport are inadequate, overcrowded, and ludicrously expensive. They are a testament to the failure of the Aer Rianta monopoly. The Irish taxpayer – through Aer Rianta – is investing heavily in hotels and airports in Birmingham and Düsseldorf [a reference to Aer Rianta's expansion overseas] – yet we are subjected to Third-World facilities at this nation's principal airport.

Ryanair has submitted a proposal to the Government which would see us finance and build a second terminal at Dublin [he reminded readers, in case they had managed to miss the acres of media coverage which had been dedicated to the issue]. Immediately after its construction we will hand this building, free of charge, back to Aer Rianta to own and manage. In return we would obtain a long-term low cost base, save Aer Rianta from the capital expenditure, launch at least ten new routes from Continental Europe to Ireland, carry over one million additional visitors to/from Ireland, and create over 500 jobs.

He concluded:

In recent years competition has transformed Ireland's airline sector, our telecommunications industry, our bus services, health insurance and broadcasting. Even the ESB will shortly be in a competitive environment.

Competition will transform our airport infrastructure by improving facilities and lowering costs. Aer Rianta now needs a similar discipline. Why not introduce competition now at Dublin? The facilities will be improved, the costs will fall, and low fares to a wide range of European cities will underpin the continuing success of our tourism industry.

Noel Hanlon, Aer Rianta's chairman, rose to the bait. Three days later he made his own appearance in the letters page of the *Irish Times*. It was a peculiar way for the leaders of two major companies to conduct business but such was the level of animosity between the two that direct negotiation was not on the agenda. Hanlon wasted no time in getting to the point.

Independent consultants have concluded that Ryanair's proposal to build its own terminal at Dublin Airport would mean the transfer of between £70 million and £80 million by Aer Rianta to Ryanair over a short period, hence Mr O'Leary's enthusiasm for such a proposal. Aer Rianta is the most competitive commercial airport company in Europe and frequent reference to the airport monopoly by Mr O'Leary does not change that fact.

Hanlon charged, 'Mr O'Leary's quite extravagant claims about bringing in one million additional visitors from Europe is, I would suggest, a nice round figure but one which is very hard to accept.' He finished his letter by spelling out what he claimed were Ryanair's true motives. 'I can only conclude that the constant barrage of spurious claims, frequently couched in superficially plausible language, from Ryanair and its highly paid spin doctors is more to do with Ryanair profits and its share price than with bringing in additional tourists to Ireland.'

Hanlon was correct, up to a point. O'Leary was primarily concerned with Ryanair's profits and not Irish tourism, but the two were not mutually exclusive. He wanted to exploit opportunities in Ireland but believed that he could not do so profitably enough unless Aer Rianta compromised.

★

Three days later Ryanair announced yet another set of record results, this time for the first quarter of the new financial year. Its pre-tax profit for the three months to the end of June had risen by 13 per cent to £14.2 million.

O'Leary always attributed Ryanair's success to its 'simple' business model.

We have the lowest cost base of any airline in Europe. Business is simple. You buy it for this, you sell it for that, and the bit in the middle is ultimately your profit or loss. We have low-cost aircraft, low-cost airport deals, we don't provide frills, we pay travel agents less [than other airlines], our people are well paid but work hard and we deal in efficiencies. A second low-cost airline will only survive in Ireland as long as it is prepared to keep losing money. Britain is a tougher market, but even there nobody can match our efficiency.

Other airlines were failing to implement the same formula with success because, he said, 'nobody else has our discipline.' It was a fair point. As Kerry had discovered, no airport was too small to escape his notice, no charge too minimal to be ignored. O'Leary's pursuit of lower costs was relentless. 'It was a war, a daily war,' says one former executive. 'Michael never stopped hunting for ways of cutting costs or boosting revenues, and his message was really simple: lowest costs means lowest fares.'

Aircraft turnaround time had been reduced to twenty-five minutes, compared with the one-hour turnaround that major airlines were used to at large airports. To achieve this Ryanair refused to sell peanuts, chocolate and other food so that it would take less time to clean the plane before take-off. 'We can fly six aircraft a day where Aer Lingus or British Airways could fly four,' O'Leary explained. 'Where they can get six in the air, we fly eight. So we're 20–25 per cent more efficient from the very start. It's so simple a four-year-old could work it out.' Ryanair's flights were staffed by three flight attendants, compared with the five used by other carriers; its planes were all one type, so that crews and pilots could move seamlessly from one to another without retraining, while maintenance costs were kept to a minimum.

No employee was in any doubt about the company's mission, or its style. Where rivals baulked at the simplicity of the Ryanair model, they paid the price with higher costs. For O'Leary there was no middle ground. He did not want to be a little bit cheaper and a little bit more efficient than the major airlines. He wanted revolution, not evolution: fares that were eye-wateringly low, matched by costs that were lower still, generating ever-rising passenger traffic and ever-rising profits. There was no magic formula, no creative accounting, just hard work, obsession and relentless aggression.

The airline industry had begun to notice Ryanair's skill. At the Paris Air Show the following June the airline was presented with the Best Managed National Airline award, a rare accolade from its peers. But far from becoming complacent, O'Leary's plans for the airline were more ambitious than ever.

I think we can revolutionize Irish tourism to and from Europe, and I think it is a cause worth fighting for. We have a plan over the next five years to double the size of the airline again. This year we'll carry six million passengers; in five years time we want to carry twelve million passengers. That will make us Europe's fifth-biggest airline. My hope is that one million of those passengers will be on low-fare services from the Irish airports to Europe, but if not we'll continue to grow out of Stansted, and from points within Europe.

Ryanair's plans were all the more ambitious against the backdrop of an increasingly competitive European aviation market. When talking to investors, O'Leary expressed caution about the changing situation, pointing out, 'the trading environment is not all blue skies' and yields would be affected by the competitive nature of the market. He was much more bullish when talking to journalists. When asked in December if he was worried about competing with low-cost carriers out of Stansted, he responded with a laugh.

Hardly . . . Competition from other low-cost carriers is just not an issue. We compete with British Airways, Alitalia, Lufthansa, SAS on routes all over continental Europe. Why the hell would we fear Go? It's lost GB£21 million on a GB£41 million turnover. And Virgin Express is a tiny airline which has issued twelve profit warnings in the last four quarters. It's not an airline that anybody in Europe would fear or acknowledge as a serious threat.

The emergence of a flurry of new low-cost carriers had also concentrated some minds on possible alliances and mergers between the start-ups. Not O'Leary though. When asked about the prospect of a merger he replied, 'No thanks. I'd rather have a social disease.'

15. Dot-Com Revolution

As the end of the millennium drew near, technology swept all before it. The dot-com boom, which would implode in early 2000, was in full swing. The Internet, still a relatively new but fast developing phenomenon, was unavoidable; every business wanted to understand how to exploit its possibilities and was prepared to invest millions in the hope of hitting the Internet jackpot. The dot-com boom was based on the premise that profits did not matter. It was, in effect, a land grab, as new businesses raised money from credulous investors and then spent lavishly to achieve brand recognition. No matter their losses, the share prices of Internet companies were driven into the stratosphere on a wave of irrational exuberance. Few really knew how to make any money from the Internet, but investors were convinced that it represented a new world order.

O'Leary, though, was not prepared to rush in. EasyJet, his main rival in Europe's emerging low-cost industry, had sold its first seat online in April 1997 and even the slow-moving Aer Lingus had joined the information superhighway with a website, albeit with-out a regular online booking facility. O'Leary could see the possi-bilities but saw no need to be an innovator. 'Michael was hugely resistant to the Internet; he didn't sign on at all,' recalls Tim Jeans. 'Michael took a lot of convincing,' agrees Ethel Power. 'At that stage he didn't have a computer in his office.'

His opposition was not based on fear of technology or fear of the new; O'Leary was simply far from certain that the Internet could deliver what he wanted. He had dabbled the previous year, launching a brochure site which gave information on the airline's route network but had no booking facility. It was a presence, a toehold in the market, but nothing more.

By 1999, the case for a genuine Internet presence was growing stronger. EasyJet had led the way, and now other airlines had begun to successfully sell tickets online. Senior managers at Ryanair could see the Internet's promise as a business tool and knew that their company was in danger of being left behind.

Power says that Caroline Green, then chief executive of Ryanair Direct, was 'very very pushy about the website' and instrumental in getting it up and running. But Jeans says it was O'Leary's acceptance that the Internet had evolved into a serious proposition that could provide a quantum leap in cutting costs which ultimately propelled Ryanair into the digital age. 'We were trying to get better deals from [booking system companies] like Galileo and Amadeus. Michael and I traipsed around, and they really didn't take us seriously and would not budge on costs. They really didn't think that an airline could be run without them. What convinced us about the Internet, and what convinced Michael, because he needed to be convinced, was that easyJet were clearly making a very good fist of distributing their product entirely over the Internet.'

O'Leary could wait no longer. 'There are two different stories, both of which are actually true,' says O'Leary.

The truest is that for the first three or four years of the Internet I blocked any Internet development here. When easyJet first started off with its site, I said we are not doing the Internet for a very sane and obvious reason. At that stage 60 per cent of our sales were driven through travel agents. The software didn't exist to sell half of your tickets online . . . If you were selling through the travel agents you had to have the old tickets with the dye on the back of them and all our tickets had to be like that. We weren't set up to have both – old-style tickets through travel agents and email tickets as well. So I said that until we have the technology to get rid of the old tickets, we wait. Then later the technology came along where we could sell ticketless flights through the Internet and sell through travel agents as well. And that's when we went into the Internet. And [from that moment] I pushed the Internet in here. I blocked the Internet for about three years, and it was the right thing to do.

O'Leary wanted a site that was simple and cheap, and he did not want to be surrounded by computer consultants with ponytails and cargo pants. The first quotations for the Ryanair site came in at around £3 million, and O'Leary said no. There had to be a cheaper way. In order to minimize costs Ryanair opted to entrust the website design to two students – seventeen-year-old secondary school student John Beckett and twenty-two-year-old dentistry student Thomas Linehan.

'Michael couldn't bear having these dot-com guys come in with fancy brochures, talking about the corporate model. He just wanted a simple website that worked,' said Power. 'He used to get a great kick out of talking to the guys that did the website, I think he recognized the genius in them.'

Beckett and Linehan came to Ryanair's attention through the airline's recently appointed human resources director, Eddie Wilson. Wilson had previously been at computer firm Gateway, where Beckett and Linehan had worked during the summer. 'There was no tendering process for the contract,' recalls Beckett. 'They mentioned they had had these ridiculously high quotes of up to £3.5 million. They came to us because in the middle of a management meeting Eddie [Wilson] said, "I know a guy who might be able to do this for us, there's no harm in chatting to him."' The next day, while Beckett was sitting in a classroom in St Andrew's secondary school in Dublin, his mobile phone rang. It was Wilson, inviting him to come for a meeting with O'Leary and the Ryanair management.

'They wanted it done yesterday, is the quote they used,' says Beckett. 'So I gave them three prices: one was for setting up a site in a month, a slightly cheaper price for two months and cheaper again for three months.'

'Michael said, "Yeah, we want you to do it, but you'll have to reverse the cost of the three-month deal with the one-month deal."' O'Leary wanted the fastest job and the cheapest price, and the two students were no match for his negotiation techniques. 'I just said yeah, fair enough.' Beckett laughs. 'The prices we quoted – £17,500, £16,500 and £15,500, I think – were basically figures that we plucked out of our head, and we thought great. It was a smashing payday for us.'

Beckett and Linehan dealt mainly with Wilson, Michael Cawley and Sean Coyle, a rising young executive known as 'Mini-me' because of his ability to ape O'Leary's mannerisms. 'O'Leary's main concern was how long would it take and how much would it cost, and he was going to let everyone else worry about how it worked and what it did,' says Beckett.

The students' task was to create a website that would combine a simple marketing function – information on routes and special offers – with a sophisticated computerized booking system. Ryanair's telesales department was already using the Open Skies system, and the objective was to integrate it with the website. It was a complex job, and IBM was retained to create the bridge between the marketing element of the website and the booking system.

Despite the stories of O'Leary's technophobia, Beckett doesn't recall him as particularly computer illiterate.

I didn't get that from him. But maybe when I thought he was being shrewd by only looking at the things that affected him, like price and time, he was actually avoiding like the plague the technical side of things. He certainly seemed to know what he was talking about, but we were talking basic Internet design terms, 'We'll put the logo there, we'll put the links there,' that kind of thing. We didn't discuss platforms or anything like that with him. When we tried, he got up and left the room and said, 'I'll leave you to sort that out.'

When the job was done, O'Leary tried to hardball Beckett and Linehan, offering to pay £12,000 instead of the agreed £15,500. 'At that stage I knew he was in the wrong, so I stuck to my guns. They had signed what effectively was a purchase order – somebody signed the quote we had given them which outlined the price – but it was very informal.'

Beckett, however, did not stick too hard to those guns. Even though he and Linehan had produced a website for a fraction of what a design company would have charged, they were still beaten down on their original tender. 'Two schoolkids couldn't go up against Ryanair,' says Beckett, and O'Leary had no qualms about hardball negotiations with a schoolkid and student.

'Eddie gave us a cheque signed by Michael and Cawley,' he says. 'The last thing Eddie said to us, because we had invoiced them plus VAT, was, "I hope you're registered for VAT, are you?" They thought we were trying to squeeze an extra few pounds out of them.'

Beckett and Linehan thought the cheque signalled the end of their dealings with Ryanair, but they had forgotten one thing. Ryanair had been given a site designed to sell seats, not one that encouraged, or envisaged, interactivity with the airline. 'When we finished the site they didn't have a single email address at all for Ryanair on it,' recalls Beckett. 'And the phone number led to Ryanair reception. Sometimes you'd get an answer and sometimes you wouldn't.'

The only online contact details were for the site designers, Beckett and Linehan. 'A month after the launch we asked them to remove our contact info from the site. It was huge publicity for us but it was getting ridiculous. We would get hundreds of emails every day saying, "This is a disgrace, my ticket blah blah blah, my flight was delayed." We were like, what do you want us to do about it, we are web designers, we've got nothing to do with Ryanair at all . . .'

To drive Internet sales up, Ryanair began to shut down their other sales channels. It was a high-risk strategy. Just under half of Ryanair's business came through travel agents, with the balance coming from direct telesales. Internet penetration in Ireland was still well below the European average and years behind the US, but having made the decision to go with the Internet, O'Leary would tolerate no half measures.

'We were taking nearly 40 per cent of our passengers through Galileo and most of the [other] airlines were too,' says Jeans.

We took the decision to turn Galileo off. Travel agents could still book seats for their clients, but they would have to use Ryanair's own Internet site rather than the Galileo system. But booking direct meant there would be no commission. The theory was that if people wanted low fares there was only one place to go, and that was Ryanair.com. The carrot was the low fares and the stick was you couldn't get it from anywhere else.

The booking options had been reduced to just two routes – Ryanair's own Internet site and its telephone sales operation Ryanair Direct. There would be no more travel agents and no more commissions. Just as significantly, the new technology would give Ryanair complete and instant knowledge of every booking on every route, as soon as that booking was made.

Online booking catapulted the airline's accessibility to a new level. People no longer had to traipse down to a travel agent to make a reservation or endure long periods on hold for Ryanair's reservation centre. Instead, they could choose to book a ticket whenever they wanted, and the whole transaction could be completed in a few minutes.

With the aid of the Internet, Ryanair's growth was beginning to change the lives of a generation. For decades scheduled air travel in Europe had been the preserve of the moneyed classes, but now hopping on a plane was becoming as easy and familiar as hopping on a bus. Importantly, too, the young Irish had money to spend because the economy was booming.

Once one of the poorest and least progressive in Europe, Ireland's economy had been growing at a phenomenal rate. The country was in the grip of a virtuous economic cycle, with surging employment delivering high tax revenues for government, which in turn spent ever more on the nation's infrastructure, further fuelling the boom. The demographics were young – in 1999 40 per cent of the population was under twenty-five – and the traditional powers in Irish society were falling away. The Roman Catholic Church, the moral power behind Irish governments up until the late 1980s, had been brought to its knees by emerging stories of systemic child sexual abuse by parish priests and in Church-run institutions, and Ireland's political class was rocked by allegations of corruption at the highest levels of the establishment, allegations that prompted the creation of a series of public tribunals of inquiry which would expose a rotten culture of self-aggrandizement.

Freed of the inhibitions that had governed their parents and grandparents Ireland's youth was letting down its hair. Instead of being forced to emigrate, as half a million had in the decade from 1979 to 1989, they were able to get jobs at home and had money to spend. They had the world at their feet, and Ryanair was the airline to help them explore it.

Irish pilots were among the direct beneficiaries of the airline's growth. In the late 1990s opportunities for pilots in Ireland were few and far between. Aer Lingus, which was finally carving out a modest profit after its latest reconstruction, was not expanding, and carriers with smaller planes, such as Aer Arann, were not an attractive prospect to men and women who dreamed of flying the newest jet aircraft. 'I joined in 1999,' says one pilot who is now a captain with the airline. 'It was the only job for pilots. It was a different time. Before that there was no jobs. You got a job with Aer Lingus if you were very lucky, or you flew little aeroplanes for small companies like Iona. When Ryanair [started to expand] there was lots of jobs.'

Aer Lingus was still offering a small number of highly coveted cadetships, which included fully paid training for new pilots, but at Ryanair things were different. 'It was do it yourself,' says one pilot. 'Ryanair would train you on the 737, and the cost of the training was taken out of your salary over the next three years.' Ryanair's pilots also learned that flexibility was an absolute require-ment of the job. 'You join the company, and the contract says you can be sent to any base at any time,' says the pilot. Back in 1999 the only other base was Stansted.

'I hated Stansted,' says one staff member who was based there. 'It is not London, it is forty minutes on the train from London. It's like living in Naas [a satellite town some thirty miles from Dublin] and saying you live in Dublin.'

O'Leary's doggedness, his refusal to let even the smallest irritation remain unscratched, came as a shock to Kerry airport in the late summer of 1999. The airport's management had hoped that the temporary furore caused by its decision to introduce a £5 levy on passengers would fade away and that O'Leary would learn to live with a minor inconvenience.

'The levy had operated peacefully for a couple of months,' says a former Kerry executive. Ryanair's pamphlet campaign against the charge had had an impact – about half the passengers at the airport refused to pay, while the other half handed over their £5 without a murmur. Those who would not pay were still allowed to board their flights as Kerry sought to raise money and avoid controversy. 'And then,' he says, 'without much discussion either way, Ryanair went down the legal route. In a way we weren't surprised, because to be honest nothing would ever surprise me with Ryanair.'

O'Leary, frustrated by the airport's persistence, had decided to force the issue to a conclusion. Ryanair, according to the executive, argued that 'the terms of the particular agreement they had with us stipulated that additional charges could not be imposed. They argued that even if they were not imposed directly on Ryanair they could not be imposed on passengers using Ryanair.'

What had started as a minor row, a scuffle over a small charge at a relatively unimportant airport, escalated into a bitter dispute that would now demand a disproportionate amount of Ryanair's management time. O'Leary, though, was sending out a clear message to all other regional airports. In early August he had threatened to 're-evaluate' Ryanair's future at Kerry if the levy was not dropped, but his threats had been ignored.

So he took his battle to the High Court. The Irish courts are practically dormant in August, as barristers and judges swap the Four Courts for their annual holidays, so Ryanair applied for a temporary injunction to prevent Kerry airport from levying the fee until the courts returned to normal service in September. The job of marketing the legal challenge to the media fell to Michael Cawley, Ryanair's then commercial director. 'We left a legal challenge until now because we thought the airport management would come to their senses,' Cawley told journalists. 'At this stage, however, things have got out of hand.'

The legal battle was to prove complex and costly. The High Court initially granted Ryanair's injunction in September, but the airport was subsequently granted a stay against the injunction so it could appeal to the Supreme Court. The Supreme Court backed Ryanair, and Kerry airport was once again prevented from applying the charge until a full hearing had been arranged in the High Court.

As costs rose, settlement became a priority for the airport, which did not have the deep pockets required for a lengthy legal battle. 'It got very bitter towards the end,' says the executive, 'and it was going to start getting very expensive. On top of that Ryanair had cut back some flights, so it was down to three or four days a week. It just didn't make any sense for them or us to prolong it.' He says that it came to a head when Peter Bellew, a senior manager at the airport, received notice that he was going to be a star witness at the legal hearing. 'Bellew just said enough was enough. He was about to go on holiday, his wife was pregnant and it was a stupid dispute,' the former executive says.

Bellew reckoned that a full legal hearing could be embarrassing and potentially damaging for Ryanair because once 'you get into the discovery of documents, we could have sought discovery of all the deals they had made across Europe. It didn't make sense for two Irish companies to be fighting each other like that.'

With a settlement his sole objective, Bellew called O'Leary. 'He said, "Listen, lads, I don't know anything about the lawyers, but can we not sort this out?" He had to listen to a bit of a tirade for a few minutes and then he said, "So what do you want?" And O'Leary mentioned a figure to sort it out that was ridiculous. Bellew said a figure and O'Leary said, "No no no, I can't do that." And Bellew said, "Go on go on go on go on" like Mrs Doyle [a character in *Father Ted*] and he started laughing. Michael Cawley was on the speaker phone as well and he started laughing as well.'

Eventually, a figure was agreed and O'Leary insisted on immediate closure. 'He agreed the figure, and then said, "If we don't get all the paperwork done by four o'clock it's double that, and if we don't get agreement by tonight it's treble that."' Bellew met the deadline, and peace was re-established. 'They [Ryanair] very publicly acknowledged that it had been sorted out and that we were back on level ground,' says the executive, 'and they acknowledged very publicly that even while the legal [dispute] had been going on that operationally our relationship had always gone well. And then they had a seat sale.'

Once again, O'Leary capitalized on media coverage of a dispute to promote routes and sell tickets. At the same time he won his battle by eradicating the levy. It was a comprehensive victory over a tiny, vulnerable airport operator. For once O'Leary had been Goliath, and he had shown no mercy.

While Kerry rolled over, Aer Rianta was a much more resilient foe. The trigger for renewed hostilities was the government's plan to break up the state monopoly, replacing it with separate authorities to run the airports at Dublin, Cork and Shannon. There was widespread speculation that Shannon would be the first piece of the Aer Rianta jigsaw to be hived off.

Shannon's fortunes were largely dependent on an archaic quirk of Ireland's bilateral air travel agreements with the United States, which required a large percentage of flights to the US to touch down there even though it was just twenty minutes' flight time from Dublin airport. The rule had been designed to save Shannon from closure. Europe's westernmost airport, technological advances in air and jet travel since the 1950s had made it redundant. Modern airliners could travel with ease from the US to Dublin, London or any European capital without the need to refuel at Shannon. Ireland, however, had continued to insist on the rule because successive governments feared that the airport had no future without it.

O'Leary disagreed. He announced that he would bring five new routes to the airport in a move that would create 150 jobs – but only on condition the government supported his plan for a second, independent, terminal for Dublin airport. 'The Shannon proposal was O'Leary's idea,' Tim Jeans says. 'Shannon was on its knees, and we thought we could use it for leverage. Dublin was the big prize. If we could transform Dublin into a long-term low-cost base, no stone would be left unturned.'

It was a smart piece of opportunism. O'Leary was confident that Shannon could sustain new routes – lying on Ireland's western coast, the airport is well located for tourist traffic heading north towards Galway or south to Kerry – and he knew that without new route development, Shannon's future was in serious peril.

The Irish government faced a stark choice. On one side they had TDs and businesses from the west of Ireland lobbying for the salvation of their airport; on the other they had Aer Rianta and SIPTU, who were both determined to resist Ryanair's vision for Dublin, no matter the cost. O'Leary further stirred the waters by claiming that Mary O'Rourke, the minister for transport, had invited him to make proposals that could help Shannon. 'She came to us last May and asked us to come up with a plan in Shannon,' he said. 'Shannon will always be politically sensitive until someone goes in and puts some traffic in there. We can do that.'

But O'Rourke baulked at the price that O'Leary wanted to extract. 'I think it is awful that Mr O'Leary is asking for a slice of Dublin airport as part of the deal,' she said. 'It would seem that he doesn't want to come back to Shannon, and he seems determined on the coupling of the Dublin and Shannon proposals.'

In the event, O'Leary held back on developing routes from Shannon and the government ignored the mounting pressure to develop new facilities at Dublin.

O'Leary's style in his dealings with the state was very unIrish: instead of lobbying ministers politely he chose to ridicule and harangue them, appealing instead to the ordinary voters and travellers, to whom he promised lower fares if inefficient state monopolies could be broken down.

'What mystifies me in Ireland is we have this complacency,' O'Leary said in an RTE radio interview in 1998. 'Why doesn't somebody call our bluff? If they think we are not serious about [building a terminal at Dublin airport] why don't they say, "Ryanair, off you go, build your terminal, spend your twelve million."?'

His question went unanswered but it touched on one of the central criticisms of O'Leary's attitude to Dublin airport: was he serious or was he just making mischief?

At the end of October O'Leary was given a chance to make his case for the second terminal in a more conventional arena when he was invited to appear before the Dáil committee which dealt with transport affairs to outline his plans. He broke with his normal check shirt and jeans and donned a suit and tie for the occasion. While O'Leary was keen to discuss Terminal Ryanair, the members of the committee were more interested in hearing about Ryanair's tumultuous relationship with the British advertising watchdog, the ASA.

Emmett Stagg, a Labour party TD, was particularly concerned that Ryanair had been censured by the ASA thirteen times. Shane Ross, an independent senator who doubled as a business journalist, said the company's relationship with the Irish ASA was equally 'deplorable', resulting in six complaints, three of which were upheld. This, according to Ross, meant that half of the company's ads were 'misleading, untrue, dishonest and unacceptable to an independent body', casting a considerable shadow over O'Leary's credibility.

'What you say is very impressive,' Ross said, 'but can I believe a word you are saying when an impartial body says you are lying?'

Ross and Stagg set the tone for a hostile grilling, but O'Leary refused to be drawn into apologies. Talking about one case, where an error by an employee in an advertisement had resulted in a GB£18,000 ASA fine for Ryanair, O'Leary left the committee in little doubt as to where his priorities lay. 'All advertising is now being vetted by three different people in the company, not only because we do not want to mislead consumers but because we do not want to waste £18,000.'

Two weeks later Aer Rianta had the chance to make its own presentation to the committee on Ryanair's terminal proposal. Noel Hanlon, its chairman, did not hide his contempt for O'Leary's plans: Ryanair was telling 'blatant lies', he told the committee, and the airline wished to design a 'cowshed' and not an airport terminal.

O'Leary was incensed and responded with a terse letter to the committee on 22 November threatening legal action if an apology from Hanlon was not forthcoming. 'Failing this, Ryanair will have no alternative but to initiate legal proceedings against Aer Rianta for libel so that we may have this untrue accusation laid to rest and Ryanair's good name and reputation restored.'

Once again, what had begun as a matter of vital importance for Ireland's infrastructure and the future of its tourism industry had become a personality clash between Hanlon and O'Leary. 'There was a lot of personal antipathy between O'Leary and Hanlon,' recalls Tim Jeans. 'It probably was a big obstruction to the whole process.'

Instead of following through on his threat to launch a libel action, O'Leary moved his battle to the not unfamiliar territory of newspaper advertisements.

The Bank of Ireland branch at Dublin airport had been robbed in late October, with armed raiders making off with up to £250,000. Another airline CEO might have felt some sympathy for the bank's workers, but O'Leary saw the robbery as yet another PR opportunity. 'It's not just the Bank of Ireland which gets robbed at Dublin airport,' his new advertisement proclaimed. The Irish Advertising Standards Authority denounced the ad as a breach of its code of practice.

The government was due to give its initial verdict on the proposed second terminal project by the end of the month, but instead of a decision it kicked for touch. O'Leary had been confident of a swift decision. 'I think the chances [of a second terminal] are very strong,' he had told RTE's *Moneymakers* programme in September. 'It is going to be politically very difficult for the Irish government to tell the people, "No, you must continue to pay three hundred, four hundred, five hundred pounds to fly direct to Germany, France and Italy, when Ryanair can do it for £19 out of Stansted." And it is going to be very difficult for the government to turn down 500 new jobs.'

He was wrong. For the next six years the government would do nothing. Congestion at Dublin airport would intensify and its development as a low-cost base would stall. O'Leary, finally recognizing the inevitability of delay after the government had failed to make a decision by the end of the year, opted for irony, liberally laced with doom. 'We're quite happy to wait it out for a year, two years or three years, if that's what it takes. Airfares will rise, traffic will decline, we'll cut back flights and tourism will start to suffer. Then Aer Rianta and the minister will ask Ryanair to come back into Ireland. And we'll consider it.'

Stansted had become the base of Ryanair's European expansion and the airline had five planes based there. But despite this Aer Lingus had stubbornly maintained its Dublin–Stansted service, which it had reintroduced in 1992 after Ryanair's exclusive access deal had run its course, and it had stubbornly refused to be forced off the route. In November, that stubbornness was finally replaced with pragmatism when the flag carrier announced it would be dropping its Stansted service in favour of increased services to Gatwick from January 2000. O'Leary was quick to fill the gap by promising to add four new Ryanair flights a day between Dublin and Stansted from January, bringing their daily total to sixteen. He also pounced on the opportunity to take some PR shots against his ailing rival. Aer Lingus's talk of 'a customer-driven plan with a clear business focus' was 'Japanese for high fares', O'Leary said.

In November Ryanair reported a 17 per cent rise in pre-tax profits for the first half of the financial year, to £42.9 million. The airline was in the midst of its aggressive European expansion, had just launched its latest Scandinavian service, to Aarhus in central Denmark, and by the end of 1999 O'Leary told journalists that Ryanair was in talks with twenty European airports with a view to flying into ten of them in 2000.

Financially, Aer Lingus was also being outperformed by Ryanair. In April Aer Lingus had released full year results which showed a pre-tax profit of £52.4 million, up 14 per cent. But the airline's chief executive, Garry Cullen, warned that margins, at 6 per cent, were too low. To solve the problem of low margins, Cullen wanted a review of pay scales, a proposal which put him on a collision course with trade union SIPTU, which represented most of the airline's workers.

Cullen also had to contend with mounting speculation that the airline was to be sold by the Irish government, with sources saying in December that Aer Lingus would be floated on the stock market the following year. The airline had managed to claw its way back from bankruptcy thanks to a large injection of state aid, but a flotation would strip away its safety net and leave the airline, and its unionized workforce, at the mercy of the market. The day of reckoning appeared close, but the unions would fight the sell-off, and they could count on formidable political allies.

Shouting and screaming at state monopolies and poking fun at cabinet ministers might have won O'Leary some popularity, but his hostility to all-comers was more problematic when it was directed at customers. In October Ryanair had incurred the censure of Ireland's *Daily Mirror* when the airline refused to refund the ticket of a young boy who missed his flight because he was too ill to travel.

'FAMILY'S FURY AS AIRLINE TELLS ASTHMA ATTACK BOY, 7: SORRY, YOUR FLIGHT'S GONE, YOU'LL HAVE TO BUY ANOTHER TICKET; FATHER BRANDS RYANAIR "HEARTLESS"', the headline raged, in bold capital letters. The piece detailed the story of 'little Liam Nolan', who had travelled to Ireland for a family wedding. The day before he was due to return to the UK he had an asthma attack and doctors declared him unfit to travel. Ryanair chose to follow its no refunds policy to the letter, refusing to allow the Nolan family to change their tickets and outraging Liam's parents. 'I just can't believe Ryanair can do this,' his father Joseph told the *Mirror*. 'I am absolutely furious with the way we have been treated. I'm never going to fly with them again because of this.'

The airline was unmoved by the family's plight. 'We have different types of tickets,' a Ryanair spokeswoman said. 'I presume the family bought the non-flexible ones, which means they are valid only for that flight . . . there is nothing we can do about it. The family could have opted for travel insurance which Ryanair offer their passengers. We recommend it because you don't know what can happen.'

A public row was thus turned into a sales exercise but Ryanair was unrepentant. To those outside the company, it seemed heartless, but for O'Leary there was method. Publicity, he still believed, was good, and he needed to reinforce the message that low fares meant that the passenger got what he or she paid for. The public needed to be educated, and if Ryanair had played for a simple PR victory by giving the family a free flight, hundreds more would have sought similar concessions. O'Leary wanted his airline to have an uncompromising reputation: cheap but no concessions. 'What part,' he would say, 'of "No refunds" do you not understand?'

In mid-December Ryanair attracted more public anger by announcing the halting of services to Knock airport in the west of Ireland. The surprise announcement came on 14 December and was prompted by Knock's decision to follow Kerry airport's initiative and levy a £6 passenger charge from mid-January. Local politicians condemned Ryanair's decision as 'disastrous for the west' and as the save Knock airport campaign gathered pace, Ryanair performed a swift U-turn, changing its stance within days. 'Ryanair has, this evening, announced that there will be no suspension of its twice-daily service from Knock to London, Stansted,' a company statement said. 'Passengers will continue, therefore, to enjoy Ryanair's low access fares to and from the West of Ireland, without interruption.'

The airline also softened its position on the levy. 'Ryanair continues to believe that the proposed passenger levy at Knock is fundamentally wrong. If Knock airport received the same parity of treatment in terms of regional support from the Government as airports like Sligo, Galway and Kerry, it would not have a shortfall and then would not have to introduce this unjust levy on passengers.'

It was a stunning reversal of policy, and in a very short space of time. Was O'Leary mellowing? Had he been swayed by public opinion? Hardly. The change of heart was not prompted by an attack of conscience about the potential devastation of County

Mayo's economy. In fact, O'Leary had miscalculated: he thought that if he pulled out Knock would be forced to come to him, cap in hand, begging for a return of the service. O'Leary could then screw an even better deal from the airport and consign the levy to history. It would be, he reckoned, a salutary lesson to any other airport, anywhere in Europe, that tried to take on Ryanair.

Competition, though, was beginning to bite and O'Leary quickly recalculated. 'If you pull out you want to make sure that nobody else replaces you,' says Jeans.

And we thought wrongly that if we pulled out of Knock the airport would probably shut. But at the time quite a number of people were leaving Ryanair for Virgin Express and Virgin Express was in expansion mode, and they were going to open up in Shannon. It became abundantly obvious that far from Knock suffering, what would happen would be that Virgin Express would come in. So rather than let Virgin Express in, Michael changed his mind and stayed. It was a total U-turn but it was a pragmatic U-turn.

16. Vulgar Abuse

There is more to Michael O'Leary than the art of making money. There had been rumours of romance and of an impending engagement towards the end of 1999, but confirmation that O'Leary planned to marry Denise Dowling, his girlfriend for more than two years, still came as a shock to his colleagues in Ryanair. They had been aware of Denise Dowling's presence – she had helped O'Leary host his annual party in Gigginstown the previous summer – but none was close enough to the chief executive to know his private thoughts.

Despite, or rather because of, the intensity of his working week, O'Leary still maintained as rigid a divide as he could between his professional existence as Michael O'Leary, chief executive of Europe's fastest-growing and most mischievous low-cost airline, and Michael O'Leary, ordinary bloke, who lived in Mullingar and happened to work at something in Dublin during the week.

His colleagues, in any case, were pleased. 'We were all thrilled for him,' says Ethel Power. 'We teased him about having to do a pre-marriage course and several funny notices went up on the internal Ryanair TV slagging him.' Romance, however, was only a private distraction. There was to be no reduction in the hours he worked, no easing of the obsession that drove the airline and no softening of O'Leary's approach to business. 'I certainly didn't notice any change in him,' says Tim Jeans. 'It was just another thing that he added to the portfolio of things that were going on in his life.'

That portfolio now included nesting as a priority; if O'Leary was to be married then Gigginstown had to be transformed from a bachelor pad into a marital home fit for a wife and perhaps a family. Redevelopment had been on his mind for a few years. Funding the work was not an issue; in June he had sold shares which had grossed him £16.6 million, and in September he had received a 25 per cent pay rise for 1999 which gave him a salary of £314,000 and £136,000 in bonuses.

Love, though, was to prove a more complicated affair than business. In January while preparing to tell the world of his engagement O'Leary had joked in an interview with the *Guardian* that he was 'depressingly single and living in hope that a woman will find me sufficiently attractive to settle down'. He might have been trying to deflect attention from the imminent change in his private life, but in fact he would have cause to recycle the quote many times over the next few years. For the moment, though, plans were moving apace for a summer wedding. That same month O'Leary contacted Pat and Marie Cooney, well known Mullingar hoteliers and caterers, to ask them to prepare for his wedding. O'Leary knew he could depend on the Cooneys for discretion – they had worked for him before, catering his midsummer garden parties – and the couple already knew Dowling. 'He was seen around a lot with Denise,' Pat Cooney says. 'They used to come in to us a lot.'

The Cooneys started to plan a menu for the big day. Dowling was 'very precise', they recall, while O'Leary had 'simpler tastes'. 'It was to be a buffet, like the garden parties,' says Pat Cooney. 'They wanted Aberdeen Angus and exotic fish. Michael is big into the fish. There was lobster, prawns, caviar – his father and mother love fish too. Denise likes chicken and they were having a chicken dish, but he hates chicken because he had it in boarding school, so they [compromised and] decided on a chicken salad to start.'

By early spring, with the engagement public knowledge, Ireland's tabloid press started to probe for details of the wedding plans. The ceremony, the *Sunday Mirror* announced in March, would take place in a church in Mullingar and would be followed by a lavish reception at Gigginstown. The paper also interviewed an unnamed 'friend of the couple' who revealed that O'Leary and Dowling 'have been an item since last summer'. They had, in fact, been involved for several years. The same friend went on to inform the *Sunday Mirror*'s readers, 'They have never been photographed together. Denise isn't the publicity-seeking kind . . . She's blonde and very attractive, more in a girl-next-door way than a glamorous model.'

It was tame stuff, an early build-up to what would have been the wedding of the year for an Irish media desperate to foster a celebrity culture in a country still coming to grips with its new-found wealth. Newspapers wanted superstars, and O'Leary was an obvious target. Young, dynamic, successful and already rich by Irish standards, he could have been the perfect playboy. Instead, he was resolutely private, steered clear of establishment events and charity balls, dressed down and talked of nothing but his company and occasionally his cattle.

And then O'Leary called a halt. 'I think there was suddenly a realization that she wasn't the right person,' says Tim Jeans. 'But no one was close enough within the business to know the whys and wherefores. And nobody really sought to find out either. We were all extraordinarily sorry for him. It was his decision and clearly it was not one that was taken too easily. I just remember saying, "Michael, I'm really sorry it hasn't worked out." And he wasn't dismissive, he was clearly quite affected by it.'

O'Leary has subsequently refused to discuss the reasons for the split, arguing that Dowling is entitled to her dignity and her privacy. She was, he said, 'too good for him'. Dowling returned to her previously anonymous life, working as a secretary for Gerry Purcell, the son of a successful beef trader. For O'Leary there would be no time for mourning; his philosophy was that it had happened, it had hurt, now move on.

Marie Cooney recalls a brief phone call from O'Leary to tell her the news. 'All he said was, "Marie, I don't know how to tell you this but we're not going ahead with that."'

Meanwhile, O'Leary's business life was moving at increasing speed. In January he had set the template for the year by announcing Ryanair's biggest ever seat sale. The prices were the lowest Ryanair had ever advertised – flights between Dublin and Stansted were to cost just £4 return, plus taxes and charges, a total fare of about

£24.99 – and the sale was rolled out across most of Ryanair's European network, with twenty-one routes included.

'The economics of the operation appear to defy explanation,' the transport editor of the *Guardian* noted at the time, but the economics were blindingly obvious to O'Leary. He wanted publicity, he wanted passengers and he wanted Ryanair.com, the website launched three months earlier, to become instantly recognizable as the place to surf for cheap flights. O'Leary had previously recognized that airline passengers represented a captive market for as long as they were on his planes; now, with the Internet, he saw that they could be a captive market while they booked their flights as well.

The dryly dubbed 'ancillary sales', already a significant factor in Ryanair's profits, were about to become their driving force, and every pound earned from selling more than just a seat could be used to reduce the cost of selling those seats. By February O'Leary was able to make public the next development: Ryanair.com would no longer merely sell tickets, it would also offer travel insurance, hotel accommodation and car hire. Unlike Richard Branson, the entrepreneurial brains behind the Virgin group of companies, O'Leary had no interest in stretching the Ryanair brand beyond the core business of flying passengers from airport to airport. Other companies could compete for the privilege of a presence on the Ryanair.com website; all O'Leary wanted was a large slice of cash.

Immediately, stockbrokers started to speculate that Ryanair.com could be floated on the stock market as a separate company – the dot-com bubble was a month away from bursting. O'Leary quashed the speculation: 'We want to concentrate on being Europe's largest low-fares airline,' he said. 'Selling tickets online will help us cut some £10 million in costs, but there is scope for using Ryanair.com to sell a variety of products.'

O'Leary's conversion from apparent technophobe to full-blooded embracer of the new world of the web was complete. So complete, indeed, that he decided his cows deserved a website of their own. Sean Coyle, then O'Leary's personal assistant, was given the job of arranging it, and he turned again to the two young men who had created the Ryanair site. 'He wanted pictures of the cattle, their family history, their vital statistics, contact numbers for the farm,' recalls John Beckett. 'It took a couple of weeks. The pay wasn't nearly as much as the Ryanair site but it was actually harder to get paid.'

Coyle was learning at the feet of his master. He knew that the two boys had been hammered on the Ryanair website, and he was determined to prove that he could be as tough a negotiator as his boss. 'I was surprised how aggressive Sean was in his negotiations after we finished the site,' says Beckett. 'A price had been agreed before we began, but Sean was trying to negotiate the price down severely after we had done the work. I was just seventeen and I was way out of my depth. I made one of the worst decisions in my life by not walking out but I didn't see it that way at the time. I thought I'd better try and get paid something, so I accepted a reduced rate.'

Within weeks of the seat sale O'Leary announced seven new routes to Europe from Stansted and an additional 250 jobs at the London airport. It was a stunt designed to capitalize on the publicity he had already generated at the start of the year and create the impression of unstoppable growth. The routes and the jobs would happen, but not for another year when Ryanair was to take delivery of another five Boeing 737s.

O'Leary's timing was also intended to place additional pressure on the Irish government and Aer Rianta. Jobs and routes that could have gone to Dublin were moving to the UK, he said, because of the Irish government's refusal to introduce competition at Dublin airport by agreeing a second terminal, and because of Aer Rianta's decision to eliminate its rebate scheme and increase its charges.

We were disappointed that the Irish government permitted the Dublin airport monopoly to increase costs for all airlines from 1 January, and this has already resulted in the average cost of air travel to and from

Ireland rising for the first time since 1986. The Irish government has got it wrong. The days of protecting these state-owned monopolies are gone. Dublin airport will once again lose out as all our new routes this year will operate between the UK and Europe.

What mattered for the company, though, was not snubbing Dublin but the sheer scale of the planned expansion. At the start of 2000 Ryanair operated eight routes to continental Europe. The new launches would almost double that number and set the airline firmly on the path to O'Leary's stated ambition of becoming Europe's dominant low-fare airline. In his mind dominant meant more than being the biggest in a growing but still small market; it meant reaching a scale that would represent a serious challenge to the traditional airlines. Some fretted that O'Leary was moving too fast, that the thin layer of senior management would not be able to cope with the multiplying organization beneath them. But O'Leary was unconcerned. To him the growth was as controlled as it was essential.

The trick was to keep the business model simple and to keep chipping away at costs. Ryanair was a point-to-point airline, and would stay that way. Passengers could choose to fly from Dublin to Stansted and then onward to a European destination of their choice, but they did so at their own risk. Landing at Stansted, passengers planning to fly on to Sweden would have to collect their bags, clear customs and then check in again at the Stansted departure desk. If their Dublin flight had been delayed and the connection was missed, tough. It was not Ryanair's problem. No Ryanair staff would ease passenger transfers, no planes would be held back to facilitate delayed passengers and no refunds would be given for flights missed. It was a reiteration of Ryanair's existing policy, but as the airline expanded its route network, offering destinations across Europe, it would attract a new generation of customers who would have to be educated in the ways of the low-cost airline business. The O'Leary mantra was unforgiving: low fares meant basic service. It was a novel approach to public relations, but it was working. O'Leary had decided he did not need to be loved; all that mattered was that Ryanair was well known for what it delivered.

In mid-February 2000 O'Leary announced the airline's results for the third quarter of 1999. Pre-tax profit had risen by more than 29 per cent, compared with the same period in the previous year, to almost £16 million, helped by some exceptional gains on foreign exchange and by the sale of shares in a communications company. The results also revealed that Ryanair's fares had risen by 18 per cent during the quarter to an average of £45 – a rise that had given O'Leary the room to launch his January sale.

A week later Ryanair announced the destinations for the seven new routes it had flagged up. Flights would operate from Stansted to Lübeck ('near Hamburg') in Germany, Malmö (nowhere near Stockholm) in Sweden, Nîmes and Perpignan in southern France, and Brescia and Lamezia in Italy. Further north, Ryanair also added a flight from Prestwick to Frankfurt Hahn. The routes were an eclectic mix, but with the exception of Prestwick–Hahn were linked by a common factor: substantial population centres were being offered cheap flights to London, one of the world's greatest tourist destinations as well as one of its most important financial centres. British tourists might want to visit Nîmes or Perpignan or even Malmö, but Ryanair's expectation was that the seats would be filled mainly by Europeans travelling to London – a point missed by sceptics who wondered how O'Leary planned to fill his planes on such seemingly unglamorous routes.

The noise of the early months of 2000, with the seat sale, website relaunch and route announcements, set the scene for O'Leary's decision to ask the stock markets to fund the acquisition of ten more Boeing 737s and 'to exploit opportunities for the purchase of second-hand aircraft'. Ryanair, he said, wanted to raise GB£100 million. 'We are facing into a period of great opportunity,' O'Leary said. 'The successful launch of Ryanair.com has the potential to transform both Ryanair's business and European air travel.'

The new shares were to be offered to new and existing institutional investors in Ireland, the UK and continental Europe, but not in the United States because European rules on the ownership of airlines meant that the majority of shareholders had to be European. O'Leary also planned to liberate some of his own assets by selling five million Ryanair shares at the same time, in a move that was to earn him £38 million and reduce his stake-holding below 10 per cent. O'Leary's sale came less than a year after the share placement in 1999 which earned him £25 million but analysts were unconcerned at the move. 'The company decided now is a good time to raise some cash because the share price is full and fair and since the chief executive makes the decision for the company, it's logical that he also thinks it is a good time to sell some of his own shareholding,' airline analyst Shane Matthews said.

The share placement raised €122 million for Ryanair, while O'Leary's sale raised €48 million.* After previous share sales, O'Leary had always insisted his money was hoarded away in his local post office. This time O'Leary told investors that he had serious plans for his money – paying for his upcoming wedding. The post office, however, would not be disappointed. Within weeks of the sale, the wedding had been called off.

If Michael O'Leary had been about to walk up the aisle of his local Roman Catholic church on 1 July, he might have paused before launching his May advertising campaign. It was a classic of its type: cheap, crudely executed and mightily effective. Placed on the front page of the *Irish Independent*, Ireland's largest-selling daily newspaper, the advertisement was headlined, 'Pope reveals Fourth Secret of Fatima', and showed the pontiff whispering to a nun, 'Psst! Only Ryanair.com guarantees the lowest fare on the Internet.'

The advertisement sparked outrage among members of the Roman Catholic Church, and the publicity flowed for Ryanair. 'It is surprising that a reputable airline couldn't have found a more appropriate way of reaching the public than the use of advertising

* Ryanair switched to reporting in euros when the new currency was introduced in 2002.

copy linking the Pope and a facetious reference to Fatima,' a statement said, describing the advertisement as 'pointless and without particular focus'. How wrong that was. The advertisement was both pointed and focused. Ryanair had a foothold in the Italian market and had just announced two more routes, and a spat with the Catholic Church was a sure-fire way to generate plenty of free publicity.

Back home, the sisters of La Sagesse Convent in Sligo complained to the Advertising Standards Authority that 'the advertisement was an affront and a gratuitous insult to the Pope and the thousands of practising Catholics and was in poor taste. It trivialised and demeaned the head of a worldwide religion, and it attempted to make a joke of the Fatima experience which for many was the focus of devout respect.'

The Catholic Church was not alone in failing to see through a transparent piece of attention-seeking. The advertising standards authorities on both sides of the Irish Sea regularly complained about Ryanair's advertisements, rising to whatever bait O'Leary threw their way. The previous year the Irish ASA had said that an O'Leary advertisement that made fun of a bank robbery had been 'gravely offensive' and in June, just after the Fatima campaign, Tom Kitt, a junior minister in the Irish government, launched an attack on Ryanair's advertising policy. Kitt said there was 'widespread dissatisfaction' about the way its fares were advertised, claims dismissed by O'Leary as 'rubbish'. The UK ASA was on hand to back up Kitt's assertions, denouncing Ryanair as the 'most complained about airline' and revealing that it had issued a special alert to British newspapers advising them to seek advice from the ASA before publishing the airline's advertisements.

They just did not get it. Kitt and both ASAs were trying to protect customers from misleading advertisements – complaints ranged from Ryanair's destinations, like Beauvais being sold as Paris, to its fares, which excluded taxes and charges, making the advertised fare significantly lower than the price actually paid by the customer – but by engaging with Ryanair, they played its game. Ryanair wanted as much controversy as possible by spending as little money as possible. 'We track coverage sometimes,' says Paul Fitzsimmons, Ryanair's former head of communications. 'I don't mean hiring a research company to track it, I mean googling it and seeing where it is getting to and putting cost estimates to it. On the Pope one, we tracked it [as being worth] four or five million dollars.'

The simplest way to have restrained O'Leary would have been to refuse to react to any campaign unless it breached a certain impact point: one or two cheap advertisements, no response; a multi-million pound campaign, response. O'Leary would have been stumped. Instead, he cast the flies and those he offended swallowed them whole. 'Bookings peak for big ads,' says O'Leary, 'and they'll peak even more if somebody reacts badly to them.'

Publicity could come from any quarter, and O'Leary would seize it gratefully. Just before he offended the Pope he had happily capitalized on the success of Brian Dowling, a Ryanair employee who had been chosen as a contestant in the second series of *Big Brother*. In a format which has been replicated across the world, Dowling and others would live together in a house, their every moment recorded on camera. Each week, viewers would vote to eject one contestant from the house, and the last man or woman standing would take the spoils.

Ryanair pledged to give GB£1,000 to a children's charity for every week Dowling stayed in the house, and painted a *Big Brother* logo and a good luck message on one of its aircraft. 'Everyone here is delighted that Brian made it into the house,' said O'Leary. 'He's been two years in the Ryanair madhouse, which is perfect training. We will be holding his job for him and hope that he will be returning to us – unless, of course, he becomes an international superstar through this.'

Dowling, an early favourite and the only gay contestant, duly won. 'I don't imagine he will want to come back if he is making a fortune,' said O'Leary. 'If he does, then we would be glad to have him, and perhaps we would use him in promotion. But if he is looking for appearance money he can feck off.'

★

The promise of the third-quarter results for 1999, released in February, was confirmed by the full-year results O'Leary announced in June. Pre-tax profits had grown by 19 per cent to €90.09 million. Passenger numbers were up by 13 per cent to 5.6 million for the year, turnover was up 25 per cent to €370.1 million and Ryanair now had forty-five routes serving eleven countries. Investors, who had driven the shares from €3.85 the previous November to €8.22 by the close of business on the day of the results, had been rewarded for their faith. Ryanair.com was a success, generating 50,000 seat bookings a week and rising.

'We intend to make Ryanair.com the largest air travel website in Europe,' O'Leary said. He was also able to put flesh on his earlier promises that the website could become a profit centre in its own right by formally announcing that a deal had been done with Hotel Systems International on the first website tie-in. The deal would allow Ryanair's customers access to 13,500 hotels worldwide from 28 June, and Ryanair would earn money on every booking made.

Media commentators and stock market analysts were impressed. 'The Ryanair formula of low fares and no frills continues to carry all before it, and there are few clouds on the immediate horizon,' said the *Financial Times*. 'The oil price risk is fully hedged, airport charges are under control, the cost of aircraft acquisition is locked in and the older parts of the fleet are almost fully depreciated.'

At the airline's AGM later that year O'Leary announced that Ryanair was exercising options to buy three more Boeing 737-800s at a cost of €136 million. The airline had already taken delivery of eight 737-800s in 2000. Profits, too, continued to rise and analysts were forecasting that the result for 2000 would exceed €120 million on a turnover of more than €480 million.

In O'Leary's seven years as chief executive the company had been transformed beyond recognition. The chaotic losses of the early years had been turned into modest profits by the time O'Leary stepped into the main job, but progress since 1994 had been exponential and the effect on European air travel had been revolutionary. As the *Wall Street Journal* wrote that summer, 'Ryanair's

rise from Irish puddle-jumper to Continental contender is more
than one airline's growth story. The Gaelic upstart and its followers,
such as London-based easyJet, are fundamentally shifting the economics of flying around Europe.'

The shifting structure of the European aviation industry, prompted
by the emergence of the low-cost carriers and intensifying competition on the lucrative intercontinental routes, was forcing the flag
carriers to think the previously unthinkable. Mergers were now
on the agenda and in the summer of 2000 the possibility of British
Airways joining forces with KLM, the Dutch carrier, was floated.

O'Leary professed to be unconcerned about the creation of a
European aviation giant. 'I can't for the life of me think why they
[BA] would take it over,' O'Leary said in mid-June. 'KLM is a
basket case. BA is a basket case too. You put the two together and
you get an even bigger basket case.' He was, however, conscious
that a low-fare airline backed by the two giants could pose a
commercial threat. Each of the two potential partners already had
its own low-cost airline, BA's Go and KLM's Buzz. 'With BA
and KLM's deep pockets to tap, these low-fares units could sell
tickets at a loss in order to drive carriers like us, with no rich parent
to call on, from certain air routes,' he said. 'While we are keen to
take on Goliath, we want a fair fight.'

With or without a BA–KLM merger, competition was already
intensifying in the low-cost market. EasyJet had grown impress-
ively from its humble beginnings in March 1995 when it had
started operations with two leased Boeing 737s. Two years later
the airline had ordered twelve new 737s, followed by an order for
fifteen more in July 1998 and a further seventeen in March 2000.
EasyJet had also expanded through acquisition, buying 40 per cent
of Swiss airline TEA Basel AG in 1998 and rebranding it easyJet
Switzerland. In June 1999 easyJet strengthened its Swiss position
by increasing its stake to 49 per cent, and acquiring an option to
buy out the remaining 51 per cent. Under the deal, easyJet Switzerland also moved its operations to Geneva, which became easyJet's
first continental European base.

The airline's success meant that it too could plan for a stock market flotation. Stelios announced his flotation plans that summer, telling the market that the carrier was on course to make profits before tax of GB£20 million that year. It was an impressive number for a five-year-old airline, but still way behind the GB£100 million Ryanair would make in the same year. Yet easyJet's success was not a hindrance to Ryanair because it demonstrated that low-cost aviation was not a one-company phenomenon. Meanwhile, the well-funded loss makers, like BA's Go, helped highlight Ryanair's key differences. It was, in stark contrast to most of its rivals, a low-cost airline which delivered profits for its shareholders.

Go, launched in 1998, had been a marketing and promotional triumph, but it lacked the rigour and ruthlessness that marked out Ryanair. By the autumn of 2000 Go was flying to twenty-one European destinations, employed 650 staff, had a turnover of GB£150 million, and was speculatively valued at about GB£200 million, a sizeable return on the £25 million BA had invested just two years previously. But the airline had yet to turn a profit.

The BA group, under chief executive Rod Eddington, was in cost-cutting mode by the summer of 2000, with BA chairman Bob Ayling signalling compulsory redundancies across the group. Barbara Cassani, Go's chief executive, was not impressed and began to speculate publicly about the benefits of BA selling off its low-cost wing. Throughout the summer speculation about a sale continued to mount, with Cassani expressing interest in a management buyout and easyJet reportedly considering a takeover bid.

While Go's future was in the balance, Richard Branson's Virgin Express was haemorrhaging cash. In the first quarter of 2000 Virgin Express racked up losses of GB£8 million – more money than the airline had lost in the whole of 1999 – and was now culling routes in a desperate attempt to stem its losses.

Ryanair's profits demonstrated that the airline could thrive in a competitive market place. Mergers, however, could change the dynamics and O'Leary was not prepared to be rolled over by the giants. Ryanair, he said, would go to the European Commission and ask that 'any merging airline' surrender slots at London's Stansted and any other airports where both of the merging carriers were present. 'If the European Commission does not act, we may be pushed out of Stansted and other airports,' he said. O'Leary also asked the EU to insist that Buzz and Go be sold if the BA–KLM merger went ahead. Before long, however, the merger talks collapsed.

In the autumn of 2000 O'Leary chose to reignite the Dublin airport row with his usual flair for controversy. In an interview with the *Wall Street Journal* O'Leary said that the best way to settle his differences with Aer Rianta was 'with Semtex' – 'preferably during a board meeting'.

Aer Rianta spokesman Flan Clune said he 'wouldn't stoop so low as to respond to that remark'. Clune's colleagues, however, were happy to stoop. O'Leary's comments were 'malevolent and shocking', said Rita Bergin, an Aer Rianta director. '[O'Leary proposes] to resolve business differences in a manner which is far too fresh in the minds of people on the island of Ireland,' she admonished, referring to the terrorist campaigns that had blighted the country for the previous thirty years. 'Here we have an individual worth well in excess of £100 million behaving in a shockingly irresponsible manner.'

O'Leary was unmoved and refused to apologize. A week later at Ryanair's AGM he renewed his attacks on Aer Rianta and Dublin airport. Conditions at the airport were 'shambolic', he said. 'They've spent £50 million on a five-storey extension which nobody wants to use,' he said, adding that the new baggage hall was 'something designed by Russian architects', while 'Pier C was designed by Aer Rianta to win an architectural competition rather than serve the needs of airlines.'

Could Ryanair accomplish more with a bit of diplomacy, wondered the *Wall Street Journal*. 'Nahhh,' said O'Leary. 'You want to take on monopolies, you've got to be ready to fight.' The fights, he told the paper with a laugh, 'are good for the soul'.

★

In November 2000 Ryanair's staff policies came in for sharp media coverage when it emerged that Ryanair's pilots were considering going on strike. Until then, Ryanair's pilots had negotiated directly with O'Leary, and with reasonable success. 'We used to have what were called "town hall meetings",' recalls one pilot.

O'Leary would come and he would negotiate with pilots, and there was an ERC [employee relations committee] who sat down with him. The ERC wasn't elected as such by the pilots, but they were pilots and they used to talk with O'Leary. They never did a very good job, and we got these pay agreements, two-page things, but we had a bit of power. If O'Leary turned around and said, 'No we don't want to do this any more,' then we turned around and said, 'Screw you.' In the early years, because Dublin was the main hub, we could do that.

In 2000 the Ryanair pilots were due to negotiate another wage agreement and O'Leary was not in a generous mood. 'He did one of these sweeps of the pen, changing the amount of hours we could work in a week,' recalls the pilot. The pilots were not impressed, and in mid-September it was reported they were considering a go-slow. The pilots had also beefed up their negotiating power by bringing in the pilots' union IALPA and its larger affiliate IMPACT, the largest public-sector union in Ireland, to help defeat the changes.

They had hoped that with the experience and organization of IALPA they would be better equipped to fight their corner. But they were quickly disappointed. 'IALPA just didn't deal with it very well,' recalls another pilot. 'There was a few meetings and then, "Right, we'll go out on strike."' A strike was first mooted in late September, but IMPACT then announced that it was being deferred because Ryanair had reached an agreement with its pilots on working hours.

For Ryanair, the simple fact that IMPACT, with SIPTU the dominant union at Aer Lingus, was saying anything at all about the airline's internal industrial relations was an unwelcome development. 'As always these matters were discussed and clarified directly between Ryanair and our pilots and this will continue to be the case. Rumours of disruption within Ryanair which emanate from an Aer Lingus trade union should be seen for what they are,' Ryanair said in a statement. But despite the airline's denials pilot unrest continued, and in early November the pilots voted by 77 to 1 to reject the company's pay deal and take industrial action.

O'Leary professed bafflement at the development. It was, he said, 'quite extraordinary that Ryanair's pilots would fail to accept a five-year pay package which included all captains rising to £100,000 per annum'. But reject it they did, and strike action was set for 23 November. Faced with an imminent and potentially ruinous dispute O'Leary switched to diplomatic mode and success-fully convinced the pilots to call off their strike on the promise of fresh negotiation.

As a gesture of goodwill, the pilots pledged to donate their flight allowances from 23 November to the North Dublin Hospice. O'Leary had taken a public relations hammering during the bag-gage handlers' dispute two years previously, and was forced to admit to RTE radio in 1999 that 'if you look back you'd have to accept that it was a PR disaster'. Keen to avoid a repeat of that error and ever keen for a publicity coup, O'Leary said that Ryanair would match the amount donated. He then went on a promotional offensive, determined to make what use he could of the press cover-age of the dispute, and offered free flights on all available seats between Ireland and the UK on 24 November, with passengers paying only taxes and charges.

His tactics worked. Direct negotiations with the pilots produced marginal improvements in their pay and conditions and the dispute was settled. The deal included a €100,000 share option package for all pilots and a 15 per cent increase in basic pay over its five-year term, which would see pilots' annual pay increase to more than €127,000 per year. The pilots signed up, and the unions were eased back out of the company. IMPACT's Michael Landers said pilots would be 'reasonably happy', and conceded there were 'significant improvements on roster patterns and working hours'.

For the pilots it had been a bruising battle, and not all of them were satisfied. 'A really bad pay agreement and a really bad working agreement was signed,' recalls one pilot. For Ryanair, however, the battle had proved something of a coup. The airline had attracted some decent publicity from its charitable donation, the original terms of its pilots' package had been altered only minimally and, most importantly, Ryanair had once again managed to steer its way out of industrial strife without having to sit down with the trade unions.

O'Leary's growing skill at turning even the worst story into a positive publicity stunt would be tested more and more in the months to come.

In September Ryanair's attempts to place advertisements in Glasgow's central railway station had been met by a sniffy letter from Malden Outdoor, agents for the sites, which said, 'Regrettably we are unable to accept any form of advertising within the station which is deemed as direct competition to the train services provided.'

Ryanair's flights from Glasgow to London were of course a competitive threat to the trains, but it was naive of the agency to spell this out. O'Leary made the affair public. 'We're knocking the stuffing out of the rail competition with our £9 plus tax return fares from Scotland to London,' he said, 'and the best Railtrack can come up with is "You can't advertise that here."' The result was that the refusal to carry advertisements drew more attention to Ryanair than the advertisements themselves would have generated.

Soon afterwards O'Leary had another opportunity to practise the art of turning bad news to his company's advantage. In late October 264 Ryanair passengers, including 49 school students, were stranded in Beauvais, the tiny airport on the outskirts of Paris, for two days due to bad weather. Mike O'Hara, the leader of the school party, complained that they were 'practically ignored' by the airline. 'I am furious about the treatment we received from Ryanair staff at Beauvais airport,' he told the *Sun*. 'The handling staff were absolutely brutal and made no effort with us whatsoever. We weren't offered any food, not even a cup of tea, and no one tried at all to accommodate us.'

The *Irish Times* ran a 1,100-word story on the 'trauma' endured by one passenger, David Gibbons. 'The accommodation we were offered for the night was in a hangar in the airport with beds like army cots and no showers,' Gibbons complained. 'Anybody with any money went into Beauvais. I got a two-star hotel for £30 and paid £10 on taxis.' The airline eventually offered passengers a roll and 'a thimbleful of tea' according to Gibbons.

Any other airline faced with a hostile media onslaught and images of distraught passengers would have made conciliatory noises and perhaps offered compensation. Not Ryanair. The affair was instead another opportunity to hammer home the company's mantra: low fares, nothing more, nothing less. 'It's not part of our service to provide accommodation or even a cup of tea in these circum-stances,' O'Leary said. 'Some people paid as little as £9 return for their fares, so they can't really expect such extra benefits.'

O'Leary's attack was considered: if you paid a pound for your flight, how could you expect the airline to pay £50 to put you up if the weather was bad? He was also irritated by the Irish media. Ryanair's success did not receive the attention or praise it deserved from a domestic media fascinated by the negatives and bored by the positives. O'Leary's opposition to trade unions, his refusal to become part of the cosy establishment, his wealth and his aggression had turned most of the media against Ryanair.

O'Leary's competitors seemed incapable of learning that the best defence was simply to ignore him and his airline. In September BA had announced it was suing Ryanair in London's High Court for running advertisements which it claimed amounted to trade-mark infringement and 'malicious falsehood'. Britain's biggest air-line, which liked to call itself the world's favourite, had been irritated by a number of Ryanair advertisements, but the one that stuck in its corporate throat had been run the previous year under the simple but effective headline: 'Expensive BA——DS'.

BA wanted the courts to give Ryanair a public and expensive dressing-down and calculated that a successful action might take the wind out of O'Leary's billowing sails. Big mistake. In December Mr Justice Jacob delivered his ruling, and it was devastating for BA. The 'Expensive BA——DS' campaign centred on a comparison of Ryanair's and BA's fares, with O'Leary's company claiming that BA was five times more expensive on certain routes. Jacob said it was 'particularly odd commercially' that BA should complain that the comparisons were misleading. 'The complaint amounts to this: that Ryanair exaggerate in suggesting BA is five times more expensive because BA is only three times more expensive,' he said.

The advertisements 'might amount to vulgar abuse' but they did not constitute malicious falsehood. And then came his withering conclusion. 'I suspect the real reason BA do not like [the advertisement] is precisely because it is true.'

O'Leary was a happy man. 'They did not think we could afford to fight them in court,' he said outside, playing his David card even though he would make profits of more than GB£100 million that year, easily enough to fund a few days in London's High Court. 'It is an age-old dirty trick by BA. But we did fight them and we won. It's game, set and match to us.'

Win some, lose some. On the same day as Justice Jacob made his ruling, Ireland's High Court found against O'Leary in a case brought by Aer Rianta. The airports company had sued Ryanair for £459,885 it claimed was owed to it for unpaid fees due on various routes. Ryanair had subsequently paid just over £103,000 for fees on the Dublin–Bristol route, but Aer Rianta had returned to court in December to claim the remaining £350,000.

O'Leary had claimed that he had held discussions with Aer Rianta's assistant chief executive Brian J. Byrne in which the two men agreed a variation on the standard landing charges for Ryanair and that therefore the £350,000 was never in fact due. Byrne's recollection was somewhat different. He denied any special deal had been agreed. Mr Justice Kelly took the same view, found that there was no written agreement between the airline and the airport, and that correspondence demonstrated there was no evidence of any amendment to landing charges.

The verdict was squarely against Ryanair. What Ryanair was saying was not credible, Kelly said, and was undermined by documents exhibited by O'Leary. Kelly ordered the airline to pay the full £350,000, as well as 8 per cent interest and Aer Rianta's costs. He also refused to give the airline leave to appeal and refused a stay on his order. For once, O'Leary stayed silent, concentrating instead on milking his victory over BA.

17. Customer Care

In October 1988 P.J. McGoldrick, Ryanair's then newly appointed chief executive, had marched across the tarmac at Dublin airport to greet an incoming flight. As the passengers disembarked, McGoldrick scooped Jane O'Keeffe, a twenty-one-year-old, into his arms and carried her towards the terminal building, while press photographers clicked away for the next morning's newspapers.

O'Keeffe was the millionth passenger to use the new airline. Her reward, McGoldrick said, would be 'free flights for life' for her and a partner. 'What would that cost the company?' a journalist wondered. 'We don't nitpick over the gifts we give,' McGoldrick replied rather grandly.

At the time money did not really matter in Ryanair. McGoldrick had just taken over from the profligate, if occasionally inspired, regime of Eugene O'Neill and had no idea about the true state of the airline's finances. Simple things like organizing a contract with O'Keeffe that might specify the precise nature of her entitlement and how she could claim it were bothersome details with which the young Ryanair did not concern itself.

For the next ten years O'Keeffe made use of her free flights, nominating first her sister then her new husband as her travelling companion. In the absence of a contract O'Keeffe and the airline had come to a mutually acceptable compromise. If she gave a couple of weeks notice, Ryanair would put her on the flight of her choice. But then came a crunch in the summer of 1998. 'It blew up one weekend,' O'Leary says.

Our records say she called up on the Friday of a bank holiday weekend insisting on two flights to Prestwick and we had only two seats left, and we said, 'No, you're not getting it; you have to call in advance.' She claimed she had called two weeks earlier and nobody had gotten back to her . . . We couldn't prove it, she couldn't prove it. The difficulty with [the case] was that we inherited it from back in the days when nobody [in Ryanair] had a sheet of paper. The only evidence that she had anything from us was some video clip from the nine o'clock news with P. J. McGoldrick saying she had free flights for life. There was no terms, no conditions, nothing.

.O'Keeffe remembers it differently, 'I did get a contract originally but then they had to make changes [and] they never issued a new one,' she says. 'It worked very well for many years. It was all very easy, very straightforward. I didn't ask for anything in writing after that because it was all working fine.'

Her troubles started with that Easter flight to Prestwick.

I was due to go over to Scotland and they had told me two days or so before that I couldn't travel. I kept ringing up trying to find out what was going on and one day I was put through to Michael O'Leary. He wasn't expecting me. I was working in Today FM [Ireland's independent national radio station] at the time, sitting in an open-plan office. We had such an argy-bargy on the phone; we were shouting, and when I hung up everybody in my office was looking at me, asking what was that all about? When somebody is shouting at you, it's intimidating and I was trying to make myself heard. The only way I could do that was to raise my voice. Of course I got nowhere. He was saying, 'Stop ringing me, stop ringing my employees.'

O'Keeffe did not travel with Ryanair after that: the refusal to accommodate her Easter plans had rankled, and she believed that the airline, and O'Leary in particular, could not be trusted to honour McGoldrick's 1988 promise. O'Keeffe's solicitors exchanged letters with Ryanair, seeking a new agreement or compensation. 'Whatever about the logistics of it, it wasn't right, it wasn't fair,' says O'Keeffe. 'I wanted to work out something that was workable but we had reached an impasse. There was no real option [but to issue proceedings] because nobody was budging.' So in September 2000 she instructed lawyers to write to Ryanair, saying that the airline had broken the agreement and seeking compensation of up to £500,000.

'We said fuck off,' says O'Leary.

In December 2000 the newspapers were alerted to the story, and the feeding frenzy began. 'It's Ryan-unfair: Woman sues airline as free travel is cancelled,' the *Mirror* proclaimed on 18 December. 'Stingy Ryanair bosses have grounded a woman who was given free travel for life by the budget airline,' the paper said.

O'Leary was not bothered by the hostile coverage and refused to countenance a settlement with O'Keeffe. He knew the publicity would be bad, but he believed he had to make a stand, if only to show other would-be complainers and litigators that Ryanair never backed down. If you want to take on this company, he was saying, be prepared for a long and expensive fight. It is a strategy that newspapers use against libel claims: they may not fight every claim, but occasionally they pick one to go all the way, just to show that they are prepared to fight and that there is no easy money to be made from suing them. O'Keeffe says she was not after easy money:

They were trying to shaft me for no reason. Halfway through the case they tried to settle and they said, 'We'll give you back the free flights, you can have them back.' After all I had put up with on the TV and the radio during the last few days [of the court case] ... I decided, 'They don't like me, I don't like them. I don't really want to fly with them any more.' Whatever trust there had been was gone. I'm not small-minded and petty, but when I walked up those court steps I didn't feel good about them.

O'Leary's belligerence was not shared by his colleagues. 'It was one of those things where Michael really didn't carry the rest of the company with him,' says Tim Jeans. 'Nobody could see the point of it. Why put us through all this grief and all this bad PR?' Jeans might have been right, but O'Leary was not for turning.

The O'Keeffe case would fester in the background for many months as it wound its way to the courts, but it would not be the only generator of bad publicity for O'Leary. His hostility to

O'Keeffe was mild compared to the contempt he reserved for Mary O'Rourke, Ireland's minister for transport. She was his bête noire – a woman for whom he had no respect yet who had power over key decisions that could make a real impact on his company's growth and its earnings. The loathing was mutual.

Originally a primary schoolteacher, O'Rourke's family connections – recently her brother had been a senior cabinet minister – ensured her a power base within the governing Fianna Fáil party. As transport minister O'Rourke was the majority shareholder in Aer Lingus and the sole shareholder in Aer Rianta. If O'Leary were to get a second terminal at Dublin airport he would either need O'Rourke's support or he would have to undermine her to such a degree that she lost her job or simply buckled under the pressure.

At the start of the year she had again rejected O'Leary's proposals for a new terminal, claiming that the European Union would not allow the government to give Ryanair special treatment. 'I will be writing back asking her whether or not she wants to support our proposal to open ten new routes from Ireland to Europe and the UK, creating 500 new jobs and carrying two million passengers a year,' he replied.

At the end of January 2001 O'Rourke was at her most vulnerable. Enda, her husband of forty years, died suddenly after suffering a brain haemorrhage. His funeral drew crowds of mourners, including Mary McAleese, the Irish president, Bertie Ahern, the taoiseach, and senior politicians from all the major political parties. O'Leary, to O'Rourke's surprise, joined the mourners. It was a momentary ceasefire.

A few days later he launched a series of personal attacks on O'Rourke through full-page newspaper advertisements depicting her in a bathtub, with the headline, 'Mary, Mary, quite contrary, how does your monopoly grow? It doesn't'. O'Rourke was appalled. 'He did it four days after Enda died, and he saw me; he was at the funeral and I was roaring crying,' she says. 'If you wrote a novel about a man who four days after this woman's husband had died, that he set out to torture her, you'd think it was unbelievable, because you would say nobody could be that cold or that horrid, but he was. He didn't care.'

O'Leary, as his various battles with rivals and the political establishment confirmed, liked to project himself as the underdog scrapping for a fair chance to take on the big guys. That sense of smallness, of being an entrepreneurial company in a world of state-owned or recently privatized behemoths, was critical to the company culture fostered by O'Leary, but as Ryanair grew quarter by quarter, racking up higher profits and passenger numbers, so the challenge to maintain that culture intensified.

In an interview with the *Wall Street Journal*, his second in less than a year, O'Leary explained how he coped with the changing shape of Ryanair.

We try to keep a lot of the bull out of the organization. We keep the management structure extremely flat. As we grow, we're only adding aircraft, pilots, inflight people and engineers. We don't need these layers of bureaucracy or layers of management.

So hopefully we'll avoid the bull – by keeping our feet on the ground and not losing the run of ourselves. The downside of success that we really worry about is the danger that the more successful you are, the more likely you are to lose sight of the things that made you successful . . . Someone wrote a book in the States twenty years ago and said the three things you can always use to tell the time when a company turns from being a success to a failure are when they build a headquarters – the glass palace headquarters office – helicopter outside of it, and the chief executive writes a book. So I think as long as we stay away from all those things, we're fine.

O'Leary was true to his word. Despite the airline's success, Ryanair inhabited a drab headquarters building at Dublin airport, using the same furniture acquired by Eugene O'Neill back in 1987, with the exception of the grandiose chief executive's desk, which had been ditched. There was no corporate helicopter and no corporate jet, and no prospect of O'Leary penning a guide to corporate success. 'Business books,' he says, 'are bullshit and are usually written by wankers.'

His management structure had helped ensure that the same senior managers who had helped float the airline two years earlier were still on board, while growth came through adding bases and adding routes. Alongside the release of third-quarter results – which revealed a 39 per cent increase in passengers and a 23 per cent increase in pre-tax profits – O'Leary announced yet another share sale, this time to raise £113 million, which he said would be used to part-fund the purchase of thirteen more Boeings and launch six more European routes. He was also able to announce Ryanair.com's first full-year figures, and said that the website had sold 3.3 million seats online.

Growth also required a strengthened board of directors. O'Leary was the only executive to sit on the board, not out of hubris but largely because directors were required to reveal their levels of pay to shareholders. O'Leary had a relatively modest pay package, content in the knowledge that adding value to his shareholding was the real route to wealth. His management colleagues, however, required substantial remuneration. By staying off the board, the scale of those packages and the rate of their pay increases were shielded from public scrutiny.

Just before the results Ryanair recruited to its board Kyran McLaughlin, a stockbroker with Davy, Ireland's most successful broking firm; Michael Horgan, a former Aer Lingus executive; and Paolo Pietrogrande, a senior Italian businessman. McLaughlin, hugely respected in the Dublin financial market, was the most controversial appointment. The previous year he had been required to resign as joint managing director of Davy after it emerged he had invested almost €320,000 in a Liechtenstein-based trust which was being investigated by the Irish Revenue Commissioners. Ryanair, though, 'couldn't care less' about his Davy resignation, according to their then spokeswoman. 'The issues surrounding his resignation have no bearing whatsoever on the matter,' she added. 'To secure someone of Kyran McLaughlin's skill and expertise is a tremendous coup for Ryanair.'

The announcement of the sale knocked the Ryanair share price back a few pence to £7.45, a fall blamed on O'Leary's decision to sell another chunk of his shares. O'Leary told the market that his sale should not be seen as an attempt 'to get the hell out of here quick'.

'I'm in the tragic position of selling 10 per cent of my holding a year and still having 90 per cent of my wealth tied up in this airline,' he said, referring to the steady rise in the airline's share price each year. 'I'm selling shares for good, boring portfolio-management reasons.' Later, O'Leary would say that his frequent share sales were in part prompted by the experiences of the dot-com paper millionaires – the entrepreneurs who had been worth millions because investors had chased up the value of their companies, only to wake up penniless one morning because the market had collapsed. 'I'm not going to be like those dot-com gobshites,' he said.

Banking his cash was an essential part of the O'Leary approach. He had enough money tied up in Ryanair, and he instinctively made sure that no matter what happened to the company, he would still be a wealthy man. Making more, much more, from his Ryanair holdings remained his first priority, but he would continue to cash in his shares if the stock continued to rise.

Farmers like cash, and O'Leary was no different from his forebears. February's sale meant the chief executive had taken almost €115 million out of the company in the previous three years, and had spent just a fraction of it on the fripperies of life. The rest was his nest egg, his rainy-day money, his marker.

'Ryanair shareholders can't say they haven't been warned,' the *Irish Independent* said. 'When a chief executive sells €46m of stock within a fortnight, it's not a vote of confidence. No compelling technical explanation was offered. The sales go beyond all normal requirements of cash need or diversification. Michael O'Leary is not retiring. Even a Dublin house is not that expensive . . . Believers put their money where their mouth is.' O'Leary was unruffled: he remained a large shareholder, he remained committed to driving the company forward, and he had the unequivocal support of his board and his shareholders. Newspapers could write what they like, but O'Leary pointed only to results.

With the money for the new planes banked, O'Leary was ready to take his next step forward. On the day of the results he had said that Ryanair was close to finalizing details of its first continental European base. He had narrowed down the search to three airports: Stockholm's Skavsta, Frankfurt's Hahn and Brussels' Charleroi. On 28 February 2001 Charleroi, owned by the regional Walloon government, was unveiled as the victor. For the airport the prize was considerable – Ryanair's first-year target was seven routes, up to thirty flights a day and one million passengers – and the victory was the culmination of months of tough negotiation.

'At the end of the year 2000 we were put on a short list of several European airports located near big cities,' recalls Pierre Fenemont, Charleroi's PR manager. 'The negotiations started in November 2000 and ended at the end of January 2001. It was a long and strong and hard negotiation but it was a friendly negotiation.'

The key issues were financial: how much would Charleroi charge, how much would it contribute to Ryanair's marketing costs and what would it pay towards the cost of establishing the base? O'Leary knew that his business had already transformed an airport that had been atrophying. Charleroi was about to become a significant and profitable European airport, and the surrounding area would benefit from Ryanair's decision. Logically, therefore, the owners of the airport should pay Ryanair for the privilege of its business.

The deal, which would soon be referred to the European Commission by jealous rivals, was the template for Ryanair's future European expansion. The Walloon regional government agreed that landing charges at Charleroi would be fixed at €1 per passenger, about half the standard rate. It also agreed to pay €4 per passenger towards Ryanair's marketing and promotional costs for fifteen years for up to twenty-six flights a day; a further €160,000 for up to twelve new routes – a flat fee paid regardless of the cost of establishing the routes; €768,000 towards pilot training; and

€250,000 towards hotel costs for Ryanair staff. On top of that, Charleroi would charge Ryanair just €1 per passenger for its ground handling services, compared to the normal rates of between €8 and €13 per passenger.

It was a remarkably sweet deal for O'Leary, and was concluded as a bilateral private contract between the airline and the airport. The details were not published and the incentives not made available to other airlines. O'Leary has always maintained that any other airline could have negotiated a similar deal with Charleroi, and that the discounts on ground handling and landing charges were a red herring because the published tariffs were strictly notional. Charleroi's published rates applied to an airport that had no business; the rates he negotiated applied to an airport that would handle a million passengers a year, all delivered by Ryanair.

Charleroi and the Walloon government believed the incentives were a worthwhile investment; their money and flexibility on charges would deliver an airline, a base and passengers. The airport's growth would stimulate the local economy, create employment and increase tourism. The airport's business plan, which was used to justify the deal, expected revenues to surge, not from Ryanair but from other carriers drawn to the airport.

But the plan was optimistic and economical with the truth. It ignored the potential risks attached to the deal, understated the scale of its incentives for new routes and was overly bullish about the earnings that might accrue from other, hypothetical, airlines. In short, the Charleroi business plan was a political document. It was designed to put flesh on a political decision to back Ryanair and its development of the airport – a decision that would require millions in taxpayers' money but which the Walloon government decided was money well spent if it delivered a bustling airport to a region that had been depressed ever since the demise of its coal mines.

Three years later the European Commission would have to decide how much of the incentives would have been paid if Charleroi had been thinking like a private company rather than an instrument of government. For the moment Ryanair had a deal that boosted its profits and reduced its costs, a deal not made available to any other airline.

'A lot of work and energy went into the Charleroi base,' says Tim Jeans.

The great thing was that Ryanair would parachute people in from various departments – they would take a pilot and someone who works in the accounts department and say, 'Right, you're going out to Charleroi.' I effectively moved my sales team out of Stansted and across to Brussels and we lodged in hotels in Brussels for several weeks and prepared the ground in terms of PR, holding press conferences, alerting the media, launching competitions and just getting the name out there.

O'Leary's tactics for promoting the Ryanair brand were tried and tested. Sabena, Belgium's struggling flag carrier, would be his whipping boy; as long as it rose to his bait, he would be able to promote Ryanair cheaply and dramatically. Christophe Mueller, Sabena's president and chief executive officer, should have been prepared for the onslaught, but he proved easy prey for O'Leary.

Ryanair's opening campaign was low key by its standards: newspaper advertisements carried the relatively uncontroversial message, 'Welcome Ryanair and its really low prices. Good-bye Sabena and its really expensive flights.' The second round of advertisements was more typically confrontational. They featured a picture of the famous Brussels statue of a small boy urinating and said, 'Pissed off with Sabena's high fares? Low fares have arrived in Belgium.'

Mueller was furious and sent a fax to O'Leary claiming that the advertisements were defamatory. The game had begun, even if Mueller was not yet aware what he had started. O'Leary faxed back his rebuttal. The advertisements, he said, were 'valid criticisms of Sabena's outrageously high airfares'. If Mueller had expected the faxes to remain a private matter between two chief executives, he had failed to do his homework on O'Leary. With his fish hooked, O'Leary could start to play. The faxes were speedily translated and sent out to the Belgian press.

Sabena would not let up, however, and Mueller eventually took his complaint to court, where he won a truly Pyrrhic victory. In October, eight months after the Charleroi base had been announced and eight months after the advertisements had first run, Ryanair was ordered to discontinue the campaign or face a fine, and was also instructed to apologize to Sabena. O'Leary complied with the court order, but gave it his own twist. 'We're sooooo sorry Sabena!' his advertisement said, and listed seven one-way fare comparisons with Sabena. 'Ryanair is really, really sorry and promises to include this information in our future advertising.'

Once again the easily pricked vanity of a national airline had guaranteed Ryanair months of controversial coverage. By the end of the court case Ryanair had become a well-known brand in a country where it now had a base, and its message of low fares was clearly understood.

The airline industry is used to endemic crises: war, terrorism and the vagaries of the oil market all create painful losses from time to time. In February 2001 a different crisis took hold, with the confirmation that in Britain there had been an outbreak of foot and mouth disease.

Highly contagious, foot and mouth afflicts cattle, sheep, pigs, goats, deer and prompts a panic reaction from governments. Once confirmed in Britain, Ireland went on red alert to prevent the spread of the disease across the Irish Sea. The Irish government banned the importation of live animals and animal products. Disinfectant mats were placed at all points of entry and across farm gates, schools, offices and shops, and the movement of animals was restricted. People were asked to cut down on unnecessary travel and public events cancelled.

The seriousness of the situation was evident from the decision to call off the annual St Patrick's Day festivities in Dublin, while Joe Walsh, the minister for agriculture, banned hunting and fishing and shut down national parks. Dublin Zoo shut on 1 March, and then Walsh called on racing fans not to travel to England for the

Cheltenham racing festival. In Britain measures were less draconian, but the nightly television news carried gruesome images of herds of cattle being destroyed and their carcasses burnt in massive pyres.

Sporting events, too, started to fall victim to the foot and mouth outbreak. Ireland's rugby internationals against Scotland, Wales and England were postponed so that thousands of fans would not travel. The match against Wales, scheduled to take place in Cardiff, was called off just a week before the game was due to take place. In a show of patriotism Aer Lingus immediately offered to refund the tickets of travelling fans or at least to change the dates so that they could make the rescheduled game. Ryanair, however, refused to make any concessions. 'It may turn out to be something of a PR disaster for us,' said Ryanair spokesman Enda O'Toole. 'But these are all scheduled services we have to run anyway. We had a flight into Cardiff on Friday morning with 130 booked and only sixteen travelled. We have to protect ourselves against that.'

The stock market feared that Ryanair, which relied on the Ireland–UK routes to generate more than 40 per cent of its revenues, would suffer. O'Leary disagreed. 'We will continue to deliver shareholder value despite foot and mouth – it isn't impacting Ryanair,' he told an investor conference. He said that 6 per cent of passengers weren't turning up for Ireland to UK flights, but because the airline refused to give refunds, the no-shows had no impact on revenues. O'Leary was more concerned about the effect of foot and mouth on his own herd of Aberdeen Angus cattle. A prize bull he had bought in Canada was stranded on the other side of the Atlantic until travel restrictions were lifted, and an outbreak of the disease in Ireland would have forced him to kill his entire herd.

There was, though, a moment of light relief at the height of the crisis. On 21 March, O'Leary's fortieth birthday, his fellow directors organized a surprise. In the middle of a Ryanair board meeting the door was thrown open and in marched Mary O'Rourke, O'Leary's political nemesis. His shock quickly turned to laughter when he realized it was actually Minister Rourky from RTE's satirical programme *Bull Island*, who bears more than a passing resemblance to O'Rourke despite being played by a male actor.

O'Leary spends a lot of time talking to the media, but interviews rarely offer a new insight into the man or his company, and he recycles the same stories and the same explanations, often word for word. His objective remains the same: to promote the brand and the mantra of low fares, preferably via free publicity. Occasionally, however, he will float a new idea and see what happens. In May 2001 he decided to use an interview with Fiona McHugh of the *Sunday Times* to test some radical thoughts.

In 2001 Ryanair passengers were choosing to spend an average of £4 each on ancillary services. O'Leary noted that an extra pound per passenger on those services would raise revenues by more than £9 million. 'If we can increase the average spend per passenger by enough, then we could afford to cut fares to zero,' he said. 'Ultimately, we are trying to get to a situation where we can give away tickets, not on Monday mornings or peak times, but on midweek seats. All the other airlines are asking how they can get up fares, we are asking how we can get rid of them.'

To get this extra pound per passenger, O'Leary proposed to introduce a host of paid inflight services, ranging from satellite television to Internet services to gambling. 'I'm working on a [cinema] multiplex model,' said O'Leary. 'They make most of their money from the sale of popcorn, drinks and sweets, not cinema tickets.'

O'Leary was thinking aloud, floating the concept of free flights and guaranteeing headlines for his airline. It was not wishful thinking. He believed that if the package on offer to each passenger was compelling enough, he could turn a profit simply by having people on his planes, even if they paid nothing to get there. By no means would all seats be free and Ryanair would still squeeze every last cent out of last-minute travellers, but as the airline expanded and opened new routes, the prospect of filling planes on a wet Wednesday afternoon from Stansted to Malmö or Charleroi appeared a daunting task. Free, or virtually free, flights would draw the numbers; the challenge was to make so much money from passengers while they were a captive market that the giveaway became a profit centre.

Encouraged by the deal with Charleroi, by May 2001 O'Leary was talking to thirty airports that wanted a Ryanair service, fourteen of them in Italy. He was happy to let them compete for his attention and was candid about his intentions. 'We don't view any airport as a long-term arrangement per se; the biggest incentive for us to use an airport is a package of low charges. All of our existing arrangements are interchangeable so if, for example, Belfast was to come up with a better package [than Derry] then we would certainly consider it.'

Ryanair wanted low charges, quick turnaround times and money for its promotions and new routes, and it was also saying it would turn its back on any airport that tried to ratchet up charges once it had got their business. To make sure his new suitors were aware of his single-mindedness, O'Leary was able to provide an example. In mid-June he announced that he was terminating the service between Rimini and Stansted, a route launched in 1998. Ryanair claimed that Rimini's new management and board had tried to break the terms of its deal with Ryanair. It was commercial director Michael Cawley, and not O'Leary, who presented Ryanair's case to the public.

Here we have the spectre of a misguided airport management and board seeking to break its contract with Ryanair. Ryanair has built up Rimini airport from the provincial backwater that it was prior to 1998 and has transformed tourism in Emilia-Romagna with tens of thousands of new visitors to the region from the UK, not just during the peak summer periods but throughout the whole year.

The airport management and board now feel that they can renege on the terms of the agreement which Ryanair signed originally in 1998 with the airport and expect Ryanair to continue to fly there under some new financial arrangements. What they do not understand is that with ten existing airports and in excess of ten further airports seeking our business Ryanair has more demands for its flights than it can supply for the foreseeable future.

The Rimini flights were immediately moved to Ancona airport, an hour's drive away.

Rimini was not the first Italian airport to feel the ire of Ryanair. In November 2000 Ryanair had terminated its flights between Stansted and the southern Italian airport of Lamezia, just four months after the airline had begun flying there. Ryanair claimed it was 'impossible to maintain a satisfactory arrangement with the board of Lamezia', complaining that the airport had sought to renege on the terms of Ryanair's deal just months after it was signed.

The disagreements with Rimini and Lamezia were no worse than the problems Ryanair had had over the years with Stansted and Manchester, and they were certainly no worse than the various wranglings with Dublin airport. But while Stansted, Manchester and Dublin were vital parts of the Ryanair network, Rimini and Lamezia were expendable. The number of people living within an airport's catchment area mattered but not hugely. London was the draw, and London was the market, not Ancona, Rimini or Lamezia. And the message to hopeful airports was emphatically clear. stay cheap, stay amenable or Ryanair will leave.

On 25 June 2001 Ryanair delivered yet another set of solid full-year results: pre-tax profits rose by more than 37 per cent, to €123.4 million, and turnover was up by 32 per cent to almost €487 million. It had been an eventful year for Ryanair, O'Leary said when announcing the figures. Ten new aircraft were purchased; ten new European routes were launched; and a five-year agreement was signed with pilots, cabin crew and ground operations staff. O'Leary said there was 'no cap on us growing at 25 per cent a year for the foreseeable future'. He stressed, though, that the airline's growth was being judiciously managed.

Trading conditions over the past twelve months have been difficult, characterized by significantly higher oil prices, fears of an economic downturn, significant retrenchment in the technology sector and the outbreak of foot and mouth disease in the UK in the last quarter. Most of our European competitors have issued profit warnings or reported losses. Despite these negative market conditions, Ryanair has continued to deliver disciplined growth in fleet, new routes, traffic, revenues and profitability. During the last six winter months of the year, when all of the other low-fare airlines in Europe have been recording losses, Ryanair's traffic increased by 35 per cent and profitability by 37 per cent. What makes Ryanair different from other low-fare airlines is that although our average air fares are some 30 per cent lower, our profits rise as our traffic grows, and we continue to be profitable in all four quarters.

As usual, O'Leary was not content with just talking up his airline's performance.

I could not let these results pass without highlighting the lost opportunities to the Irish economy and tourism due to the disastrous effects of the present Irish government's policy of increasing costs at Dublin airport, and protecting this high-cost airport monopoly which has resulted in higher fares and the ending of Dublin airport's fifteen-year record of annual double-digit traffic growth. This policy is catastrophic for a small island nation like Ireland, whose tourism industry is central to the growth of our economy ... It is time for the Irish government to change this disastrous policy before any further damage is inflicted upon Irish tourism.

It was a predictable rant, and it fell on deaf ears. The *Irish Times* and *Irish Independent* failed to mention O'Leary's tirade against government policy in their coverage of the results the next morning. O'Leary's passion was becoming a private one.

In November 1999 the appointment of Bill Prasifka to the new position of independent aviation regulator for Ireland had promised to change the dynamics of Ryanair's tumultuous relationship with Aer Rianta. Ryanair had supported the concept of an independent regulator and Prasifka seemed like a natural ally for the company. A newcomer to aviation – something O'Leary always valued – Prasifka had served as director of Ireland's Competition Authority, and his appointment indicated that competition issues would now become central to Irish aviation policy. Prasifka's brief would include the thorny matter of airport charges. From now on if Dublin airport or Shannon or Cork wanted to raise their charges they had to get approval from the regulator, and he would lay down maximum charges.

Prasifka's first year and a half was spent fact-gathering and familiarizing himself with the industry, and his office was only formally established in February 2001.

Despite the regulator's power over Aer Rianta, the airport authority did little to endear itself to Prasifka, who was forced to seek a court order in March 2001 to force the company to release information to him. Aer Rianta caved in and gave the files to the regulator just before the case reached court, and at the end of June Prasifka gave his much-awaited draft determination on airport charges for 2000–05. He gave all three airports the right to increase their charges, but what he allowed for did not come close to the doubling Aer Rianta had wanted. Under the draft Cork was allowed to raise prices by a maximum of 94 per cent, to €9.08 per passenger, Shannon by 37 per cent, to €7.68 per passenger, and Dublin by just 9 per cent, to €6.30.

The rates were maximums only, and Prasifka said the airports were free to negotiate lower rates with individual airlines if they wanted to. He also set Dublin airport a target of efficiency gains of 15 per cent over the five years after finding that the airport was 30 per cent less efficient than peer airports of a similar size, and chopped €21 million from its proposed capital expenditure budget.

On that point, O'Leary applauded Prasifka's efforts but his pleasure did not extend to the new charges. 'The regulator's draft report fails miserably to facilitate the development and operation of cost-effective airports which meet the requirements of users, and unless his final report meets this statutory obligation, then we will be calling on him to resign his position and allow someone who is willing to challenge the Aer Rianta monopoly – and promote the needs of airport users – to take over.'

At a meeting called to discuss the report, O'Leary went even further with his criticisms of Dublin airport. 'Dublin is ridiculously expensive,' he ranted. 'Dissatisfaction with Aer Rianta by the users is widespread.' O'Leary was particularly outraged by Aer Rianta's proposed extension at Dublin airport, which involved spending more than €200 million on a new pier to accommodate flights to Heathrow and some continental European airports. 'What you want is low-cost facilities, not gold-plated mausoleums. Where in the legislation does it say Aer Rianta can subsidize the fat cats waddling down to Pier C to board their British Midland morning business flight to Heathrow?' he asked. O'Leary wanted cheap facilities that could handle the needs of a low-cost airline. He did not want elaborate piers for aircraft; passengers could walk to their plane and board by the stairs. He wanted what his critics described as a 'shed' – a building where passengers could assemble for check-in and boarding, but nothing more.

Much to O'Leary's disappointment, the arrival of a regulator had failed to resolve his increasingly bitter dispute with Aer Rianta and its chairman Noel Hanlon. With Mary O'Rourke also a confirmed enemy, O'Leary's ambitions for Dublin were stymied. He was stuck with an airport management and a transport minister with whom he could not do business, and now he had a regulator who thought it was acceptable for airports to increase charges rather than reduce costs. Prasifka may have trimmed Aer Rianta's spending but he had not changed the airport's direction: instead of low-cost facilities, it would press ahead with elaborate and expensive expansion that delivered only marginal increases in capacity.

By the summer of 2001 Ryanair had grown to become one of Europe's largest airlines. It was carrying upwards of nine million passengers a year, taking in hundreds of millions of euros in fares, making profits which were the envy of the aviation world, and expanding its route network at a fast clip. The one thing the airline lacked, though, was glamour. EasyJet projected a friendlier, hipper image; Go was all touchy-feely and consumer-friendly; Ryanair was just cheap.

And then came the sprinkling of celebrity magic. In August 2001 Tony Blair, Britain's then charismatic prime minister, announced that he and his family would be taking a Ryanair flight to Carcassonne for their summer holiday. Blair had been expected to choose easyJet, prompting an advertising campaign boasting that 'even Tony Blair got a bargain this summer', but in an embarrassing U-turn for the British airline Blair switched to Ryanair – 'probably because it is convenient', according to a Downing Street spokesman. It was a stroke of luck and a massive publicity coup for O'Leary. Ryanair was undoubtedly cheap, but if it was good enough for Blair and his children then it was good enough for most.

Ryanair's reaction to the news was remarkably restrained – 'Downing Street aides have confirmed Tony Blair will be flying with us, but we cannot discuss any details,' a spokesman said – but it still used the opportunity to get across its message. 'If he wants a cup of tea or a sandwich he will have to pay for it; this is a very egalitarian airline,' the spokesman told the London *Times*.

Some high-profile travellers, however, refused to use O'Leary's airline. Des Geraghty, president of SIPTU, reacted furiously when O'Leary said he was a Ryanair regular. O'Leary claimed on radio that it was 'breathtaking' that Geraghty had 'flown six times with Ryanair in the past six months' yet continued to criticize the airline so vehemently. Geraghty said he would seek an immediate retraction of O'Leary's 'misrepresentative claim', or failing that an apology in the courts. He insisted he had never travelled on a Ryanair flight 'before, during or since' the baggage handlers' strike in 1998.

Characteristically O'Leary refused to apologize. If Geraghty hadn't flown Ryanair, why were the hard-earned dues of union members 'being frittered away on higher fares for SIPTU bigwigs'? Or did Geraghty get a 'special deal' on Aer Lingus and 'travel with the other fat cats in business class'?

'I don't travel with fat cats, skinny cats or any other cats,' Geraghty replied. 'Actually, I usually take my car and the ferry when I go on holiday. I would normally travel economy class and I travel with Aer Lingus because that's where our members work.'

O'Leary could not have cared less. His airline was growing, his profits rising and his routes expanding. Disease and high oil prices had not knocked Ryanair off course; Blair had given the airline his blessing; and while O'Leary was bogged down in a long war over Dublin airport and its development, this was not distracting him from the main prize. European domination was the goal, and O'Leary was on his way. What could go wrong?

18. Terror in the Skies

Just before 9 a.m. on 11 September 2001 American Airlines Flight 11 was flown into the North Tower of New York's World Trade Center. Fifteen minutes later United Airlines Flight 175 crashed into the South Tower, and thirty minutes after that American Airlines Flight 77 hit the Pentagon in Arlington, Virginia.

In less than an hour the world changed. Almost 3,000 people died in the attacks, which had been planned and executed by members of al-Qaeda. The consequences were immediate and far-reaching: death and devastation in New York, Washington and in the fields of Pennsylvania, where United Flight 93 had crashed after its hijackers had been overwhelmed by passengers, followed by the launching of US-led invasions of Afghanistan and, eventually, Iraq.

The attacks sent the airline industry into a tailspin. Who would want to fly in their aftermath? And what levels of security would have to be introduced to prevent a repeat of the easy hijackings that had made the attacks possible? 'The US airline industry is in an unprecedented financial crisis,' said Continental's chairman and chief executive Gordon Bethune. 'This patient is dying very quickly. We all are going to be bankrupt before the end of the year. There is not an airline that I know of that has the excess cash to handle this.'

Before 9/11 that crisis had already been well on its way. The major American airlines had consistently failed to bring their costs into line with their revenues and were racking up losses at a remarkable rate. Yet, thanks to the generosity of America's bankruptcy protection laws, their financial incontinence did not force the collapses or mergers that would have rationalized the industry and allowed healthier and leaner carriers to emerge in their place. Smaller airlines went to the wall, and some larger ones; but the majority struggled on, fighting with their employees, staving off their creditors and trading at a loss.

For them 9/11 was also an opportunity, because it allowed them to blame external factors for their own deficiencies, gave them an excuse to announce large-scale redundancies already in the pipeline, and encouraged them to put out the begging bowl for government assistance. Within days of the attacks American Airlines and United Airlines both announced they were shedding 20,000 jobs, while Continental and Delta said they would cut 12,000 jobs each. Industry analysts estimated that the attacks would cost America's airlines a further $3 billion in losses and that 100,000 jobs would be lost.

European airlines were also preparing for the worst. British Airways' share price tumbled by almost 40 per cent in the four days after the attacks and the company responded by announcing 5,200 job cuts on top of the 1,800 voluntary redundancies revealed just weeks before. Alitalia, Italy's long-suffering flag carrier, announced plans to cut 2,700 jobs and grounded thirteen jets in response to what it termed 'by far the worst crisis commercial airlines have faced since the end of the Second World War'. And in Ireland Aer Lingus suspended a quarter of its flight schedule and said it would shed 600 temporary workers.

Back in Ryanair headquarters, however, the reaction to 9/11 was somewhat different. O'Leary's immediate response was classic: he launched a seat sale, offering one million seats at the then low price of GB£9.99 each and using the iconic image of General Kitchener calling men to war with the tag line 'Your country needs you.'

O'Leary had no sympathy for the flag carriers' woes and was sceptical about their motives in calling for help. 'There is little doubt that tragic events in the US are being used by a number of European flag carriers as an excuse upon which to blame their long-standing cost problems and an opportunity to look for subsidies and handouts,' he said. 'We intend to fly our way out of this crisis by giving passengers even more reasons to travel at even lower prices. I think a lot of airlines are making hay out of what happened and trying to create their own crisis. This is our chance to send out a clear message to the big, fat flag carriers who are looking for state subsidies.'

It was a response that prompted accusations that O'Leary was trying to use the atrocities to grind his rivals into the ground. He was, but he was also doing what he did best: using any opportunity to sell seats, calculating that people's fear of flying would be tempered by low prices. 'You might be scared of flying at £200 return, but you'll be a lot less scared at £20 return,' he said. And he was right. While the high-fare airlines saw sharp falls in bookings, the Ryanair seat sale was an instant success.

A million cheap flights was, however, a small stroke of opportunism compared with O'Leary's major coup. In the months before 9/11 O'Leary had been engineering a Dutch auction between Boeing, the aircraft manufacturer which supplied all Ryanair's current fleet, and Airbus, its European rival. O'Leary's expansion plans required scores of planes over the next five years and he was focused on securing the cheapest possible price. His tactics were crude but effective. During July he had cancelled options that Ryanair held on nineteen new Boeing 737s and then stated publicly that he would be trawling the second-hand market to find fifty planes to meet his growth targets. In August, just before the 11 September attacks, Ryanair had placed full-page advertisements in trade publications for fifty second-hand Boeings and within a month had 600 to choose from, all priced at under $15 million each. At the same time he informed Airbus that he was open to offers. He said he would not deviate from his policy of operating a uniform fleet, but if Airbus wanted to convert Ryanair from an all-Boeing to an all-Airbus carrier, now was the time to make its proposals.

He was not bluffing. The list price of a new Boeing was $60 million, with an Airbus A320 marginally cheaper at $58 million, both far more than he was prepared to pay. But the attraction of new aircraft was that ongoing maintenance charges and running costs would be significantly lower than with second-hand planes.

For both manufacturers the stakes were remarkably high. Each had studied Ryanair's growth, subjecting its business model and projections to exhaustive testing. They knew that the airline would be a major customer in the years to come and also that O'Leary would not deviate from his conviction that Ryanair should operate only one type of aircraft. Winning O'Leary meant not just hundreds of millions of dollars in orders from the Irish airline, it meant that the winner could claim to be the provider of choice to Europe's most dynamic airline.

For Airbus, the pressure to win was intense. Boeing already had Southwest, America's most successful low-cost airline, as its largest customer. Airbus had no significant presence in Europe's low-cost market – its home patch – and it needed to shoulder its way in.

Technically, O'Leary believes, there is little to choose between the planes. His criterion was price. 'In the autumn of 2001 Ryanair started to involve us very seriously in the evaluation of sourcing additional aircraft,' says Chris Buckley, a vice president with Airbus. 'I would say that the main reason for doing that was to put tremendous pressure on Boeing so they could get the deal they wanted from Boeing for additional aircraft.'

It would have been a tumultuous battle even without the intervention of 11 September, but the terrorist strikes gave the negotiations added bite. The manufacturers' plight was fast becoming desperate as carriers cancelled aircraft orders and dumped their options. Boeing was in crisis. Its order book had halved almost overnight and it was about to embark on a massive redundancy programme that would see 50,000 workers lose their jobs in Seattle. Airbus, too, was being pushed to the brink, although the company's chief commercial officer, John Leahy, insisted there would be no job cuts.

O'Leary could smell blood. 'As soon as either one of them came up with a price, O'Leary would fax their offer through to the other and say, "That's what I'm being offered, better it,"' says one former executive. The manufacturers knew that they were being played, but could not afford to back away. The second-hand market was bloated with planes, their customers were in retreat and there were no new ones on the horizon. O'Leary was the only buyer in a buyers' market.

In O'Leary's book state aid was a mechanism to keep inefficient airlines in business. It distorted the market and was, he argued, illegal under European competition laws. When Sabena secured a €125 million 'bridging loan' from the Belgian government after 9/11, he complained to the European Commission. And he was preparing another tirade against 'lazy incompetent national airlines' when the waters were muddied by news that Ryanair itself was a beneficiary of a form of state aid.

The 9/11 attacks had prompted insurance companies to withdraw their war risks cover from airlines, and governments stepped in to provide the insurance indemnity without which airlines could not fly. As Ireland's largest airline, Ryanair was the greatest beneficiary of the Irish government's decision to provide the indemnity.

O'Leary insisted that Ryanair had offered to pay the government for its cover, and vigorously denied that the temporary provision of insurance cover in such exceptional circumstances could conceivably be termed state aid. 'It is not state aid, because it is not costing the state a penny,' he said. 'We would be happy to pay in any case.' Such subtleties, however, did not find favour in the Irish media. The *Irish Times* report was typical: 'Ryanair wins under state aid cover plan', and it followed up its news coverage with an opinion piece that argued that Ryanair and O'Leary were hypocritical about state aid.

'Let's get one thing clear,' the article began. 'Michael O'Leary is not opposed to state aid to Aer Lingus. He is opposed to anything that gets in the way of profit at Ryanair, be it state aid to the national carrier or ice in his customers' drinks.' Ryanair, it argued, had no objection to state aid when the Walloon regional government gave it subsidies of about €12 million per year to operate from Charleroi airport. And the airline's ideological objections to state aid were muted when it accepted the government's insurance indemnity.

O'Leary was not prepared to let the paper's views go unchallenged, and three days later his own article appeared on its opinion pages. 'We are indeed opposed to [state aid],' he wrote. 'Not . . . because it would get in the way of profit at Ryanair (it wouldn't), but because it will threaten some of the jobs of 1,700 – mainly Irish – people employed at this company. How would [the *Irish Times*] feel if the *Irish Independent* or the *Irish Examiner* were to receive Government subsidies to compete with the *Irish Times*?' He then addressed the issue of state aid from the Walloon government.

The low-cost arrangement we have entered into with Brussels South Charleroi Airport is not State aid. It is a low-cost arrangement (which in turn is passed on in the form of low fares) which is available to every airline – including Aer Lingus – that wishes to fly there. This is not, as asserted, State aid.

State aid does not result in efficient airlines or lower fares – it props up inefficient airlines and high fares. I object to State aid for our principal competitor, when it is quite clear that this aid will be used to assist it to compete against Ryanair.

His argument was passionate but failed to deal with the newspaper's most pointed accusation – that O'Leary and Ryanair were hypocritical in their approach to state aid. O'Leary did not explain how state aid for Aer Lingus threatened Ryanair jobs but not profits. Without doubt, Ryanair's profits would have suffered if Aer Lingus, or any state-owned airline, was given unlimited resources by its government to compete with it. His objective was to ensure that as little state assistance as possible found its way onto state airlines' balance sheets, because the weaker they were, the better equipped Ryanair was to compete with them aggressively. There were, too, semantic distinctions that O'Leary took seriously: he saw his deal with the Walloon government not as a subsidy or state aid, but as a commercial deal that would benefit both sides. Ryanair would get the opportunity to build a new market at low cost and with financial help, but the long-term winner would be the Walloon region. It was not a subsidy to prop up an ailing airline or to distort competition, but an investment by the Walloon government in a profitable future.

O'Leary also said that he was calling a truce with Mary O'Rourke, the transport minister. 'We have requested a meeting to explain in detail how – by working together – Ryanair and the government can deliver two million new passengers and 500 new jobs for Irish airports and Irish tourism over the next two years. I hope she will respond magnanimously in the national interest.'

The day after his article appeared, O'Leary and O'Rourke attended a political fund-raising event hosted by Charlie McCreevy, Ireland's finance minister and a friend of O'Leary. 'Reports say they [O'Leary and O'Rourke] were not observed in friendly conversation, or indeed any conversation at all,' the *Irish Times* noted. By early November, however, reconciliation was back on the agenda when O'Leary said he had decided to stop 'slagging off' government ministers. His comments came during a conference call with stock market analysts, as he was discussing the prospects of Ryanair's terminal and the location of Ryanair's next base.

'Our view remains unchanged that Aer Rianta is a high-cost, inefficient monopoly, but perhaps the Irish government's view is changing,' he said, according to a transcript of the conference call.

There is a new atmosphere and it's time to stop slagging off the government and certain Cabinet ministers and work more cooperatively with them. If not, we could see 15,000 to 20,000 tourism jobs lost. The government is giving some consideration to our plans to break the Aer Rianta monopoly and our plans for a second terminal. But I'm guessing that the government will not be able to move quickly enough to meet our deadlines.

O'Leary, in any case, was not prepared to wait. He was hunting for a new continental base to complement Charleroi, and in late 2001 he chose Hahn, the former NATO airfield in southern Germany he preferred to call Frankfurt Hahn.

The two sides signed a twenty-year deal which would create 200 jobs and provide at least thirty flights daily to more than ten destinations from February 2002. Ryanair promised these flights would deliver 1.5 million passengers in the first year. For the airline it meant a guaranteed low-cost base for twenty years in Europe's largest market. For the airport, the deal with Ryanair guaranteed its future.

'A deal is a deal,' says Hahn's Helfer.

And of course it includes some provisions for inflation, and there are provisions in the deal concerning what happens if they grow to a certain level of base aircraft and so on, but basically it is a deal. It doesn't make sense for an airport to handle Ryanair as a customer, give it a low-cost deal, and then increase your charges by 100 per cent two years later, because then their business model wouldn't work. We have a passenger charge of €4.35 and that is it.

Helfer says Hahn offered Ryanair a cheap deal because it was the only airline flying there. 'That's the problem of conventional airports,' says Helfer. 'They have, let's say, one daily flight from Lufthansa going to Frankfurt or one daily flight from Aer Lingus going to Dublin and they have to be very careful not to deteriorate their price base with the traditional customers when they start doing business with Ryanair. We did not have this problem.'

O'Leary was happy with the outcome, and happy to use it as a stick with which to beat Aer Rianta. 'What makes Frankfurt Hahn different is that everything they said they would do from day one they have delivered on,' he said. 'This new German base means that four more aircraft, 200 new jobs and over one million tourists have again been lost to Ireland by the high-cost Aer Rianta monopoly.'

His relationship with Dublin airport deteriorated further at the end of November, when the two disagreed about the creation of a special low-cost facility within the airport, prompting Aer Rianta to state that a low-cost deal for Dublin did not necessarily have to involve Dublin airport. 'It is worth noting that Shannon airport is only marginally further from Dublin than many of the European airports Ryanair flies to [that claim to be city airports],' a spokesman said, referring to airports like Malmö, Hahn and Beauvais. It was a valid, if mischievous, point. It also highlighted the differences between an established airport like Dublin and a transformed military base like Hahn. Dublin had an international market, a host of carriers as customers and far less flexibility to manoeuvre. Hahn, starting virtually from scratch, could offer dramatically cheap deals because it was desperate to build a business.

O'Leary is a supreme pragmatist who never worries that his actions might contradict a previously stated policy. He will do whatever he thinks is best at the time and execute a perfect U-turn moments later if conditions change.

In his long-running battles with Aer Rianta, O'Leary used a familiar refrain. The airport company's refusal to reduce its charges and the Irish government's inability to deliver a second competing terminal in Dublin was, he said, depriving Ireland of both new airline routes and consequent tourism growth. When he announced the new bases in Charleroi and Hahn he reiterated that Ireland had once again lost out on the opportunity to have more routes because of the intransigence of Aer Rianta and the government. He would not, he said, launch another route from Dublin until there was a change in policy, and other countries would benefit instead from Ryanair's growth. He had also denounced both Glasgow and Edinburgh airports as far too expensive and had opted instead to base Ryanair's Scottish operations in Prestwick.

Barbara Cassani, unfortunately for her and her fledgling airline, believed O'Leary's rhetoric and decided that Go would launch a route from Dublin to Edinburgh. Her decision was announced in July, with the service due to start operating at the end of September.

O'Leary's response was immediate and brutal: Ryanair would crush Go, no matter what it cost. In part, his determination to see off Go was simple machismo. Ryanair wanted to retain its dominance of the low-fare market between Ireland and the UK and would brook no competitive threat. His response was as consciously predatory as Aer Lingus's earlier attempts to knock Ryanair out of the skies, and showed that O'Leary only liked competition when it was on his terms.

'Go foolishly decided to come into Dublin,' recalls Tim Jeans. 'David Magliano, the Go marketing director at the time, apparently told Barbara Cassani not to worry. Go could do Edinburgh and Glasgow because Ryanair wouldn't follow. We had often said quite publicly that we would never darken Edinburgh's doors because [its landing and passenger charges] were far too expensive and it wasn't our kind of airport.'

Cassani's decision to launch a Dublin–Edinburgh service was not illogical. At the time the route was served by Aer Lingus, which operated two Fokker 50s and ran four flights a day. It was an expensive route – a typical return fare was more than £200 – and it seemed ripe for competition. Instead of a battle with Aer Lingus, however, Cassani got a price war with Ryanair, or as Jeans says, 'a competitive response of biblical proportions'. The number of planes ploughing the route ballooned from two Fokkers to thirteen Boeing 737s daily, with a capacity of 1,500 passengers each way, as Aer Lingus, Go and Ryanair battled for supremacy.

'We certainly weren't making money,' says Jeans. 'But this was very much part of the cost of defending our territory. The costs of the exercise were never calculated and it was only a question of when would Go pull out.'

Ryanair's fares undercut Go, tumbling to £5 each way. Eighty-four days after launching the route, Go admitted defeat and withdrew. 'We got a thrashing,' Cassani wrote some years later in her book about Go.

Going head-to-head cost us millions and we withdrew wounded. We learned another crucial lesson about discounting. You can't take on someone with lower costs because they dig deeper than you to lower their prices and still make money, while you're bleeding.

We seriously misjudged how seriously and how angrily they would take the incursion into Dublin. It was just a really tough lesson in business.

For Ryanair the battle had been a resounding success and had created a firm precedent – mess with us and we will crush you.

Prey had turned predator, and would use its power to drive away competition by cutting fares to the bone. O'Leary's response, though, was only possible because of his obsessive attention to costs. Ryanair had become the lowest-cost operator in Europe, and so could charge less than any competitor on any route without losing money. Even where it dropped its fares to loss-making levels, it could still recoup revenue from its ancillary deals. Critically, its low costs allowed it to sustain a price war longer than any rival could bear.

'It sent a warning shot to everybody,' says Clifton.

If you step on our toes we can sustain lower costs and lower fares better than anybody else. It's particularly true when you've got a guy like Michael on top. Airline executives have to decide if they'll compete with Ryanair or not. They look at the cash balance and they look at the guy running it. And [after Go's experience] it wasn't a very good idea to go into your board and say, 'I've decided to take these guys on, because they'd have to fly for free for ten years to beat us off,' because a number of people sitting around the board table would say, 'Well, maybe they just will.'

For O'Leary, route dominance mattered. It gave him extra power with the airports served by his airline, and it gave customers in search of a cheap ticket no option but to choose Ryanair. It was not, however, predation in the old style. Where Aer Lingus wanted to crush Ryanair so that it could restore high-priced travel, O'Leary's philosophy was fundamentally different. He wanted volume, and the way to drive passenger numbers ever higher was to reduce ticket prices. He wanted dominance on a route not so that he could push up prices, but so he could have far greater control over the airports and their charges. The result would be higher profits, but they would come from squeezing his suppliers for extra savings and from boosting passenger numbers, not from raising ticket prices.

While O'Leary and his colleagues basked in their swift victory over the pretender, Aer Rianta complained to Ireland's

Competition Authority that Ryanair had 'launched services on the same routes with the sole purpose of putting its competitor off the routes'.

Aer Rianta chairman Noel Hanlon had already written to the government to complain. 'Ryanair publicly stated that they would not allow another low-cost airline to operate on these routes, and proceeded to offer fares at £5 return with the sole purpose of putting its competitor off the route. To do so, Ryanair pulled capacity from three other routes which had an overall effect, from Ryanair's point of view, of not increasing capacity but of undermining its competitor.'

O'Leary was unfazed. 'The thought of our airport monopoly making a complaint to the Competition Authority fills me with joy and wonder,' he said.

For Cassani, the battle with Ryanair was a defining defeat. The barbarians had trampled all over the nice people and Go's credibility had taken a battering from which the company would struggle to recover. O'Leary just banked the victory and moved on. It had been important to win, but he had had no doubts that he would. Securing a deal for new aircraft was far more important, and demanded his full attention. By the end of the year Airbus had won, or at least it thought it had. It had offered to sell Ryanair its planes for just under $30 million each – effectively half price – and Boeing had come up short.

Chris Buckley suggested O'Leary and his team come out to Toulouse to finalize the deal. 'And that is exactly what we accomplished. That day in Toulouse, Michael and our president at the time, Noel Forgeard, shook hands on a deal for a hundred A321s.'

As far as Airbus was concerned the deal was done, but O'Leary had other ideas. Airbus's offer was attractive, but it gave him the ammunition for one last shot at Boeing. 'As far as I know, Michael called Boeing on the day, and said he had been in Toulouse, had a deal with Airbus,' says Buckley. 'Boeing came back on the following day, knocked some more money off, and Ryanair called us up, and said they were going to stick with Boeing after all.'

Boeing, like Airbus, was up against the wall. Production at the 737 plant in Renton, Washington had been cut in half, morale was at rock bottom and tens of thousands of employees had already lost their jobs. It was not a situation Boeing was used to. It was the dominant player in world aviation, having snapped up old rival McDonnell Douglas – maker of the infamous DC10 – in the 1980s. Airbus, a European consortium driven together by political desire rather than economic compulsion, was the new kid on the block, and its aggressive sales techniques made Boeing look patrician, old-fashioned and complacent.

But this time, Boeing knew it could not afford to lose. Alan Mulally, Boeing's chief executive, decided to do the deal with Ryanair whatever the price. Boeing had one extra shot in its locker that Airbus could not match.

The 737–800 series, with its slightly elongated body, could carry 189 seats in Ryanair's tight configuration – sixty more than the older 737s and thirty more than the Airbus A320. This would put enormous pressure on O'Leary to fill the new capacity, but his calculation was that those extra places reduced the average cost of each seat on the plane. They also gave added firepower against his competitors, allowing him to ramp up seat availability and flood the market on chosen routes with low fares and the capacity to match. It was a risk, but a calculated one. 'We were getting the extra seats almost for nothing,' he says. 'The challenge was to fill them.'

For Airbus, the memories of the deal that never was are still painful.

'This was an unprecedented event for Airbus, because after having two chief executives shake hands, it's normally left for everybody else to quickly do the paperwork and make sure everything else happens,' says Buckley. 'When the Ryanair delegation left Toulouse we were elated, we actually thought we had a deal. But then our reaction was one of massive disappointment that we had not won as we thought we had. And [there was] massive disappointment that the handshake we had thought we had was not even a handshake at all.'

Unusually for O'Leary, he showed Airbus some compassion in

their loss. 'We had a letter from Michael a few days later,' says
Buckley. 'It was thanking us for all our efforts, apologizing but
business is business, and the Boeing offer was much better. At least
[we had] something in writing from Ryanair, but that only goes
5 per cent of the way to mitigating our disappointment about not
winning.'

The result was a spectacular coup for Boeing, but it was even
more spectacular for O'Leary. 'We raped the fuckers,' he crowed
shortly after securing a deal that delivered him a hundred brand
new Boeing 737–800 jets, and an option for fifty more, for less
than half price – just over $28 million a plane. Boeing, however,
did not care. Asked how he felt about the 'rape', Toby Bright,
then Boeing's vice president in charge of sales, replied with a
straight face, 'We enjoyed the experience.'

The deal had stabilized Boeing's Renton plant and, just as
importantly, had given the company a solid platform in Europe.
For Boeing's employees, oblivious to the high-wire negotiations
that had delivered the deal, news of the Ryanair order caused
jubilation when it was announced at the end of January 2002. 'It
was a fantastic feeling,' says one Renton veteran.

For months there had been a sense of unimaginable doom. It's difficult
for people outside Boeing to understand, perhaps, but when we watched
those planes hit the towers on September 11 we were watching planes
that we had built being turned into weapons. It was a sense of violation.
And then came the cancelled orders and the trauma of the layoffs.

The spirit here in Renton is great, but nothing could withstand those
sort of setbacks. We badly needed a lift, and Michael O'Leary gave us
that lift. He came to us when we were at our lowest, and he said, I
believe in you and I believe in your product and I want to do business
with you. More than that, though, he promised us he would take our
fight with Airbus to his heart. It was like something out of *Braveheart*
rather than something you'd expect from an airline boss.

When O'Leary arrived in Renton to address the Boeing staff
in February 2002 he was given a rousing ovation by a crowd of

almost 2,000 employees, who cheered as he regaled them with tales of lazy state-owned airlines and hammed up Boeing's victory over Airbus. 'We love Boeing,' he told the crowd. 'Fuck the French.'

On 25 January 2002 Ryanair went public with its new Boeing deal. Ten days later, after announcing yet another set of record-breaking quarterly results which showed that profits had risen by 35 per cent to just under €30 million for the third quarter, the company seized the opportunity to place another thirty million shares on the market to raise €162 million, with a secondary offer raising an additional €25 million when demand for the new shares once again exceeded supply. For a change, O'Leary did not participate by selling any of his own stake in the company.

Ryanair had another cause for celebration in February – a partial victory in its long-running battle with Aer Rianta, when the airport operator agreed to provide a designated area in Dublin for low-cost carriers.

The agreement came on the back of a report by international aviation expert Professor Rigas Doganis which had recommended the initiative. The new facility would be operational for the 2003 season, Aer Rianta promised, and would give low-cost carriers a quicker, no-frills service. The key to the proposal was speed and convenience; lower charges were not on the agenda. Doganis's report ruled out Ryanair's plans for an independent low-cost terminal, but a partial victory was better than no victory at all.

'This will be a physical area which low-cost flights on any airline, including Aer Lingus, will be able to access and exit quicker than in other parts of the airport,' Mary O'Rourke explained.

O'Leary had no time for the normal business of Irish politics. Instead of courting political leaders, he lambasted them publicly and loudly. Mary O'Rourke had felt the full force of O'Leary's contempt, and Bertie Ahern, Ireland's popular taoiseach, was regularly lampooned by O'Leary as a dithering idiot in hock to the trade union barons. O'Leary, however, did have some political friends. His most important ally was P. J. Mara, a former government press secretary who had branched out into the world of public relations and political lobbying. Mara had retained powerful links with Ahern's Fianna Fáil party, acting as its director of elections, and he was also a close confidant of Ahern. His relationship with O'Leary – both friend and paid adviser – put him in a peculiarly awkward position with Ahern, but Mara is a man who can serve two masters with poise and charm.

O'Leary was also on friendly terms with Mary Harney, leader of the Progressive Democrats, a right of centre party which had been instrumental in delivering the country's low-tax regime, and Charlie McCreevy, the finance minister who had implemented the low-tax policy and was an avowed supporter of entrepreneurs and the free market. O'Leary's friendships, therefore, were with like-minded politicians; he did not go out of his way to seek access or favours from those he disdained.

Traditionally businessmen sought political favours by lavishing cash on political parties and on individual politicians. Ireland's planning system was systemically corrupt, with zoning decisions bought by land developers who bribed both local and national politicians. O'Leary's attitude to politics stemmed from a perhaps idiosyncratic view of what motivated politicians. In a radio inter- view in 1999 he said, 'I have never yet come across a politician who will make a political decision in your favour or against your favour unless it was in their interest, or in what they consider to be the national interest. They just don't make decisions based on the fact that you sponsored something, or that they stayed in some holiday home of yours.'

It came as a surprise then when it was revealed in early February that, through Ryanair, O'Leary had made a substantial donation to Harney's Progressive Democrats. Details first emerged in a parliamentary debate, and within a matter of days the scale of the contribution became public knowledge.

Ryanair had donated £50,000, the maximum allowable under Irish law. O'Leary refused to comment at the time, but he now says Ryanair has made donations to Ireland's two largest political parties – Fianna Fáil and Fine Gael – as well as to the Progressive

Democrats. 'If the party is going down the right road we should try and support it,' he says. 'The only two I wouldn't give a contribution to would be Sinn Féin and Labour. Sinn Féin are a bunch of mindless morons and they have the economic policies of a two-year-old. Labour have my sympathies, but that'd be about the height of it.'

If O'Leary appeared to be softening in Ireland, he showed no sign of changing his tactics in Ryanair's new markets. The airline planned to launch fourteen new routes from Hahn on 14 February – a move that prompted Lufthansa to mount a new legal challenge against Ryanair's decision to refer to Hahn airport as Frankfurt Hahn.

Since Ryanair had announced the new routes in November 2001 tensions had been steadily building between the two airlines. Ryanair opened hostilities in early December by slashing fares on existing routes from Hahn to Stansted, Glasgow and Shannon. Lufthansa responded by lodging complaint after complaint about Ryanair's advertisements, which resulted in Ryanair lodging three complaints with European regulators about the sheer volume of Lufthansa's complaints.

'This is basically chapters one and two of the big airlines' book on how to stamp out competition,' O'Leary said.

All they're trying to do is keep us tied up in the courts for a couple of months because they know that if they can head us off for the first few months we'll never get these new routes off the ground. Lufthansa went to a court in Cologne [where it is headquartered] where it can get these things done at nine o'clock on a Friday night by convincing some dotty old judge that Lufthansa will face irreparable damage because Ryanair is slagging it off.

Unnerved by the emergence of low-cost rivals in its home market, Lufthansa had responded aggressively on a number of routes, slashing its prices by up to 60 per cent. This was too predatory for the German Cartel Office, which ruled in February that Lufthansa would have to raise fares on the Frankfurt–Berlin route because its new fares did not cover its costs. Its strategy, the Cartel Office said, was to force its rival off the route and then recoup its losses by raising fares once it had succeeded. Lufthansa had cut its one-way fares from €254 to €100 in response to the €99 fare offered by newcomer Germania. The Cartel Office decided that Lufthansa would have to charge at least €35 more than Germania.

For O'Leary the skirmishes with Lufthansa were all part of the game. Each time Ryanair was hauled into a German courtroom and served with an injunction against producing advertisements which compared Ryanair's fares to Hahn with Lufthansa's fares to Frankfurt, it would drop them and then produce yet more comparative advertisements and find itself back in court yet again. But the fighting escalated in mid-January when a German court banned Ryanair from advertising Hahn airport as Frankfurt–Hahn. O'Leary's initial reaction was to downplay the ruling – 'As is the case with all of these ludicrous injunctions, Ryanair will appeal,' he said – but this case had the potential to be far more damaging than arguments about comparative advertising. Ryanair's expansion strategy had been based around flying to small, low-cost, airports and marketing them as their nearest local cities. Flights from London to Stockholm or Brussels to Glasgow were easy to sell, but flights from Stansted to Skavsta or Charleroi to Prestwick were an entirely different proposition.

For Hahn airport the battle was even more critical. It had ambitious expansion plans for itself, and any interruption in Ryanair's growth would hurt it more than it hurt the airline. 'Ryanair had trouble in court, so we thought, How could we help them?' says Andreas Helfer, manager of Hahn. 'And we decided, let's rename the company. So we went to court and said we wanted to rename the company. Not Hahn but Frankfurt Hahn. And the judge said, "Oh you are good guys, you bring lots of jobs to the region so I find for Frankfurt Hahn . . ."'

On 11 February Ryanair announced victory when an injunction against the use of the Frankfurt Hahn designation was thrown out by a Cologne court. 'We're delighted with ourselves this morning,' O'Leary said. 'I feel like the Michael Owen of the airline industry, beating the Germans on their home turf. Through all these court cases, Lufthansa has probably created more [publicity] for us than we've had on any other route we've launched.'

A month later, on 19 March, the courts delivered another verdict which attempted to balance the competing demands of the two German parties central to the case – Lufthansa and Frankfurt Hahn airport. With the wisdom of Solomon, it found that Ryanair could use the name Frankfurt Hahn as long as it clarified that Hahn was actually a long way from Frankfurt. But the court also agreed with Lufthansa that the use of the name was 'misleading'. This was enough for O'Leary. Once again, he had been allowed to generate acres of free publicity that hammered home the basic Ryanair messages.

Michael O'Leary's belief that all publicity is good publicity was tested to the limit at the end of February 2002, when Jane O'Keeffe, Ryanair's millionth passenger, entered Dublin's High Court. The case was guaranteed extensive media coverage, none of it favourable for Ryanair. 'We were shooting ourselves in the foot,' says one former executive, but O'Leary was unrepentant. He thought O'Keeffe's demands were unreasonable – he claimed that she had broken an understanding that the airline would be given at least two weeks notice of her flight requests.

From the very first day the case went badly for O'Leary. O'Keeffe told the court that when she had spoken to O'Leary on the telephone he had shouted, 'Who do you think you are, ringing up demanding flights?' On the second day Ryanair dangled an olive branch by offering O'Keeffe free flights for life plus €4,000, which she rejected immediately; she wanted £500,000. O'Leary then had to take the stand and answer allegations that he had bullied and abused O'Keeffe. Asked if his manner had been 'hostile', O'Leary replied, 'I had no reason to be hostile. I knew the call was coming through and what it was about. I knew she was not getting satisfaction and we would not be offering her a free flight on the basis that she was ringing up the day before [the flight].'

O'Leary said the first he had heard of the bullying allegation was 'when I read it in the papers at Heathrow last Friday'. He added, 'I'm not sure how it's possible to bully someone on the phone.'

Several other Ryanair staff members were called to give evidence, including Tim Jeans. 'That was the nadir of my career,' he says.

I'll never forget, I walked up and I was so nervous going up to the stand. And the judge had clearly taken an instant dislike to us. Nothing we were going to do or say in that courtroom was going to win over that judge. And the first thing he told me to do was take my hands out of my pockets. For some reason I had walked onto the stand with my hands in my pockets. It started badly and it went downhill from there.

Jeans sympathized with O'Keeffe's position. 'I had negotiated one to one with Jane O'Keeffe, who was actually a perfectly decent human being. I really couldn't argue with her,' he said. 'She had been given free flights for life and Michael decided she wasn't going to have them any more.'

It would take Justice Peter Kelly more than three months to deliver his verdict, and it contained no good news for O'Leary. Kelly concluded that he had indeed been 'hostile and aggressive' to O'Keeffe, and awarded her €67,500 in compensation. The money was irrelevant to Ryanair and substantially less than O'Keeffe had been hoping for, but Kelly's criticism of O'Leary was damning.

'I found the plaintiff [O'Keeffe] a more persuasive witness than Mr O'Leary and I therefore find as a fact that the version of events given by the plaintiff is what occurred,' Kelly said. 'I reject Mr O'Leary's assertion that he was not hostile or aggressive or bullying towards the plaintiff. I find that he was.' The judge also indicated he was wise to O'Leary's media games. 'The whole event was designed to, and did in fact attract enormous publicity,' he said, in a written judgment.

'I think of all the things that Ryanair has done this was one of them with the fewest upsides,' says Jeans. 'I think we just looked mean, which we were. We looked vindictive, which we were. And the individuals involved, myself and Michael, came out of it with no credit whatsoever.'

Those close to O'Leary say that privately he recognized the case had been a mistake, but felt it was an unavoidable one. It is a position that O'Leary still clings to. No matter the bad publicity, no matter the perception of meanness and vindictiveness, he still believes he had no choice. And he also claims that his position was proved correct. 'For three days we got the worst publicity any company has ever had in its life, our bookings soared by 30 per cent day by day by day,' he claims. 'The more we were in court the bigger the bookings were.'

19. Taking on the EU

Despite the animosity between Bertie Ahern and Michael O'Leary, the two men shared a common ambition: both wanted rid of Mary O'Rourke.

Ahern's reasons for wanting to see the back of the transport minister were a little more complex than O'Leary's, but the taoiseach was in a better position to get what he wanted – though it would not be easy. O'Rourke's deep family connections within Fianna Fáil and her longevity as a minister and TD meant that dropping her from the cabinet would provoke some internal party strife and would also create a troublesome presence for Ahern on his party's backbenches.

Confrontation was never Ahern's style, so he allowed P.J. Mara, Fianna Fáil's director of elections, to engineer a situation in O'Rourke's constituency – which happened to be O'Leary's home county of Westmeath – that would make it extremely difficult for her in the next general election, expected to be called in May 2002. Donie Cassidy, an ineffectual but loyal member of the party, would stand alongside O'Rourke in an attempt, so the party said, to maximize the Fianna Fáil vote and win a potential extra seat in the constituency.

Ireland's proportional representation voting system is a complex affair, with voters marking their candidates in order of preference so that their votes can be transferred to other candidates once their first choice has been either elected or eliminated from the race. Maximizing the vote among two or three candidates is a difficult and imprecise science for a political party, and fraught with danger.

O'Rourke knew that Fianna Fáil's decision to run Cassidy would create problems for her, and she fumed about being 'shafted' by the taoiseach. Her fears were realized when she was defeated, although Cassidy was elected and her party was swept back into government in what was as close to a landslide victory as the Irish system can deliver.

'Ahern would not have reappointed her to cabinet in any case,' says one close adviser, 'because she was a loose cannon. But he was too pragmatic to actually organize a defeat. Like her or loathe her, he wanted as many Fianna Fáil seats as possible, and if she had won he would have been very close to an overall majority. But to achieve that, he had to win extra seats from constituencies like hers, and if it didn't work, he wouldn't shed a tear if she was the loser.'

O'Leary has consistently denied that he played a role in O'Rourke's political demise. He did not fund Cassidy's campaign for election, although his victory certainly suited his agenda. And even though Mara, who worked for O'Leary from time to time as a political lobbyist, had helped engineer her defeat, O'Leary claims there was no connection and no hidden agenda. Cassidy concurs.

I didn't talk to [O'Leary] much during the election campaign and he didn't actively support me. What can you do, only call to a person's door and ask them for their vote? I most certainly did call to his door. I was looking forward to calling to it because I knew I was coming home to a friend. We had a cup of coffee and we sat down. He said, 'You have a big challenge on your hands.' I said, 'I know it's not going to be easy.' He would have had lots of points to raise in relation to Ryanair, what the government should be doing. He raised those and very forcefully. I knew exactly where he was coming from and what he was doing.

Cassidy's election ensured that the department of transport would get a new minister. No one, O'Leary reckoned, could be worse than O'Rourke. In fact, her replacement was a lot better for O'Leary. The early candidates were Mary Harney, leader of the Progressive Democrats, and Seamus Brennan. Either would suit O'Leary. Harney's party were free-market liberals who would embrace the concept of competition at Ireland's airports, while Brennan, the architect of Ireland's two-airlines policy years earlier, had already proved his credentials as a politician who was not afraid to challenge and reform state monopolies.

On 6 June Ahern announced his new cabinet, and Brennan was appointed minister for transport. The mood swing was immediate. Within two weeks of taking over at the department Brennan had invited O'Leary to a private meeting to discuss the airline industry and the *Irish Times* could report that Brennan wanted 'to make peace with Ryanair'.

O'Leary accepted Brennan's olive branch, but Ryanair's attacks on the government did not cease; O'Leary just had to find a new target. It was hardly a shock that Ahern should replace O'Rourke as the butt of O'Leary's humour. 'The hate beam turned from O'Rourke to Bertie,' says one former executive. 'It was a very smooth transition.'

On 18 June 2002 the London *Times* published on its front page a confidential safety report by an air traffic controller which claimed that pilots 'working for at least one low-cost airline' were disobeying air traffic control instructions because they were under 'extreme pressure on the flight deck to achieve programmed sector flight times'. The *Times* said that 'the report is understood to refer principally to Ryanair and its base at Stansted in Essex'.

The controller claimed that pilots were sometimes forced to abandon landings because they approached too quickly and came too close to the aircraft in front. Pilots, he said, were also ignoring longer flight paths designed to reduce noise disturbance, and were flying too low or passing directly over villages. He also claimed controllers were receiving 'overly aggressive responses' from pilots, who were repeatedly challenging information on visibility and whether the aircraft in front had successfully cleared the runway. The air traffic controller said he had filed his report with the industry's Confidential Human Factors Incident Reporting Programme (Chirp) because he was concerned that the growing number of incidents involving budget airlines could result in a crash.

Stelios Haji Ioannou, the founder of easyJet, decided to engage in some Ryanair bashing. 'Combine a low-cost airline with old aircraft and the odds of your reputation surviving an accident are against you,' he told *The Times*.

Ryanair's only input in the original article was from Tim Jeans: 'We don't cut corners while the aircraft is airborne. Turnaround times are tighter but safety and security are an absolute priority and there is nothing we would do to compromise that. There is no more pressure on our pilots to depart on time than there is on British Airways.'

As soon as the article was published, O'Leary went on full offensive. The controller, he said, was 'loony' and Chirp was 'the equivalent of a PPrune chat room' – a reference to the Professional Pilots Rumour Network website where pilots exchange industry gossip anonymously. O'Leary also attacked the controller for not reporting his concerns to the UK Civil Aviation Authority. 'The report from one single air traffic controller is subjective nonsense with no basis in fact or evidence,' he said. 'The controller is duty-bound by procedures to file a report to the Civil Aviation Authority. He's broken the law if he hasn't filed this concern with the CAA.'

He also rejected claims that Ryanair's pilots were under more pressure than anyone else's. 'Our pilots are under less pressure because we don't operate to the busiest airports like Heathrow, Charles de Gaulle or Frankfurt,' he said. 'I don't even know how we would put our pilots under pressure. What do you do? Call him up as he's coming in to land?'

The Times story caused no lasting damage but would have proved explosive if Ryanair had been involved in a serious safety incident in its aftermath. O'Leary's strongest argument that safety is paramount comes from the bare statistics: in more than twenty years of flying Ryanair has never experienced a serious or fatal crash. There have been blips – planes sliding off runways, pilots landing at the wrong airport or botching approaches – but they have been isolated and rare.

On 29 August 2002 a Ryanair flight was due to leave Stockholm's Vasteras airport at 15.55 local time, bound for Stansted.

As the passengers filed through the security point, a guard noticed that one of the passengers, who appeared to be travelling as part of a large group of Muslim men, had a gun in his hand luggage. Kerim Sadok Chatty was arrested immediately and the flight was grounded. Inevitably, the media fed on the drama, their stories fuelled by briefings from unnamed security sources who revealed that Chatty had taken flying lessons in the United States. The parallels with the previous year's attacks on 11 September were unavoidable. The *News of the World*, Britain's largest-selling newspaper, ran the headline: 'Gunman plotted to fly Irish jet into US embassy, 189 Ryanair passengers escape death by a whisker'. Chatty, however, maintained that it was all a mistake, and that he had simply forgotten he had a gun in his luggage. A known criminal with previous convictions for gun-related offences, Chatty had no known link to Islamic terrorism, and his flying lessons had taken place years earlier and resulted in ignominious failure. In time the terrorism charges against him would be dropped because of a lack of evidence, but for the moment Ryanair and all other airlines, were once again under the spotlight.

There was more bad news for Ryanair on 1 September, when it emerged that the airline was facing a landmark legal action by Bob Ross, a cerebral palsy sufferer who had fallen victim to its policy of charging passengers for the use of wheelchairs. The combined effect of the near-hijacking and the Ross litigation wiped 9 per cent off Ryanair's share price on 3 September, the shares' largest drop in seven months.

'Ryanair has been very publicly highlighted because of the Swedish incident, even though that could have happened to any airline, and it's being sued by a wheelchair user,' said Kevin McConnell, an analyst at Bloxham Stockbrokers. 'The worry that something serious will happen is enough to keep investors away.'

Faced with a tumbling share price and hostile press coverage O'Leary reacted as he always did: he launched a million-seat give-away on 17 September. Free fares, available for the next three months, with the passenger just paying the relevant taxes and airport charges. Predictable but effective.

The rapprochement between Ryanair and the department of transport instigated by Seamus Brennan's appointment as minister in June bore early fruit. In July Brennan introduced proposals for temporary facilities at Dublin airport for low-cost airlines until permanent facilities were built. O'Leary for once was happy with the government. 'It [Brennan's appointment] has been very positive,' he said. 'We have seen more action in one month than in the previous five years. Certainly, it [the temporary facility] is welcome but we also want a long-term fix.'

Brennan was listening. In early August the department of transport tendered for expressions of interest in developing a new terminal at Dublin airport. At long last, it seemed, Ryanair was going to get what it had been pursuing so relentlessly for six years. O'Leary was pleased but he wanted more. He hoped that Brennan would not 'stop at a second terminal but consider third and fourth terminals as well'.

Brennan's request for tenders met an enthusiastic response. By late September, at the Ryanair annual general meeting, O'Leary could tell his shareholders that eleven companies had expressed interest in building the second terminal. Ryanair made its tender and remained prepared to build the terminal itself if no one else could do it as cheaply, but O'Leary was unconcerned about who actually won the contract – as long as it wasn't Aer Rianta. 'If nobody would do it, we'd pay for it, we'd build it, we'd give it to somebody else to operate it. We just wanted some competition with Aer Rianta out there and we have been consistent in that for years.'

At the end of October the final list of thirteen interested bidders was unveiled, and O'Leary wanted to proceed at speed to actual construction. He would be frustrated. As he complained to Brennan in a letter, 'Your department now proposes to waste two further years appointing consultants, designing, planning and tendering, with the result that even allowing for no slippages in planning, etc. a new terminal won't be available until summer 2006, almost the entire life of the present government. This is ridiculously lethargic.'

He backed his call for immediate action with his own proposals for the second terminal. Under Ryanair plans the facility would cost €114 million to develop, would be able to handle ten million passengers a year and would be operational by 2004. The airline also backed plans to build a third terminal at the airport, but to no avail. Brennan's spurt of activity, his promise of early action and his sense of urgency had swiftly dissipated. The debate about a second terminal went far deeper than economics and passenger comfort; it was a political argument and a deeply divisive one. Brennan faced formidable opposition from the unions and from Aer Rianta and, by extension, from members of his own government, who had no interest in going to war with the unions, particularly if the main winner of that war was Michael O'Leary.

O'Leary's belief that all publicity was good publicity had been severely tested in the preceding months. Earlier in the year he had stumbled into a political row when his decision to open a route to Austria's Klagenfurt airport had turned into a publicity stunt for Jörg Haider, the far-right Austrian politician. The alleged attempted hijacking in Sweden had caused another flurry of headlines, resurrecting fears of another 9/11-style terrorist outrage, and then came news of the court action against Ryanair by Bob Ross. Passenger bookings were holding up, but the company's share price was not.

O'Leary needed to review his public- and investor-relations strategies, and he needed to improve the share price performance. At the time the company's in-house communications unit was low key, reporting to Michael Cawley, and not directly to O'Leary, who dealt mainly with Murray Consultants, Ryanair's external PR advisers. The challenges that lay ahead required a new strategy and O'Leary decided to appoint a communications manager who would report directly to him, and to give the position senior executive status. O'Leary judged candidates on two main criteria: they had to be strong-willed enough and self-confident enough to handle him, and they had to have an instinctive understanding of how the media worked.

His choice was Paul Fitzsimmons, a young Northern Irish man who knew nothing about the airline industry. Fitzsimmons, who worked for Today FM, a young independent radio station, had been a journalist and understood the media, but he also had to handle Eamon Dunphy, Today FM's explosive and unpredictable star performer. Dunphy, a former footballer, was Ireland's self-styled media maverick: abrasive, opinionated and addicted to controversy. Fitzsimmons says,

He thought if I could handle Dunphy I could handle him. Dunphy is tough and he's demanding and he rants and he raves. And also he wanted someone who really could understand media. I'm a journalist by profession. I didn't know anything about airlines. I did my usual read-up before the interview, but when I got there I realized I knew nothing about it. And he said that's a distinct advantage, we don't want people with baggage and the old way of doing things.

Apart from the steady onslaught of poor publicity, O'Leary was also conscious that his own high profile had created the impression that Ryanair had metamorphosed into O'Learyair – a perception which was accurate but dangerous for the company, and particularly for its relationship with investors. A key part of Fitzsimmons' role would be to withdraw O'Leary from the media spotlight and build up other managers in the company so that Ryanair would be perceived as a mature business rather than a one-man band.

The overriding strategy was to withdraw him and build up [Michael Cawley and Howard Millar]. If I had an investment magazine from the US ringing up asking lots of financial stuff, I'd have said to O'Leary, 'Let Howard handle this one.' If it was something they were comfortable with, no problem. But if it was anything outside of that, or a sticky situation or anything we needed to put our dancing shoes on for then it would have been me and O'Leary all the time.

O'Leary left Fitzsimmons in no doubt about his publicity philosophy.

In my first week there was a huge article in the travel section of the *Sunday Telegraph*, O'Leary's dream paper. They'd spent a day at Stansted, and it was shitty weather and there were lots of flight cancellations and delays and stuff and this was two pages in a big important travel section.

I said to Michael, 'Did you see that piece in the *Telegraph*?' And he said, 'What was wrong with it?' And I said, 'We were slated, the flights were late, there was no information, it was awful.' He said, 'Come here and have a look at the booking figures for Sunday.' [The *Telegraph* story] was the only story about us that Sunday. And the figures had actually gone up. He said, 'There's no such thing as bad publicity.' And so, on the premise that there is no such thing as bad publicity, we went after everything.

We'd have done anything to get publicity. We were complete full-on prostitutes for publicity.

Ryanair's relentless expansion into Europe was now more than just an irritant to the major airlines who had failed to anticipate the growth of low-cost travel. Air France, Lufthansa and British Airways had all been forced to slash airfares on short-haul routes to stave off the competition from Ryanair, easyJet and the growing number of small low-fare carriers who were eating away at their business. Now the fightback was about to move to a different level.

In October Ryanair launched a twice-daily service between Strasbourg in north-eastern France and London Stansted. Amid the fanfare of the launch Ryanair mentioned that it would receive €1.4 million in marketing support from the airport for the launch of the new route. Brit Air, the Air France subsidiary which was Ryanair's main competitor at Strasbourg, was not impressed. In November Brit Air's chairman Marc Lamidey publicly denounced the marketing support as a 'subsidy' and threatened to sue the local chamber of commerce, which owned the airport, unless the same offer was made available to his airline.

Lamidey's complaint, which would grow into a legal action, was the first strike in Air France's campaign against Ryanair. Weeks after Brit Air complained about Strasbourg the EC confirmed that anonymous allegations had been made about Ryanair's relationship with Charleroi, the state-owned airport near Brussels. 'What we are doing is opening investigation proceedings into the advantages granted by Wallonia [the regional government that owned the airport] to Ryanair operating from Charleroi,' Transport Commissioner Loyola de Palacio announced. She said that her commission had been conducting informal investigations into the situation at Charleroi for about a year, having received a complaint from an unnamed Ryanair competitor. That informal probe had raised 'doubts regarding the nature of the measures taken by [the Belgian authorities] which exclusively benefit Ryanair and might constitute state aid incompatible with the proper functioning of the internal market'.

For O'Leary, de Palacio's decision to launch a formal investigation represented a serious worry. It was one thing to scrap with competitors, slashing fares and running in and out of court, but it was quite another thing to do battle with the EU. The European Union's commissioners tend to be seasoned politicians, often former cabinet ministers in their own countries. Nominated by their governments, the commissioners preside over the vast Brussels bureaucracy and have wide-ranging powers. De Palacio would be a dangerous foe for O'Leary, and was less vulnerable than elected politicians to his normal tactics of denigration and mockery.

Ryanair's operations at Strasbourg and Charleroi went to the heart of its business model. O'Leary used small regional airports for straightforward operational reasons – lack of congestion made for fast turnaround times – but a central motivation was money. Small underutilized airports were desperate for business and open to negotiation. Landing charges could be reduced to nothing or next to nothing, and O'Leary could also extract marketing contributions for each new route opened. Minimal landing charges combined with marketing incentives meant that Ryanair's costs were substantially lower than the costs of airlines that flew to more traditional and more expensive airports.

'People always think the marketing support is a bit fishy but it actually isn't at all,' says one executive.

What we say is we're going to advertise your destination because we're the carriers, but you actually get the benefit. If €20,000 is spent on a newspaper advertisement selling flights to somewhere, the benefit from those passengers does not stop the second they hop off the plane. The beneficiaries are the airline *and* the region. Essentially we are saying that if we're charging £19 for a flight to Strasbourg and Brit Air are charging £119, that's an extra £100 that the passengers are going to spend in your shops, in your hotels and restaurants and therefore there's a benefit.

At Charleroi, though, the benefits to Ryanair had been extensive. The airport had agreed to pay hundreds of thousands of euros towards Ryanair's recruitment and training costs and €160,000 for every new route. Ryanair was provided with free offices, and landing charges were set at €1 per passenger, less than a tenth of those at larger airports.

Most alarming was the realization that de Palacio's investigation had the potential to spread to every state-owned airport with which Ryanair had struck deals, and could unravel all of them. 'We were in Milan doing a press conference when [news of the investigation] broke,' says Fitzsimmons. 'We were fielding phone calls from journalists. We were trying to get holding statements put in place, and then when we got back to Dublin we thought, Oh fuck, this is going to be serious.'

O'Leary was for once uncertain how to respond. Should he choose all-out aggression or feign indifference? Initially, he went for indifference. 'The arrangements at Charleroi airport are competitive, non-discriminatory and available to all,' he said. 'Ryanair have no concern about any formal or informal inquiries made by the EU into our successful operations at Brussels Charleroi. Firstly, [the inquiry] will have no impact on Ryanair. Secondly, we welcome it.' He told the *Financial Times*, 'Someone here is looking for a smoking gun and there isn't one.'

He also resorted to his favourite diversionary tactic of launching a seat sale, offering 200,000 seats to or from Charleroi for €9.99. O'Leary's public sangfroid, however, did not placate the markets. Stock market analysts fretted that challenges to Ryanair's lucrative deals with state-owned European airports could destroy its business plan, and the airline's share price subsided.

Indifference was clearly not going to work and O'Leary changed tack. The investigation, he decided, had to be portrayed as yet another David versus Goliath battle. He had to paint Ryanair as the champion of cheap fares for the common man, and the commission as the bureaucratic bad guys who, if they made the wrong decision, would be punishing the people. O'Leary put out a statement:

Ryanair and Brussels Charleroi Airport have been the champions of low fares choice and bringing the cost of air travel within the budget of ordinary consumers and not just the rich. Ryanair will continue to fight for low fares in Europe. We remain confident that the politically motivated investigation launched by the Commission this week will ultimately confirm that Ryanair's low-cost base at Brussels Charleroi is not in breach of state aid rules and we hope that Commissioner de Palacio will move quickly to expedite this investigation and allow Ryanair to get on with the process of rolling out competition, consumer choice and low fares all over Europe.

More than a quarter of the airports with which O'Leary had struck deals were state-owned, and therefore liable to investigation by the EU, whose remit was to prevent government subsidies from distorting the market place.

The irony was not lost on O'Leary. The EU was using powers it had been given primarily to prevent governments from bailing out national airlines to attack a private airline that had brought competition to Europe's skies. It was a legalistic and bureaucratic twist that infuriated him but that he could not avoid. He could argue that Ryanair's planes brought hope and prosperity to regions, like Charleroi, which had been dying before his airline's arrival; he could argue that low fares were egalitarian, that they worked in favour of closer European integration by making possible a mobile labour market; but he could not deny he was receiving payments from airports. And since a number of those airports were owned by the states in which they were located Ryanair was in receipt of state money. The key questions were whether that money was a subsidy that distorted the market, and whether it was available to all airlines or just to Ryanair.

For the commission, its investigation of Ryanair would be a precedent-setting case that would establish the ground rules for the new low-fare market as it expanded across Europe. Its difficulty, however, would be in distinguishing competition between airports and competition between airlines. Was Ryanair's deal with Charleroi a problem for other airlines or a problem for rival airports? And how to balance the needs of a small airport trying to break into a new market with the needs of an established airport? Ryanair's case was further complicated by the fact the regional government was accused of giving illegal aid to a foreign rather than to a Belgian airline, an unusual twist on the more common accusation of governments propping up their own national carriers with taxpayers' money.

O'Leary knew he needed to construct a scenario that allowed Ryanair to emerge as the winner no matter what the commission finally decided, and he needed to position Ryanair as the uncrowned king of low fares and competition. 'The ramifications [of an adverse decision] for the other airports loomed large,' says Fitzsimmons. 'So it had to be fought. There could be no rolling over here.'

The Strasbourg and Charleroi cases had temporarily derailed O'Leary's plans to retire from the spotlight. Now, while the commission started its lengthy probe, he got back on track. In January 2003 Michael Cawley, the chief financial officer, and Howard Millar, the finance director, were promoted to the newly created positions of joint deputy chief executive. Cawley also assumed the title of chief operating officer, with Millar taking over as chief financial officer.

The promotions, which reflected O'Leary's determination to highlight the strength and depth of the company's management, came after a period of some turbulence in the senior ranks. Conor McCarthy, the Aer Lingus executive poached just before the flotation in 1997, had been the first significant major departure, leaving his role as operations director just over two years earlier. 'After four and a half years I got pretty tired of doing the job that I was doing and wanted to try and move on to other things,' McCarthy says. 'I've never regretted leaving.'

The next senior casualty was Tim Jeans, who quit his position as sales and marketing director in July 2002. And then Charlie Clifton, a Ryanair veteran, resigned as director of ground operations and inflight in December 2002. O'Leary shows uncharacteristic regret at Clifton's departure. 'Charlie was a good guy,' he says. 'Of them all I was sorry to see Charlie go. It just got too much for him. He'd done so much, he'd just had enough of the stress and the hassle and the remorseless grind of it all.'

Cawley and Millar's promotions put a new structure in place, one designed to both reassure the markets that there was more to Ryanair than its noisy chief executive and establish a stable management structure to steer the company through a period of exceptionally rapid growth. That both men had a firm grounding in finance was no accident; careful financial management was the key to Ryanair's profitable growth.

Below the top team of three sat O'Leary's 'Z team': the executive management layer who gathered each Monday to review the airline's operations. The regulars were Jim Callaghan, head of regulatory affairs; David O'Brien, director of inflight; Ray Conway, the chief pilot; Mick Hickey, engineering director; Caroline Green, head of customer services; Eddie Wilson, head of personnel; Bernard Berger, head of route development; and Paul Fitzsimmons, head of communications.

The Monday meeting was, and remains, a fraught affair O'Leary's approach is abrasive and dismissive. Echoing the cry of Margaret Thatcher to her cabinet ministers, he wants solutions not problems, and is relentless in his demands for fresh ideas to curb costs and raise revenues. 'There were people who had been there for ages, who should really know better, who either walked into trouble or wouldn't know when to stop digging,' recalls one Z team member. 'You could either let him hear what he wanted to hear, whether or not it would actually happen, or drop the subject.

If you fought him he'd just keep going and keep going. But there's only ever one winner.'

O'Leary chaired the meetings from the head of the table in his starkly furnished glass-walled office, which looks onto a busy open-plan work area. To his left was O'Brien, who was usually first to be called upon for his operations update. O'Brien was promoted to operations director in December 2002, and had arrived at the senior management table via an unusual route. From 1992 to 1996 he had been director of ground operations and inflight with Ryanair but had then defected to Aer Rianta, O'Leary's bête noire, from 1996 to 1998 before returning to Ryanair in 1998 as director of UK operations.

'David's soft-spoken, good at his job and he has a huge task to try and control. But he's a bit of a digger,' says one team member. 'Michael would ask, "Have you got the answer to that?" David would say, "No," and Michael would say, "Don't come to the fucking meeting without the actual stats."' Instead of retreating, O'Brien would plough on. 'David would say, "But—" [prompting] Michael [to] say, "David, shut the fuck up." And so it would go on.'

Next to O'Brien sat Conway, the chief pilot, who joined Ryanair in 1987 and was promoted to the top table in June 2002. O'Leary's natural disdain for pilots did not make life easy for Conway. 'He was too slick, too good-looking, he was all the things Michael hated,' says one executive.

Conway, who served as an officer with the Irish Air Corps for fourteen years before joining Ryanair, was immune to O'Leary's hostility. 'He had a nice life, earned nice money and had a flash car. He'd argue a bit but then he just couldn't be bothered. He'd say, "Right Michael, if that's what you want that's what you'll get,"' says the executive.

To Conway's left was Mick Hickey, one of the more experienced executives, who had joined the company in 1988 and had established a rapport with O'Leary that few enjoyed. 'He got off relatively lightly,' says another executive. 'Michael had a lot of respect for him.' It helped too that Hickey was responsible for safety, an area where O'Leary would not compromise.

Next to Hickey, at the end of the table, was Michael Cawley, who became known as Daddy because part of his role was to protect other executives from O'Leary's explosions. 'If he saw that O'Leary was being unreasonable he would try and interject,' says one executive. 'He'd defend you or he'd try to deflect it. He'd say, "Come on, Michael, we should really come back to this . . ."' and O'Leary was usually okay with that.' Cawley had no qualms about tackling O'Leary. 'Cawley argues back with him a bit and is quite dogmatic,' a colleague says. 'He'd say, "Michael, you're not listening, you can't do that." His priorities were always commercial, what routes weren't working, what airports weren't giving good deals.'

Next to Cawley, at the opposite side of the table, sat Jim Callaghan. A lawyer trained in the US, Callaghan had been head of regulatory affairs since May 2000 and company secretary since June 2002.

The only woman at the table, Caroline Green, was to Callaghan's left. Green's brief was and still is customer services, or 'the warm and fluffy department', as O'Leary calls it. 'She wouldn't get it that much,' says a colleague. 'She stood her ground quite well with him but he would have her in tears a couple of times. He would stop once she started crying. He'd say, "Don't take it too personally." And afterwards he'd make sure he'd be nice to her.'

Paul Fitzsimmons, the newly arrived head of communications, sat next to Green. 'He never really got it too bad from him at the meeting,' says an executive. 'He'd say, "I hear what you're saying, Michael. I'll do that, Michael."'

Next to Fitzsimmons was Eddie Wilson, who had assumed the position of director of personnel and inflight on Clifton's departure in December 2002. 'Eddie would have been like David [O'Brien],' says a source. 'He would have got it in the neck a lot. He would have been a digger. It'd be like, "But Michael, but Michael—" "Eddie, just fucking do it." "But Michael, but Michael—" "Eddie, just fucking do it."'

To Wilson's left and O'Leary's right, sat Millar. While Millar lacks O'Leary's dynamism, insiders say he is cut from very much the same financial cloth as his chief executive. 'Howard is very

close to O'Leary in the financial sense,' says one former colleague.
'He trusts Howard. Howard does the fuel hedging, the stuff like
that . . . O'Leary knows a fair bit about it but not as much as
Howard does. If you want someone moving money around and
investing and making money on money, in the money market,
hedging, bonds, Howard is brilliant at that.'

The dynamics of the meetings never changed: O'Leary
demanding answers, ideas and innovations, his executives scrabbling for answers and hoping to be left alone. Outside the company
he was trying to create the impression of a team, but inside Ryanair
remained as driven as it had ever been by the obsession and
determination of one man. The others made it happen – striking
deals with airports, organizing schedules, juggling the finances,
keeping the planes in the air – but the glue that bound them into
Europe's most aggressive and successful young airline was still
O'Leary. His executives did not have to like him, and did not have
to know him personally (few did), but they had to respect and
respond to his urgings.

The promotion of Cawley and Millar did however provide
some ballast in upper management. For investors, their grasp of
the finances projected an image of a company that cared more
about substance than style. Internally, though, little changed:
O'Leary led, others followed. But Cawley and Millar had become
the front-runners to replace O'Leary if disaster were to strike, and
investors now had the opportunity to assess them.

20. Home Fires Burning

At the start of 2003 O'Leary was poised to increase the tempo of Ryanair's expansion with an opportunistic bid for a dying rival.

Rumours had been circulating for a number of months that Buzz, a low-cost offshoot of Dutch airline KLM, was in deep financial trouble and would be closed or sold by its parent. Gambling that consumers would be prepared to pay a little more for extra comfort, KLM had positioned Buzz well away from Ryanair's low-cost, no-frills service. The strategy failed to understand the simple dynamics of the new market: price was paramount.

'Buzz had additional services and better conditions for passengers who wanted to change seats,' says KLM spokesman Bart Kotser. 'They had inflight catering. They served both primary and secondary markets whereas Ryanair was only flying from secondary airports. Buzz was seen as the chic low-cost product, versus the non-chic from Ryanair.' Big mistake.

Buzz had enjoyed some success in the French and Spanish markets, conveying the British middle classes to their holiday homes. But as the low-cost market became more and more crowded, it began to feel the strain. 'At that time there were so many start-ups that it was very hard,' says Kotser. 'The economy, the political situation, made people very reluctant to fly anyway, and in the end it wasn't possible for Buzz to make money.'

Almost as soon as rumours of Buzz's impending sale or closure began to circulate, Ryanair was linked with the Dutch airline. The Irish initially remained coy, claiming that while they were indeed talking to Buzz, it was about cooperating on common issues such as passenger compensation. But behind the scenes furious negotiations were taking place.

O'Leary had repeatedly rejected the idea of Ryanair engaging in mergers and acquisitions. His principles, though, were always ready to be sacrificed to pragmatism. He could see the value of Buzz's slots at Stansted and of its routes into France and Spain. He was not alone. Ryanair was just one of a number of buyers interested in taking over Buzz. According to Kotser, KLM looked at three main factors. 'One was a social one, how to keep as many people at work as possible. And the second was long-term risk management for those same people. And the third one was we wanted to do it quick and transparent, and so you look at the financial risks that you have there.'

At the end of January, the deal was announced. Ryanair had bought Buzz for just €23.9 million, substantially less than the list price of one Boeing 737. Buzz came with €19 million in cash, so O'Leary was quick to boast that he had effectively acquired it for less than €5 million. On the same day Ryanair placed orders for another twenty-two Boeing aircraft and secured options on a further seventy-eight. 'Fortune favours the brave,' he said later. 'The time to buy is when everyone else is selling and prices are low. I believe this is one of those times.'

Less than a week after Ryanair announced it was buying Buzz, O'Leary announced a survival plan for the airline. Top of the list was the immediate culling of a hundred jobs, reducing Buzz's workforce from 570 to 470. Buzz's trade unions were indignant but O'Leary was clear.

If Balpa [the UK pilots' union] wants to go strike on 1 April, when Ryanair formally takes over, it will not be a question of sacking them, we will close down Buzz. We are not hanging around for long negotiations; it is take it or leave it. It is losing shedloads of money [its losses were running at €1 million a week] and must be turned round. It is tough and unfortunate to lose a hundred jobs, but the alternative was to lose all the jobs.

Airports were in line for a similar message, as O'Leary sought to drastically reduce the number of routes served by Buzz. High-cost airports were first to go while the others were invited to fight it out for a place in the Ryanair network, with price as the key determinant. 'They had twenty French destinations; we were going to cut that down to about ten,' says O'Leary. 'We would have an auction and get cost deals out of them.'

The victorious airports ended up with a better proposition than Buzz, O'Leary argues. 'Buzz had loads of routes they were flying twice a week and three times a week and we were going to go daily,' he says. 'We had bigger aircraft, lower cost base; we knew what we were at.' As for the airports that lost, they could 'fuck off'.

The original plan for Buzz would have seen the Dutch airline acting as a subcontractor to Ryanair, with its own UK air operator's certificate. But as the indignation of Buzz's Stansted staff became increasingly hard to drown out, O'Leary's plans began to evolve. By the end of February, the plan to make a hundred of Buzz's staff redundant had changed. Now, O'Leary decided, two thirds of the airline's workforce would have to go.

The cuts extended to every area of the airline – 25 per cent of the pilots were out along with up to 80 per cent of cabin crew, 50 per cent of ground operations staff and all of the cargo and sales staff. The remaining 200 staff would be offered new contracts with 'significant' increases in pay and productivity allowances. Predictably, the unions screamed. Paul Kenny, who represented Buzz's administration and ground staff, said it was an 'absolute outrage' and accused Ryanair of treating staff with 'contempt'. Balpa general secretary Jim McAulsan said the takeover was being approached 'as if it was a fire sale'.

Ryanair was unconcerned. 'The poor old staff were working for a basket case company,' says Charlie Clifton, who had by then resigned as director of Ryanair's ground operations.

It's the classic, 'Ah, how could you?' Well, if we didn't they were all going to be made redundant. So now some of them had an opportunity to work, to sign on the dotted line and say we're going to work the Ryanair way because Ryanair is successful. And a number of people have and will always find that absolutely too awful a medicine to take. Good luck to them. Nobody's putting a gun to their head.

Ryanair's new plan specified the axing of fifteen of Buzz's twenty-four routes and the reduction of Buzz's fleet from twelve to eight aircraft. Fares on the remaining routes were to be cut by 50 per cent and seat capacity doubled. The plan, however, hinged on the 200 staff agreeing to sign up to Ryanair's offer. In early March Ryanair wrote to the chosen few. 'If we don't get sufficient acceptances, we would go ahead and close it down, and operate it ourselves by hiring in pilots and cabin crew,' O'Leary said.

By mid-March, the verdict was in and O'Leary could boast that 90 per cent of the Buzz pilots offered new contracts had signed on the dotted line, along with 50 per cent of the invited cabin crew. There was, however, another issue: Ryanair's due-diligence trawl of Buzz's accounts had discovered losses far greater than those expected. O'Leary managed to whittle KLM down to €20.1 million from the previously agreed €23.9 million. He then decided to implement his doomsday plan, and shut Buzz down completely for the duration of April, ahead of a planned relaunch in May.

'The unions would have played ducks and drakes with us if we were trying desperately to keep it going,' says O'Leary. 'We said, "Fuck that, we're going to shut it for a month." The unions realized, "Shit, this is serious." And shutting it down was the master stroke, because then we weren't dealing with any of the bullshit.'

Despite O'Leary's tactics, Kotser said KLM had no regrets about the choice it made. 'Ryanair was the best option,' says Kotser.

We were aware of redundancy plans. We also were aware that if we had chosen any of the other options the same thing would have happened and even more people would get made redundant. If you decide to withdraw from a market and you cannot make money, then the options are limited of course. In the end, we only would have been happy if Buzz had turned out profitable. Knowing that was not the case we still think it was the best decision from the options we had.

O'Leary, with his new acquisition on board and with new planes arriving by the month for his ever-expanding Ryanair fleet, had taken on a huge challenge. Buzz accelerated Ryanair's expansion into Europe, increased its dominance at Stansted and made the Irish airline a fixture in the lives of Britain's growing army of French homeowners, but it was also about to give O'Leary a severe bout of indigestion.

On 1 May 2003 Ryanair relaunched Buzz. Or, more accurately, it relaunched a handful of Buzz routes, staffed by a handful of Buzz staff now kitted out in Ryanair uniforms. The relaunch was without fanfare; former Buzz routes restarted alongside a tranche of new Ryanair services. The result was the most intense two days of Ryanair's eighteen-year history. On 30 April and 1 May Ryanair launched twenty-one routes from Stansted and a further two from Pisa and Hahn. The flurry of launches was the culmination of Ryanair's aggressive march through Europe, which had intensified dramatically in previous months.

In February the airline had launched eight new routes; in March, two more and early April had seen a further eight. The frenzy continued throughout the summer, and by the start of June forty-seven new routes had been launched in 2003, almost double the twenty-four inaugurated in the whole of 2002.

'It was all about the deals on offer from the airports,' says one executive. 'O'Leary had no time for demographics or detailed market research. He needed routes for his planes, and he needed money from the airports to keep his costs down. So the airports prepared to offer the best deals got the routes.'

As always, though, there was method in O'Leary's apparently chaotic approach. His trump card, he believed, was Ryanair's strength at Stansted. The British capital was a magnet for tourists and businessmen alike, as well as being a vast catchment area for potential airline customers. Routes to and from London, almost no matter where they went to, were certain to attract passengers. Low airfares were still a novelty in continental Europe, and Ryanair was offering people who had never flown before an opportunity to travel and explore at prices too tempting to refuse.

The business model remained as simple as before: Ryanair would fly point to point, offering no complicated connecting flights;

turnaround times on the ground would be kept to a minimum so that the planes spent as much time as possible in the air; bases would be established in European countries so that planes, pilots and cabin crew could be grouped locally and cheaply; small airports would be used because they wanted the business and were prepared to pay handsomely to get it; ticket sales would be handled directly, with Ryanair.com growing in importance by the day and simultaneously providing an ever-growing profit centre.

The airline's accelerating expansion made it easier for O'Leary to punish airports who dared challenge his demands for low charges and marketing support. In February Ryanair reduced frequency on the Shannon–Hahn route over a row with the Irish airport about charging levels. O'Leary had originally planned to move the extra capacity to Italy, but the personal intervention of an executive at Kerry airport – only seventy miles from Shannon – swayed his plans in just a matter of hours.

'I was following the Shannon row and I had heard that the plane was going to Italy,' says Peter Bellew, a former manager at Kerry airport.

The plane was a Hahn-based plane, so rather than flying Hahn–Shannon they were going to fly from Hahn to Bergamo, and I thought, Jesus, that's a bit of a dog. A friend of mine operates walking holidays in Kerry and west Cork. And he said to me, 'What am I going to do, this flight's gone and that's where I'm getting all of my customers from.' So I said to him, 'We'll try and see what we can do to get it to Kerry.'

Bellew had dealt with O'Leary before and knew he was not averse to an unconventional approach to business. Bellew recalls:

I started thinking about it on the Monday, and on the Tuesday I knew Michael was speaking at a function in Trinity. So I decided I'd doorstep him. He was walking into the lecture theatre and he saw me outside and he just said, 'What the eff are you doing here?' I said, 'We want your Hahn flight.' And he said, 'You can't have it, the plane is gone to Italy.' I said, 'I want it.' And I actually grabbed him by both arms and I shook him and said, 'We want it,' and he said, 'Well, you have to give me a deal.' And I said, 'What deal do you want,' and he mentioned a figure and I said, 'We'll do it.'

Bellew stayed for the rest of the talk, and the details of the deal were hammered out in a car with O'Leary on the way back to Dublin airport.

For Kerry the deal was a coup as the airport only had three destinations – Dublin, London and Zurich. The deal was also a winner for Ryanair, who could now claim that reducing services at Shannon would have almost no impact on passenger numbers as the Hahn passengers would simply fly to Kerry instead. And the move also served to put manners on Shannon by reminding the airport how easily it could be replaced by its privately owned neighbour and rival.

The deal was typical of the airline's casual attitude to route selection. Ten of the forty-seven routes launched in early 2003 were to last less than a year, but the scale of Ryanair's expansion meant that they were swiftly replaced by other services. Because Ryanair operated point to point, closing one route had minimal knock-on effects on the rest of the network. 'There was an element of churning, of course, but the pace of expansion was being dictated by the arrival of new aircraft and the determination to fill them,' says one executive. 'We were going to make mistakes, but so many airports wanted our business that the failures could be replaced quickly.'

Coupled with the acquisition of Buzz, the speed of expansion was putting Ryanair under intense pressure to fill seats. The result was tumbling fares and soaring passenger numbers. Between January and March 2003 average fares fell by 6 per cent, while passenger numbers were up by 50 per cent. The trends were matched between April and June, when fares fell by a further 8 per cent while passenger numbers rose by 60 per cent.

The pressure to sell seats demanded a high-profile publicity campaign to generate free publicity, and O'Leary was willing to act the fool if required. The anonymous accountant of the early years had been transformed into a showman. O'Leary did not care how ridiculous he appeared as long as seat sales went up. His personality was a tradeable commodity and he was determined to exploit himself to deliver the maximum profile for his company across Europe. One of his more controversial stunts took place on 13 May 2003, when publicity for the new route launches was essential. That morning O'Leary changed his jeans and check shirt for the military fatigues of a tank commander, climbed on board a Second World War tank and set off for Luton airport, the headquarters of easyJet.

O'Leary's message was as crude as his tactics and was certain to provoke a hostile response. Terrorist attacks remained the authorities' greatest fear and the sight of a tank trundling towards an airport was hardly going to meet with widespread approval. Unsurprisingly, police refused to allow O'Leary to enter the airport and for a moment he weakened. Turning to Paul Fitzsimmons, O'Leary suggested pulling out of the stunt. 'He said, "We can't do this, it's gone wrong." I said, "No, we have to fucking do it,"' says Fitzsimmons. And so O'Leary, megaphone in hand, berated easyJet from the turret of his tank outside the airport's perimeter as the theme tune from *The A-Team*, an old American TV series, blared from speakers. It worked. O'Leary was rewarded for his poor taste with the newspaper and television exposure he craved and his business needed.

However, O'Leary recognized that it was going to take more than stunts to fill Ryanair's ever-expanding fleet. In early June, announcing the full-year results for 2002/03, O'Leary spelled out the evolving picture to investors. The airline would go through a period of 'abnormal' traffic growth in the 2003/04 financial year, he said, with passenger numbers growing by 50 per cent to twenty-four million, and fares would be between 10 to 15 per cent lower in 2003/04 than in the previous year.

Investors were spooked, prompting an 8 per cent fall in the share price on 3 June. But later that day the share price rallied and closed just 2.2 per cent below its opening price. The damage, however, had been done. The pace of Ryanair's expansion was unsettling investors. Their mood was not improved when a few days later O'Leary announced that the cost of acquiring Buzz was actually €46.7 million, and not the €20.1 million he had previously claimed. The extra was for 'excess lease and acquisition costs', O'Leary told an investor roadshow on 7 June. 'I think it is cheeky,' one analyst told the *Irish Times*.

Investor unease had also been stoked by a critical report on Ryanair by Andrew Lobbenberg, an airline analyst with ABN-Amro, who published his views on the company under the provocative title 'The Emperor Has No Clothes'. He advised his clients to sell Ryanair shares because he believed the company would not be able to sustain the levels of profit growth its share price implied. Lobbenberg was not arguing that Ryanair was a busted flush – he admired its business model and management – but he believed that the share price had been overinflated by expectations which the company would be unable to meet. O'Leary responded furiously to Lobbenberg's assessment, demanding and receiving an opportunity to address ABN-Amro's stockbrokers directly so that he could rebut his analysis, but O'Leary's irritation did not sway the analyst's views. The market, for once, had to balance contrasting views of Ryanair's future, and the new air of uncertainty ensured that any difficulties would be amplified.

O'Leary, however, was not going to change course. He wanted to stamp his mark on the major European markets, establish the Ryanair brand and use his low cost base to frighten competitors away from his routes. Relentless expansion had its risks, but he saw no alternative. The planes arriving from Boeing had to be put to use, and changing perceptions of the low-cost airline market meant that a host of potential competitors were lining up to get their slice of the new market. Ryanair's expansion was an aggressive land grab before competitors could establish their own presence. Expansion would, in the short term at least, damage yields and profits, but he had no time for a more measured approach. He told investors that rapid expansion was indeed choking yields, but then said that Ryanair was negotiating with forty new airports and nine potential new bases, and aiming to carry 30 million passengers within three years.

While championing competition in the market as a whole, O'Leary had no desire to engage in direct competition on specific routes. He wanted dominance of individual routes and airports so that he could maximize his bargaining and pricing power. But, unlike traditional capitalists, his objective was not to achieve dominance so that he could later increase his prices. He remained fervently committed to lowering prices as the only sure stimulant of new demand, and his objective was to increase the scale of his operation and the size of his passenger pool.

The new challenge was to exploit the opportunities that his expanding passenger base gave the company. Getting more money from every passenger was critical to future profit growth, but he was not going to go down the traditional path of simply raising prices. He sought painless extraction, not straightforward extortion, and his tool of choice was the Ryanair.com website.

O'Leary was determined not to fall into the same trap as the early Ryanair, which had failed to turn rising passenger numbers into increasing profits. The key was the amount of money that could be extracted from each passenger for services and products other than the airline ticket. In 2003 Ryanair planned to carry 24 million passengers – a captive market who would book their flights directly with Ryanair and then sit for between one and two hours on its aircraft. The task of maximizing ancillary revenue fell to Conal Henry, who was hired as commercial director at the start of 2003. As one Ryanair manager remembers,

When Henry walked in [ancillary revenue] was seen as a big opportunity but it was felt that we probably weren't delivering on it, even though the market probably felt that we were. The feeling inside was that we could make more out of this. [Ryanair's executives] aren't consumer marketing people. They're not sitting there going, 'Well, that customer proposition doesn't match with our customer base and our brand.' They're much more traders than marketeers.

Henry was determined to transform the website so that the products offered were of a higher quality and a better fit for Ryanair. He was up against the company's ingrained obsession with short-term profit. 'Sean Coyle [Henry's predecessor] had basically just said yes to anybody who would write him a cheque,' says a Ryanair manager. In the spring of 2002 Ryanair had started selling Bank of Scotland mortgages on the website because 'a friend of one of the senior guys in Ryanair bent his ear at a dinner party one night'.

The mortgages were marketed through a link to the website of a Dublin-based broker, Richardson Insurance. Ryanair and Richardson Insurance pledged to pay the property valuation charges for any customer who organized a mortgage through the new system. Unlike Richard Branson's Virgin, however, O'Leary was not stretching his brand with company money; the Ryanair website was available to partners who could market their products if they were prepared to pay for the privilege. It was a cash stream not a financial risk, and it required no management time other than the negotiation of the deals.

Henry wanted to change the way Ryanair sold additional services to its customers. When Henry started, 15 per cent of passengers who booked with Ryanair Direct booked a car or a hotel or bought travel insurance, but on Ryanair.com it was less than 2 per cent, despite the fact they were the same products. A senior Ryanair manager says,

The reason was because in the call centre they were selling it as part of the same booking process. On the website you had to go off onto a different website, pull out your credit card a second time and complete a second transaction. People just didn't bother and the product wasn't so compelling as to drive you to it. What Henry wanted to do was like Expedia. If you booked a flight to Venice in May, he wanted to show you within that booking the price of a hotel for three days in Venice, [and you would just] tick to buy.

Henry's proposal would have involved root and branch changes to Ryanair's online booking system – a gamble that O'Leary was not prepared to take. 'Michael was very wary to change it,' says a Ryanair executive. 'If you think about the Ryanair model it hasn't really changed that much since 1995. Michael doesn't know what bits of it actually work and what bits don't so he's very wary to change any of it.'

With radical change ruled out, Henry turned his attention to the deals Ryanair had struck with Need a Hotel for hotel rooms and with Hertz for car hire – with links to both companies' websites carried prominently on Ryanair.com. There was clearly a problem with both. Despite climbing passenger numbers, the number of hotel rooms being booked on Ryanair.com was falling and Henry was determined to find out why. 'Every week Henry would go in [to the website] and show the hotel prices on Ryanair.com and the hotel prices on easyJet and the others,' says one of Henry's colleagues. 'And we were always out on price. And the reason we were always out on price was that we had nailed [Need a Hotel] for so much margin that they had to keep their prices up.'

Henry arranged a meeting with Andrew Collins, financial director of Need a Hotel, and told him that he had to get his prices lower. 'He said he couldn't afford to. Then he said, "Conal, give me a chance to get my prices down and I'll make you more money,"' says a manager who attended the meeting.

The previous deal had been based on a complex formula whereby Ryanair got a different percentage of Need a Hotel's earnings depending on how many rooms were sold, with the percentage rising as higher targets were hit. Ryanair's success had made the formula unworkable: its percentage take was so high that it was no longer worthwhile for Need a Hotel to sell the rooms. The two men set about creating a simpler deal, which was signed off in spring 2003.

Henry's position was simple: he was interested in the cash. He didn't care about the percentage structure, just how much cash he could make for Ryanair. Henry proposed a deal that guaranteed Ryanair the same minimum cash from Collins's company, with additional payments triggered by passenger growth. Released from the straitjacket of the earlier deal, Collins could afford to drop his prices and fill his rooms. Suddenly Ryanair was making more money and the customer proposition was cheaper.

While negotiating with Collins, Henry was simultaneously trying to hammer out a new deal with Hertz, which was also hampered by a similarly restrictive deal struck when Ryanair's growth was more modest. The deal with Hertz was that the more cars Ryanair shifted to its passengers, the higher the payment Hertz had to make. For the first 10,000 cars rented, the percentage was set at around 20 per cent of revenue, rising to 30 per cent for the next 20,000 cars, and then, at what both sides first thought was an unachievable target, Ryanair's share would rise to 50 per cent.

Like Need a Hotel, Hertz was now actively avoiding new business from Ryanair because it made no financial sense. 'So you had a situation in Charleroi where Avis were renting more cars than Hertz despite the fact the only airline in Charleroi was Ryanair, and our deal was with Hertz,' says a Ryanair executive. 'They pulled back their availability because it wasn't worth their while, but Avis were making loads of money because they weren't paying us commission.'

A new deal was essential. Ryanair needed the profit growth and Hertz needed the incentive to make its cars attractive to Ryanair's customers. 'We were all looking at each other saying, "This is fucking mad," ' says one of the team. 'Ryanair's ancillary revenue per passenger was going down because the number of cars rented was going down. So we flipped it the other way round. We said to Hertz, the more cars you ship the lower margin we'll take – provided you guarantee a minimum income per passenger, which is the income per passenger generated today. So the way for Hertz to make money is to ship loads of cars. And that's what they did.'

This time Henry's proposals met with O'Leary's approval. 'Once he could see he was guaranteed to make at least as much as he made on his own original deal he said, "Fine, do whatever you want, boys." He was very happy,' says one of the negotiators. A new five-year deal was signed in the summer.

With the core hotel and car-hire contracts tied up, Henry turned his attentions to the other products on Ryanair's website. The previous years had seen a steady stream of products advertised. Some worked, some failed, and there was no overall strategy, just a suck it and see approach to what was a still new and unproven system.

'O'Leary understands the airline product really well, but get him outside of airlines and he doesn't see a good product from a bad product,' says one airline analyst.

Ryanair is much more interested in the deals that they make than the value they bring to their customers. And they want nice big fat slabs of cash. So rather than seeing the long term, like here's how we can get 70 per cent of our customer base into this franchise, they see the money. It devalued the quality of the real estate. Henry's role was to bring order to the chaos, and to bring fewer, better links to the Ryanair website. He did a good job.

Slowly, Henry began to pick off the underperformers. As he cut, he created new revenue streams. His first innovation was Ryanair affinity credit cards, which offered a free flight for every ten booked on the card within a ten-year period. The agreement with MBNA, the credit card provider, proved a template for future deals. Ryanair was paid up front for access to its customers, with more cash to come after certain thresholds were reached. All it had to provide in return was free flights, which were already part of its marketing strategy.

The cards were launched at a press conference in mid-February 2003, with O'Leary and Fitzsimmons lining out for Ryanair. 'I remember there was a gold card and a regular card,' says Fitzsimmons. 'MBNA came around to us all to make sure we had them and gave us stupid limits, scary limits. They gave me €100,000. I could have bought a house. We had to have the cards at the press call, not to be caught out if someone said, "And do you have one?" O'Leary was given a gold one that just said "Ryanair" on it. And he said, "Fuck, get me a regular one with the fucking plane on it."'

The cards were an immediate success. 'It was the fastest-growing affinity card in the UK and Ireland,' says Fitzsimmons. 'It grew like a weed.' Within eighteen months O'Leary would be able to report that ancillary revenues were shooting ahead, rising by 35 per cent in 2003 to contribute just under €150 million in revenue – a figure that would have been even higher had it not been for the weakness of sterling, which accounted for two thirds of the revenue generated.

Ryanair's European land grab was the dominant feature of 2003, but it did not mean that O'Leary's traditional enemies in Ireland could rest easy. His home country's significance to Ryanair's immediate expansion plans was small, but O'Leary never lost sight of the future. Ireland had the potential to be a dynamic growth market for Ryanair if O'Leary could strike the right deals. The country's dramatic economic growth had stalled around the turn of the century but was swiftly regaining momentum and there was a burgeoning market of newly affluent Irish consumers ready to board flights, if they were available.

The targets of O'Leary's domestic venom remained constant: Aer Rianta, the state-owned airport operator, and Aer Lingus, the state airline. Aer Rianta caused him the most frustration because he believed that its inability to grasp the dynamics of low-cost travel was preventing him from building a bigger presence on his home turf. Aer Lingus was a different matter. The airline was a competitor, and for the moment an ineffective one. Its high costs and heavily unionized workforce meant that it struggled to respond to competitive threats. Its passengers were there to be taken, if only O'Leary could get better access to Ireland's airports.

For the moment O'Leary contented himself with sporadic mischievous attacks on the national airline, accusing it of ripping off its customers and then watching with amusement as the row played out in the media, all the time generating publicity for Ryanair on its chosen battleground of price. He did not always win. To O'Leary's consternation, Aer Lingus won an award that year as the best-value airline on routes between the UK and Ireland. 'Only a bunch of complete idiots could possibly vote Aer Lingus as best-value airline,' said Paul Fitzsimmons, his spokesman. 'Aer Lingus's fares are four times higher than Ryanair's. If this is what passes for best value among the top thousand chief executives in the survey, then maybe they're still drinking too much free champagne on Aer Lingus's overpriced flights.'

These were minor squabbles, but they demonstrated that no fight was too small for O'Leary, and they set the tone for the larger battles that still had to be fought. The main areas of disagreement between O'Leary and Aer Rianta – and by extension with the Irish government – were the continued failure to develop a second, independently operated terminal at Dublin airport; the expense of Aer Rianta's expansion at Cork airport, which O'Leary argued was a waste of money that would have to be paid for by the travelling public; and the break-up of Aer Rianta, which had been proposed by Seamus Brennan, the minister for transport.

Despite years of campaigning a second terminal in Dublin appeared as remote as ever and in mid-May O'Leary launched yet another assault: 'It's time for the government to put the interests of the 16 million passengers – who have to use the third-rate Dublin airport facilities – above the sectional interests of those trade union leaders who seek to protect the Aer Rianta monopoly. It's time for the taoiseach to stop talking about the problem and deal with it. Irish tourism is in a serious crisis. We need more action, not dithering, and we need it now.' To illustrate his point, O'Leary dispatched a hearse and coffin to Aer Rianta's annual results meeting – his way of showing that the authority was killing Irish tourism.

Brennan was sympathetic but seemed powerless to help. Aer Rianta, under Noel Hanlon, its combative chairman, wanted to press ahead with extensions to its existing terminal – dismissed by O'Leary as a 'gold-plated' waste of taxpayers' money. The trade unions backed Hanlon. Allowing Ryanair to control a new terminal would be like giving a blood bank to a vampire, said Joe O'Toole, a trade union leader. 'Let him [O'Leary] continue flying airplanes, he does a good job there, keep at it. I don't want to give him the airports. I do not, frankly, trust Mr O'Leary on the issue of Aer Rianta. It's just as simple as that.'

In the face of trade union condemnation and Hanlon's accusations, O'Leary took his battle to the people with a television advertisement that called for public support. In the advertisement O'Leary spoke about increasing competition at Dublin airport, and then gave out the telephone number of the taoiseach's office so that viewers could call and demand action. State-owned RTE refused to air the advertisement, arguing that it contravened the broadcasting code. TV3, a new independent station, broadcast the advertisement in early July, but was then advised to pull it by the Broadcasting Commission of Ireland.

Cork airport, too, was becoming a battleground between Ryanair and Aer Rianta. Once again charges, competence and efficiency were at the heart of O'Leary's complaints – with his objective, as always, to reduce his own costs. Aer Rianta had proposed a €140 million overhaul for the airport, a figure that prompted howls of outrage from Ryanair.

Fitzsimmons was quick to raise his chief executive's concerns in the letters page of the *Irish Times*. 'The latest madcap scheme to squander money is plainly insane,' he wrote.

The planned extension to Cork Airport, which currently has passenger traffic of 1.9 million a year, will allow growth to a new capacity of 3 million passengers a year at a proposed cost to the taxpayer of €140 million. To put this ludicrous plan in perspective, Ryanair began flying to Frankfurt Hahn airport in 1998, taking that airport's traffic from zero then to 2.5 million passengers this year. Fraport, one of the largest airport operators in Europe, only yesterday opened a new terminal extension to its Frankfurt Hahn airport, increasing its capacity to four million passengers a year, at a cost of €11 million. Yet Aer Rianta is proposing to spend twelve times as much, for one million fewer passengers.

John O'Connor, director of Cork airport, replied with his own letter to the newspaper.

Perhaps Mr Fitzsimmons is unaware that the development plans for Cork Airport were formulated in consultation with airlines and their

representatives and that their combined views significantly influenced
the ultimate plan. We had proposed a less ambitious expansion at Cork
but the airline users vehemently objected and demanded a new building
rather than the planned extension to the existing building.

O'Connor went on to detail where the €140 million would be
spent at Cork – €70 million on the new terminal and €70 million
on a road network and car parks – and listed the various facilities
which would be built at Cork which were superior to those
constructed at Hahn. He also included a jibe certain to provoke
O'Leary. 'At a time when it has emerged that Ryanair is paying
substantially more for Buzz than it disclosed two months ago, the
airline continues to play fast and loose with statistics to suit its own
political purposes.'

O'Leary's concerns had been dismissed, and the airport's expansion plans would continue, though the cost would rise to more
than €170 million. It was an extraordinary sum for a small airport
to spend, particularly since the proposed increase in passenger
numbers was so small, but Aer Rianta was not in the habit of
building cheaply. O'Leary believed that the airlines would be stuck
with the costs because Cork would be forced to raise landing
charges to cover its debts, and he knew what Ryanair's response
would be: if prices rose, services would be cut.

O'Leary's spats with Aer Lingus and Aer Rianta delivered
plenty of publicity but few policy breakthroughs. Yet change,
however incremental, was on the way. On 10 July Brennan formally announced that Aer Rianta would be broken up into three
separate airport companies – one each for Dublin, Shannon and
Cork.

Noel Hanlon, Aer Rianta's chairman, had made his feelings on
a potential break-up clear in an interview with the *Sunday Tribune*
on 22 June. 'Shannon will not survive,' he said. 'Cork is also facing
a difficult situation in the short term, because it needs investment,
but long term it should be self-sufficient.' O'Leary, however, was
pleased. 'The break-up of the Aer Rianta monopoly and competing terminals at Dublin will allow Ryanair to introduce over

twenty new low-fare routes to Europe,' Fitzsimmons wrote in a letter to the *Irish Times*. 'We will deliver up to five million new visitors for Ireland, and this will in time create over 5,000 new jobs in Irish tourism.'

His optimism was premature. While the end of the airport monopoly was now government policy, it would take months to effect the change. Under the new arrangements the three airports would remain under state ownership, but they would be free to compete with each other for new routes and free to set their own charges. Brennan also had to grapple with the borrowings attached to Shannon and Cork airports. He could not encumber new companies with massive debts but nor could he saddle Dublin with a disproportionate share of the liabilities. Critically, too, the changes did not guarantee the Holy Grail of a new terminal in Dublin independent of the new Dublin Airport Authority. That remained embroiled in politics and no closer to resolution. All the break-up guaranteed was that there would be competition between the airports – competition that would give O'Leary the opportunity to play one off against the other, but not the seismic shift in Irish airport policy he felt he needed to take Ryanair's operations to another level.

While O'Leary fought his political battles in Ireland and expanded swiftly across Europe, he was also preparing for the first legal fight that seriously threatened to stall his progress. By the summer of 2003 the case filed against Ryanair by the Air France subsidiary Brit Air, charging that the marketing support offered to it by Strasbourg airport constituted illegal state aid, was ready for court.

Ryanair protested its innocence. The deal was a simple volume proposition, the company said. Ryanair carried 20,000 passengers a month compared to Brit Air's 2,000, so they received the marketing subsidies their efforts deserved. However, in mid-June the verdict was returned: the court ruled that the deal had indeed involved illegal subsidies.

Ryanair and Strasbourg immediately began to prepare their legal replies, with O'Leary also embarking on a two-pronged public relations offensive, appealing to French politicians and asking the French public to protest at this attack on their right to low fares.

When the appeal came to court in Nancy in late September, Ryanair opted for a typical way of garnering public support. 'We offered free flights to anyone who turned up to support us on the appeal,' recalls Paul Fitzsimmons. 'We were mobbed. There must have been 3,000 people waiting there. We got out of the car and they were all cheering and clapping. We were handing out all these vouchers and they were [chanting], "Justice, this is for the people." It was hilarious. You couldn't but hear it in the court.'

Ryanair had used the tactic successfully in Germany in previous legal spats with Lufthansa, but Strasbourg airport Director Alain Rusell felt it wouldn't do the airline any favours in France. 'It went down very badly with the French administration,' he says. 'We advised them that they shouldn't do things like that. But sometimes he [O'Leary] is impossible to control.' The publicity surrounding the case and O'Leary's tactics ensured that it would be watched closely, but would count for nothing when the verdict was delivered. The appeals court found against Ryanair and Strasbourg.

Before the case Ryanair had made it clear that it would no longer fly to Strasbourg if the case was lost, a position which the airport understood.

We had signed an agreement and the terms of that agreement included sharing marketing costs. If the tribunal forbade us from doing that it is normal that we would face the consequences. We tried to come up with a different contract, but it would have risked another appeal. We have kept good relations with the airline, we have always had good relations with them. And if tomorrow we could find a way that would let us get them back here, we'd do it.

With Strasbourg off its route map, Ryanair had to find another airport to fill its shoes. The solution was just across the border in Germany, where Baden Baden airport was ready and waiting. Brit Air would still face the heat of Ryanair's competition, Ryanair would still have its route, and the only losers would be Strasbourg.

21. Poor Little Rich Boy

The journey from O'Leary's home in Mullingar to Ryanair's starkly functional offices at Dublin airport is less than sixty miles, but unless he left home at the crack of dawn and his office in the late evening, it could take more than two hours, such was the weight of the rush-hour traffic. It was frustrating wasting time sitting in traffic in his chauffeur-driven Mercedes, but O'Leary was reluctant to take the flashy option of acquiring a helicopter. And then he had a moment of inspiration. 'I was sitting there in traffic one day. [The government] had deregulated the taxis and I saw that taxis could use the bus lane. There's a bus lane and it would save me half an hour coming into the office in the morning. And I'm thinking, Why don't I?'

So O'Leary paid €6,000 for his taxi licence and stuck a taxi plate on the back of his Mercedes when it was licensed by Westmeath County Council on 18 February 2003. For two weeks no one noticed, but then, on 2 March, the *Sunday Business Post* broke the story. 'Ryanair boss, millionaire Michael O'Leary, has found a cunning way to elude Dublin's notorious traffic jams without resorting to a plane,' the paper said. 'The intrepid airline boss has just bought a €6,000 taxi plate for his 02 black Mercedes to fly him through the capital's snarl-ups – a bargain price for high-net-worth business people who make their fortune on the principle that time is money.' The article went on to report, accurately, that the taxi had been registered to a company called Tillingdale, which was owned by O'Leary.

O'Leary did not anticipate the media storm that would follow. Although a self-professed prostitute for publicity, he had seen his acquisition of a taxi plate as a logical move for a time-starved businessman, not a national and then international story. Once again he could not have bought a fraction of the publicity that followed, though this time he had stumbled into the spotlight rather than leapt under it. Taxi drivers and their unions professed outrage and politicians climbed onto the bandwagon, happy to take swipes at O'Leary once they thought the public was on their side.

'Someone like O'Leary coming up and passing by cars stuck in traffic jams is a disgrace,' said John Usher of the Irish Taxi Drivers' Federation. 'Not only is it offensive to people in the business, it is also offensive to every motorist on the roads. It is equal to giving the two fingers to everyone else,' he said. Vinnie Kearns, of the National Taxi Drivers' Union, shared his sentiments. 'It is a shocking abuse of the taxi licence. It will only defeat the whole purpose of the bus lanes and makes a complete mockery of the rules of the road. It is a kick in the teeth for taxi drivers out there trying to earn a crust.'

Opposition politicians attacked O'Leary and eventually the minister for transport was drawn into the frenzy. Seamus Brennan asked his officials to establish the exact position in law of 'the issuing of taxi licences to business concerns or individuals for their own private use and not for the provision of a service for the benefit of the general public'.

The criticism washed off O'Leary. 'It's a black taxi,' he told a radio phone-in show.

It's registered in Mullingar. I have a driver who drives it for me and if they want to amend the regulations which say I'm allowed to pick up people in Dublin, I'll be happy to do it, and I'll do it a lot cheaper. At a time when there is about to be a war in Iraq and there is a crisis in the health service, Michael O'Leary's taxi is capable of exciting everybody. I have a taxi because it's a good investment. I own the car. I own the plate and I operate a taxi as do about 12,000 other people in Ireland. As far as I understand it, people are upset because my taxi uses a bus lane on the way to Dublin airport. But if I rent a taxi in Mullingar he can drive a taxi up the bus lane to Dublin airport and there is no problem. The problem appears to be that it's all right if I rent a taxi, but if I own a taxi there's a problem.

Three years later O'Leary still travels to work in his taxi and claims that anyone who books a trip in advance can travel with him. The criticism of his brainwave however still rankles. 'Everybody expects you to be all humble and ashamed. Bollocks. I bought the plate, it operates perfectly legally. It picks me up, it drops me off.' To many observers it was just another little stroke that showed that O'Leary was always a step ahead of the pack, always looking for ways to get a better deal. And the global coverage – the story was carried in newspapers across Europe and as far afield as Delhi and Melbourne – was a bonus. The taxi controversy was not planned, but it fitted his agenda: acres of newspaper coverage and prime-time television, all promoting the Ryanair brand.

As the taxi controversy waned, O'Leary was invited by the Irish Dáil's Transport Committee, drawn from politicians on both sides of the house, to discuss aviation policy. It was an opportunity for O'Leary to engage with policymakers on their home ground, rather than just attack them in speeches and press releases. The committee existed to explore policy options and make recommendations to government. Its invitation to O'Leary was a recognition that Ireland's aviation policy was no longer an issue that could be subcontracted to Aer Lingus. Ryanair's growth had given it equal status on routes out of Ireland, while its relationship with Ireland's airports had been the dominant factor behind the eventual reform of their management structure. O'Leary decided that education would be the order of the day.

'Probably the best way to deal with this is to give a brief presentation on Ryanair, partly because the extent of the ignorance of what Ryanair does here is breathtaking,' O'Leary began.

Ryanair is Europe's number one low-fares airline. We are number one on almost every front. We are by far and away the longest established. The airline started in 1985 as a loss-making high-fares airline and it was turned around starting in 1990 as a low-fares airline. It is number one for traffic and this year we will carry 24 million passengers. That is six times the total population of this country and is four times the total number of passengers carried by Aer Lingus.

Statistics, though, were never enough for O'Leary. Within minutes he had received a warning from the committee because he chose to describe Mary O'Rourke, the former transport minister, as 'particularly incompetent'. O'Leary apologized briefly, and continued with his passionate promotion of Ryanair, prompting Fianna Fáil's Peter Power to say, 'I think we should charge an advertising rate.'

His presentation over, the politicians probed for weaknesses. Róisín Shorthall, transport spokeswoman for the Labour Party, wanted to know about Ryanair's refund policy. O'Leary explained that Ryanair kept all of the money paid by customers, including airport charges, when a trip was cancelled. Power took exception to this, saying he did not see how Ryanair could keep money supposed to be destined for airport authorities or insurance authorities. 'There is a misunderstanding here,' O'Leary said. 'We do not take money – passengers give it to us voluntarily. This could not be any clearer.'

Soon the subject turned to Aer Rianta, which was in line for its break-up. 'Aer Rianta. Is it possible for the company to be run better?' asked O'Leary sarcastically. 'Where do I start? Let me give an example. Aer Rianta is the Iraq of Irish tourism. It is an inefficient dictatorship.'

His audience was not amused. 'We have never tolerated such remarks from anyone who has made a presentation to the committee,' complained Noel O'Flynn, a government TD. 'Perhaps you would remind Mr O'Leary that he should conduct himself in a proper manner in the Houses of the Oireachtas.'

O'Leary's language soon caused further offence when he suggested that 'if the government wants to develop its spatial strategy [a plan to spread development around Ireland, away from Dublin], it should fly the buggers straight to Shannon'.

'Mr O'Leary's language is unparliamentary,' the committee chairman said.

'Sorry, what did I say?' O'Leary replied, appearing genuinely puzzled.

'You used the word "buggers",' came the reply.

'That is a term of endearment in Mullingar,' O'Leary responded.

The following day it was O'Leary's use of the word 'bugger' which attracted most coverage, followed by his confident assertion that Ryanair would be the world's largest airline by 2005. The *Irish Independent* ran a satirical piece headlined 'Poor little rich Mick with no friends'. The article began:

Pity poor rich boy Michael O'Leary – he has everything money can buy but no friends. At times, the chief executive of Ryanair sounded like the kid with all the new toys but nobody to play with . . . He sat before the transport committee yesterday like a bold lad at a boarding school carpeted by the prefects for trousering the takings of the tuck shop. But as the class show-off, Mick O'Leary was determined to put on a performance and he didn't disappoint his inquisitors . . .

For O'Leary it was a minor victory. He had had an opportunity to place on public record Ryanair's success, even if his language and demeanour caused more discussion than the fact that Ireland had produced Europe's most successful airline. The next day, however, his taxi returned to the headlines, and this time O'Leary had to choose contrition over aggression when it was revealed that he had been caught speeding. His driver was ill, so O'Leary had taken the wheel himself. When he appeared in court, the judge heard that O'Leary had overtaken fifteen cars on a blind bend, prompting two witnesses to call the police on the emergency 999 number.

Convicted and fined, O'Leary managed to keep his driving licence because he had been 'courteous' to Gardai. Uncharacteristically subdued at the outcome, O'Leary steered clear of his normal self-promotion. 'I'm very sorry,' he said. 'I feel the court was very fair, the judge was very fair, the guards were very fair and the two people who gave evidence were very fair.'

Contrition was a temporary affliction. By the end of April O'Leary was at war with Ireland's department of transport because he refused to cooperate with procedures the government had put in place to reduce the risk of Severe Acute Respiratory Syndrome (SARS). A highly contagious and potentially deadly virus, SARS had first emerged in China in November 2002 and was being billed as a major threat to aviation as governments took measures to prevent its spread. Although fatalities were few, it had provoked a global media storm that threatened to scupper the aviation industry's slow recovery from the 11 September attacks – a recovery already imperilled by the invasion of Iraq by United States and British forces. O'Leary insisted Ryanair could weather the storm, but the market disagreed and Ryanair's shares fell along with other airline stocks, encouraged downwards by British Airways claims that SARS had contributed to its low passenger numbers the previous month.

The Irish government had responded to the epidemic by requiring airlines to broadcast a 48-second SARS alert to passengers and to distribute leaflets. Hardly onerous, but O'Leary was unimpressed and determined to prevent what he saw as a low-risk disease spreading panic among European air travellers. On 29 April he wrote to John Brown at the Airports Division of the department of transport.

Your letter dated 25 April (which we received by fax at 17.00 hrs on Friday) to all airlines and their handling agents was both unnecessary and ridiculously disproportionate.

At a time when Irish tourism is trying to fend off the adverse effects of the war in Iraq and the international economic downturn we are now to be hindered by a bunch of incompetent civil servants designing irresponsible and unnecessary leaflets/passenger announcements solely to appear to the local media like you are actually doing something, instead of sensibly analysing and addressing the actual threat to Ireland or Irish people from SARS in a proportionate and realistic fashion.

The (non-existent) threat to Ireland from SARS is a media invention which is in danger of running riot because of the absence of any common-sense response from panicked civil servants and spineless politicians ... More people in Europe got killed falling off barstools this weekend than got killed from SARS. What's next, leaflets on Irish aircraft to warn visitors about the threat of Legionnaires' Disease in Irish hospitals? Why don't you get a grip of yourselves?

O'Leary made it clear that his airline would not be cooperating with the department's demands. When Micheál Martin, the health minister, intervened on the side of the transport department and appealed for cooperation, O'Leary's response was withering.

We would appreciate it if, the next time the Department of Transport wants to panic and pander to some manufactured media controversy in order to threaten even further international confidence in the Irish tourism industry, you might consider actually consulting with one or two of the larger airline/ferry operators and then put in place proportionate and realistic measures that bear some relationship to the magnitude of the threat to the health and safety of our passengers, our staff and the population of this country. I have never read such a ridiculous, spineless, load of nonsense.

Unloved by the media and feared by the establishment, O'Leary was nonetheless a celebrity. His public persona was now well established, but little was known about his private life. In April an Irish journalist decided to exploit the fact that O'Leary's house outside Mullingar was designated a 'heritage home', which meant it was open to the public on a certain number of days each year – a concession which allowed the owner tax breaks on the costs of maintaining the house. When O'Leary had bought Gigginstown in 1993, he had been 'to the pin of his collar' to pay for it. The house needed to be renovated and modernized, so O'Leary had signed up to the heritage scheme. 'I had spent a couple of hundred thousand that I really didn't have doing it up,' he says. 'And so the tax relief was very important to me at the time.'

Gigginstown remained open to the public in 2003 because the tax relief scheme required houses to remain open for five years after the final claim. 'People think that I pulled out of the scheme because I'm a celebrity,' O'Leary says. 'I didn't. I pulled out of the scheme five years earlier because at that stage I thought, I want to get married and have a family down here. It's not so much that I don't want them coming into my family home, frankly I don't much care. But it's not fair to your [future] wife and kids to have people traipsing up and down the place for three months in the summer.'

While O'Leary went through the process of withdrawing from the scheme, Liam Collins of the *Sunday Independent* decided to take a look, bringing his wife and children for the tour. Instead of bringing a photographer from the newspaper, Collins asked his wife to take pictures. 'They went berserk at the office, and they dispatched a photographer down to take fresh pictures,' says Collins, whose visit had gone unnoticed by O'Leary.

[The photographer] arrives at the gate of Gigginstown and demands to be let in. They say, 'You're from where?' He says, 'The *Sunday Independent*; there was a reporter down here and he's done a piece.' 'Oh really . . .'

So the next thing O'Leary gets on to the *Irish Independent* [the *Sunday Independent*'s sister paper], the eejit. He rings them up to complain. Vinny Doyle, the editor, listens to O'Leary, puts the phone down and says, 'That's a great idea, get our reporter down there.' So one of the girls was sent down and they wouldn't let her in.

When O'Leary finally got through to Collins's editor, he made much of the invasion into his privacy and the potential for the article to tip off burglars. 'Then he started sending solicitor's letters, he sent about three, saying not to publish it, that we were putting him in danger,' says Collins. 'As if. I mean, if you were any way intelligent you'd know where he lives.'

Despite O'Leary's entreaties, the article was published on 13 April. 'There is nothing to indicate that this is the entrance to Gigginstown House, home of Michael O'Leary – Ireland's wealthiest bachelor,' Collins began.

But you can guess by the pristine state of the stone walls and the extended gate lodge that it isn't the seat of some decrepit old Anglo-Irish squire.

Gigginstown is not a big house. In fact, it's rather small, but perfectly pro-portioned. But [O'Leary] is currently extending it to at least twice the size. There is a long columned swimming pool facing on to the walled garden and, on the other side, suites of bedrooms and offices. A tall crane hangs incongruously over the house as workmen toil in the sunshine . . .

Collins then provided his readers with a detailed description of the interior of the house. 'You ascend the steps and pass through a stone porch and into the hallway, where dozens of portraits soar up the stairway towards a glass dome,' Collins wrote.

Michael O'Leary fills his walls with old portraits in much the same way as he packs his Ryanair flights with cut-price travellers. In big ornate gilt frames, blue bloods from the 17th and 18th century soar towards the beautifully corniced ceilings . . . As befits a stud farm owner of note, virtually the only other paintings on his walls are of horses. Derby winners, famous sires and old nags, whose names are now long forgotten, jostle for space on his elegantly papered walls. The room on the left-hand side of the hallway is the dining room and it goes on into a second reception room. Neither is very large, but the ceilings are high and there are lovely Waterford chandeliers and glassware by Louise Kennedy. An Ascot Gold Cup from the 1840s is one of the trophies on a side table.

The atmosphere is slightly spoiled by a large television and video, with horse videos and a cassette of *Ben Hur*. Among the CDs is Burt Bacharach. And beside it the *Who Wants to Be a Millionaire* game . . . Across the hall is another reception room filled with more paintings. The rooms are rather impersonal. It's like walking through a miniature version of the National Gallery in Dublin.

Behind this is Michael O'Leary's study, complete with desk and computer. One side is lined with old bound volumes, including the *Annals of the Four Masters*, while in the far corner his modern bookshelves are crowded with business tomes and biographies of, among others, Churchill. In the four downstairs rooms there are only two personal photographs – one of him as a member of a golfing team and the other with a female friend on a skiing holiday. There are a few tacky Ryanair mementoes, but they are hardly noticeable . . .

O'Leary was not happy. Despite his willingness to prostitute himself for the Ryanair brand, he drew a clear distinction between his public and private lives. He believed he could court the media for business purposes, but turn them away when he decided that he wanted to retreat.

After a relatively brief courtship – they had met a year earlier at the wedding of Shane Ryan, Tony Ryan's youngest son – O'Leary announced that he was engaged to Anita Farrell, a banker who had some experience of the aviation market.

O'Leary understood that the media interest would be intense. 'You cannot on the one hand court publicity as I do for Ryanair and then on the other hand say, "Oh, I want to be alone,"' he says. The attention was 'a pain in the arse', but also 'a small price to pay'.

It was an opportunity for the media to peek behind O'Leary's image of a committed, if demonic, businessman and glimpse the man. The tabloids announced that O'Leary was 'head over heels in love' and that he had showered his fiancée with presents – including a racehorse. The *Daily Mirror* proclaimed that the wedding was 'not to be a no frills affair' and the *Sunday Independent* said it would be 'the grandest event'. The papers were desperate for photographs of Farrell, with the *Mirror* appealing to its readers for help. Background details on the future Mrs O'Leary were thin on the ground. Anita Farrell was an understated woman – attractive, intelligent and single. She also knew the airline business, working in the aviation leasing division of Citigroup, the giant American financial institution, from its offices in Dublin's Financial Services Centre, and she liked horses, another O'Leary passion. In the past she had worked with Andrew Lobbenberg, the London stockbroker whose critical analysis of Ryanair had caused a share-price wobble.

O'Leary was smitten. 'Underneath that arrogant, aggressive exterior you have to remember that like most Irish men he's a mammy's boy at heart,' says one school friend who has stayed in touch with O'Leary through the years. 'Mick wanted to be loved and he wanted to be looked after, he wasn't looking for a trophy wife like a twenty-three-year-old supermodel. That's all bullshit. He wanted a woman who could settle down, lead a quiet life and bring up his kids, not someone who wanted a society life. He nearly managed it with Denise [Dowling] and he was really lucky with Anita.'

The marriage would take place less than six months after the engagement. 'I think he desperately wanted to get married and get the heir to the empire under way,' says Paul Fitzsimmons. 'I think that was a driver for him.'

It was, O'Leary claims, the most nerve-racking day of his life. A man who had negotiated billion-dollar deals with Boeing, who had fought trade unions, governments and airline rivals, had been brought to his knees by a woman. On 5 September 2003, in a small church in the village of Delvin, County Westmeath, Michael O'Leary was about to get married.

For the Irish media O'Leary's wedding was a rare opportunity to record the wealthy at play in their own backyard. It would not be the celebrity wedding of the year – that distinction would belong to Georgina Ahern, daughter of the taoiseach, and Nicky Byrne, a singer with Westlife, an Irish boy-band – but it would be close. Ahern and Byrne's wedding was in France, not Ireland, and the rights had been sold to a celebrity magazine. The O'Leary wedding was home-grown and free. 'I never thought about selling it to *Hello!*,' he says. 'That's for the ones who can't afford to pay for their own weddings.'

And so a mob of television crews and reporters crowded outside St Livinius's, held back from the steps of the church by security guards and crash barriers, while a small army of smartly dressed women in black suits vetted guests and fitted them with wristbands as if they were going backstage at a rock concert. O'Leary arrived at the church ten minutes early, fresh from a game of golf at his local club, accompanied by his brother and best man, Eddie. Sporting a pink waistcoat beneath his black morning coat, he looked at the media scrum behind the barriers mingling with local well-wishers, shouted a greeting and then could not resist using his wedding day as yet another marketing opportunity.

'Will your bride be late?' he was asked.

'Yes,' he replied. 'She's flying Aer Lingus.' She arrived a respectable thirty-seven minutes late, and RTE, which had sent a camera crew and reporter to cover the wedding, dutifully carried O'Leary's jibe on its main evening news bulletin.

One hour later Mr and Mrs O'Leary emerged from the church and faced the throng outside. Until that moment on the steps of the church O'Leary and Farrell had never been pictured together by a press photographer, as had been the case with Denise Dowling. Since the wedding they have continued to guard their privacy jealously and photographs of the couple remain a rarity. When asked to give his bride a kiss, O'Leary refused, saying, 'That's for the wedding album only.' The line between public and private had been drawn again.

The formalities over, the couple made the ten-minute journey to Gigginstown in a vintage Bentley. The best-known of the 300 guests were Mary Harney, Ireland's then deputy prime minister and leader of the Progressive Democrats; Charlie McCreevy, then minister for finance and now Ireland's European commissioner; and J.P. McManus, the billionaire financier and racehorse owner. O'Leary insists he wasn't aiming for A-list guests. 'I didn't want a bunch of politicians at my wedding for the sake of having politicians at my wedding,' he says. 'I know Charlie and Noleen [McCreevy]; I know Mary [Harney] and Brian [Geoghegan], so they got invited. And I know J.P. [McManus] for donkey's years – if you were involved in racing then you know J.P. There were no celebs there.'

Gigginstown had been transformed for the reception, with marquees to accommodate the guests and a small army of staff to serve them. 'Between the house and the garden there was an awning – it was carpeted – and every ten or fifteen feet there were flowers draped along,' recalls one of the contract staff hired for the day.

After the tunnel there was the walled garden, and there's a pond in the centre, and the waiters were standing there with the champagne when the guests arrived. Then they were called into the first marquee which was forty foot wide and eighty foot long, that's where the bar was. From there they went into the courtyard, they had to go up big granite steps, over a bridge of the swimming pool, specially made. The courtyard is enclosed, they put on a marquee roof. There's a fountain in the centre, three big gods round it. And the pool has all Italian statues round it – the gods of this, that and the other – you'd think you were in Rome. Then they went into the second huge marquee and that's where they had their meal.

O'Leary had also laid on a champagne tent and a chill-out tent for those who needed respite from the festivities.

Twelve hours after they arrived, the last of the guests headed wearily home. It had been a success, with O'Leary talking passionately about his wife, ignoring his business and surprising some with his lightness of foot on the dance floor.

The morning newspapers gave the wedding celebrity status, and the O'Learys headed off for their honeymoon – a trip to the Maldives and unaccustomed calm for O'Leary.

22. Baying for Blood

Back from his honeymoon O'Leary was immediately embroiled in crisis. Competition in the European low-fare industry was growing ever more intense as scores of new airlines tried to mimic Ryanair's success, while the traditional carriers and Europe's charter operators tried to fight back. More seats for sale and lower ticket prices could lower profits, as O'Leary was forced to slash seat prices to fill his steadily expanding fleet of planes.

Simultaneously, he had to engage with the European Commission's deliberations on Ryanair's covert agreement with Charleroi airport – an issue that had assumed far greater significance now that its timing coincided with a period of bloated capacity and falling fares.

O'Leary would be able to ride out one storm, but could he handle two if the financial markets were baying for blood? If Ryanair ran into difficulty, no matter how short term, would the enemies that O'Leary had made over the years emerge to bury him? 'He has got a lot of free publicity for Ryanair, but he's pursued a very risky strategy from a personal point of view. He's made so many enemies and offended so many people that if for any reason the financial performance of the company isn't what is expected, I think there will be quite a few people who will begin to believe he's a loose cannon – and not worth the risk as chief executive of a public company,' said Stelios Haji Ioannou.

The potential damage from an adverse commission ruling on Charleroi was hard to gauge. If the ruling went against Ryanair, in itself this would be costly but hardly catastrophic – at worst the airline would be forced to repay about €10 million to the Walloon government. The unknown factor was the effect it could have on other deals that Ryanair had negotiated with state-owned airports across Europe. About a quarter of the airports served by Ryanair were under state ownership, and O'Leary had negotiated low charges and marketing support with each one, deals no different to those agreed with privately owned airports. Underlying each was the same basic business philosophy: Ryanair would bring large amounts of passengers, and the airports could make money from those passengers.

The pressure on Ryanair started to build when news of the European Commission's deliberations began to leak to the media. In early September unnamed commission officials briefed the financial press and set the tone for a fight that would spill over into viciousness. 'We are in favour of low-cost airlines but we must be sure that nobody is breaking the rules,' one official was quoted as saying. 'We have to decide whether the tax breaks and other public money which Ryanair receives are acceptable or whether it constitutes illegal state aid.'

Another official who asked not to be named said the commission also had concerns about the manner in which Charleroi airport had granted Ryanair the subsidies. 'It's one thing to make an investment, but it's another to do it secretly. When the negotiations took place they were not public and a lot of people did not know what was available, and now all the slots are taken. It's too late.'

As the weeks went by, the news from Brussels became confused and conflicting. By the end of September some newspapers believed that Loyola de Palacio, the commissioner charged with making the decision on Ryanair's dealings with Charleroi airport, had emerged as a possible ally of O'Leary. 'It's believed,' wrote Conor Sweeney in the *Irish Independent* on 28 September 2003, 'that Ms de Palacio and her officials in the transport directorate have championed the Ryanair example, arguing that the airline has successfully created a new low-cost model that can attract passengers to obscure airports, if the price is right.'

The next month, however, the mood had apparently grown tetchier between the commission and Ryanair. Gilles Gantelet, Ms de Palacio's official spokesman, responded tersely to an O'Leary suggestion that the commission was considering shortening the terms of Ryanair's agreement with Charleroi from ten to five years. 'He does not have any idea of what the commission is going to decide, mainly because the commission does not have an idea of what it is going to decide. I think it's very dangerous for everyone to have these declarations and strange speculations,' Gantelet said.

Gantelet was rattled. A talented civil servant, he was used to the traditional ways of Brussels. When investigations were under way, companies would lobby behind the scenes, applying discreet political pressure. Meetings with company executives would be formal, polite and suitably deferential. A diplomatic man, Gantelet struggles to hide his distaste for the tactics employed by Ryanair and O'Leary. At the mention of their names his face creases as if he has inadvertently taken a bite of something deeply unpleasant. O'Leary, he says, was disrespectful and his approach counterproductive. Ryanair's case, he says with conscious understatement, 'could have been handled better'.

O'Leary was not interested in subtle diplomacy or playing the Brussels game. His experience with politicians had taught him that they did not like public pressure and that nothing could be achieved by staying silent. He decided to increase that pressure dramatically, ensuring that his fight with the commission would grow ever more hostile. As usual his aims were to generate extensive media coverage and portray Ryanair as the defender of the rights of the consumer against a collection of bureaucrats who cared nothing for the little people, but were beholden to the corporate interests of the major airlines and Air France in particular.

The Charleroi case, O'Leary claimed, could destroy the low-fare airline industry in Europe. He fumed in print about the time it was taking to make a decision – promised in November 2003, it was not announced until February 2004 – and warned of Armageddon. He was deliberately overstating his case. The commission was aware that its ruling on Charleroi would have ramifications for the low-fare market, and it was trying to strike a balance between the need for competition and the need to ensure that competition was not distorted by secret deals and misuse of state funds. It was a delicate balance, affecting airlines, airports and European consumers.

In October O'Leary said that 'while delay and uncertainty persist Ryanair and our regional airport partners will continue to fight and overturn all of the anti-competitive measures attempted by our high-fare flag-carrier competitors. The commission's decision on Charleroi is crucial. It will be our Waterloo and we will win it,' he declared, twisting history to suit his argument. He made it clear that Ryanair would fight any negative ruling. 'If it does [rule against us] we'll be off to every European court in every hill and valley,' he said, adding that Ryanair would not be 'shouldered with stupid legislation' coming out of Brussels which would only make air travel less competitive.

As decision day drew nearer, O'Leary increased the pressure. 'He is terribly irritating,' said Philippe Busquin, Belgium's commissioner. In November O'Leary said that the only basis for a negative judgment against Ryanair would be political and not legal, implying that de Palacio and her fellow commissioners would be motivated by political considerations rather than the facts of the matter. It was standard O'Leary hyperbole. He believes that most politicians are fools and that political institutions like the European Commission are irretrievably left wing and anti-business.

The following day a commission spokesperson responded angrily:

It's complete rubbish. The commission will not be swayed by political considerations, but also it will not be pressurized by Ryanair. What they are doing will only be counterproductive and will not bully the commission to change its stance. We're still working on the details, but I don't know why O'Leary presented the thing in this way – but anyway the commission does not take into account the rumours, wherever they come from.

But O'Leary's war of words had been effective. His constant attacks on the commission had generated enough media interest to ensure that an important, if narrow, decision by the EU on the legality of discounts and alleged illegal subsidies paid by one small airport to one low-cost carrier had been elevated into a life and death battle for the survival of the low-fare industry. Much to the commission's discomfort it found itself on the wrong side of the argument. Its role, so it said, was to ensure fair competition and free choice for Europe's citizens, yet O'Leary's campaign had portrayed it as an institution determined to destroy low fares.

O'Leary argued persuasively that low-cost airlines, led by Ryanair, had shattered the high-price airline cartel which had ruled Europe before the market was deregulated. Ryanair and its rivals were proof positive, he claimed, that enlightened policy on a European level could change the lives of ordinary people – a tangible example of the European Union working for the benefit of Europeans. So why, he asked, would the commission want to end that, unless it was improperly influenced by the concerns of the traditional airlines? Significantly the benefits of that European policy were being felt most dramatically in the United Kingdom, where scepticism about the EU is traditionally greatest, and O'Leary played to that scepticism. The British press delight in stories that make Europe's rulers look like bureaucratic buffoons – particular favourites were claims that Europe would outlaw British sausages, insist that all bananas be straight, deny British chocolate makers the right to call their products chocolate and outlaw pints of beer.

De Palacio was shaken by the onslaught but determined not to be turned. Under the media spotlight and faced by uncontainable leaks from within the commission to Ryanair, she pressed ahead with a decision that would unleash the full force of O'Leary's fury on her and her fellow commissioners. O'Leary, though, was playing two games. In part he wanted to make life as uncomfortable as possible for de Palacio. He wanted to politicize the debate and force the commission to side with populism – low fares – and not focus on the legal intricacies of his dealings with Charleroi. Just as important for O'Leary was the gathering sense of crisis that had the media hanging on his every utterance. By December 2003 Ryanair was suffering acutely from its heavy expansion in 2002 and 2003.

O'Leary knew that he would have to think the unthinkable and issue his first ever profits warning. Ryanair was in no danger of losing money – its annual profits would remain healthily above €200 million – but its unblemished track record of profit growth was about to be broken. Shares in publicly owned companies are valued by their growth potential – the higher the profits growth a company is expected to achieve, the higher its share price. Ryanair, as a fast-growing company, enjoyed a high market rating, reflecting its perceived ability to generate earnings growth of 20 per cent a year. If that earnings growth disappeared overnight, then the share price would tumble as analysts rushed to reassess their valuation of the company.

The stock market shuns companies that cannot grow their profits quickly, but it saves its ultimate dislike for companies that spring surprises. O'Leary could afford one shock, but no more. It was, he realized, imperative to get all the bad news out of the way in one dramatic week, rather than hope for the best and be forced to drip feed disappointing news over the months ahead. Fortunately for O'Leary, de Palacio's tardiness in making her decision suited his timetable. The Charleroi announcement was now expected at the end of January or early February 2004, precisely when Ryanair announces its preliminary results for the preceding financial quarter.

This gave O'Leary his opportunity: the markets could be warned that profits would fall, the Charleroi decision would be known. Ryanair shares would, he knew, fall sharply but if he played it right that would be the end of it. And so he went for the meltdown strategy.

On Wednesday 28 January, six days before de Palacio was expected to announce her decision on Charleroi, O'Leary issued his profits warning. Ryanair's share price fell 30 per cent that day, wiping €1 billion off the value of the company.

O'Leary's comments to the media were laden with doom. Ryanair, he said, was now facing 'an enormous and sudden reduction' in its income of 25 to 30 per cent in the January to March quarter. There was a vicious price war under way and there would,

he predicted, be a 'bloodbath'. His warning to his competitors was
stark: no matter how low they cut their prices, Ryanair would cut
even lower, throw ever more planes into service, and would be
prepared to sacrifice short-term profit for long-term survival and
dominance.

The following week, with the media and the markets still fren-
zied by the profits warning, de Palacio announced her ruling:
Ryanair had breached European rules, she said, and would have
to repay more than €4 million to the Walloon government. It
was a blow but it could have been worse. An early draft of the
commission's decision had indicated that the sanctions against
Ryanair would be more draconian, but intense lobbying by
O'Leary and by Ray MacSharry, a Ryanair director and former
EU commissioner, had helped to lighten the penalties. Publicly,
though, O'Leary was apoplectic with rage.

He railed against the 'fucking Kim Il-Jungs' in the commission,
who were, he claimed, determined to destroy the low-fare industry
– a garbled reference to the communist dictator of North Korea,
Kim Jong-Il, and/or his dead father, Kim Il-Sung. 'You cannot
have civil servants trying to design rules that make everything a
level playing field,' he told stockbrokers in a conference call.
'That's called North fucking Korea, and everybody is starving
there. This market works well. The European Commission has
successfully followed a policy of deregulation and competition for
the last twenty years that has transformed air travel in Europe, and
has transformed regional airports.'

O'Leary was damaged by suggestions that his tactics had actually
hindered Ryanair's case rather than helped it. Ms de Palacio said
that O'Leary had 'overplayed his hand. He thinks this is good for
him; I am not sure that is the best for his company, but this is up
to him.' De Palacio was not alone in thinking O'Leary had gone
too far. For the first time in his sixteen-year career at Ryanair he
faced shareholder unrest, with a number of institutional shareholders privately briefing journalists that the time had come for
O'Leary's stewardship of the company to draw to a close.

Ryanair's rivals, who had been waiting patiently for the day when O'Leary's world started to sunder, were ecstatic. Chris Walton, the finance director of easyJet, suggested that Ryanair's famed business model was creaking at the seams and stock market analysts rushed to downgrade their profit forecasts. The *Financial Times* warned that Ryanair's 'air of invincibility' had been 'finally shattered'.

O'Leary was unrepentant. In interview after interview he stoked the markets' fears rather than calming them. He vowed to cut Ryanair's fares by a further 25 per cent and refused to acknowledge, let alone bow to, pressure that he should be more restrained. 'I love this,' he said, referring to the chaos in the markets and the consternation caused by his doom-laden warnings. 'It is much more fun when the world is falling apart than when it is going boringly well. We had been saying fares and margins would fall. What we didn't foresee was that they would come down this bloody quickly.'

And his message to investors was unapologetic. In his conference call to stockbrokers, recorded and transcribed so that all investors could have equal access to company information, he said,

Hey, live with it. Remember, Tesco had a drop in profits four years ago and nobody said its business model was bust. Our profits have fallen for the right reason – not because we have a cost problem but because fares have gone through the floor. We expected that to happen but we did not expect it to happen in the space of one quarter. It is our job to show that this is a bump in the road and not some hole we have fallen into.

I fully accept that the share price will take a beating today and over the next couple of weeks, but we think it is an investment in the medium and long term. Southwest has had periods in its history where profits have taken a dip for a period of time, or the share price has taken a dip for a time – it's still the mother and father of low-fares airlines, and by now [indiscernible] the largest domestic airline in the US. I might believe that Ryanair is building a similar position here in Europe.

If O'Leary's attitude to the media remained bullish, his mood with stockbrokers became more considered. It needed to. In a meeting

with London brokers the week after the Charleroi ruling he was
finally asked the dread question: did he think that investors would
be 'thinking about whether or not you should be CEO of the
company, considering that you have been very, very confrontational with the commission on this issue? You started out saying
that you would definitely win this, no problem. You handled it in
such a way that it may have contributed to the size of the defeat,
if it's as big as you say. Is this a time to reconsider your post as
CEO of Ryanair?'

O'Leary's response was direct.

Personally, I don't think it's a time to reconsider, I think it's a time of
interesting times and very interesting challenges ahead for the next couple
of quarters. Will there be some people out there who believe that my
performance or my handling of the case hasn't contributed or has caused
a negative decision in the Charleroi case? Yes, I'm sure there are. And I
would find it hard to disagree with some elements of that. I think if we
lose that case, ultimately the responsibility rests with me. And it would
be up to the board and the shareholders. If they want to change me,
they can change me at any time.

And as I think on my feet, I think my defence just over the last twelve
months would be that the company is still growing at over 50 per cent;
we still have the lowest cost base in Europe; we have the number-one
operational delivery in Europe in terms of on-time, fewest cancellations;
fewest lost bags; no other airline in the world makes a 20 per cent margin;
and we have got 1.1 billion in cash. I accept that some people may
question my performance, but I think I am happy to stand over it.

Rumblings about his stewardship of Ryanair were a price
O'Leary was prepared to pay for a high-risk media strategy. It was
a calculated gamble, but still a brave one. O'Leary was painting
Ryanair's situation in the blackest possible light. Stripped bare of
rhetoric the profits warning was less than calamitous. O'Leary
was telling the market that profits had been hit by a temporary
combination of factors. Clearly he was being cautious but the
underlying message remained strong.

Despite the warning that profits would fall by as much as 10 per cent, Ryanair would still record profits of more than €200 million. Its profit margins, at 20 per cent, would remain the highest of any airline in the world. Its passenger numbers were growing spectacularly, with traffic up a remarkable 54 per cent. It had more than €1 billion of cash on the balance sheet and O'Leary's relentless war on costs was still paying dividends, with a further reduction of 8 per cent in non-fuel-related operating costs.

It was clear from a sober reading of the Ryanair statement that the airline's business model, far from being broken, was robustly intact. The factors that had caused profit growth to stall were the speed of Ryanair's expansion over the previous two years, when capacity grew by more than 50 per cent each year; the British pound's weakness against the euro, the currency in which Ryanair reported profits; the launch of two new European bases in Spain and Italy; and intense competition in the market.

As O'Leary said at the time,

We've seen a number of these cycles in the industry before. Ryanair continues to grow strongly and profitably, even during periods such as now when fares and yields are being lowered at a faster rate than we originally predicted. Our response to these market conditions will be to continue to lower fares and yields. We will continue to exploit our huge cost advantage over our competitors and tightly manage further cost reductions so that we can continue to deliver industry-leading low fares and profit margins.

It was O'Leary rather than his competitors who was actually contributing most to market turbulence. Ryanair was leading the market by boosting its capacity and by cutting fare prices in a determined attempt to put its rivals under pressure. The noise that O'Leary generated around the Charleroi decision and the profits warning that preceded it helped drown out the market's real difficulties, and deliberately so. O'Leary wanted investors to believe that low-fare airlines were engaged in a fight to the death and he wanted consumers to believe that the European Commission was

trying to drive a stake through their hearts as well. Terrifying the
market ensured that potential rivals would find it difficult to raise
money to launch new airlines, while demonizing the commission
might, he believed, encourage it to soften its approach to Ryanair.

The main message, as always, was that Ryanair would continue
to cut airfares, and there were few people in Europe during the
last week of January and the first week of February 2004 who
would not have heard that message, such was the blanket television
and newspaper coverage generated by Charleroi and the profits
warning. When O'Leary landed in Charleroi airport on 3 February
he was met by thirty-five television crews from around the world
and countless newspaper reporters. An impromptu press conference was broadcast live across Europe and the company's brand
recognition soared ever higher.

The high-wire act worked. O'Leary's public protestations of doom
deflated expectations of Ryanair's performance to rock bottom,
and the only way was up. It was as close to perfect market manipu-
lation as any chief executive could hope for: facing a difficult
twelve months, Ryanair had managed to unload all its bad news
in one concentrated seven-day period at the end of the first month
of the year. The share price had collapsed, but it would recover.
The only losers were those who had bought stock in the days
immediately preceding the profits warning, and those who felt
most sore were those who had purchased their shares from
members of the founding Ryan family, who had sold two weeks
earlier when the price was €6.90, netting €40 million. The Ryans
had been unaware of the impending profits warning, but buyers
were unimpressed.

Over the next few months, as Ryanair's traffic figures improved,
profits recovered and rivals started to feel the pain, the flurry of
sniping about O'Leary's stewardship subsided. There had, however, been questions for the first time about O'Leary's longevity
at the company that he had transformed, and these had prompted
some investors to look more sharply at the management structure.
O'Leary was not about to be forced out and his aura of invincibility

had been barely dented, but the question of the succession had been raised. What would happen to Ryanair if O'Leary walked away or fell under the proverbial bus? Was it a one-man band?

O'Leary claims he is not essential to Ryanair. When asked about his role at the company he says he is 'just a big mouth on top of a fantastic group of people'.

I think it is shite to say that I'm indispensable. This company stands on its own. It may have needed me ten years ago. There is a much deeper, wider management team at this company now than me. I am sadly and depressingly replaceable and dispensable, and at some point in time in the future it will replace me. I suspect it won't be in the near-term future, although I don't doubt there are some people who would like to see me resign or fired.

O'Leary had weathered the storm, and succession receded as an issue almost as soon as it had arisen. Charleroi had been a catastrophe, but only because he said it was. The airline sector was facing Armageddon, a perfect storm and a bloodbath, but only because O'Leary wanted it that way.

He controlled the capacity which was savaging fares in the market, and he was prospering because his costs allowed his fares to undercut anyone else's. His competitors would feel the pressure, and anyone thinking of launching a competitor would think twice.

23. Town Hall Showman

Just after 8.30 on a bright October morning in Boeing's Renton production facility, four miles outside Seattle on the north-west coast of the United States, Michael O'Leary walked through a clutch of senior Boeing executives and jumped lightly on to a stage. Wearing his trademark jeans and open-neck check shirt and clutching a bottle of Coke, O'Leary acknowledged the applause from the crowd, smiled, took a drink from his bottle and settled into his act.

As a measure of its respect for its second most important customer, Boeing had decided to transmit O'Leary's presentation live across its company intranet to other Boeing plants, and he had promised to keep his swearing to a minimum. 'So I won't say screw Airbus,' he shouted, 'or bleep the French.'

We like to think in Ryanair we have a number of traits in common with Southwest [Boeing's largest customer]. Firstly it's run by the drunken Irish, and we like to pride ourselves on our ability to party, and fly while over the limit. Secondly the Irish and the Texans have a number of other things in common, like humility, religion, gun laws.

His audience lapped it up, clapping and laughing as O'Leary beguiled them for an hour with his peculiar mix of hard business facts, stage-Irish showmanship and frequent declarations of love and respect for the men and women ranged in front of him.

There is no doubt that you people build the best goddam aircraft in the entire world. The thing that made Ryanair stand out from the crowd in Europe, instead of being just another small shitty European regional airline, was our decision back in 1994 to go with Boeing 737s. We are an oasis of Boeing in a sea of Airbus all over Europe. We are an oasis of punctuality and profitability in a sea of losses and shitty delays all over Europe.

Apart from the front row, where the aircraft manufacturer's senior executives had gathered to watch, his audience was blue collar, the production workers who put the finishing touches to Boeing's 737 series of passenger jets after the various parts had arrived from around the globe. More than a thousand thronged a small corner of the vast production facility that sprawls across 230 acres of former marshland, downing tools to listen to the man they see as both hero and saviour. O'Leary may not be Boeing's biggest customer but he is arguably closest to their hearts.

'We love Michael,' says Carolyn Corvi, then Boeing's vice president in charge of the huge Renton facility. 'He can connect with the workers, he is at ease with everybody and he's such good fun. He's the only chief executive who has ever picked me up and dumped me in the engine of a Boeing 737.' Ever the showman, O'Leary repeated the trick a couple of hours after his speech at the official handover ceremony for the new aircraft at Boeing's airport, Seattle Field.

O'Leary for once seemed faintly embarrassed by the adulation. Where Boeing sees him as a saviour, as the perfect customer who will promote their cause with evangelical zeal across Europe, extolling the virtues of their 737 over the rival attractions of Airbus's A320, he sees Boeing as a deal. Where they seek a close customer relationship, a bond that will see them through the rough times together, he seeks ever-lower costs. O'Leary will stand and deliver for Boeing in Europe, he will tell anyone who cares to listen that Boeing's planes are the best, but in return he wants discounts, not love.

He may look and sound like a showman, but O'Leary is at heart an accountant, with an eye for detail and a nose for savings that make him an uncompromising negotiator who will take brinkmanship to the highest level. Boeing might love him, but they also know that if the price is right he will, without blinking, switch his allegiance to their arch-rival.

Amid the jokes, O'Leary had a serious message. His business philosophy, he said, was simple: keep reducing costs, keep lowering fares and the competition will be blown away. He told the Boeing employees that they would work together to take those costs lower still and begged them to come up with a solution for the one part of the Boeing 737 that drives him mad – the forward airstairs, which are cumbersome to use. 'I don't know if there is anyone there who has anything to do with the installation of the forward airstairs – if there is I'd like you to stick your hands up so that I know where you're sitting, cos when I'm finished talking here I'm coming after you people,' he joked – but he was also deadly serious. Those airstairs – which allow Ryanair to unload its passengers without relying on ground staff at the airport – are an important cog in the airline's machine-like efficiency.

As he neared the end of his session with the Renton workers, O'Leary was running short of inspiration. His questioners were polite but hardly probing and the mood was in danger of shifting from rapt attention to listlessness. The showman, however, had to end on a high note.

He rallied the crowd once again by telling them that he would take one of the new Boeings, painted in the aircraft manufacturer's new Dreamliner livery, to every airport in Europe and 'kick the shit out of Airbus'. The workers hollered their approval. Carcassonne, a small airport near Toulouse, the French city where Airbus is headquartered, would be festooned with posters calling it 'Boeing country' and he planned a similar fate for Luton, home base for easyJet, the rival that had chosen Airbus over Boeing.

Then came his showstopper. He could not fly a plane, he re-minded them, and he could barely drive a car – in reality, of course, O'Leary drives a Mercedes – but he could certainly dance. And with that he started to jig on stage, kicking high with his hands by his side, shouting above the rising noise that the only reason the Irish drank so much was because there was 'no sex in Ireland'. The standing ovation that followed was short but heartfelt. Once again, as he had done two years earlier in their darkest hour, O'Leary had made the Boeing workers feel good about being raped. He was a saviour not a savage and, better still, a customer who could lead their fight against Airbus into Europe.

Ryanair's planes are the most basic that roll down the Renton production line, which moves at a constant two inches an hour. O'Leary will not compromise on safety, but everything else is up for grabs. The new Ryanair planes come with no window blinds, seats that do not recline and have no back pockets.

While O'Leary spoke at Boeing in October 2004 the production lines were temporarily halted, but the evidence of his European revolution was lined up in the 760,000-square-foot factory. On the far side of the factory floor stood a row of Boeing 737s, each near completion and each bearing the logo of a low-cost carrier – Virgin Express, Gol, the new low-cost carrier in Latin America, the familiar orange and white livery of Southwest Airlines, and Ryanair.

Southwest is still the biggest low-cost carrier in the world and continues to grow in the United States, but the inspiration for the new generation of airline entrepreneurs who have appeared across Europe and Asia is now Michael O'Leary, not Herb Kelleher. 'About five years ago there was a change. Up until then every new airline wanted an introduction to Kelleher and asked us to arrange it,' says Boeing's Toby Bright. 'Now they only want to see Michael. He's the one they want to emulate.'

Kelleher and Southwest were willing tutors, taking time to explain the low-cost industry and their own success to Boeing's new customers, just as they had with O'Leary twelve years earlier. O'Leary, though, is no Kelleher. He has no time for upstarts who want to pick his brains – 'They can fuck off and do their own work' – and has no interest in being feted.

O'Leary is as unlikely a champion for Boeing as the airline manufacturer could have found. Boeing is a true corporate giant, a bureaucratic and political corporation which moves slowly and believes in its own greatness. It represents everything O'Leary has despised and ridiculed in the traditional airline network carriers like Lufthansa, Air France and British Airways. Boeing is too institutionally polite to be aggressive, too smooth to be foul-mouthed, too big to be hungry.

O'Leary is astonished by its culture and its passivity, but is prepared to fight its corner if his bravura helps him shave a few more dollars off the price of his next plane. In O'Leary's world the idea that a massive production facility should down tools for almost two hours just to hear him run through a tried and tested routine is beyond comprehension. Even more astonishing was his performance at the dinner that Boeing had laid on for O'Leary the previous night in one of Seattle's finest restaurants.

O'Leary was seated between Toby Bright and Carolyn Corvi and the conversation soon focused on the developing low-cost market in the Far East. Bright had been charged by Boeing with the task of reeling in Tony Fernandes, chief executive of AirAsia, who was about to place an order for up to a hundred new planes. As always, Boeing was in a head-to-head battle with Airbus, and it was a battle that it looked like losing.

O'Leary grew increasingly exasperated as Bright explained how the negotiations were going. 'Just do the fucking deal,' he said. 'Get on a plane to Hong Kong and don't leave Fernandes's side until he signs, and just undercut every Airbus offer. And tell him I said just fucking buy Boeing.'

Bright listened politely and then pulled out his BlackBerry and started tapping away at the keys. 'What are you doing?' O'Leary asked.

'I'm texting Fernandes,' said Bright.

O'Leary, who barely knows how to turn on a computer and refuses to use email because his inbox 'just fills up with shite', rolled his eyes. 'Gimme that,' he said, and proceeded to tap out a simple message: 'Just buy fucking Boeing.'

For almost forty minutes Bright's BlackBerry maintained an intercontinental conversation with Fernandes, with messages alternating between O'Leary and the Boeing man. Four weeks later, Air Asia made its decision: it would be buying Airbus.

'It was an unbelievable performance,' O'Leary said afterwards. 'Boeing needed to do the deal, it needed to stop Airbus getting a bigger slice of the Asian market, but what did they do? Sent bloody text messages back and forth. Crazy, but that's Boeing. They're being eaten alive by Airbus because Airbus know how to do a deal.'

O'Leary may fly only Boeing and he may tell the world that only gobshites fly anything else, but if Airbus came forward with a deal that slashed his costs, he would listen. 'Ryanair will never fly two types of aircraft, but that's not to say we would never switch. It would take a few years to make a smooth changeover, but if it made sense we'd do it without hesitation,' he says.

Just before he left the Seattle airfield, O'Leary toured Boeing's private jet facility, admiring the 737s that had been converted into sixteen-seater planes for the uber-rich.

Instead of the non-reclining chairs and parsimonious interiors he was used to, each of these planes had walnut panelling, leather sofas, armchairs, a bedroom, bathroom and a bar. 'It's great to see how the other half lives,' O'Leary said, as he marvelled at the luxury, blithely ignoring the fact that he was one of the very few who could easily afford the $70 million price tag and the annual running costs.

O'Leary then boarded his new Ryanair jet – complete with non-reclining seats – and set off for Dublin via Iceland, catching what sleep he could by stretching out in the centre aisle. He had paid to fly to Seattle but was not going to turn down a free trip home as a member of the delivery team. He was returning to a new political landscape: Seamus Brennan, the transport minister with whom he had managed a civil relationship, had been replaced in a cabinet reshuffle by Martin Cullen. Ireland, which had faded from O'Leary's view while Ryanair had expanded aggressively in Europe, was once again a market ripe for further exploitation. His difficulties with the new Dublin Airport Authority had yet to be resolved, but at least Brennan had started a process of change that might lead to better opportunities. Ireland's economy continued to boom, and O'Leary was fully aware how Aer Lingus had success-fully launched almost forty routes from Ireland to continental Europe.

Events in Ireland were about to give him the impetus he required to revisit that market with renewed ambition. EasyJet had already tweaked his tail by announcing routes from London to Ireland, a challenge that would be fought viciously, and now Aer Lingus was embroiled in a battle between management and government that could only play to his advantage. Willie Walsh, Aer Lingus's chief executive, was at war with Taoiseach Bertie Ahern about the airline's future, and O'Leary reckoned that no matter how it panned out, there was one certain winner from their disagreement.

24. The Last Socialist

By the end of 2004 Aer Lingus should have been moving smoothly towards privatization. The sale of the airline had been on the government's agenda, and off it again, from the moment Bertie Ahern had become taoiseach in 1997. There had been a number of false dawns and the whole process had been derailed by the 11 September terrorist attacks in 2001, but under the astute leadership of Willie Walsh Aer Lingus had returned to profitability, and its management was keen to take the next commercially logical step: free the airline from state ownership and give it the capacity to expand. Ahern, however, was not in a hurry, and Walsh was contemplating resignation as the year drew to a close. If he had harboured doubts about his impending decision, his copy of the *Irish Times* on Saturday 13 November 2004 would have banished them.

Ahern, the pivotal player in the future of Aer Lingus, had just declared himself 'one of the few socialists left in Ireland'. It was a declaration that would be greeted with hilarity and disbelief by Ahern's critics – 'If Bertie Ahern is a socialist the moon is a balloon, Ian Paisley is a member of Opus Dei and Tony Blair never told a lie in his life,' said Eamon McCann, a well-known Irish writer and socialist – but for Walsh it was confirmation that his plans for Ireland's state-owned airline had little chance of success.

Ahern's self-proclaimed socialism, which included a peculiar homily on state-owned parks and gardens, which could, he explained, be enjoyed equally by rich and poor, was unlikely to result in a speedy privatization of Aer Lingus. The prime minister had placed himself firmly, or so it seemed at the time, in the camp of continued state ownership.

Three days after Ahern's interview was published, Walsh and his two most senior colleagues, Brian Dunne and Seamus Kearney, submitted their resignations to John Sharman, Aer Lingus's acting chairman. It was an explosive end to Walsh's three years as chief executive, a term of office that had transformed Aer Lingus from a stumbling flag carrier on the brink of bankruptcy to a low-cost carrier that would report profits of €130 million for 2004.

Walsh and his management team had slashed costs, laying off more than a third of the workforce, and had cut fares to boost passenger numbers. A month before his resignation Walsh had appeared before the Dáil's Transport Committee to explain what he had done as soon as he took office in October 2001, and what still needed to be done.

'In the immediate aftermath of the tragic events of 11 September 2001 it was clear that if Aer Lingus took no action, operating losses were likely to exceed €90 million. Losses in 2002 would have exceeded €150 million,' he said.

At the time Aer Lingus had no credit facilities available to it and was burning cash at a rate of approximately €2.5 million per day. We also had a shareholder [the Irish state] who was unable to provide financial assistance to the airline because of restrictions on state aid.

Aer Lingus was associated with failure and identified by all media sources as a likely casualty along with Swissair and Sabena. The action required had to be urgent, radical and, more significantly given this was not the first time we had faced into a major downturn, the change had to be permanent. Since then, it is fair to say we have delivered a more sustainable business which is profitable and has a much stronger financial position.

It was a succinct summary of a business plan conceived and executed in the midst of a crisis that threatened to destroy the company. Just thirty-eight years old when he was made chief executive, Walsh had joined Aer Lingus in 1979 as a cadet pilot and had worked his way from the cockpit into management; on the way he had also spent time as a union representative for the pilots in their negotiations with the company. His potential as a manager was tested and proved in the two years immediately prior to his appointment as chief executive. In 1998 Walsh had been put in charge of Futura, a troubled Aer Lingus subsidiary. Under

Walsh's guidance, loss was turned to profit and Aer Lingus was able to sell 80 per cent of its holding. As his reward, Walsh was appointed chief operations officer in 2000.

Despite that success, his elevation to overall chief executive had been a surprise to those outside the company who had never heard of Willie Walsh. However, Aer Lingus had few options in 2001. Recent years had been marked by a succession of management and board changes, culminating in the tragic drowning of Bernie Cahill, the airline's chairman and author of its mid-1990s survival plan, in 2001. Cahill's death was compounded by the resignation of Michael Foley, Aer Lingus's chief executive, when he was accused of sexual harassment.

Walsh had taken over a company which, quite apart from the global crisis in aviation sparked by 9/11, was in internal turmoil. His response had been calmly efficient. Walsh knew that costs had to be taken out of the business if Aer Lingus were to survive, so he cut. At first his determination to reduce staff numbers met with little more than token opposition from the airline's trade unions. They knew the prospects for survival were bleak and that without change Aer Lingus was doomed. But as Walsh continued to make cuts and the airline's financial performance started to improve, so union intransigence started to reassert itself.

Within a year Walsh had faced down his first strike action – 360 flights were grounded in May 2002 when pilots opposed to redundancies went on strike. He was a victim of his own success: no sooner had he removed the prospect of collapse than the old complacency had started to reassert itself. But Walsh was not like his predecessors. He believed that Aer Lingus's transformation had to be deep and permanent if the airline was to free itself from the debilitating cycle of boom and bust that had characterized its previous twenty years. His style was understated. He chose not to hire a secretary, answered his own phone, typed his own letters, drove to work in a ten-year-old car and continued to live in his modest family home in Donabate, north Dublin.

His remit, as he understood it, was to make Aer Lingus a viable commercial airline, with a cost base that would allow it to compete profitably on European short-haul routes with low-cost carriers like Ryanair and with the flexibility to exploit opportunities on its long-haul operations. Further airline liberalization between the United States and Europe – known as Open Skies, because it would literally open the skies to competition by removing restrictions on routes between the two continents – would be necessary for Aer Lingus to mount an aggressive push into the US market, but there were ample opportunities to expand long-haul operations into Africa and the Far East, if only he could get the trade unions to agree more flexible working conditions.

'We do not consider that we have a public service commitment,' Walsh said, just over a month before he resigned.

We believe we have a commercial mandate. While I do not wish to give the impression that the company is driven solely by profitability, profitability is critical. It is more important to highlight that we are driven by viability, and that for us to be viable, we must be profitable. Aer Lingus has a commercial mandate and operates commercially. Clearly, our view is that the company must generate a profit on all of its activities, for which I make no apologies. This perspective became very clear to us in 2001 when we were faced with closure. I have stated this before, but it must be said again.

Walsh's profitability and Ahern's socialism, however, were not happy bedfellows, and the escalating tension could not stay hidden for long.

Walsh knew that future growth had to be positioned away from Ryanair until Aer Lingus's costs were substantially lower. O'Leary's constant battles with the airport authority and the Irish government meant that Ryanair growth out of Dublin was not part of its immediate agenda. That gave Walsh the opportunity to establish Aer Lingus as a low-cost carrier direct from Dublin to Europe, and he launched routes into France, Germany, Italy and Spain, offering relatively cheap fares, an increasing Internet presence and, by 2004, a service which no longer included a business class cabin. Travel agents' commissions were also cut from 9 to 5 per cent, new plane orders postponed and poorly performing routes replaced with new ones. Growth was not just out of Dublin; Walsh's plan envisaged more continental destinations available from Cork airport by 2005 than there had been from Dublin in 2001.

On short-haul operations Aer Lingus was becoming a new kind of hybrid. Where other flag carriers, both in Europe and the United States, had tried to combat the rise of low-cost airlines by launching their own low-fare subsidiaries, Aer Lingus would transform itself. It was a bold decision, one that risked public hostility and political resistance. Walsh was aware of the dangers. 'Much has been said about the positioning of Aer Lingus,' he said. 'The old Aer Lingus had been a 'traditional full-frills model. The type of words associated with this type of carrier is impressive, sophisticated, flexible but expensive. In other words, pricey but smart.'

The modern low-cost alternative, he said, could be 'cranky, basic, unapologetic, tolerable, cheap and nasty' – in other words Ryanair. His ideal was to position the new Aer Lingus 'as a friendly, practical, fair and relevant airline to its customers that is cheap and cheerful'. The new Aer Lingus would by necessity be a leaner and harsher airline, but Walsh wanted to do it with a smile, not a sneer, and wanted to combine Aer Lingus's self-styled tradition of friendliness and good service with low fares.

His survival plan was clearly time sensitive. He knew that before long O'Leary would launch new routes out of Dublin, regardless of his public hostility to the airport's development plans. He knew too that while the Open Skies negotiations between Europe and the United States might take many years before they came to fruition, Aer Lingus had to be in a position to take advantage of any arrangements as soon as they were agreed. That would require forward planning: new planes to service the potential routes between Ireland and a host of new American locations would have to be ordered quickly because delivery could take at least three years.

Plane orders required access to capital, and that necessitated a decision from the Irish government to either invest in the airline itself or allow the company to raise outside capital by selling shares to investors. Direct investment by government was the route favoured by Aer Lingus's trade unions and Ireland's opposition Labour Party, but was resisted by Ahern and his coalition partners.

Under European Union rules this would have been legitimate by the summer of 2004. Aer Lingus had been returned to profit, was on a stable footing and was a candidate for private investment. While governments were precluded from shoring up failed companies with taxpayers' money, because such investment distorted competition, there was nothing to prevent the state investing in a profitable company on the same basis, and using the same rationale, as a private investor.

Although the sums required were relatively small – an injection of €500 million would have given Walsh the ability to fund aircraft purchases through a mix of cash and debt – political objections were intense. Ahern and his cabinet believed it would be difficult to justify spending taxpayers' money on aircraft when there were more pressing priorities like hospitals, schools and roads. It was even less politically palatable given the willingness of private institutions to provide Aer Lingus with money in return for a shareholding in the company. Privatization, though, was as politically unpalatable for some as direct investment.

For the first two years of Walsh's tenure the government's reluctance to deal with the airline's future funding was an irritant, but it paled beside the urgent need to repair its finances and implement a new business plan. By the early summer of 2004, however, Walsh's frustrations had started to mount. In two years he had transformed the airline, turning losses into substantial profits as his cost-cutting and route expansion combined to increase passenger numbers, revenues and profits.

In 2003 Aer Lingus had made profits of €90 million and in 2004 it would make more than €100 million. As Walsh had explained to the parliamentary committee,

Despite all of this and the fact that we reduced our cost base at the end of 2003 by more than 30 per cent or €344 million, it is clear that our cost base is still too high and our efficiencies are too low. Significant further unit cost reduction is required. Our average fare in Europe at €83 in 2003 was significantly higher than that of our competitors. Competition particularly in Europe and from new European low-cost operators is intensifying. It is important to point out that there are now more than ninety airlines serving Ireland. Ireland is not served by Aer Lingus and Ryanair alone. Urgent action is needed to address this situation.

Time was running out. Walsh needed a commitment from Ahern and he needed it quickly.

In his days as a pilot and union negotiator Walsh had written in a staff publication, 'a reasonable man gets nowhere in negotiations'. Now his frustration with Ahern's inactivity prompted Walsh into unreasonableness. It was a course of action which might have been tempered if Aer Lingus had not lost another chairman. Tom Mulcahy, a seasoned businessman and former chief executive of AIB, had tendered his resignation earlier that year after details of an offshore remuneration scheme for senior bank executives had been published. It was a serious blow for Walsh, who had come to rely on Mulcahy for his sound and clear-headed advice.

'If Mulcahy had remained as chairman, none of what followed would have happened,' says one of Walsh's former colleagues. 'Without that, Walsh would still be chief executive and Aer Lingus would be recognized as one of Europe's stellar performers. It would have been the only state-owned airline that had managed to create a new hybrid: a dynamic low-cost European operator combined with a more traditional long-haul presence. And it would have been privatized far more quickly.'

Frustrated by the government's lack of urgency, Walsh decided to press for action. In June 2004 he and his senior managers requested permission to develop an investment proposal for Aer Lingus that could resolve its requirement for fresh capital. Walsh did not call it a management buyout and was careful to avoid the term. His plans were neither concrete nor well advanced; he just wanted to create some momentum towards a government decision that would allow Aer Lingus to continue on its recovery path.

While the government's public stance was neutral, privately Ahern was furious. He believed that the privatization of the airline was purely a political decision and that the company's management had no place in pointing a gun at his government's head. Maintaining good relations with the trade union movement was a political priority for Ahern and the pace of privatization would be dictated by political, not commercial, priorities. Privatization, if it happened, would have to be endorsed by the unions, and Ahern needed time to persuade them to come on board.

Within days of Walsh's request Irish newspapers were reporting conflict between government and management. Instead of urgent action, the government's public response was to create a cabinet subcommittee to consider the airline's future. It was an exercise in procrastination and delay, a tactic later confirmed by Ahern when he told the Dáil, 'the day Willie Walsh and his colleagues proposed the management buyout, I shot it down'.

Ahern's anger at being pushed towards a decision he did not want to make prompted a concerted public relations campaign against Walsh. His request to develop a proposal was swiftly transformed by government spin doctors into a request to lead a buyout that would personally enrich senior management. Walsh's plan may indeed have developed into a management buyout, but it may also have led to the sale of Aer Lingus to another airline. It was unformed. 'Willie just wanted to get things moving,' says one former colleague.

The government formally requested Walsh not to advance his plans until the cabinet had made a decision on the ownership of the airline and Brennan said, 'They [Aer Lingus management] would have to get in the queue and make their bids like anybody else. You could not do a deal or make an arrangement with management on their own. One of the things the cabinet subcommittee will have to consider is the appropriateness of senior management remaining inside were they to be involved in such a process.'

Walsh had succeeded in placing Aer Lingus's future firmly on the government's agenda, but his approach had alienated him from Ahern and had seriously undermined his standing with the rest of the government. Ahern was still smarting from Fianna Fáil's poor showing in local and European elections that summer and he was in no mood for further trouble. In September he announced a reshuffle of his cabinet. Out went Charles McCreevy, the controversial finance minister, who was sent to Europe, and Seamus Brennan was shifted from transport to social welfare. The electoral setbacks had prompted Ahern to try and reposition his party as caring and left of centre. McCreevy was perceived as right wing, and had to go.

In such a climate management buyouts of prized state assets were beyond the pale. Walsh's timing may have been dictated by frustration and commercial necessity, but it was inopportune. His head buried in the task of transforming Aer Lingus, he had missed the political nuances and lacked the guidance that Mulcahy could have provided. His call for action was, to Ahern, a slap in the face. Bad enough that Michael O'Leary should rail against his dithering and lampoon his indecisiveness, but it was unacceptable for a state employee to join the fray. Though Ahern's style favours consensus and negotiation, when angered he can be a vicious opponent. Walsh would discover just how vicious Ahern could be.

For two months Walsh's proposal faded from view, but in October it returned to the front pages with a vengeance. When Ahern was questioned about it in the Dáil his reply was emphatic. He did not believe that a management buyout would be 'appropriate in the situation of Aer Lingus. I do not believe it is compatible with the mandate of Aer Lingus to have a management buyout.'

Ahern's timing and choice of words were remarkably inflammatory because, two days earlier, Walsh had formally withdrawn his request to prepare an investment proposal for the company. As Walsh explained, 'We did not seek permission to develop an MBO. We sought the consent of the government to prepare an investment proposal for Aer Lingus. Nothing was done with regard to that . . . I repeat that there was never a question of a management buyout.' But the issue would not go away. Ahern's hostility to Walsh meant that relations between government and Aer Lingus management had reached a nadir.

The row should have been defused by a report commissioned for the government by Goldman Sachs, the US investment bank, which recommended partial privatization as the best route forward for Aer Lingus, but it was timing, not the already conceded principle, that concerned Walsh. 'Any number of reports could say that Aer Lingus needed to be privatized,' says one former government adviser. 'That was blindingly obvious, given that government was not prepared to invest. What mattered to Walsh was when. His business plan required funding and flexibility, not indecision. That was the nub of the problem, and Ahern was not prepared to give a commitment on timing while he was going through his public conversion to socialism.'

Ahern did not understand Walsh's sense of urgency, or if he did, he could not accommodate it. Walsh's views were straightforward. 'The short-haul model of European flag carriers is broken and the companies concerned are inherently loss-making. A price war is anticipated which my good colleague in Ryanair, Michael O'Leary, expects to be a bloodbath. Ryanair and Aer Lingus are among only a handful of airlines which make a profit on short-haul operations in Europe.'

Walsh needed planes, he needed money and he needed operational independence from the government. There was an inherent conflict between what Walsh saw as his commercial mandate and what the unions and many politicians saw as Aer Lingus's social mandate. Where Walsh wanted a stand-alone airline that could compete with the rest of the market, they wanted an airline that could continue to meet different needs – whether by subsidizing services into airports within their constituencies or maintaining staffing levels and wage rates more appropriate to an old-style airline. Where Walsh wanted permanent change, a new culture and a new airline, they wanted to believe that compromise was possible: that Aer Lingus could achieve a comfortable level of profitability, but not too much; that change could be agreed, but not too much; that there was a halfway house between success and failure.

Above all, though, Walsh wanted clarity. That clarity was not forthcoming and by 16 November Walsh believed that it would not come soon enough to allow him to build on his early successes and secure Aer Lingus's future. And so Walsh, Brian Dunne and Seamus

Kearney considered their options. If they stayed, they believed, they would be stymied. Ahern's dismissal of their request to prepare an investment proposal was disappointing in itself, but it had also tilted the balance of power in the airline away from management and back towards the unions. Further progress on costs, staffing and flexibility was now dubious despite the success of Walsh's autumn redundancy programme, which had elicited 1,500 volunteers.

What, Walsh wondered, was the point? What was he trying to create if he could not be certain that money would soon be available to complete the transformation? Would he start going backwards rather than forwards, and would his strategy – and hard work – simply unravel in the face of relentless Ryanair competition? Was he now an obstacle to progress at the company he had served for a quarter of a century?

The answers came with the joint resignation of Walsh, Dunne and Kearney. Ahern's response was an all-out assault on Walsh.

The workers and the unions are concerned that the very people they were dealing with as management wanted to sell out to make themselves extremely rich. That was the underlying position of the trade union movement to which I have been listening all year. The level of trust between management and unions is non-existent. There is huge resentment that the management team has claimed virtually all the credit for the rescue of Aer Lingus after the events of 11 September 2001, ignoring the huge effort by union leaders and staff to make the changes work. That is what I have been dealing with . . . [The unions and staff] are also determined not to yield up savings which they perceive are intended to enrich a management team concerned with its own position rather than the company's future.

Not content with impugning Walsh's motives, Ahern also launched an attack on his business plan. 'There is much evidence of some unease in the business community about the reduction in both the nature and quality [of Aer Lingus's service],' he said, without providing any evidence. 'The government is trying, based on last month's Goldman Sachs report, to make the necessary and right decision – it is a big decision for the staff, management, the board and the country – on the national airline. I will not just click my fingers because some right-wing economists believe we should privatize it.' And in a direct attack on Walsh's contribution to the airline's transformation, Ahern continued:

No player is indispensable. A new management team will be appointed and the government will proceed to take the necessary decisions as shareholder. Aviation policy and, by extension, the future of Aer Lingus are major strategic questions for an island nation that is heavily dependent on trade, investment and tourism. Policy decisions will be taken with an eye to the long-term future. We will not be stampeded by anyone.

Walsh responded calmly and stuck to the fundamentals. 'Given the brutally competitive nature of the industry, we need to move faster not slower. It was clear the government [does] not share our sense of urgency,' he said.

Seamus Brennan confirms that in Walsh's original request, he did not raise a management buyout. 'They didn't even use the word MBO. So we knew where we stood from day one.'

Brennan believes that Walsh, Dunne and Kearney were right to resign. 'My [government] colleagues would not agree with this, but I thought they behaved very honourably. It became clear the government was not going to make an early decision on any equity sale, and the guys thought that if there is no early decision then maybe it won't happen at all and maybe we can't take the airline any further so we can go our separate ways.'

The consequences for Aer Lingus were catastrophic. It had lost the management team that had guided it from the brink of bankruptcy to sustainable profitability, and had lost it at a time when it needed it most. With Aer Lingus in turmoil, O'Leary was ready to pounce.

25. Full Frontal Assault

Two months after Willie Walsh tendered his resignation, Michael Cawley, Ryanair's deputy chief executive, hosted a low-key morning press conference at Dublin airport. Ryanair, he said, would be launching six new routes out of Dublin. The new services were hardly dramatic – two of them, Doncaster and Eindhoven, were not likely to set the travelling public's pulses racing – but the decision to expand from Dublin was the first signal that a new front was being opened in Ryanair's fight for European domination. It was also a signal that Michael O'Leary's pragmatism continued to win out over principle. He had consistently and very publicly maintained that he would not develop Dublin airport as a base until the Irish government had made a decision about building a new, independently owned terminal there.

O'Leary's boycott of new services from Dublin would have been effective if it had brought a halt to the airport's growth, but it had not. Aer Lingus's aggressive expansion had swollen Dublin's passenger numbers, and foreign airlines continued to open routes to Ireland's capital city. O'Leary liked to claim that government dithering on the building of a second terminal had cost the Irish economy thousands of jobs and millions of euros in tourist revenue, but growth had continued without him.

His neglect of Dublin had not troubled Ryanair's own expansion, because the growth opportunities within Europe remained apparently bottomless. New bases in Italy and Germany soaked up the new planes arriving from Boeing and Ryanair's passenger numbers continued to climb month on month. The Irish market was but one growth possibility in a sea of opportunity. Ireland's continued economic success and the rising levels of disposable income which that generated for its citizens made it an attractive market, but for O'Leary the poor economic performance of Italy,

France and Germany made those countries even more attractive for a low-fare airline. As Cawley said on the morning of the route launches, 'If anybody thinks that Ryanair needs Dublin, think again. The half-million passengers through Dublin is neither here nor there. Dublin, with all due respect to Dubliners, is a fairly insignificant city.'

O'Leary, though, had miscalculated. He had allowed himself to believe that Ryanair was critical to Dublin's growth as an airport, and that he had the power to dictate the pace of that growth. He had underestimated the stubbornness of the Irish government, the resolve of the trade union movement and, more fundamentally, the airport's ability to grow without Ryanair's involvement.

A former Aer Rianta executive says that negotiations between O'Leary and the airport's owners over the previous five years had been characterized by O'Leary's unflappable belief that he created the market. 'We said you can either participate in the growth in this market, or you can go to less attractive markets, we don't mind. Nobody creates the market, the economy creates the market. As an economy grows, the demand for travel grows with it and that's one of the most robust statistics in international economics. The question is, who's going to service it. If Michael doesn't service it, somebody else will.'

Tim Jeans agrees. 'Michael thought that because Ryanair wouldn't expand from Dublin, effectively Dublin airport wouldn't expand. And that was wrong. The fact was, other airlines, including Aer Lingus, did fill the void. And Dublin airport continued to grow despite Ryanair.'

Publicly, O'Leary did not waver from his position that Ryanair would not expand from Dublin until there was regime change, but Jeans says that his private views were far more considered. 'He did listen to opposing points of view and he would frequently come into my office or Michael Cawley's office, particularly of an evening, and we would debate these things rationally.'

Ryanair's position as Europe's dominant low-fare airline had not, however, changed O'Leary's passion for his home country. Growth in Europe produced the results that satisfied his shareholders, but O'Leary's patriotism fuelled his frustration at the failure to develop Dublin to its full potential. His battles with Bertie Ahern and the Irish government, with Aer Rianta and with Irish trade unions stemmed from his deep belief that Ireland could be so much better if its leaders only had the courage to strip away the obstacles that held it back from even more dramatic growth.

'The [fighting] with Aer Rianta transcended business,' says Jeans. 'It went to the very heart of what Ryanair was about. It was about Ireland, it was about Ryanair as an airline delivering growth . . . I thought O'Leary and the management team were passionate about Ireland and the difference that we would make to Irish tourism. It wasn't an altruistic, misty-eyed view of the mother country. It was based on the fact that we knew we could make money. The two interests coincided.'

By January 2005 O'Leary could point to some movement from the Irish government – the break-up of Aer Rianta the previous year into separate authorities for Dublin, Shannon and Cork had been a nod towards change because it would allow the three airports to compete against each other for new business – but he had begun to accept that his vision for Dublin airport simply would not be realized. O'Leary's competing terminals, with one dedicated to the needs of the low-cost industry – rudimentary infrastructure and speedy turnaround times – were not going to happen.

Dublin was also edging towards a new slot-controlled system, which would create a more rigid structure for airlines flying in and out of the airport, rather than the more flexible, negotiated system that had existed for years. O'Leary was firmly opposed to slot control – 'Dublin doesn't need slot control because there is no problem with access to the runway; it's the terminal that's the problem,' he says – and he would fight legal actions to prevent it, but Ireland's aviation regulation authorities were in favour. If it came to pass, incumbent airlines would be in a stronger position than new entrants. The pressure on Ryanair to increase its presence at Dublin was mounting inexorably.

★

Three years after Seamus Brennan, as minister for transport, had sought tenders for the building of a second terminal at Dublin airport, the Irish government was finally ready to make a decision in May 2005. After studying all the proposals it decided to award the tender for a new terminal to the state-owned Dublin Airport Authority.

O'Leary's response was withering:

the Taoiseach has dithered for three years on providing a second terminal at Dublin airport. As a result, Dublin airport today is not just a slum; it is a testament to the failure of Bertie Ahern to keep his own election promises . . . Another terminal provided by the people who brought us the Black Hole of Calcutta is not competition, it's still the Black Hole of Calcutta. The government has been forced to open up telecoms, electricity and other sectors to competition and airports shouldn't be any different. This is anti-competitive and anti-consumer.

It had also always been a fait accompli. The Irish government's slowness to make a decision did not mean that it was ever in any doubt about what that decision would be. It was not that it could not make up its mind, just that it wanted to give the appearance that it had considered all the options and that, on balance, the proposal from the Dublin Airport Authority was the best. In truth, private tenderers did not have a hope of winning the contract. The trade union movement was vigorously opposed to private competition at Dublin airport and would have reacted aggressively to anything other than a continuation of the state monopoly that gave it and its members power and influence over the airport's affairs. SIPTU, the strongest union at the airport, had toyed with suggestions that it should participate in the ownership of a second terminal, but had always been determined that union control would not be diluted by private competition.

O'Leary knew that continued opposition to the government's plans was probably futile, but he was not prepared to retreat quietly. 'We'll go to the Competition Authority and the European Commission and challenge this on the basis that it contravenes competition and public procurement rules,' he said. 'It's time for this monopoly to be tested in the courts and in Europe. It's a state monopoly and it's illegal.' In July O'Leary confirmed that Ryanair would bring full proceedings under Section 82/86 of the Competition Law under the European Treaty. 'Competition works, but Bertie giving in to his buddies in the trade unions doesn't,' he said.

O'Leary's case to the courts alleged that Ahern 'entered an arrangement with the trade union movement in relation to union work practices'. The agreement, O'Leary alleged, meant that similar if not identical work practices would be applied to the new terminal as were already in place in the existing terminal. He also claimed that Ahern 'wrongfully and in breach of duty' imposed the agreement on his minister for transport.

The case was adjourned, and the Dublin Airport Authority pressed ahead with its plans, revealing details in September and prompting another O'Leary tirade. According to the DAA, the new terminal would not be completed until 2009, and would cost €1.2 billion. 'We, as the largest airline in the country, have not been consulted on either the location, the cost or design of this terminal. It's an absolute bloody disgrace that it's not going to be here until late 2009 [and] how you can spend €1.2 billion when the private sector has offered to build it for €200 million with no extra cost to the taxpayer is equally a disgrace.'

He said that the DAA's terminal would be built in the wrong place, and would not meet the requirements of its airline customers. 'It's a shambles,' he said. But it was a shambles he would have to live with.

At 8.50 a.m. on 7 July 2005 three bombs exploded in London's Underground within fifty seconds of each other, and one hour later a fourth bomb exploded on a bus. The attacks killed fifty-two people and paralysed London's transport system. Fourteen days later four more bombs went off, again targeting London's public transport, but this time the main explosives failed to detonate and there were no serious injuries.

Inevitably, the stock markets reacted by marking down the value of airline companies, fearing that terrorist attacks would cause an immediate slump in travel, but the impact of the bombings on air travel was not as calamitous as the fallout from 9/11. Ryanair reported a sharp fall in bookings to London in the days after the attacks, but the slump was not matched for other destinations. Quickly, too, London traffic returned to the pre-bombing levels as travellers seemed to shrug their shoulders, accept the risks inherent in the new age of terrorism and carry on regardless.

Far more serious for airlines was the linked problem of rising oil prices, pushed ever higher by the continuing instability in the Middle East. In 2004 steadily rising prices had forced long-haul carriers to introduce fuel surcharges on their ticket prices, and after a brief lull the oil price had started to spike alarmingly through 2005. Fuel surcharges on international routes were hiked up again in March 2005, and soon spread from long- to short-haul flights. 'Our fuel bill next year is expected to be an extra £300 million,' said BA's commercial director, Martin George. 'With prices continuing to rise, a surcharge increase is regrettably unavoidable.'

In May Giovanni Bisignani, director general of the International Air Transport Association, had said that the high oil price was 'destroying' the profitability of the global airline industry, which was facing losses of $6 billion in 2005, its fifth successive year of net losses. Ryanair, though, was revelling in its rivals' discomfort. Its advantageous price hedging on oil had allowed it to report a 29.5 per cent increase in pre-tax profits to €295.9 million on the last day of May and O'Leary was confidently predicting further growth in 2005/06. In O'Leary's view high oil prices could even be seen as a positive. 'At $60 a barrel there will be even less pressure on pricing, there will be no new entrants and some [recent start-ups] will disappear. The bloodbath in Europe is continuing and will get worse at $60 a barrel. It is not pretty out there. If oil stays at $60 per barrel over the next twelve months, most of Europe's airlines will show enormous losses,' he said. In America, while the traditional airlines struggled Southwest was also reporting strong profits, despite a 25 per cent rise in its fuel costs.

By the summer of 2005 BA's fuel surcharge had increased

fourfold to £24. O'Leary's response was predictable. 'Only Ryanair guarantees no fuel surcharge on all of our fares, not now, not ever,' he said in a statement. 'Why don't BA reduce other costs instead of always gouging their passengers?' He then rammed home his point by wearing a highwayman's outfit to a press conference in London, where he lampooned BA's 'skyway robbery'. 'While oil prices have doubled, BA fuel surcharges have gone up twelvefold,' he said. 'BA and other airlines are simply using oil price increases to jack up fares.'

If war had created the impetus for the rising oil price, natural disaster soon sent it higher still. Hurricane Katrina, which crashed through the southern states of the US in September, sent oil above $70 a barrel, and analysts were quick to predict that $100 was now a distinct possibility. In mid-September IATA predicated the global airline industry was now heading for losses of $7.4 billion for 2005 and said that oil was 'once again robbing the industry of its return to profitability'. Worse, there was no end in sight as the oil price remained stubbornly high. War, terrorism and natural disaster ensured that airlines would have to come to terms with a new price regime, one that would increase pressure on the weakest players in the market and re-emphasize that the future lay with the leanest, lowest cost operators.

The previous year O'Leary had generated acres of press coverage by saying he was thinking of charging for baggage, an idea that sparked heated debate across the travel industry. The travel supplement of the *Sunday Times*, which has more than four million readers in Britain and Ireland, devoted its cover story to the idea of travelling with hand baggage only.

Author Dan Ryan and his partner struggled to cope on a weekend away, despite carrying O'Leary's mooted ten kilos of free carry-on luggage. Sweating and uncomfortable from layers of clothing worn to bolster his weekend clothing options, Ryan was irritated by the sight of two amply built passengers who clearly weighed more than he and his baggage combined. Why, he wondered, do airlines not charge fat people more than they charge thin people?

O'Leary, who has the lean physique of a man with a high metabolism rather than a body honed by hours spent in a gymnasium, was quite taken by the idea. He also delights in telling audiences that he cannot wait to show pornography on late-night flights (adding that he would be its best customer) and wonders aloud about the possibility of his fleet of aircraft becoming flying casinos, using international airspace to evade gaming laws, as soon as the technology to extract instant settlement of inflight debts is foolproof and cheap. 'These things may happen, and some of them certainly will,' he says. 'Paying for baggage is logical, because if we can persuade people to fly with what they can carry, we can carve another chunk off costs and take fares lower still. But yes, it generates publicity, and every time we get publicity, good or bad, bookings spike up.'

Some ideas worked, some failed. At the end of 2004 O'Leary, with some ballyhoo, had announced the arrival of inflight entertainment on a select number of flights and plans to roll it out across the whole fleet throughout 2005. It was a carefully planned project but within months had been abandoned. The average Ryanair flight was simply too short to encourage passengers to part with cash for a portable player with modest amounts of programming. And those who were prepared to pay for a player were less likely to buy anything else on board – like food or a drink – and so the revenue impact even on flights where they proved popular was negligible. 'It was a good idea but not fully thought out,' says Paul Fitzsimmons. So inflight entertainment was dropped, without remorse or apology, because it did not work. Charging for baggage, however, would become a firm fixture.

Adding revenue streams went hand in hand with reducing costs, and O'Leary was always on the hunt for ideas, big and small. Aspirant pilots applying for a post with Ryanair had to pay a non-refundable fee of €50 with their applications, and if they landed a job had to pay for their own retraining on Ryanair's fleet of Boeings. Finding cabin crew for his ever-expanding fleet drove O'Leary into the eastern European labour market, as Ryanair started to employ hundreds of Latvians, Lithuanians and Poles to staff the planes. They too were expected to pay for their training, subsidize their uniforms and work punishing schedules to earn their wages. The more they flew, the more they earned, but it was a far cry from the gentle work rosters of traditional airlines.

Success, though, seemed to have blunted O'Leary's edge. He started to muse aloud about leaving the company that he had led to such dominance in such a short space of time. He told the *Sunday Times* he would be gone by 2008, sparking a flurry of speculation about who could replace him and confirming a growing view among stock market analysts that O'Leary was bored. 'Ryanair is maturing into a solid business, one that will grow steadily and which no longer needs the sort of a driven personality that O'Leary gives it,' said one. 'Mature businesses need a different style of leadership.'

O'Leary's life was starting to change as well. His marriage had been followed that autumn by the birth of his first child, a son, and by a shift in priorities. In an interview that year he said,

I'm nearly certain I won't be here in five years' time. I'll be fifty! I think it'll be partly staleness, partly boredom. I think it will be time for a change in here. There are good people coming up through the system here; they need to be able to see there's something. There are about four guys on the senior management team here who could run this place tomorrow morning. The best businesses have a logical sequence of succession. One of the weaknesses of the company now is it is a bit cheap and cheerful and overly nasty and that reflects my personality.

But if O'Leary's competitors thought they could relax, they were wrong. Far from laying down a template for the three years to come, O'Leary was simply doing what he always does with the media: mischievously thinking aloud and letting the press coverage flow. He may be gone by 2008 or he may still be driving the airline forward; he just does not plan that far ahead. 'There's no point in having some long-term plan because that long-term plan gets knocked on its ass. We have a five-year plan here, the next twelve months is set in stone, years two to five are fluid. There is no point in having too many plans.'

One plan, though, was about to be unveiled.

Five days before Christmas O'Leary announced he would be hosting a press conference the following morning. It had already been a busy month: he had finalized a new ten-year deal with Charleroi airport in Belgium, had announced seventeen new routes from Glasgow, Stansted, Shannon, Stockholm, Beauvais, Frankfurt-Hahn and Liverpool, had signed a new five-year deal with Hertz and had revealed another 25 per cent increase in passenger numbers for the previous twelve months. But he had kept his most dramatic announcement for the final week before Christmas, when news media are traditionally starved of information and desperate for a story.

'This is a momentous day for Ryanair,' he said, as he revealed that he would launch eighteen new routes from Dublin the following year, basing five new aircraft at Dublin airport. 'This is the largest ever single investment in Irish tourism. The five new aircraft to be based in Dublin represent an investment of over \$300 million. The eighteen new routes from Dublin to Europe together with the additional flights on seven existing routes will mean an additional 1.5 million passengers a year at Dublin airport.'

It was, he said, a direct assault on Aer Lingus.

These new routes from Dublin to Europe mean that Ryanair's operations at Dublin airport will become substantially larger than Aer Lingus's. Ryanair will carry over seven million passengers on fifty-two routes from Dublin next year compared to Aer Lingus's less than six million passengers on just forty-three year-round routes. Ryanair's average fare of €39 is less than half Aer Lingus's average European fare of €80. Ryanair now offers more routes and services than Aer Lingus to both the UK and now continental Europe. With these new routes and passengers, Ryanair will now carry more passengers than Aer Lingus at each of the main Irish airports (Dublin, Cork and Shannon) as well as serving the bigger regional airports (Derry, Kerry and Knock) which Aer Lingus no longer operate to. Ryanair is now twice the size and just half the price of Aer Lingus here in Ireland, and has long since displaced any claims Aer Lingus might have had to being Ireland's national airline. Aer Lingus's only remaining title is that of Ireland's highest-fare airline. Aer Lingus can't compete with Ryanair's prices, they can't match our punctuality, and now they can't match our route network from Dublin to the UK or Europe.

Not content with the impact of his words, O'Leary hammed up for the occasion, wearing a Santa Claus outfit, while Peter Sherrard, his newly appointed public relations executive, wore an elf's costume. Stacks of gift boxes emblazoned with the names of the new routes were stacked on either side of the top table.

For Aer Lingus, the news could not have been worse. Under Willie Walsh the airline had successfully expanded away from Ryanair, concentrating on new route launches to European destinations. Walsh knew that O'Leary would not ignore Dublin for ever, but he had been determined to move at speed and secure the routes before Ryanair changed its tactics. Since his departure, however, the airline had wobbled. Dermot Mannion, Walsh's replacement as Aer Lingus chief executive, had not taken up his post until the late summer and barely had time to grow accustomed to his new job before O'Leary struck. Mannion's background as a senior executive in Emirates, the successful long-haul airline, had not prepared him for the viciousness of the new European short-haul market. Mannion believed Aer Lingus could expand its way to a profitable future and was convinced there were opportunities to launch long haul routes to the Middle East and further afield, and to America too once deregulation was agreed between Europe and the US. It was a credible strategy, and one that he would use in the coming months to persuade international institutions to back the privatization of the state-owned airline.

But he had not factored in a full frontal assault on his most profitable European routes by Ryanair. 'O'Leary's aggression was breathtaking,' says one Dublin analyst. 'He was picking off Aer Lingus's best routes – to Madrid, Berlin, Rome – and launching head-to-head competition. It was a blow to the solar plexus for Mannion.'

'We were confident in our own model that it would work,' says one Ryanair executive. 'And we were confident because our costs were lower and we could sustain a head-to-head competition with anybody else longer than anybody else could.' Mannion and Aer Lingus were about to discover just how long, and how painful, that competition could be.

26. Mischief and Mayhem

It was an unusual night for a party, an otherwise quiet Monday evening in early February 2006, but Michael O'Leary was in attack mode. That night Channel 4, a British television station, was broadcasting a documentary on Ryanair, the result of a five-month investigation by two undercover reporters. According to the programme makers, the documentary would expose serious flaws in Ryanair's safety practices, showing scenes of overworked pilots and cabin crew, dirty aircraft and security lapses.

O'Leary had decided that the best way to defuse the programme was to ridicule it. Instead of chastising those members of staff who had been caught on hidden cameras moaning about their working conditions, he organized an 'Oscars' night to be held in Stansted, where the airline employs close to 1,000 staff. The prizes would include an award for the Ryanair staff member 'who tells the best whopper on air', as well as a special award for the staff member who delivered the best chat-up line to one of Channel 4's 'undercover investigative dollies', the term O'Leary had coined for Charlotte Smith and Mary Nash, the two reporters who had trained and served as Ryanair cabin staff.

'The Oscars night wasn't for the press, it was for the staff,' said O'Leary. 'Either they'd all be sitting at home worried that they were going to be sacked, or we could deal with it the best way we know how. So we said, "Right, we're going to have a free bar; everybody comes in and nobody gets fired." We were not going on a witch-hunt. And it was great.'

O'Leary's counter-attack against Channel 4 had started weeks earlier, when the allegations were put to him by Steve Boulton Productions, the programme makers. In a letter to O'Leary the company said that Smith and Nash had uncovered incidences of pilot and crew fatigue including crew falling asleep on duty, inadequate staff training, breaches of safety and security and a cynical attitude to passengers. During one flight, they alleged, vomit had been discovered on the floor of a plane but had not been cleaned up because of the constraints of the twenty-five-minute turnaround time, and the undercover reporter had been told to spray aftershave to disguise the smell. A Ryanair pilot said on air that if he refused to fly because he was tired he would 'probably be fired and definitely demoted'. Most dramatically, Smith claimed that during her training she was told that any passenger sitting in seat 1A on a Ryanair flight would be killed on impact in any crash because a piece of metal used to attach a handrail would go straight into their head.

O'Leary responded directly, and caustically, to each allegation and offered to appear on the programme in an unedited interview to combat them. He dismissed the claim about seat 1A as 'ludicrous', saying the handrail attachment was not on aircraft used by Ryanair, and described the pilot's claim that he would be sacked or demoted as 'without foundation'. His offer of an unedited interview was rejected – Channel 4 said it was logistically impossible to guarantee an unedited version, though it was prepared to carry an edited interview that fairly reflected his point of view – and O'Leary decided on a pre-emptive assault instead. The programme's claims were rubbished in advance by Ryanair, and the Oscars night was organized to show that neither he nor his airline cared about them. Channel 4 had, however, struck a raw nerve. Three times in the previous twelve months Ryanair flights had come close to danger.

On an approach to Rome the previous summer a co-pilot had been forced to take the controls from his senior officer, who had been suffering from stress; in December a flight to Glasgow had suffered a loss of cabin pressure after the captain and co-pilot had failed to carry out checks which could have identified the problem; and earlier in the year a flight to Beauvais airport in France had had to abort its landing because the pilot failed to line up his approach correctly. All three incidents had been resolved safely, and O'Leary could claim that Ryanair's internal procedures and failsafes had ensured that crises were averted, but they revealed how close the airline – any airline – was to disaster.

Safety always gnawed at O'Leary. He always maintained that the one thing that could ground Ryanair was a crash, particularly if it could be shown that the crash had been caused by scrimping on safety. The perception of Ryanair was that it was cheap and occasionally nasty, but was also safe. Its Boeing 737s were fast becoming the youngest fleet in the skies as aircraft arrived each month, and while the new planes delivered operating efficiencies – primarily through lower fuel and maintenance costs – they also created an aura of safety around the airline. Bright shiny Boeings reassured passengers that while their tickets might have been cheap, they were not expected to fly in ageing rust buckets.

O'Leary's obsession with safety transcended his normal approach to costs; it was a corner that he was not prepared to cut, yet it could destroy his airline if something went wrong. It was, in short, his Achilles heel, and there was nothing he could do about it other than ensure he could not be faulted if the worst happened. By exposing sloppiness in Ryanair's training procedures and tiredness in its staff, Channel 4 was creating an uncomfortable context if anything did go wrong. Trade unions, particularly the pilots' unions, were also acutely aware of O'Leary's vulnerability on safety. In any dispute about union recognition – and despite the individual issues that might arise with pilots, every dispute was ultimately about recognition – the unions would use safety, particularly pilot fatigue, as a weapon.

That was why Channel 4's documentary had to be attacked so aggressively and publicly. O'Leary's approach would prove successful, but he was greatly assisted by the programme's failure to convince Ryanair's critics that it had uncovered anything of substance. The media response was desultory, while the Irish Aviation Authority, the regulator responsible for ensuring that the airline conformed to international safety standards, said it had investigated the allegations and was satisfied that no safety breaches had occurred. 'I do not accept that there is a slack approach to safety in the low-cost sector,' said Lilian Cassin, a spokeswoman for the IAA.

Simon Evans, of the consumers' rights organization the Air Transport Users' Council, concurred. 'I didn't see anything horrendous. You would have heard the same comments and apparent disregard for customers at any low-cost airline and, indeed, most organizations. It's not a bad thing if the airline realizes it is under scrutiny by the public and the media, but the show will have no effect on the industry and I don't think it will affect Ryanair's bookings.'

O'Leary was not content with simply ridiculing the programme and exonerating his staff. 'We're doing a follow-up,' he said the following week. 'We have pulled in all of our cabin-crew trainers this week; we've sat down with the safety instructors and we've gone to the handling agents. And we sold 20,000 extra seats yesterday.'

One month later the publicity was even better. The Cheltenham Festival, held annually in March, is the marquee event for fans of National Hunt, or jump, racing. Each race in the four-day festival is a championship final, with the best horses from Britain and Ireland battling for supremacy. While the Grand National at Aintree is the most famous jump race of them all, the Cheltenham Gold Cup is the ultimate event for racing fans, and particularly Irish racing fans. Tens of thousands make the journey each year to the Cotswolds, thronging the racecourse for the duration of the festival and filling bars and hotels for miles around. Drinking and gambling to excess – the all-night poker games are legendary – they crave Irish victories but enjoy themselves no matter what. Although held on British soil, it is a quintessentially Irish affair that bemuses the British media. Each year the racing coverage is peppered by stereotypes, as newspapers tell tales of gambling priests, straying husbands and outrageous betting coups, and they are always on the hunt for the story that justifies the clichés.

This year, 2006, with the Gold Cup scheduled for St Patrick's Day and Irish challengers hot favourites to take the prize, they did not have to look far for the main story.

Michael O'Leary's family had always kept horses, but unlike his siblings he had never taken to riding. 'I fell off a horse at the age of four and I realized it was a stupid activity. My brothers and sisters didn't realize how stupid it was and kept going.' Eddie O'Leary had kept going all the way, becoming a respected breeder and owner in an industry that still holds a special place in Ireland. Eddie's involvement was the key to his brother Michael's conversion. 'If Eddie wasn't involved, I wouldn't be,' O'Leary says.

He's the judge. He decides what we buy or don't buy. It's important to have someone like that. Someone you can trust. It's like any walk of life. There are great people in racing and there are messers. Eddie's advice is vital. It's 90 per cent frustration and 10 per cent fun. But then the 10 per cent does vastly outweigh the other side. The owner is the mug at the bottom of the food chain. As long as you know that, you'll be okay. But you have to know you will lose your money. Which makes me an idiot.

Four of the first five horses O'Leary owned had to be put down. 'Deaths and injuries are what I hear about most of the time. It's very hard to take. But it's what you have to accept as part and parcel of the game. If you can't deal with them, you shouldn't be in it,' he says.

For the first time at Cheltenham O'Leary would have a horse challenging for the Gold Cup. His horse, War of Attrition, had been an unlikely runner-up two years earlier in the Supreme Hurdle but had failed to live up to its promise when being roundly beaten the following year in the Arkle Chase. This time O'Leary was not sure whether to run him in the Gold Cup or in the lesser Ryanair Chase – which carried an obvious attraction.

The weekend before the festival he told the *Irish Times* he was 'leaning towards the Ryanair, I think it's the more sensible option'. Michael 'Mouse' Morris, the horse's trainer, had other ideas. 'I was always going for gold,' said Morris.

O'Leary's claims of ignorance about horseracing and his relative indifference – he says too many people 'obsess' about Cheltenham and he prefers smaller meetings – sit uneasily with his character. He is a fast learner, a consumer of information who can spout at length about the intricacies of the handicap system that applies to jump racing. He may keep his obsession in check, but he is no novice owner throwing cash at the prospect of glory. O'Leary's sales and purchases, managed primarily by Eddie, are astute. It was no fluke that he came to Cheltenham that March with a chance of victory.

War of Attrition started the race as a well-backed contender but was far from favourite. As the horses came to the final fences, three Irish runners were battling for gold but it was O'Leary's that held off the challenge of Grand National winner Hedgehunter to take the cup, with Forget the Past in third. It was the first time in Cheltenham's history that Irish horses had filled the first three places. The Duchess of Cornwall was on hand to present the prize to an ecstatic O'Leary, who promptly promised free flights for all who'd backed his horse.

One gambler who had had the foresight to invest was Willie Walsh, the former Aer Lingus chief executive who had taken over as CEO of British Airways. O'Leary had told him that War of Attrition 'hadn't a hope' of winning. Walsh decided that O'Leary, as usual, could not be believed, and put down £100 for the horse to win at 7/1.

Each year Ryanair drops a few routes as it opens many more. The reasons may be straightforward – passenger numbers do not justify the route – but it is also a method of reminding airports of what can happen if they do not play the game by Ryanair's rules.

In March 2006 Michael Cawley, Ryanair's deputy chief executive, travelled to his hometown of Cork to explain the economics of modern air travel to its newly independent airport company, and to get rid of some routes while he was there. Cork's problem was that it was just completing a brand new terminal that would cost €170 million – ten times what Frankfurt Hahn had paid for a similar increase in capacity. The cost was being covered in part by increases in landing charges.

'There are three elements,' he said at a press conference in Cork. 'Supply, demand and price. We are the supplier and we create the demand by reducing the price. If somebody forces us to put up the price, the demand will go down and we've got to drop the supply. In our judgement, for the kind of increases [in charges] that we are suffering here in Cork, we should drop the supply by three flights a day on one route. It's a judgement call.'

Ryanair's view was that if it directed its routes to the cheapest airport operators, the passengers would follow. Cork had to come to terms with a new reality: it was no longer competing solely with other Irish airports; it was part of a new European market and had to compete as much with Polish airports as it did with Irish ones. There would still be some business for Cork if it chose not to compete, but if it wanted the volume of passengers that its new terminal demanded, then it had to recognize the new dynamics: volume came from low fares, and low fares were only possible at low-priced airports.

The result that day was that Cork lost its route from Liverpool to rival airport Kerry. 'It could have gone to France or anywhere else in Europe, but Kerry came up with the best deal,' says Cawley. He adds, 'It was particularly nice for us to have Kerry as an alternative, because from our point of view we have already created the demand and we'll now fill it at another Irish airport. Cork airport is going to lose these passengers.'

A potent combination of rising demand, continued instability in the Middle East, disruption of supplies in Nigeria and a global shortage of refining capacity for transport fuels pushed the oil price to new highs in April, with the price of a barrel of crude climbing above $74. Shares in airline companies suffered sharp falls, reflecting the industry's vulnerability to events beyond its control. Air Berlin, one of the new breed of low-cost European carriers, was one of the early casualties of the frosty investment climate. Forced to scale back its forthcoming stock market flotation, it cut both the number of shares on offer to investors and the price of those shares as potential buyers drifted away.

It was a dismal time for the Irish government to be planning the partial sale of Aer Lingus, and once again the airline's immediate future was clouded in doubt. The government's support for privatization had always been lukewarm, but before the latest oil price crisis it had seemed on course to sell a large part of its stake in the airline to private investors. The potential sale was not driven by ideological belief but perceived commercial necessity. Aer Lingus needed fresh investment to buy new planes, and the government had a simple choice: it could fund all of that investment from taxpayers' money or it could allow the airline to raise money from the private sector. The airline's commercial recovery under Willie Walsh's regime meant that the government had a genuine choice: while European rules precluded state handouts to failing airlines, they allowed governments to invest in successful ventures. So, if Aer Lingus could attract private investment, then it was a suitable candidate for state investment.

Ireland's booming economy and burgeoning tax receipts meant that money was not a problem for the government, but giving the state airline more cash was not an option it was prepared to consider. Aer Lingus needed new planes for its long-haul routes to America and for potential routes to the Far East and South Africa. A new fleet could cost as much as €2 billion, far more than the government was prepared to invest. And while Aer Lingus was for the moment profitable, its ambitions were not risk-free. If the government invested more money and Aer Lingus ran into difficulty, then the government would be precluded by European rules from making further investment. And if that happened, private investors would also shun the airline. The risks were too great, even if the cash was available, and the short-term political difficulties involved in pushing ahead with a sale were balanced by the realization that if the government failed to secure the airline's future by giving it the ability to survive, it could pay a far heavier price in the future. If Aer Lingus was to expand, it would need to access money from other sources, and so privatization had once again gathered momentum.

Rising oil prices were not the only difficulty. Political opposition to a sale remained intense, both within the government parties and from the opposition. Also, Aer Lingus had a pensions deficit that would have to be plugged before new investors parted with their cash, and the trade unions in the company were determined that the airline's workers should secure as large a stake as possible once the airline was sold – certainly no less than the 14.9 per cent they owned before privatization. The unions were also determined to conclude binding agreements with the airline's management on wages and redundancies so that a newly privatized Aer Lingus could not metamorphose into a ferocious cost-cutter. 'Without clarity over these issues, the company is simply not a credible investment prospect,' said the *Irish Times* in an editorial comment in mid-May.

After protracted negotiations, the airline eventually agreed that the pay and conditions of staff employed before privatization would be maintained, but that new staff hired after the sale would be subject to different terms. It also agreed that there would be no compulsory redundancies in the future, unless 'significant change' affected the company.

Despite these agreements hopes of an early-summer flotation receded, to be replaced by doubts that a sale would happen at all. The government was in the fourth year of a five-year term of office and it was highly unlikely that a politically charged privatiz-ation would take place any time close to a general election. If a flotation could not be arranged by early autumn, Aer Lingus would remain in state ownership for at least another year.

June came and went, and pressure on the government to take a decision rose inexorably. Bertie Ahern assured the Dáil that a sale would take place 'as soon as possible' and said that 'it is still the view that it can happen this year'. O'Leary watched and waited. He was not convinced the airline would ever be sold, believing the demands of the trade unions would make Aer Lingus unpalatable to private investors, and that unless those demands were conceded, the unions would not agree to a sale. It was, he figured, a classic catch-22.

But in early July Martin Cullen, the minister for transport, declared that shares in Aer Lingus would be sold in September. The unions had secured a post-privatization pay increase of 3 per cent as well as a lump-sum payment and a new profit-sharing scheme that would see up to 7.5 per cent of the airline's profits

transferred to the Employee Share Ownership Trust to buy shares
in the company. Aer Lingus management also agreed to scrap plans
for any further outsourcing of jobs to subcontractors and conceded
that the number of staff on fixed-term contracts (as opposed to
permanent positions) would not exceed 25 per cent in any
department.

The timing of the flotation was politically propitious – it would
take place before the Dáil returned from its long summer holidays
and there would be no awkward parliamentary debates until the
sale had been completed – but there was still the danger that events
beyond the control of the government or the airline's management
could conspire to scupper it, and on 10 August they almost did.
In a dramatic swoop British police arrested twenty-five people,
seventeen of whom were later charged with conspiracy to murder
and commit acts of terrorism. Police claimed that they had foiled
a plot to blow up ten planes as they flew across the Atlantic from
Britain to the United States. Just as dramatically, it was claimed
that the terrorists were planning to use liquid explosives smuggled
on board the flights in everyday containers. Immediately, Britain
raised its terror alert from severe to critical. Security at British
airports was thrown into chaos: hand baggage was banned from all
flights in the immediate aftermath of the arrests, massive queues
formed at security checkpoints and hundreds of flights were
delayed and cancelled.

Three days after the arrests, 30 per cent of flights out of Heathrow were cancelled to reduce pressure on baggage screeners. The
tightened security prompted a vicious war of words between
O'Leary and Willie Walsh of BA on one side and the British
government and BAA, the airports authority, on the other. Walsh
and O'Leary joined forces to lambaste the handling of the security
scare, calling on the government and BAA to bring in extra staff
to help ease the logjam at airports. O'Leary then threatened to sue
the British government for compensation unless it moved speedily
to ease the crisis.

He described the new restrictions as 'farcical Keystone Cops
security measures that don't add anything except to block up

airports', and ridiculed the searching of small children and elderly people in wheelchairs.

These restrictions have absolutely no impact on security, they are nonsensical and the height of stupidity, but the more you call these restrictions stupid and nonsensical the more the [UK] Department of Transport digs in its heels and says, 'Oh, we have to protect the nation, this is needed for security.' If it was they would apply these restrictions on more likely terrorist targets like the London Underground or Eurotunnel . . . If you look at where the terrorists have been striking in recent years it's the London Underground and the trains in Madrid. Yet you don't see the government confiscating lipsticks and gel-filled bras on the London Underground. Most of them couldn't identify a gel-filled bra if it jumped up and bit them anyway. It's simply a way of politicians making it look like they are doing something.

Typically, he combined his attack on government with a seat sale, using an image of Winston Churchill to make his case. It was a classic O'Leary assault, one certain to grab headlines and make Ryanair look positive in a negative story for the industry. But for Aer Lingus, which planned to sell its shares six weeks later, the news could not have come at a worse time. Once again commentators were quick to muse about the long-term decline of the airline industry, in particular the low-fare sector which relied heavily on speedy turnaround times and uncluttered airports to keep down its costs. It also revived the spectre of the 11 September attack which had had such a long and profound impact on the aviation industry.

Gradually the situation stabilized. No one had died and potential attacks had been averted. In time, too, fear was replaced by a degree of scepticism about the claims that plans for attacks had been at an advanced stage. The climate for a share sale had, however, been damaged and the price that the Irish government could hope to extract from investors was edging lower.

O'Leary, meanwhile, had more mischief to make. In August he announced twelve new routes from Dublin, to be launched the following year, signalling that Ryanair was preparing to make Dublin a key target in its relentless pursuit of passengers and that Aer Lingus's growth at its home base could no longer be taken for granted.

By the end of September, however, Aer Lingus CEO Dermot Mannion could pack his bags for a well-earned holiday. As the security crisis had eased, so too had oil prices fallen, slipping back below $60 a barrel by the time Aer Lingus shares came to market. The government had settled on a price of €2.20 a share, towards the bottom end of expectations, valuing the company at about €1 billion, but demand for the new shares had been high. Trading started officially on Monday 2 October, but in unofficial trading the previous week the price had risen gently and by the middle of the first week Aer Lingus shares were just over €2.51, a respectable gain on the offer price, with demand still heavy. The government and Aer Lingus senior managers could afford a rare moment of self-congratulation. Despite all the gloomy predictions, despite oil price scares and terror alerts, and despite O'Leary's attacks on the Dublin market, the flotation had been a marked success. Investor interest was high, the shares had risen after the sale, but not so far as to prompt accusations that the government had sold on the cheap. All in all, it was a job well done and Mannion could depart for the United States with a smile on his face.

On Thursday 5 October the telephone rang in the London home of John Sharman, the Aer Lingus chairman. At the other end of the line was David Bonderman, Ryanair chairman. It was a brief conversation, but a startling early-morning wake-up for Sharman. Ryanair, said Bonderman, had informed the stock exchange before trading commenced that morning that it had acquired a 16 per cent stake in Aer Lingus and that it was making a cash offer of €2.80 a share for the rest of the equity. Hurriedly, Sharman made contact with the rest of the Aer Lingus board and tried to contact Mannion, who had already departed. While Bonderman broke the news to Sharman, O'Leary was trying to contact Bertie Ahern to tell him. Ahern was unavailable, so O'Leary briefed his special adviser and spoke to Martin Cullen, minister for transport, as well as Brian Cowen, minister for finance, and Michael McDowell, deputy prime minister.

The shock was almost tangible; it was, says one official adviser, the government's 'worst nightmare' come true. O'Leary, the tooth and claw capitalist, was pouncing on the national airline. In the financial community, the shock was no less profound. O'Leary, the champion of low-cost, low-fare flying, was stepping outside his comfort zone and into the world of traditional national airlines, trade unions, high costs and transatlantic flights. He was in effect breaking the mould he had fashioned so successfully over the preceding thirteen years.

The supreme opportunist, O'Leary had struck when no one was expecting it. He had often toyed with the idea of buying Aer Lingus, but clearly this would never be a possibility unless the airline was privatized. His own scepticism about the flotation ensured that he had not spent too much time planning his raid. Two weeks before the shares were due to start trading he had discussed the possibility of a bid with Bonderman. Initially surprised, Bonderman had quickly warmed to the idea. Ryanair had cash reserves of more than €1 billion, so had no difficulty funding a bid. Kyran McLaughlin, a Ryanair non-executive director and senior director at Davy Stockbrokers, a Dublin firm, was also briefed on the plan, as he and his brokers would be charged with implementing it. On the Tuesday night before Aer Lingus shares were due to start trading Bonderman called a telephone board meeting of Ryanair's directors so that O'Leary could reveal the plan and seek the board's support. It was the first any of the other directors knew about it, but their initial shock soon turned to approval.

'I had a couple of conversations with David Bonderman,' O'Leary said in an interview with the *Sunday Tribune*. 'We first discussed the prospect of buying shares in the airline the Tuesday evening before it floated [on the unofficial market] on Wednesday. We first discussed the formal offer with the board only on Tuesday of this week. So it's happened that quickly. That's why nothing leaked. Because we weren't discussing it for yonks. At Ryanair we don't sit around agonizing over things.'

O'Leary argued to his board that Ryanair could not lose by buying shares and mounting a takeover bid. The Irish government was selling at a discount, so the stake could be acquired relatively cheaply. At best, victory would mean that Ryanair would get control of an overstaffed and underperforming airline, with ample opportunity to strip out costs and make it more efficient and profitable. At worst, Ryanair would be left with a minority interest in an airline that would then have to perform if it were to escape its clutches. Either way, the value of Ryanair's investment should rise.

O'Leary knew that the government would react with alarmed hostility to his bid, and knew too that the trade unions in Aer Lingus would go ballistic. That, however, was a source of amusement rather than concern. The commercial logic of securing a strategic holding in Aer Lingus was what counted, not the damaged sensibilities of politicians and trade union officials. As a large shareholder in Aer Lingus, O'Leary's hand would also be considerably strengthened in his long-running dispute with the Dublin Airport Authority, since the two airlines accounted for 70 per cent of traffic at the airport. O'Leary remained determined to block the authority's plans for a lavish new terminal building – the estimated costs of which had continued to rise over the previous month – and remained committed to his goal of a low-cost alternative terminal operated by different management.

There was, he recognized, the potential for problems with the European Commission because of the combined power of Aer Lingus and Ryanair in the Irish market, but he believed that any objections on competition grounds were surmountable. If the commission were to block the deal, it would have to tread warily, finding a form of words that did not preclude future consolidation in the European airline industry. He had, too, a major precedent on his side: the merger of Air France and KLM had created a European giant that dominated airports in Paris and Amsterdam, yet it had been waved through by Europe's regulators.

Just as important for O'Leary was the frozen terror that his bid would provoke at Aer Lingus. While its management devoted its energies to fighting off the takeover, he could concentrate on Ryanair's expansion from Dublin and new European bases, confident that a major rival was distracted. He was quick to note that the potential deal was relatively small-scale for Ryanair, and he referred to Aer Lingus as a tiny regional airline. Ryanair now dwarfed Aer Lingus, carrying almost six times as many passengers. If the airline continued to grow at 20 per cent a year, it would add the annual total number of Aer Lingus passengers in a single year's organic expansion, and O'Leary had not deviated from his ambition to double Ryanair's size over the next five years. Victory, if it came, would make him impregnable in Ireland, but would not significantly alter his European ambitions.

Some Ryanair shareholders were worried that the airline would be dragged down by dealing with the unions, that it would not be able to manage Aer Lingus's long-haul operations and that its ability to grow profits by expanding on its own terms – rather than by acquisition – would be hampered. O'Leary countered by saying that Aer Lingus would be run as a separate business, that the two airlines would continue to compete with each other, that fares would fall not rise from Dublin and that Ryanair's purchasing power and influence with jet manufacturers would ensure that Aer Lingus would be able to modernize its fleet at advantageous prices.

Ryanair's formal offer document for Aer Lingus was published on Monday 22 October, complete with cartoon cover depicting Ryanair and Aer Lingus as two small rugby players standing shoulder to shoulder against the snarling charge of three giants Lufthansa, Air France and BA. It was a disingenuous image and in stark contrast to O'Leary's claims that Aer Lingus was but a small regional airline while Ryanair was a European colossus. The details of the offer, though, were more straightforward. Ryanair would pay €2.80 a share, a premium of 27 per cent over the flotation price. The document highlighted the volatility of Aer Lingus's profits – over the previous fourteen years its cumulative losses of €616 million had exceeded its cumulative profits of €433 million – and it committed Ryanair to keeping Aer Lingus as a 'stand-alone

separate airline'. Seeking to preempt concerns about the creation
of a single dominant airline at Dublin airport, the document noted
that it 'continues to be served by over 50 other scheduled airlines
currently serving 112 international destinations'. It also claimed
that the combined airlines would account for 61 per cent of aircraft
movements at Dublin airport, well short of the 73 per cent dominance enjoyed by Olympic at Athens and about the same as Air
France's 62 per cent at Charles de Gaulle in Paris.

   In the fury that followed O'Leary's bid, however, commercial
arguments gave way to emotional opposition. Aer Lingus pilots
started to buy small parcels of shares at the inflated, bid-induced
prices, paying up to €3.00 in a desperate attempt to block Ryanair
control. Then, dramatically, Denis O'Brien, the mobile telecoms
billionaire who had started business life as Tony Ryan's personal
assistant more than twenty years earlier, announced that he had
bought a stake because of his patriotic desire to keep Aer Lingus
independent. There was in this an undercurrent of personal hostility. Only weeks before O'Leary had lampooned O'Brien's tax
exile in Malta by using an image of him to advertise Ryanair's new
route to the Mediterranean island.

   The government's 25 per cent stake, added to the employees'
15, the pilots' 2 and O'Brien's 2.5 per cent, meant that O'Leary
would have to secure almost all the outstanding equity in the
company to get a simple majority of the shares, while outright
control would remain outside his reach unless he could persuade
the government and the employees to sell. The government's
holding was large enough, under company and stock exchange
rules, to block asset sales, and without securing more than 90 per
cent of the shares O'Leary would be unable to force the remaining
minority holders to sell. At best, with more than 50 per cent but
less than 60 per cent, O'Leary would have control of the board
and the management, but he would not have the freedom to break
up the airline or sell its rights to landing slots at Heathrow airport
– a valuable commodity much coveted by airlines who could not
get access to London's major airport. O'Leary decided to increase
his stake to 25 per cent and then wait for a ruling on the bid from

the European Commission, knowing that even if the Ryanair bid were approved, there was no way he could persuade the major shareholders to sell.

Although the takeover of Aer Lingus was now only a distant possibility, Ryanair's presence on the share register had an immediate impact on Aer Lingus management. Even though it had assured the unions that cost-cutting had come to an end, O'Leary had forced Aer Lingus to recognize that far from finishing, it had barely started. As soon as management tried to negotiate fresh savings and more flexible working conditions, strike action was threatened.

O'Leary does not plan to decrease the pressure on Aer Lingus. He says that his role as a shareholder will be similar to that played by J. P. McManus and John Magnier at Manchester United when the two Irish billionaires bought a stake in the club and bombarded its board with demands for action and information before eventually being bought out at great profit by Malcolm Glazer.

O'Leary's bid for Aer Lingus was a classic example of the extreme opportunism that characterizes the man. The raid on the airline's shares was a plan cobbled together in a matter of weeks, and only formalized in the days before the shares went on sale. While he had harboured ambitions of controlling Aer Lingus for years, he was not prepared to devote any energy to the project until such time as it was a real possibility. 'I'd love to say that everything Ryanair ever does was extremely well thought out,' says one former executive. 'But the honest answer is it's not. It's seat of the pants; you make it up as you go along.'

For O'Leary, nothing is set in stone, even if he says it is. 'Having a long-term plan is a waste of time,' he says. 'I'm not a thinker. You see opportunities and you try to take them. There's no point in having some long-term plan because a long-term plan gets knocked on its ass.'

O'Leary has always taken a hard line against all trade unions, but no area of labour relations has been more vexing to Ryanair than its long-running dispute with its pilots. Although Ryanair cannot legally forbid its employees from joining unions, it can refuse to negotiate with them, and that had been its position vis-à-vis the Irish Airline Pilots Association (IALPA), which is part of the larger union IMPACT. In 2004, when Ryanair was upgrading its Dublin fleet from Boeing 737–200s to 737–800s, O'Leary decided to use the cost of retraining pilots as a bargaining chip. The pilots could either foot the €15,000 bill for the training themselves or could sign an agreement whereby the company paid for it on condition that it was not forced to deal with IALPA for the next five years. The union was outraged and plotted a legal response.

'On a scale of one to ten, O'Leary hates the pilots at least eleven,' says one former executive, 'and he hates IALPA even more. The pilots are well-paid professionals, and their working hours are restricted by law to 900 hours a year. He can't screw anything more out of them.'

In August 2004 the two representatives of the Dublin-based pilots on the Ryanair pilots' Employee Representative Council withdrew from it. IALPA, through Impact, claimed that the pilots and Ryanair were engaged in a trade dispute and asked the Labour Court to order the company to negotiate with the union now that, the pilots having withdrawn from the ERC, there was no internal company mechanism to resolve the dispute.

The retraining dispute spawned a number of separate legal battles between Ryanair and its pilots. Apart from the Labour Court case on union representation, which found in favour of the union, Ryanair was brought to court by John Goss, one of its Dublin-based pilots, and the company in turn went to court in an attempt to force a union-created website to reveal the names of pilots who had made anonymous postings on the site. Ryanair lost its attempt to unveil the pilots' identities and eventually reached an out-of-court settlement with Goss after a bruising battle that saw O'Leary threatened with jail for contempt of court and Ryanair claiming that Goss had intimidated other pilots who were prepared to accept O'Leary's retraining offer.

The major issue was not Goss or anonymous website postings but union recognition. The Labour Court had agreed with IMPACT that Ryanair should negotiate with the union but

O'Leary had immediately sought to overturn this decision. Eventually, in February 2007, the Supreme Court ruled that the Labour Court's reasoning had been flawed because it had failed to accept that Ryanair's ERCs and its willingness to negotiate with the Dublin pilots meant that internal mechanisms to resolve the dispute had not been exhausted. It was a significant victory for O'Leary in his never-ending battle to keep trade unions at bay.

The success of the Ryanair revolution has been among the factors that have pushed the aviation industry to the forefront of the debate about climate change. In January 2007 Ian Pearson, a junior minister in the British government, denounced O'Leary as the 'unacceptable face of capitalism' because of his attitude to rising carbon emissions from aircraft. O'Leary struck back, calling Pearson 'foolish and ill-informed' and claiming that Ryanair was Europe's 'greenest airline', noting that its new fleet of aircraft is more fuel-efficient than older fleets.

O'Leary dismisses the pressure as misplaced. 'It's just politicians pandering to the latest fashion. Gordon Brown wants us all to believe that he spends his days mulching his compost with his children, David Cameron's gone Dutch with his windmills and clogs. Neither of them really means it. They know that changing a light bulb isn't going to make any difference but a picture of them changing a light bulb will be a nice, cosy image,' he said in an interview with the *Daily Telegraph*. 'But the point is you can't change the world by putting on a pair of dungarees or sandals. You need to look at the real culprits and begin negotiations with them,' he said, arguing that the real battles against carbon emissions had to be fought with the Chinese, Russians and Indians, not with airlines.

Whatever happens, O'Leary believes Ryanair will be able to maintain a price advantage over its rivals because it has a lower cost base. 'We will go from 40 to 80 million passengers in the next few years. We will take them off British Airways and the other old carriers who are flying gas-guzzling, ancient aircraft and pack them into fuel-efficient planes. So Ryanair will be saving the environment – not that we care much,' O'Leary said to the *Daily Telegraph*.

Despite O'Leary's colourful protestations, however, the environmental debate will undoubtedly affect the industry in the years ahead. The Stern Review, a study commissioned by the UK government on the economic impact of climate change and required responses to it, noted in its report published at the end of 2006 that aviation's contribution to greenhouse gas emissions will rise from 1.6 per cent to 5 per cent by 2050. Environmentalists have also argued that the industry's impact on climate change could be more pronounced than the bare statistics suggest, because aircraft make their emissions directly into the upper atmosphere.

The industry is committed to using more fuel-efficient planes – its vulnerability to oil price hikes makes that a commercial as well as a politically correct imperative – but environmental taxes on flying remain a future threat to growth. There are measures that governments can take to ease the pollution – a more efficient air traffic management system in Europe would reduce emissions by as much as 12 per cent a year, according to IATA, while better management at airports, with reduced taxiing times for aircraft, would also have a significant impact – but taxes are simpler to implement than structural reform.

Environmental taxes and rationing may still be a distant threat, but the cost of air travel is more likely to increase than decrease in the years ahead. Will that kill the low-cost revolution? O'Leary believes not, claiming that the differential between Ryanair and other, more expensive, carriers will ensure that it can continue to grow at their expense, even if overall growth in the market slows.

Apart from the blip at the start of 2004, when O'Leary warned of a 'bloodbath' and cautioned that the airline's profits could fall, Ryanair's progression has been steadily upward over the past ten years. By the end of O'Leary's first year at the helm Ryanair flew 700,000 passengers on nine routes, operating as a marginally successful but relatively unknown carrier between Ireland and the United Kingdom. In 2006 he carried more than 40 million passengers, and aims to carry more than 80 million by 2012. Ryanair can claim with justification to be the most outstanding business success story that Ireland has ever produced. It is the only Irish company to be a world leader in its industry sector and has played a leading role in the transformation of the European aviation market.

Competitors have continued to join the fray, but there are just two major players in Europe's low-cost market, Ryanair and easyJet, with Air Berlin leading the next division of wannabes. The impact of the O'Leary revolution on European aviation has been felt by every traditional airline, and Europe's low-cost carriers have grown their share of the market from 7 to 20 per cent in just four years. The expansion shows no sign of abating. Ryanair and easyJet plan to double their fleet sizes over the next five years, and both have ambitions to double their passenger numbers as well. O'Leary is determined to make Ryanair Europe's largest airline, and to do that he needs to carry at least 75 million passengers a year.

His hunt for growth has taken the airline into new and more far-flung markets. He has opened new routes to eastern Europe, Morocco and even Malta, a four-and-a-half-hour journey from London. That represented a volte-face; at the 2005 Ryanair AGM O'Leary had told one shareholder that routes to distant locations were a no-go because 'people won't pay four times more for flights that are four times longer, so fuck that'. One year later, however, all had changed. 'Would we have a base in Athens? It's too far away from everywhere else, so no. Would we have a base in Malta? No. But would we do a route down to Athens if we could get a low-cost base at an Athenian airport? Yes, we probably would,' he says. O'Leary admits revenues from longer flights will be lower than from shorter routes, but 'that won't stop us going into those markets. We're not going to leave the markets out there.'

O'Leary has thought aloud about flights into former Soviet republics from continental Europe and there have even been suggestions that he would use bases there to extend Ryanair's reach into Asian markets. Far-fetched perhaps, but there is no sign yet that he has lost his thirst for new ideas. Open Skies, the long-awaited agreement between Europe and the United States to

deregulate the transatlantic market, creates other possibilities, with
O'Leary considering a low-fare, long-haul model that would fly
from smaller US airports, like Colombus in Ohio or Baltimore in
Maryland, to Ryanair's existing low-cost airports in the UK and
Europe. He says that any transatlantic venture would be set up and
run as a totally separate company to Ryanair, but he boasts that he
could make money selling seats for as little as $15 each way. His
apparent embrace of this market, however, still hovers somewhere
between publicity stunt and firm plan.

The logistics of the transatlantic market are very different to
those of the short-haul routes that have allowed Ryanair to grow
so quickly and so profitably under O'Leary's stewardship. There
would be ample opportunities to sell to a captive audience for the
duration of a six- or ten-hour flight – O'Leary's vision of planes
becoming flying casinos might be a possibility on Europe–America
flights, and there are also savings to be had from operating a
simple point-to-point service from cheap airports. Analysts may
be sceptical, but in the past his public ruminations have often
turned into solid earners. Free flights may have sounded mad three
years ago, but now tickets for just 0.1 of a cent are a regular feature
of Ryanair marketing drives. Charging for baggage in the hold,
although ultimately self-defeating if it encourages most passengers
to take hand luggage only, will generate millions, while reducing
the amount of luggage in the hold gives Ryanair scope to reduce
costs at airports. Charging for priority boarding is another new
idea to gouge a few more euros from Ryanair customers, while the
company website is constantly tweaked to drag in extra revenue,
whether through increased charges for using credit cards, or by
making travel insurance an opt-out function rather than an opt-in.
Forget to uncheck the box, and you will be charged. O'Leary's
search for new ideas will not stop, driven by the knowledge that
Ryanair, once the leader in ancillary sales, is actually slipping
behind some newer airlines in the amount of profit that it generates.

In large part this is because many of the modern low-fare airlines
depend heavily on former Ryanair managers, and they have all
developed and expanded on the original model. Conor McCarthy,

who O'Leary poached from Aer Lingus, helped create AirAsia in Malaysia, Thailand and Indonesia; Charlie Clifton, a Ryanair veteran, helped set up Tiger Airways in Singapore and is now involved in Skybus in the US. In 2006 McCarthy was involved with Mexican start-up VivaAerobus, while Warwick Brady, a former Ryanair manager, is head of operations at Air Deccan, India's first low-cost carrier. Funding many of these new airlines has been the Ryan family, using the wealth generated by Ryanair. And while the Ryans use their name and expertise to develop the low-cost model across the world, David Bonderman, Ryanair's chairman, is expected to play a significant role in any restructuring of Europe's airlines that Open Skies might prompt.

O'Leary and Ryanair have been part of deeper economic and cultural changes that transcend the airline industry. Labour-market mobility – one key to a functioning, integrated and expanding European Union – has been facilitated by the low-cost revolution, with Ryanair, easyJet and local rivals providing cheap travel for hundreds of thousands of eastern Europeans who want to earn a decent living. And 'short break' air tourism, a phenomenon that barely existed before Ryanair, is now an enormous phenomenon.

The maturing of Ryanair from irritating upstart to major European carrier causes O'Leary to muse aloud about his own future at the airline. He says he will leave Ryanair in 'two or three years' time' – though he has been saying that for a number of years. He argues that there will come a point when Ryanair requires a more conventional management style. 'When we're the biggest airline in Europe it will be inappropriate to have somebody here shouting, swearing, abusing the competition. You need more professional management than me. And that time is coming,' he says. His successor may come from the ranks of the existing management team – Michael Cawley and Howard Millar are the most likely candidates – but could just as easily come from outside the organization.

Either way, when O'Leary leaves he says he will leave completely, refusing a seat on the board or even the offer of the chair.

He says there will have to be a clean break, and the new chief
executive will not need him in the background 'banging on about
the business'. For the moment, though, O'Leary remains on course
to fulfil his ambitions. He will, too, continue to make enemies. As
Tony Ryan noted in one of his earliest proposals for a new airline,
quoting Machiavelli,

There is nothing more difficult to carry out, nor more doubtful of
success, nor more dangerous to handle, than to initiate a new order of
things. For the reformer has enemies in all those who profit by the old
order, and only lukewarm defenders in all those who would profit
by the new order, this lukewarmness arising partly from fear of their
adversaries, who have the laws in their favour; and partly from the
incredulity of mankind, who do not truly believe in anything new until
they have had actual experience of it.

O'Leary's reform of the skies is almost complete, but he still
waits for news from Brussels on his proposed hostile takeover of
Aer Lingus. It is unlikely that he will get approval. Despite his
strident claims that a Ryanair-controlled Aer Lingus would be
good for competition, the creation of such a dominant company
in a relatively small corner of the European market is expected to
prove a step too far for Europe's competition regulators.

The combined clout of Ryanair and Aer Lingus in Dublin would
not be significantly different to Air France/KLM's dominance
of Paris and Amsterdam, but O'Leary faces the hostility rather
than support of his government. EU lawmakers will, however, be
trying to ensure that any reasons they give for blocking O'Leary's
ambitions cannot be used in future years to prevent the widely
anticipated mergers between Europe's traditional airlines. Open
Skies will bring as many risks as it does opportunities and it is
likely that a number of major airlines will, in time, be forced into
defensive mergers as they face intense competition from US carriers
on the lucrative routes to North America. Europe does not want
to create a precedent that could block those mergers so will tread
warily. O'Leary professes to be unconcerned, and knows that

even if he is prevented from taking it over, Aer Lingus remains vulnerable and an attractive target for other airlines. In time, he may sell the Ryanair holding at a profit but for the moment he can sit tight and irritate the Aer Lingus management by using his position as a minority shareholder to demand improved performance.

Ryanair, in any case, is on course to become Europe's largest airline by 2011, overtaking Air France/KLM and Lufthansa, but O'Leary's hunger has yet to be sated. 'I was always driven,' he says, 'and I was always competitive. Maybe I was kicked by somebody at some stage, but if I was I don't remember it. Why are you the way you are? I haven't a bloody bull's notion. Would I want to spend a lot of time analysing myself? No. I think you make things happen. But an awful lot of things happen, and not because you are in control of them. The harder you work the luckier you get. You make your own breaks.'

He may talk of retirement, of trying new challenges and of devoting more time to his family and his farm, but as he said in November 2006, when questioned by stock market analysts, 'You just have to remember that I also said that I would retire in 1992, that I would retire in 1995, and I think again in 1998. Some of my forecasts have not turned out to be terribly accurate.'

Or as one former colleague says, 'I'll only believe it when I see him being carried out of Ryanair in a box. With a stake through his heart.'

Acknowledgements

This book would not have happened without Laura Noonan's determined research and relentless encouragement. She dug for information, talked to scores of people and assembled what she uncovered in carefully prepared files. Despite the increasing demands of her own burgeoning career she stayed with the project to the bitter end, checking, rechecking and adding new information. I am indebted to her.

I also stretched to breaking point the patience of my publisher at Penguin Ireland, Michael McLoughlin, with my disregard for deadlines and publication dates. The trouble with Ryanair and Michael O'Leary is that they never pause for breath, and there is never a natural end point for a book about a business that refuses to stop growing, changing and surprising.

My thanks too to Natasha Fairweather, my agent at AP Watt, who managed to retain her sense of humour throughout this project and whose enthusiasm never dimmed.

Many, many people have helped me along the way, providing insight (and prejudice) both on and off the record. They will recognize their contributions.

Tony Ryan kindly provided me with his original business plans for Irelandia, the project that emerged a few years later as Ryanair. Without his determination and willingness to risk his personal fortune on a dream, there would be no Ryanair, and no book.

As the epigraph suggests, Michael O'Leary had no interest in this book. I have, however, interviewed him on a number of occasions for newspapers and magazines, and have drawn extensively from those interviews.

And finally my apologies to my family, who have endured the

frustrations of the process, and who have waited with decreasing patience for me to finish so that I could honour my initial promise: that, once finished, I would give up smoking.

– Alan Ruddock

Index